Nothing Abides

Nothing Abides

PERSPECTIVES ON THE MIDDLE EAST AND ISLAM

Daniel Pipes

Transaction Publishers
New Brunswick (U.S.A.) and London (U.K.)

Library of Congress Catalog Number: 2014035994
ISBN: 978-1-4128-5673-7 (cloth); 978-1-4128-5683-6 (paper)
Printed in the United States of America

Library of Congress Cataloging-in-Publication Data

Pipes, Daniel, 1949-
    Nothing abides: perspectives on the Middle East and Islam / by Daniel Pipes.
    pages cm
    Includes bibliographical references and index.
    ISBN 978-1-4128-5673-7 (alk. paper)
    1. Middle East--Politics and government--21st century. 2. Middle East--Politics and government--20th century. 3. Arab-Israeli conflict--1993- I. Title.
    DS63.1.P574 2015
    956.05--dc23
                                                    2014035994

Alas! I have nor hope nor health,
  Nor peace within nor calm around,
Nor that content surpassing wealth
  The sage in meditation found.

—Percy Bysshe Shelley,
"Stanzas Written in Dejection, near Naples," 1818

Contents

Introduction

The English romantic poet Percy Bysshe Shelley (1792–1822) fortuitously captured two themes in his phrase that serves as my epigraph, "Nor peace within nor calm around."[1] To be sure, Shelley wrote of his inner turmoil in this poem, "Stanzas Written in Dejection, near Naples," and not his reflections on the Middle East and Islam; but he also succinctly made the two key points, about internal and external unrest, that recur throughout the following study and so might serve as this book's catchphrase.

My title, "nothing abides" derives from a lecture on the philosophy of history by the German philosopher Georg Wilhelm Friedrich Hegel (1770–1831). He said of Muslim polities: "In its spread, Mohammedanism founded many kingdoms and dynasties. On this boundless sea there is a continual onward movement; nothing abides firm (*nichts ist fest*)."[2] Almost two centuries later, instability, volatility, and perpetual motion continue to characterize Muslim communities.

Samuel Huntington (1927–2008), the eminent political analyst, coined a phrase in 1996, "Islam's bloody borders,"[3] that captures the external dimension of this phenomenon, namely the ceaseless wars waged by Muslims against non-Muslims, from the Christians of Iberia to the Hindus of Bali. Together, these three phrases convey the topic of the following chapters published over the quarter century between 1989 and 2014.

My inquiry during this period has concentrated on the Middle East as understood from a historical point of view and on the role of Islam in politics. The book contains five sections.

I. The Arab-Israeli Conflict

The Arab-Israeli conflict is the single most enduring as well as the most intensely scrutinized topic of Middle Eastern politics in the past century. Diplomatically, it compares to the Eastern Question concerning the future of the Ottoman Empire that earlier haunted

European statecraft: both endured for more than a century, engaged a large cast of regional and international players, and consumed a disproportionate amount of attention. I consider my ideas about resolving the Arab-Israeli conflict as one of my two most significant contributions to American foreign policy (the other being how to deal with Islamism).

The first chapter, "Peace Process or War Process?" argues for three points needed to resolve the Arab-Israeli conflict: realizing "that past Israeli-Palestinian negotiations have failed; that their failure resulted from an Israeli illusion about avoiding war; and that Washington should urge Jerusalem to forego negotiations and return instead to its earlier and more successful policy of fighting for victory." Victory is the key concept: only when one side wins a clear victory can the war end. And that side must be Israel. This approach dismisses the diplomacy that began with Kilometer 101 in 1973 as irrelevant at least and counter-productive at worst.

The Jewish claim to Jerusalem is well known, but what of the rival "Muslim Claim to Jerusalem"? A historical review suggests that Muslims value the city only when it has political significance to them and lose interest when it does not. "This pattern first emerged during the lifetime of the Prophet Muhammad in the early seventh century. Since then, it has been repeated on five occasions: in the late seventh century, in the twelfth-century Countercrusade, in the thirteenth-century Crusades, during the era of British rule (1917–48), and since Israel took the city in 1967." Such consistency over so many centuries and under so many diverse circumstances challenges assertions that Jerusalem has vital religious importance in Islam.

A striking contrast exists between the viciousness of most Palestinian discourse about Israel, such as, for example, comparing it to Nazi Germany, and the diametrically opposite, sober, and appreciative statements Palestinians make about Israel as an actual place to live. I focus on the latter in "The Hell of Israel Is Better than the Paradise of Arafat." Part one reviews the Palestinian preference to remain under Israeli rule and part two contains praise for Israel in contrast to Arab regimes. These outspoken statements friendly to Israel offer more than tactical ammunition for the Jewish state; they provide the potential basis for a resolution to the entire Arab-Israeli conflict. For if the Muslim Arabic speakers most affected by and knowledgeable of Israel understand and communicate its considerable virtues, the ear-piercing toxicity of their colleagues could one day find itself without a constituency.

I argue in "The Year the Arabs Discovered Palestine" that, contrary to widespread belief, the idea of a Palestinian nation between the Jordan River and the Mediterranean Sea does not reach back into hoary antiquity but rather "its origins can be traced with surprising precision to a single year—1920. In January 1920, Palestinian nationalism hardly existed; by December of that critical year, it had been born." This change in the space of one year nearly a century ago has had many implications for the Palestinian national movement, foreshadowing "some abiding themes, such as the potential for rapid change and the major role of the Western powers" and providing insight into "the most widely supported but possibly the least successful nationalist cause" of our time.

"Mirror Image: How the PLO Mimics Zionism" follows the Palestinian career as Zionism's *Doppelgänger*, a German word meaning, roughly, "evil twin." The Zionist movement was unique among national movements (notably, by establishing the *Yishuv*, a "state in the making," an informal government that prepared the way for the formal state in 1948). In many ways, the Palestinian movement mimicked these features (the PLO is its "state in the making"). For example, the Palestinian emphasis on the centrality of Jerusalem, the global status of Yasir Arafat, and the dependence on foreign backing. I argue that "the PLO can be understood only with reference to its Zionist inspiration. Indeed, imitation offers important insights into the PLO's future course."

"The Road to Damascus: What Netanyahu Almost Gave Away in 1998" contains a scoop about the Israeli-Syrian negotiations of August and September 1998. Completely secret, these talks were conducted by an unlikely pair of amateur Americans—the businessman and former ambassador Ronald Lauder and the editor of the journal *Middle East Insight*, George Nader. They approached an agreement but were thwarted in the end by the Israeli defense and foreign ministers, whose objections overrode Prime Minister Binyamin Netanyahu's hopes for a deal. Given what has occurred in Syria since 2011, Israel is very fortunate those objections prevailed. This case study remains of interest for the insights it offers into Arab-Israeli diplomacy, Israeli politics, and the man who both then and now heads Israel's government.

II. Middle Eastern Politics

"Understanding Middle Eastern Conspiracy Theories" introduces an extensive subject by examining the nature of the conspiracy mentality, the gullibility of the people who hold them, and their leaders, concluding with a case study of Iraq and Iran. This chapter provides the context for the next one, which asks how governments should respond to the irrational world of conspiracy theories. The Central Intelligence Agency commissioned me to explain how these operate, which I later published as "Dealing with Middle Eastern Conspiracy Theories." I argue that ignoring the phenomenon of conspiracism, as Washington tends to do, neglects key aspects of the Middle East; therefore, government agencies should devote serious attention and generous resources to understanding this type of thinking. Beyond paying them heed, I suggest developing policies with a specific awareness of the region's conspiracist mindset. This, in turn, leads to an interesting question: should the US government take advantage of vulnerabilities presented by conspiracism, or work to diminish this dangerous attitude? The answer is not self-evident.

Before the Syrian civil war erupted, area specialists generally scoffed at seeing the rulers' Alawi identity as defining their place in Syria, preferring to emphasize their geographic or ideological features. I begged to differ and concentrated instead on Alawi tensions with Syria's majority Sunni community. The centerpiece of my argument appeared in a 1989 analysis, "The Alawi Capture of Power in Syria." I provided background on the Alawis and on their despised place in Syrian society until 1920, then traced their dramatic and unexpected ascent over the course of the next fifty years, culminating with Hafez al-Assad's seizure of power in 1970. The most striking aspect of this analysis is that Alawis are not Muslims, which in itself led to their consequently terrible relations with Sunnis over the centuries. Two mid-nineteenth-century observations about the Alawis capture their longstanding characteristics: "They are a wild and somewhat savage race, given to plunder, and even bloodshed, when their passions are excited or suspicion roused"; and Alawi society "is a perfect hell upon earth." Westerners remained largely oblivious to these tensions through forty-five years of Alawi rule, from 1966 to 2011, only to watch them erupt in the horrific conflagration of the most vicious civil war in the modern Middle East.

First presented as my testimony to the House Committee on Government Reform, "The Scandal of US-Saudi Relations" describes a pattern of American obsequiousness—both public and private—in the areas of energy, security, religion, and the treatment of Americans in the kingdom. Example after example demonstrate how weakly the American side behaves when confronted with Saudi will. Contrary to the usual logic, Riyadh sets the terms of this bilateral relationship; a change has taken place, "with both sides forgetting which of them is the great power and which the minor one." This chapter documents that claim, explains it, and offers a specific policy recommendation to correct the problem.

I wrote "Obituary for Nizar Hamdoon (1944–2003)" for two reasons. First, I've never met a diplomat quite like him when he served as Saddam Hussein's ambassador extraordinary and plenipotentiary to Washington in 1984–87, just as full diplomatic relations between the two countries were reinstated, and as the Iraq-Iran war reached its apogee. Hamdoon took seriously his task to develop American support and did so most impressively, even as he worked for a monstrous tyrant. Second, he contacted me in May 2003, a few months after the fall of Saddam and just weeks before his own death. I did not manage to ask him the barrage of questions I had prepared but I did get some valuable information while sitting with him in a New York City Starbucks, some of which I record in this obituary.

The president of Egypt, Abdel Fattah Al-Sisi, who took office in June 2014, remains a mystery; does he fundamentally differ from Husni Mubarak, or is he but a younger clone of the longtime dictator? I look at a student paper written by Sisi in 2006 when he spent a year in the United States, to determine the answer to "What Egypt's New President Really Thinks." He turns out to be "a work in progress, a fifty-nine-year-old still trying to discover who he is and what he thinks even as he rules a country of eighty-six million. On-the-job training is literal in his case." This means he can be influenced, which offers opportunities for foreign governments.

III. Islam in Modern Life

The final three sections take up my other central interest, the role of Islam in public life. Two themes recur here: a recognition that the dream of applying Islamic law looms over Muslim life, giving it similar rhythms regardless of time and place; and the need to take Muslim experience into account, which means noting changes over time, rather than simply assuming the static authority of scripture.

"Islam currently represents a backward, aggressive, and violent force. Must it remain this way, or can it be reformed and become moderate, modern, and good-neighborly?" Against the growing and vocal body of analysts who answer that the Muslim faith cannot advance because its features are immutable, I argue that change for the better is possible in "Can Islam Be Reformed?" In it, I contend that Islam does not have an essential and unchanging core; Muslims and non-Muslims alike should work toward the reformation of the religion by building on the "medieval synthesis" that made Islam a flexible faith until two hundred years ago.

A great debate exists between those who argue that becoming modern requires emulating the West and those who disagree, saying alternative routes to modernity exist. As its title "You Need Beethoven to Modernize" implies, I come down on the side of the importance of Westernizing. To be fully modern, I find, "means mastering Western music; competence at Western music, in fact, closely parallels a country's wealth and power." I establish this point by looking at two civilizations, Muslim and Japanese. "Muslim reluctance to accept Western music foreshadows a general difficulty with modernity; Japanese mastery of every style from classical to jazz help explain everything from a strong yen to institutional stability." Beethoven's music is not in itself functional, but unless you master it, you cannot enter the inner sanctum of modernity.

I delivered "Denying Islam's Role in Terrorism: Why?" at the Institute for Counter-Terrorism in Herzliya, Israel. In it, I document and explain a curious pattern: the Establishment in the West (including politicians, the police, the press, and the professorate) routinely denies that Islamism represents the leading global cause of terrorism, even though it and everyone else knows otherwise. About five daily assaults in the name of Islam since 9/11 notwithstanding, Islamic motives are rarely noted. While euphemism, cowardice, political correctness, and appeasement all contribute to this pattern, I argue that two other, quite respectable reasons are paramount: not wanting to create even more trouble by offending Muslims and a widespread awareness that implicating Islam implies a major shift away from how secular Western societies are presently ordered. Unless the number of casualties of Islamist terrorism increases substantially, I predict no changes to the current state of denial.

Ayatollah Khomeini's 1989 edict against Salman Rushdie stands out as one of the most original and consequential political developments of recent times. Ignoring international boundaries and established freedoms, the Iranian despot sentenced to death the author of a novel called *The Satanic Verses* "and all those [knowingly] involved in the publication." While Westerners offered respectable resistance to this Diktat, I argue in "The Rushdie Rules Ascendant" that the passage of time has weakened their will, and especially that of liberals. That's because, now, "defenders of Western civilization must fight not just

Islamists but also the multiculturalists who enable them and the leftists who ally with them." This augurs badly for the continued maintenance of traditional freedoms in the West.

IV. Islam in the United States

In a sociological survey, "Faces of American Islam: Muslim Immigrants," the late Khalid Durán and I cover a range of topics: demography, geography, history, motives, religion, socioeconomics, children, sex, and institutions. We conclude that immigrants, not converts, are the key Muslim protagonists in the United States; that developing a distinctly American form of Islam will be a great challenge; and that "both the United States and Islam are likely to be deeply affected by their mutual encounter." These being two of the most powerful cultural forces in the world (along with the Chinese civilization), the result of their interaction is not only unpredictable but also very consequential.

In contrast to the grand sweep of the last chapter, "CAIR: Islamists Fooling the Establishment," written with Sharon Chadha, examines in close detail the Council on American-Islamic Relations, the most aggressive and arguably the most effective of American Islamist groups. Our exposé reveals CAIR's connections to terrorism as well as its efforts to stymie counterterrorism, its ties to non-Muslim political extremists, the irregularities about its funding, its real goals, and its reliance on intimidation. Chadha and I conclude this 2006 analysis asking, "How long will it be until the Establishment finally recognizes CAIR for what it is and denies it mainstream legitimacy?" Nine years later, that recognition has yet to be conferred, so our data retains its pertinence.

In "Barack Obama's Muslim Childhood," I establish that Barack Hussein Obama was born and raised a Muslim, provide confirming evidence for this from recent years, survey the perceptions of him as a Muslim, and place this deception in the larger context of Obama's other autobiographical fictions. In brief, the record points to Obama being "child to a line of Muslim males, given a Muslim name, registered as a Muslim in two Indonesian schools." Further, "he read Koran in religion class, still recites the Islamic declaration of faith, and speaks to Muslim audiences like a fellow believer. Between his non-practicing Muslim father, his Muslim stepfather, and his four years of living in a Muslim milieu, he was both seen by others and saw himself as a Muslim." This deception points to a deep character flaw.

V. Individuals and American Islam

US promoters of Islamism, both Muslim and non-Muslim, have great importance shaping the future of American Islam. Will they manage to keep radical interpretations dominant, or will they lose ground as other Muslims reclaim their faith?

The press lavished praise on an Egyptian-born professor of law at the University of California at Los Angeles as a moderate, but I sensed otherwise. In "Stealth Islamist: Khaled Abou El Fadl," I establish that the media's darling is in fact an Islamist, and all the more dangerously so for misleading potential critics. That he got away with this duplicity despite a long bibliography available in English, "points to the challenge of how to discern Islamists who present themselves as moderates" and the need to do serious background work before anointing anyone as a reformer. "Failing proper research, Islamists will push their way through Western institutions and ultimately subvert them." How many more individuals are like him, burrowing into the system?

"Waging Jihad through the American Courts: Iqbal Unus" tells how a nuclear physicist of Pakistani origin living in the Washington, DC, area with close links to many Islamist organizations thwarted counterterrorism work through his legal challenge to both the US government and a private counterterrorism researcher, Rita Katz. Although his legal case never had a chance of success and was, in fact, dismissed with prejudice by the presiding judge, it nonetheless brought a raft of benefits to Unus and his colleagues, from gumming up the works to gleaning information to winning public sympathy. In response, I call for changes in the legal system to prevent such predatory legal tactics.

My connection to the third individual began with a crudely written summons for me to appear in federal court in Texas. To make the crazed legal proceedings more endurable, I researched the plaintiff with the intent of publishing what I discovered about him. I held off, however, until a key ally of his switched sides, bearing important information. The result is "A Palestinian in Texas: Riad Hamad," a cautionary tale of "immigrants who bring with them the bad habits imbued by tyrannical politics and radical ideologies."

Finally, I look at an Islamist fellow traveler, an eight-term congressman from Cleveland, in "Lefty for Radical Islam: Dennis Kucinich." In his 2004 presidential effort, Kucinich set a number of precedents in his appeal for Muslim votes—claiming to keep a Koran in his office, rousing audiences to proclaim *Allahu Akbar*, and visiting Muslim organizations during his campaign travels. Although "seeking the Islamist vote in 2004 was a sure way *not* to reach the White House," his tender treatment of Islamists offered innovative methods that other Democratic Party politicians will likely adopt.

Editorial Practices

These chapters appear essentially unchanged from their original publication: I have corrected typographical errors and other minor mistakes, and added clarifications to once-familiar references that have become obscure. Further, some texts reflect the original work that the author submitted rather than the final publication. Where I have updated a text, an elevated, hollow dot, °, indicates the beginning and end of the new information.

Notes

1. Percy Bysshe Shelley, *Ode to the West Wind and Other Poems* (New York: Courier Dover, 2012), p. 15. I thank Anne Mandelbaum for pointing out this poem as well as for her generous help with the editing of my writings.
2. *Lectures on the Philosophy of History*, trans. into English by J. Sibree (London: George Bell and Sons, 1902), p. 454. In German: "Viele Reiche und Dynastien hat der Mohammedanismus bei seiner Ausbreitung begründet. Auf diesem unendlichen Meere wird es immer weiter, nichts ist fest." *Vorlesungen über die Philosophie der Geschichte* (Frankfurt am Main, Suhrkamp, 1970), p. 431.
3. Samuel P. Huntington, *The Clash of Civilizations and the Remaking of World Order* (New York: Simon and Schuster, 1996), p. 254.

Part I

The Arab-Israeli Conflict

1

Peace Process or War Process?

When Barack Obama announced in June 2009 about Israeli-Palestinian diplomacy, "I'm confident that if we stick with it, having started early, that we can make some serious progress this year," he displayed a touching, if naïve optimism.

Indeed, his determination fits a well-established pattern of determination by politicians to "solve" the Arab-Israeli conflict; there were fourteen US government initiatives just during the two George W. Bush administrations. Might this time be different? Will trying harder or being more clever end the conflict?

No, there is no chance whatever of this effort working.

Without looking at the specifics of the Obama approach—which are in themselves problematic—I shall argue three points: that past Israeli-Palestinian negotiations have failed; that their failure resulted from an Israeli illusion about avoiding war; and that Washington should urge Jerusalem to forego negotiations and return instead to its earlier and more successful policy of fighting for victory.

I. Reviewing the "Peace Process"

It is embarrassing to recall the elation and expectations that accompanied the signing of the Oslo accords in September 1993 when Israel's prime minister Yitzhak Rabin shook hands on the White House lawn with Yasir Arafat, the Palestinian leader. For some years afterward, "The Handshake" (as it was then capitalized) served as the symbol of brilliant diplomacy, whereby each side achieved what it most wanted: dignity and autonomy for the Palestinians, recognition and security for the Israelis.

President Bill Clinton hosted the ceremony and lauded the deal as a "great occasion of history." Secretary of State Warren Christopher concluded that "the impossible is within our reach." Yasir Arafat called the signing an "historic event, inaugurating a new epoch." Israel's foreign minister Shimon Peres said one could see in it "the outline of peace in the Middle East."

3

The public displayed similar expectations. Anthony Lewis, a *New York Times* columnist, deemed the agreement "stunning" and "ingeniously built." *Time* magazine made Arafat and Rabin two of its "men of the year" for 1993. To cap it off, Arafat, Rabin, and Peres jointly won the Nobel Peace Prize for 1994.

As the accords led to a deterioration of conditions for Palestinians and Israelis, rather than the expected improvement, these heady anticipations quickly dissipated.

When Palestinians still lived under Israeli control, pre-Oslo accords, they had benefited from the rule of law and a growing economy, independent of international welfare. They enjoyed functioning schools and hospitals; they traveled without checkpoints and had free access to Israeli territory. They even founded several universities. Terrorism declined as acceptance of Israel increased. Oslo then brought Palestinians not peace and prosperity, but tyranny, failed institutions, poverty, corruption, a death cult, suicide factories, and Islamist radicalization. Yasir Arafat had promised to build his new dominion into a Middle Eastern Singapore, but the reality he ruled became a nightmare of dependence, inhumanity, and loathing, more akin to Liberia or the Congo.

As for Israelis, they watched as Palestinian rage spiraled upward, inflicting unprecedented violence on them; the Israeli Ministry of Foreign Affairs reports that more Israelis were killed by Palestinian terrorists in the five years after the Oslo accords than in the fifteen years preceding it. If the two hands in the Rabin-Arafat handshake symbolized Oslo's early hopes, the two bloody hands of a young Palestinian male who had just lynched Israeli reservists in Ramallah in October 2000 represented its dismal end. In addition, Oslo did great damage to the Israel's standing internationally, resurrecting questions about the very existence of a sovereign Jewish state, especially on the Left, and spawning moral perversions such as the U.N. World Conference against Racism in Durban. From Israel's perspective, the seven years of Oslo diplomacy, 1993–2000, largely undid forty-five years of success in warfare.

Palestinians and Israelis agree on little, but with a near universality they concur that the Oslo accords failed. What is called the "peace process" should rather be called the "war process."

II. The False Hope of Finessing War

Why did things go so badly wrong? Where lay the flaws in so promising an agreement?

Of a multiple of errors, the ultimate mistake lay in Yitzhak Rabin's misunderstanding of how war ends, as revealed by his catchphrase, "One does not make peace with one's friends. One makes peace with one's enemies." The Israeli prime minister expected war to be concluded through goodwill, conciliation, mediation, flexibility, restraint, generosity, and compromise, topped off with signatures on official documents. In this spirit, his government and those of his three successors—Shimon Peres, Binyamin Netanyahu, Ehud Barak—initiated an array of concessions, hoping and expecting the Palestinians to reciprocate.

This did not happen. In fact, Israeli concessions inflamed Palestinian hostility. Palestinians interpreted Israeli efforts to "make peace" as signals of demoralization and weakness. "Painful concessions" reduced the Palestinian awe of Israel, made the Jewish state appear vulnerable and incited irredentist dreams of annihilation. Each Oslo-negotiated gesture by Israel further exhilarated, radicalized, and mobilized the Palestinian body politic to war. The quiet hope of 1993 to eliminate Israel gained traction, becoming a deafening demand by 2000. Venomous speech and violent actions soared. Polls and votes in recent years suggest that a mere 20 percent of Palestinians accept the existence of a Jewish state.

Rabin's mistake was simple and profound: One cannot "make peace with one's enemies," as he imagined. Rather, one makes peace with one's *former* enemies. Peace nearly always requires one side in a conflict to be defeated and thus give up its goals.

Wars end not through goodwill but through victory. "Let your great object [in war] be victory" observed Sun Tzu, the ancient Chinese strategist. "War is an act of violence to compel the enemy to fulfill our will," wrote his nineteenth-century Prussian successor, Karl von Clausewitz in 1832. Douglas MacArthur observed in 1951 that in "war, there is no substitute for victory."

Technological advancement has not altered this insight. Fighting either continues or potentially can resume so long as both sides hope to achieve their war goals. Victory consists of imposing one's will on the enemy, compelling him to give up his war ambitions. Wars typically end when one side gives up hope, when its will to fight has been crushed.

Defeat, one might think, usually follows on devastating battlefield losses, as was the case of the Axis in 1945. But that has rarely occurred during the past sixty years. Battlefield losses by the Arab states to Israel in 1948–82, by North Korea in 1953, by Saddam Hussein in 1991, and by Iraqi Sunnis in 2003 did not translate into despair and surrender. Morale and will matter more these days. Although they out-manned and out-gunned their foes, the French gave up in Algeria, the Americans in Vietnam, and the Soviets in Afghanistan. The Cold War ended, notably, with barely a fatality. Crushing the enemy's will to fight, then, does not necessarily mean crushing the enemy.

Arabs and Israelis since 1948 have pursued static and opposite goals: Arabs fought to eliminate Israel, Israelis fought to win their neighbors' acceptance. Details have varied over the decades with multiple ideologies, strategies, and leading actors, but the twin goals have remained in place and unbridgeable. If the conflict is to end, one side must lose and one side win. Either there will be no more Zionist state or it will be accepted by its neighbors. Those are the only two scenarios for ending the conflict. Anything else is unstable and a premise for further warfare.

The Arabs have pursued their war aims with patience, determination, and purpose; the exceptions to this pattern (e.g., the Egyptian and Jordanian peace treaties) have been operationally insignificant because they did not reduce hostility to Israel's existence. In response, Israelis sustained a formidable record of strategic vision and tactical brilliance in the period 1948–93. Over time, however, as Israel developed into a wealthy country, its populace grew impatient with the humiliating, slow, boring, bitter, and expensive task of convincing Arabs to accept their political existence. By now, few in Israel still see victory as the goal; almost no major political figure on the scene today calls for victory in war. Uzi Landau, who argues that "when you're in a war you want to win the war," is a rare exception.

The Hard Work of Winning

In place of victory, Israelis developed an imaginative array of approaches to manage the conflict:

- Territorial compromise: as proposed by Yitzhak Rabin (and incorporated into the Oslo process).
- Develop the Palestinian economy: Shimon Peres (and also the Oslo process).
- Unilateralism (build a wall, withdraw from Gaza): Ariel Sharon and Ehud Olmert.
- Lease the land under Israeli towns on the West Bank for 99 years: Amir Peretz and the Labor Party.
- Encourage the Palestinians to develop good government: Natan Sharansky (and George W. Bush).
- Territorial retreat: Israel's Left.
- Exclude disloyal Palestinians from Israeli citizenship: Avigdor Lieberman.

- Offer Jordan as Palestine: elements of Israel's Right.
- Expel Palestinians from lands controlled by Israel: Meir Kahane.

Contradictory in spirit and mutually exclusive as they are, these approaches all aim to finesse war rather than win it. Not one of them addresses the need to break the Palestinian will to fight. Just as the Oslo negotiations failed, I predict that so too will every Israeli scheme that avoids the hard work of winning.

Since 1993, in brief, the Arabs have sought victory while Israelis sought compromise. In this spirit, Israelis openly announced their fatigue with warfare. Shortly before becoming prime minister, Ehud Olmert said on behalf of his countrymen: "We are tired of fighting; we are tired of being courageous; we are tired of winning; we are tired of defeating our enemies." After becoming prime minister, Olmert proclaimed: "Peace is achieved through concessions. We all know that." Such defeatist statements prompted Yoram Hazony of the Shalem Center to characterize Israelis as "an exhausted people, confused and without direction."

But who does not win, loses. To survive, Israelis eventually must return to their pre-1993 policy of establishing that Israel is strong, tough, and permanent. That is achieved through deterrence—the tedious task of convincing Palestinians and others that the Jewish state will endure and that dreams of elimination must fail.

This will not be easy or quick. Due to missteps during the Oslo years and after (especially the unilateral withdrawal from Gaza of 2005 and the Lebanon war of 2006), Palestinians perceive Israel as economically and militarily strong but morally and politically weak. In the pungent words of Hezbollah leader Hassan Nasrallah, Israel is "weaker than a spider's web." Such scorn will likely require decades of hard work to reverse. Nor will it be pretty: Defeat in war typically entails that the loser experiences deprivation, failure, and despair.

Israel does enjoy one piece of good fortune: It need only deter the Palestinians, not the whole of the Arab and Muslim populations. Moroccans, Iranians, Malaysians, and others take their cues from the Palestinians and with time will follow their lead. Israel's ultimate enemy, the one whose will it needs to crush, is roughly the same demographic size as itself.

This process may be seen through a simple prism. Any development that encourages Palestinians to think they can eliminate Israel is negative, any that encourages them to give up that goal is positive.

The Palestinians' defeat will be recognizable when, over a protracted period and with complete consistency, they prove that they have accepted Israel. This does not mean loving Zion, but it does mean permanently accepting it—overhauling the educational system to take out the demonization of Jews and Israel, telling the truth about Jewish ties to Jerusalem, and accepting normal commercial, cultural, and human relations with Israelis.

Palestinian demarches and letters to the editor are acceptable, but violence is not. The quiet that follows must be consistent and protracted. Symbolically, one can conclude that Palestinians have accepted Israel and the war is over when Jews living in Hebron (on the West Bank) have no more need for security than Arabs living in Nazareth (in Israel).

Israel's win, ironically, would be the best thing that ever happened to the Palestinians. Compelling them finally to give up on their irredentist dream would liberate them to focus on their own polity, economy, society, and culture. Palestinians need to experience the crucible of defeat to become a normal people—one whose parents stop celebrating their children becoming suicide terrorists, whose obsession with rejection of Zionism collapses. There is no shortcut.

III. US Policy

Like all outsiders to the conflict, Americans face a stark choice: Endorse the Palestinian goal of eliminating Israel or endorse Israel's goal of winning its neighbors' acceptance.

To state the choice makes clear that there is no choice—the first is barbaric, the second civilized. No decent person can endorse the Palestinians' genocidal goal of eliminating their neighbor. Following every president since Harry S Truman, and every congressional resolution and vote since then, the US government stands with Israel in its drive to win acceptance.

This analysis implies a radically different approach from the current one. On the negative side, it puts Palestinians on notice that benefits will flow to them only after they prove their acceptance of Israel. Until then—no diplomacy, no discussion of final status, no recognition as a state, and certainly no financial aid or weapons.

On the positive side, the US administration should work with Israel, the Arab states, and others to induce the Palestinians to accept Israel's existence by convincing them that they have lost. This means impressing on the Israeli government the need not just to defend itself but to take steps to demonstrate to Palestinians the hopelessness of their cause.

That requires not episodic shows of force (such as the wars against Hamas in Gaza) but a sustained and systematic effort to deflate a bellicose mentality.

Israel's victory directly also helps its US ally, for some of its enemies—Hamas, Hezbollah, Syria, and Iran—are also America's. Tougher Israeli tactics would help Washington in smaller ways, too. Washington should encourage Jerusalem not to engage in prisoner exchanges with terrorist groups, not to allow Hezbollah to rearm in southern Lebanon or Fatah or Hamas in Gaza, and not to withdraw unilaterally from the West Bank (which would effectively turn over the region to Hamas terrorists and threaten Hashemite rule in Jordan).

Diplomacy aiming to shut down the Arab-Israeli conflict is premature until Palestinians give up their anti-Zionism. When that happy moment arrives, negotiations can reopen and take up anew the Oslo issues—borders, resources, armaments, sanctities, residential rights. But that is years or decades away. In the meantime, an ally needs to win.

2

The Muslim Claim to Jerusalem

Everyone has long agreed that Jerusalem presents the knottiest issue facing Arab and Israeli negotiators.

In part, the problem is practical: the Palestinians insist that the capital of Israel serve as the capital of their future state too, something Israelis are loath to accept. But mostly, the problem is religious: the ancient city has sacred associations for Jews and Muslims alike (and Christians too, of course; but Christians today no longer make an independent political claim to Jerusalem), and both insist on sovereignty over their overlapping sacred areas.

In Jerusalem, theological and historical claims matter; they are the functional equivalent to the deed to the city and have direct operational consequences. Jewish and Muslim connections to the city therefore require evaluation.

Comparing Religious Claims

The Jewish connection to Jerusalem is an ancient and powerful one. Judaism made Jerusalem a holy city over three thousand years ago, and through all that time Jews remained steadfast to it. Jews pray in its direction, mention its name constantly in prayers, close the Passover service with the wistful statement "Next year in Jerusalem," and recall the city in the blessing at the end of each meal. The destruction of the Temple looms very large in Jewish consciousness; remembrance takes such forms as a special day of mourning, houses left partially unfinished, a woman's makeup or jewelry left incomplete, and a glass smashed during the wedding ceremony. In addition, Jerusalem has had a prominent historical role as the only capital of a Jewish state and as the only city with a Jewish majority during the whole of the past century. In the words of one of its mayors, Jerusalem represents "the purest expression of all that Jews prayed for, dreamed of, cried for, and died for in the two thousand years since the destruction of the Second Temple."[1]

What about Muslims? Where does Jerusalem fit in Islam and Muslim history? It is not the place to which they pray, is not once mentioned by name in prayers, and it is connected to no mundane events in Muhammad's life. The city never served as capital of a sovereign Muslim state, and it never became a cultural or scholarly center. Little of political import by Muslims was initiated there.

One comparison makes this point most clearly: Jerusalem appears in the Jewish Bible 669 times, and Zion (which usually means Jerusalem, sometimes the Land of Israel) 154 times, or 823 times in all. The Christian Bible mentions Jerusalem 154 times and Zion 7 times. In contrast, the columnist Moshe Kohn notes, Jerusalem and Zion appear as frequently in the Koran "as they do in the Hindu Bhagavad-Gita, the Taoist Tao-Te Ching, the Buddhist Dhamapada and the Zoroastrian Zend Avesta"—which is to say, not once.[2]

The city being of such evidently minor religious importance, why does it now loom so large for Muslims, to the point that a Muslim Zionism seems to be in the making across the Muslim world? Why do Palestinian demonstrators take to the streets shouting "We will sacrifice our blood and souls for you, Jerusalem"[3] and their brethren in Jordan yell "We sacrifice our blood and soul for Al-Aqsa"?[4] Why did King Fahd of Saudi Arabia call on Muslim states to protect "the holy city [that] belongs to all Muslims across the world"?[5] Why did two surveys of American Muslims indicate Jerusalem to be their most pressing foreign policy issue?[6]

Because of politics. An historical survey shows that the stature of the city, and the emotions surrounding it, inevitably rises for Muslims when Jerusalem has political significance. Conversely, when the utility of Jerusalem expires, so does its status and the passions about it. This pattern first emerged during the lifetime of the Islam's Prophet Muhammad in the early seventh century. Since then, it has been repeated on five occasions: in the late seventh century, in the twelfth-century Countercrusade, in the thirteenth-century Crusades, during the era of British rule (1917–48), and since Israel took the city in 1967. The consistency that emerges in such a long period provides an important perspective on current claims to Jerusalem.

I. Koran and Muhammad

According to the Arabic-literary sources, Muhammad fled his home town of Mecca in AD 622 for Medina, a city with a substantial Jewish population. On arrival in Medina, if not slightly earlier, the Koran adopted a number of practices friendly to Jews: a Yom Kippur-like fast, a synagogue-like place of prayer, permission to eat kosher food, and approval for Muslim men to marry Jewish women. Most important, the Koran repudiated the pre-Islamic practice of the Meccans to pray toward the Ka'ba, the small stone structure at the center of the main mosque in Mecca. Instead, it adopted the Judaic practice of facing the Temple Mount in Jerusalem during prayer. (Actually, the Koran only mentions the direction as "Syria"; other information makes it clear that Jerusalem and the Temple Mount are meant.)

This, the first *qibla* (direction of prayer) of Islam, did not last long. The Jews criticized the new faith and rejected the friendly Islamic gestures; not long after, the Koran broke with them, probably in early 624. The explanation of this change comes in a Koranic verse instructing the faithful no longer to pray toward Syria but instead toward Mecca. The passage (2:142–52) begins by anticipating questions about this abrupt change:

> The Fools among the people will say: "What has turned them [the Muslims] from the *qibla* to which they were always used?"

God then provides the answer:

> We appointed the *qibla* that to which you was used, only to test those who followed the Messenger [Muhammad] from those who would turn on their heels [on Islam].

In other words, the new *qibla* served as a way to distinguish Muslims from Jews. From now on, Mecca would be the direction of prayer:

> now shall we turn you to a *qibla* that shall please you. Then turn your face in the direction of the Sacred Mosque [in Mecca]. Wherever you are, turn your faces in that direction.

The Koran then reiterates the point about no longer paying attention to Jews:

> Even if you were to bring all the signs to the people of the Book [i.e., Jews], they would not follow your *qibla*.

Muslims subsequently accepted the point implicit to the Koranic explanation, that the adoption of Jerusalem as *qibla* was a tactical move to win Jewish converts. "He chose the Holy House in Jerusalem in order that the People of the Book [i.e., Jews] would be conciliated," notes At-Tabari, an early Muslim commentator on the Koran, "and the Jews were glad."[7] Modern historians agree: W. Montgomery Watt, a leading biographer of Muhammad, interprets the prophet's "far-reaching concessions to Jewish feeling" in the light of two motives, one of which was "the desire for a reconciliation with the Jews."[8]

After the Koran repudiated Jerusalem, so did the Muslims: the first description of the town under Muslim rule comes from the visiting Bishop Arculf, a Gallic pilgrim, in 680, who reported seeing "an oblong house of prayer, which they [the Muslims] pieced together with upright plans and large beams over some ruined remains."[9] Not for the last time, safely under Muslim control, Jerusalem became a backwater.[10]

This episode set the mold that would be repeated many times over succeeding centuries: Muslims take interest religiously in Jerusalem because of pressing but temporary concerns. Then, when those concerns lapse, so does the focus on Jerusalem, and the city's standing greatly diminishes.

II. Umayyads

The second round of interest in Jerusalem occurred during the rule of the Damascus-based Umayyad dynasty (661–750). A dissident leader in Mecca, 'Abdullah b. az-Zubayr began a revolt against the Umayyads in 680 that lasted until his death in 692; while fighting him, Umayyad rulers sought to aggrandize Syria at the expense of Arabia (and perhaps also to help recruit an army against the Byzantine Empire). They took some steps to sanctify Damascus, but mostly their campaign involved what Amikam Elad of the Hebrew University calls an "enormous" effort "to exalt and to glorify" Jerusalem.[11] They may even have hoped to make it the equal of Mecca.

The first Umayyad ruler, Mu'awiya, chose Jerusalem as the place where he ascended to the caliphate; he and his successors also engaged in a construction program—religious edifices, a palace, and roads—in the city. The Umayyads possibly had plans to make Jerusalem their political and administrative capital; indeed, Elad finds that they in effect treated it as such. But Jerusalem is primarily a city of faith, and, as the Israeli scholar Izhak Hasson explains, the "Umayyad regime was interested in ascribing an Islamic aura to its stronghold and center."[12] Toward this end (as well as to assert Islam's presence in its competition with Christianity), the Umayyad caliph built Islam's first grand structure, the Dome of the Rock, right on the spot of the Jewish Temple, in 688–91.[13] This remarkable building is not just the first monumental sacred building of Islam but also the only ancient one that still stands today in roughly its original form.

The next Umayyad step was subtle and complex, and requires a pause to note a passage of the Koran (17:1) describing Muhammad's Night Journey to heaven (known as the *isra'*):

> Glory to He who took His servant by night from the Sacred Mosque to the furthest mosque. (*Subhana allathina asra bi-'abdihi laylatan min al-masjidi al-harami ila al-masjidi al-aqsa.*)

When this Koranic passage was first revealed, in about 621, a place called the Sacred Mosque already existed in Mecca. In contrast, the "furthest mosque" was a turn of phrase, not a known place. Some early Muslims understood it as metaphorical or as a place in heaven.[14] And if the "furthest mosque" did exist on earth, Palestine would seem an unlikely location, for many reasons. Some of them:

> Elsewhere in the Koran (30:1), Palestine is called "the closest land" (*adna al-ard*).

> Palestine had not yet been conquered by the Muslims and contained not a single mosque.

> The "furthest mosque" was apparently identified with places inside Arabia: either Medina[15] or a town called Ji'rana, about ten miles from Mecca, which the Prophet visited in 630.[16]

> The earliest Muslim accounts of Jerusalem, such as the description of Caliph 'Umar's reported visit to the city just after the Muslims conquest in 638, nowhere identify the Temple Mount with the "furthest mosque" of the Koran.

> The Koranic inscriptions that make up a 240-meter mosaic frieze inside the Dome of the Rock do not include Koran 17:1 and the story of the Night Journey, suggesting that as late as 692 the idea of Jerusalem as the liftoff for the Night Journey had not yet been established. (Indeed, the first extant inscription tying Koran 17:1 to Jerusalem dates only from the eleventh century.)

> Muhammad ibn al-Hanafiya (638–700), a close relative of the Prophet Muhammad, is quoted denigrating the notion that the prophet ever set foot on the Rock in Jerusalem; "these damned Syrians," by which he means the Umayyads, "pretend that God put His foot on the Rock in Jerusalem, though [only] one person ever put his foot on the rock, namely Abraham."[17]

Then, in 715, to build up the prestige of their dominions, the Umayyads did a most clever thing: they built a second mosque in Jerusalem, again on the Temple Mount, and called this one the Furthest Mosque (*al-masjid al-aqsa*, Al-Aqsa Mosque). With this, they retroactively gave the city a role in Muhammad's life. This association of Jerusalem with *al-masjid al-aqsa* fit into a wider Muslim tendency to identify place names found in the Koran, notes the scholar who goes by Ibn al-Rawandi: "wherever the Koran mentions a name of an event, stories were invented to give the impression that somehow, somewhere, someone, knew what they were about."[18]

Contrary to logic (how can a mosque built nearly a century after the Koran was received establish what the Koran meant?), building an actual Al-Aqsa Mosque, the Palestinian historian A. L. Tibawi writes, "gave reality to the figurative name used in the Koran."[19] It also had the hugely important effect of inserting Jerusalem post hoc into the Koran and making it more central to Islam. Also, other changes resulted. Several Koranic passages were reinterpreted to refer to this city.[20] Jerusalem came to be seen as the site of the Last Judgment. The Umayyads cast aside the nonreligious Roman name for the city, Aelia Capitolina (in Arabic, *Iliya*) and replaced it with Jewish-style names, either Al-Quds (The Holy) or Bayt al-Maqdis (The Temple). They sponsored a form of literature praising the "virtues of Jerusalem," a genre one author, R. J. Zwi Werblowsky, is tempted to call "Zionist."[21] Accounts of the prophet's sayings or doings (Arabic: *hadith*s, often translated into English as "Traditions") favorable to Jerusalem emerged at this time, some of them equating the city with Mecca.[22] There was even an effort to move the pilgrimage (*hajj*) from Mecca to Jerusalem.

Scholars agree that the Umayyads' motivation to assert a Muslim presence in the sacred city had a strictly utilitarian purpose. The Iraqi historian Abdul Aziz Duri finds "political reasons" behind their actions.[23] Hasson concurs:

> The construction of the Dome of the Rock and al-Aqsa mosque, the rituals instituted by the Umayyads on the Temple Mount and the dissemination of Islamic-oriented Traditions [*hadith*s] regarding the sanctity of the site, all point to the political motives which underlay the glorification of Jerusalem among the Muslims.[24]

Thus did a politically inspired Umayyad building program lead to the Islamic sanctification of Jerusalem.

Abbasid Rule

Then, with the Umayyad demise in 750 and the move of the caliph's capital to Baghdad, "imperial patronage became negligible,"[25] and Jerusalem fell into near-obscurity. For the next three and a half centuries, books praising this city lost favor and the construction of glorious buildings not only came to an end but existing ones fell apart (the dome over the rock collapsed in 1016). Gold was stripped off the dome to pay for Al-Aqsa repair work. City walls disintegrated and fell. Worse, the rulers of the new dynasty bled Jerusalem and its region country through what F. E. Peters of New York University calls "their rapacity and their careless indifference."[26] The city declined to the point of becoming a shambles. "Learned men are few, and the Christians numerous," bemoaned a tenth-century Muslim native of Jerusalem.[27] Only mystics continued to visit the city.

In a typical put-down, another tenth-century author described the city as "a provincial town attached to Ramla,"[28] a reference to the tiny, insignificant town serving as Palestine's administrative center. Elad characterizes Jerusalem in the early centuries of Muslim rule as "an outlying city of diminished importance."[29] The great historian S. D. Goitein notes that the geographical dictionary of al-Yaqut mentions Basra 170 times, Damascus 100 times, and Jerusalem only once, and that one time in passing. He concludes from this and other evidence that, in its first six centuries of Muslim rule, "Jerusalem mostly lived the life of an out-of-the-way provincial town, delivered to the exactions of rapacious officials and notables, often also to tribulations at the hands of seditious *fellahin* [peasants] or nomads. . . . Jerusalem certainly could not boast of excellence in the sciences of Islam or any other fields."[30]

By the early tenth century, notes Peters, Muslim rule over Jerusalem had an "almost casual" quality with "no particular political significance."[31] Later too: Al-Ghazali, sometimes called the "Thomas Aquinas of Islam," visited Jerusalem in 1096 but not once refers to the Crusaders heading its way.

III. Early Crusades

The Crusader conquest of Jerusalem in 1099 initially aroused a very mild Muslim response. The Franks did not rate much attention; Arabic literature written in Crusader-occupied towns tended not even to mention them. Thus, "calls to jihad at first fell upon deaf ears," writes Robert Irwin, formerly of the University of St Andrews in Scotland.[32]

Emmanuel Sivan of the Hebrew University adds that "one does not detect either shock or a sense of religious loss and humiliation."[33]

Only as the effort to retake Jerusalem grew serious in about 1150 did Muslim leaders seek to rouse *jihad* sentiments through the heightening of emotions about Jerusalem. Using the means at their disposal (*hadiths*, "virtues of Jerusalem" books, poetry), their propagandists stressed the sanctity of Jerusalem and the urgency of its return to Muslim rule. Newly minted *hadiths* made Jerusalem ever-more critical to the Islamic faith; one of them put words into the Prophet Muhammad's mouth saying that, after his own death, Jerusalem's falling to the infidels is the second greatest catastrophe facing Islam. Whereas not a single "virtues of Jerusalem" volume appeared in the period 1100–50, very many came out in the subsequent half century. In the 1160s, Sivan notes, "*al-Quds* propaganda blossomed"; and when Saladin (Salah ad-Din) led the Muslims to victory over Jerusalem in 1187, the "propaganda campaign . . . attained its paroxysm."[34] In a letter to his Crusader opponent, Saladin wrote that the city "is to us as it is to you. It is even more important to us."[35]

The glow of the reconquest remained bright for several decades thereafter; for example, Saladin's descendants (known as the Ayyubid dynasty, which ruled until 1250) went on a great building and restoration program in Jerusalem, thereby imbuing the city with a more Muslim character. Until this point, Islamic Jerusalem had consisted only of the shrines on the Temple Mount; now, for the first time, specifically Islamic buildings (Sufi convents, schools) were built in the surrounding city. Also, it was at this time, Oleg Grabar of Princeton's Institute of Advanced Study notes, that the Dome of the Rock came to be seen as the exact place where Muhammad's ascension to heaven (*mi'raj*) took place during his Night Journey:[36] if the "furthest mosque" is in Jerusalem, then Muhammad's Night Journey and his subsequent visit to heaven logically took place on the Temple Mount—indeed, on the very rock from which Jesus was thought to have ascended to heaven.

IV. Ayyubids

But once safely back in Muslim hands, interest in Jerusalem again dropped; "the simple fact soon emerged that al-Quds was not essential to the security of an empire based in Egypt or Syria. Accordingly, in times of political or military crisis, the city proved to be expendable," writes Donald P. Little of McGill University.[37] In particular, in 1219, when Europeans attacked Egypt in the Fifth Crusade, a grandson of Saladin named al-Mu'azzam decided to raze the walls around Jerusalem, fearing that were the Franks to take the city with walls, "they will kill all whom they find there and will have the fate of Damascus and lands of Islam in their hands."[38] Pulling down Jerusalem's fortifications had the effect of prompting a mass exodus from the city and leading to its steep decline.

Also at this time, the Muslim ruler of Egypt and Palestine, al-Kamil (another of Saladin's grandsons and the brother of al-Mu'azzam), offered to trade Jerusalem to the Europeans if only the latter would leave Egypt, but he had no takers. Ten years later, in 1229, just such a deal was reached when al-Kamil did cede Jerusalem to Emperor Friedrich II; in return, the German leader promised military aid to al-Kamil against al-Mu'azzam, now a rival king. Al-Kamil insisted that the Temple Mount remain in Muslim hands and "all the practices of Islam"[39] continued to be exercised there, a condition Friedrich complied with. Referring to his deal with Frederick, al-Kamil wrote in a remarkably revealing description of Jerusalem, "I conceded to the Franks only ruined churches and houses."[40] In other words, the city that had been heroically regained by Saladin in 1187 was voluntarily traded away by his grandson just forty-two years later.

On learning that Jerusalem was back in Christian hands, Muslims felt predictably intense emotions. An Egyptian historian later wrote that the loss of the city "was a great misfortune for the Muslims, and much reproach was put upon al-Kamil, and many were the revilings of him in all the lands."[41] By 1239, another Ayyubid ruler, an-Nasir Da'ud, managed to expel the Franks from the city.

But then he too ceded it right back to the Crusaders in return for help against one of his relatives. This time, the Christians were less respectful of the Islamic sanctuaries and turned the Temple Mount mosques into churches.

Their intrusion did not last long; by 1244 the invasion of Palestine by troops from Central Asia brought Jerusalem again under the rule of an Ayyubid; and henceforth the city remained safely under Muslim rule for nearly seven centuries. Jerusalem remained but a pawn in the *Realpolitik* of the times, as explained in a letter from a later Ayyubid ruler, as-Salih Ayyub, to his son: if the Crusaders threaten you in Cairo, he wrote, and they demand from you the coast of Palestine and Jerusalem, "give these places to them without delay on condition they have no foothold in Egypt."[42]

The psychology at work here bears note: that Christian knights traveled from distant lands to make Jerusalem their capital made the city more valuable in Muslim eyes too. "It was a city strongly coveted by the enemies of the faith, and thus became, in a sort of mirror-image syndrome, dear to Muslim hearts,"[43] Sivan explains. And so, fractured opinions coalesced into a powerful sensibility; political exigency caused Muslims ever after to see Jerusalem as the third most holy city of Islam (*thalith al-masajid*).

Mamluk and Ottoman Rule

During the Mamluk era (1250–1516), Jerusalem lapsed into its usual obscurity—capital of no dynasty, economic laggard, cultural backwater—though its newfound prestige as an Islamic site remained intact. Also, Jerusalem became a favorite place to exile political leaders, due to its proximity to Egypt and its lack of walls, razed in 1219 and not rebuilt for over three centuries, making it easy prey for marauders. These notables endowed religious institutions, especially religious schools, which in the aggregate had the effect of reestablishing Islam in the city. But a general lack of interest translated into decline and impoverishment. Many of the grand buildings, including the Temple Mount sanctuaries, were abandoned and became dilapidated as the city became depopulated. A fourteenth-century author bemoaned the paucity of Muslims visiting Jerusalem.[44] The Mamluks so devastated Jerusalem that the town's entire population at the end of their rule amounted to a miserable four thousand souls.

The Ottoman period (1516–1917) got off to an excellent start when Süleyman the Magnificent rebuilt the city walls in 1537–41 and lavished money in Jerusalem (for example, assuring its water supply), but things then quickly reverted to type. Jerusalem now suffered from the indignity of being treated as a tax farm for nonresident, one-year (and very rapacious) officials. "After having exhausted Jerusalem, the pasha left," observed the French traveler François-René Chateaubriand in 1806. At times, this rapaciousness prompted uprisings. The Turkish authorities also raised funds for themselves by gouging European visitors; in general, this allowed them to make fewer efforts in Jerusalem than in other cities to promote the city's economy. The tax rolls show soap as its only export. So insignificant was Jerusalem, it was sometimes a mere appendage to the governorship of Nablus or Gaza. Nor was scholarship cultivated: in 1670, a traveler reported that standards had dropped so low that even the preacher at Al-Aqsa Mosque spoke a low standard of literary Arabic. The many religious schools of an earlier era disappeared. By 1806, the population had again dropped, this time to under nine thousand residents.

Muslims during this long era could afford to ignore Jerusalem, writes the historian James Parkes, because the city "was something that was there, and it never occurred to a Muslim that it would not always be there," safely under Muslim rule.[45] Innumerable reports during these centuries from Western pilgrims, tourists, and diplomats in Jerusalem told of the city's execrable condition. George Sandys in 1611 found that "Much lies waste; the old buildings (except a few) all ruined, the new contemptible." Constantin Volney, one of the most scientific of observers, noted in 1784 Jerusalem's "destroyed walls, its debris-filled moat, its city circuit choked with ruins." "What desolation and misery!" wrote Chateaubriand. Gustav Flaubert of *Madame Bovary* fame visited in 1850 and found "Ruins everywhere, and everywhere the odor of graves. It seems as if the Lord's curse hovers over the city. The Holy City of three religions is rotting away from boredom, desertion, and neglect." "Hapless are the favorites of heaven," commented Herman Melville in 1857. Mark Twain in 1867 found that Jerusalem "has lost all its ancient grandeur, and is become a pauper village."

The British government recognized the minimal Muslim interest in Jerusalem during World War I. In negotiations with Sharif Hussein of Mecca in 1915–16 over the terms of the Arab revolt against the Ottomans, London decided not to include Jerusalem in territories to be assigned to the Arabs because, as the chief British negotiator, Henry McMahon, put it, "there was no place . . . of sufficient importance . . . further south" of Damascus "to which the Arabs attached vital importance."[46]

True to this spirit, the Turkish overlords of Jerusalem abandoned Jerusalem rather than fight for it in 1917, evacuating it just in advance of the British troops. One account indicates they were even prepared to destroy the holy city. Jamal Pasha, the Ottoman commander-in-chief, instructed his Austrian allies to "blow Jerusalem to hell" should the British enter the city. The Austrians therefore had their guns trained on the Dome of the Rock, with enough ammunition to keep up two full days of intensive bombardment. According to Pierre van Paasen, a journalist, that the dome still exists today is due to a Jewish artillery captain in the Austrian army, Marek Schwartz, who rather than respond to the approaching British troops with a barrage on the Islamic holy places, "quietly spiked his own guns and walked into the British lines."[47]

V. British Rule

In modern times, notes the Israeli scholar Hava Lazarus-Yafeh, Jerusalem "became the focus of religious and political Arab activity only at the beginning of the [twentieth] century." She ascribes the change mainly to "the renewed Jewish activity in the city and Judaism's claims on the Western Wailing Wall."[48] British rule over the city, lasting from 1917 to 1948, then galvanized a renewed passion for Jerusalem. Arab politicians made Jerusalem a prominent destination during the British Mandatory period. Iraqi leaders frequently turned up in Jerusalem, demonstrably praying at Al-Aqsa and giving emotional speeches. Most famously, King Faisal of Iraq visited the city and made a ceremonial entrance to the Temple Mount using the same gate as did Caliph 'Umar when the city was first conquered in 638. Iraqi involvement also included raising funds for an Islamic university in Jerusalem, and setting up a consulate and an information office there.

The Palestinian leader (and mufti of Jerusalem) Al-Hajj Amin al-Husseini made the Temple Mount central to his anti-Zionist political efforts. Husseini brought a contingent of Muslim notables to Jerusalem in 1931 for an international congress to mobilize global Muslim opinion on behalf of the Palestinians. He also exploited the draw of the Islamic holy places in Jerusalem to find international Muslim support for his campaign against Zionism. For example, he engaged in fundraising in several Arab countries to restore the Dome of the Rock and Al-Aqsa, sometimes by sending out pictures of the Dome of the Rock under a Star of David; his efforts did succeed in procuring the funds to restore these monuments to their former glory.

Perhaps most indicative of the change in mood was the claim that the Prophet Muhammad had tethered his horse to the western wall of the Temple Mount. As established by Shmuel Berkowitz,[49] Muslim scholars over the centuries had variously theorized about the prophet tying horse to the eastern or southern walls—but not one of them before the Muslim-Jewish clashes at the Western Wall in 1929 ever associated this incident with the western side. Once again, politics drove Muslim piousness regarding Jerusalem.

Jordanian Rule

Sandwiched between British and Israeli eras, Jordanian rule over Jerusalem in 1948–67 offers a useful control case; true to form, when Muslims took the Old City (which contains the sanctuaries) they noticeably lost interest in it. An initial excitement stirred when the Jordanian forces captured the walled city in 1948—as evidenced by the Coptic bishop's crowning King 'Abdullah as "King of Jerusalem" in November of that year—but then the usual ennui set in. °Arab states other than Jordan suggested a permanent international regime for Jerusalem in November 1949.[50°]

The Hashemite dynasty had little affection for Jerusalem, where some of their worst enemies lived and where 'Abdullah was assassinated in 1951. In fact, the Hashemites made a concerted effort to diminish the holy city's importance in favor of their capital, Amman,° prompting Anwar Nusayba, a Jordanian member of parliament for the Jerusalem region, to complain of discrimination toward the city.[51°] Jerusalem had served as the British administrative capital, but now all government offices there (save tourism) were shut down; Jerusalem no longer had authority even over other parts of the West Bank. The Jordanians also closed some local institutions (e.g., the Arab Higher Committee, the Supreme Muslim Council) and moved others to Amman (the treasury of the *waqf*, or religious endowment).

Jordanian efforts succeeded: once again, Arab Jerusalem became an isolated provincial town, less important than Nablus. The economy so stagnated that many thousands of Arab Jerusalemites left the town: while the population of Amman increased five-fold in the period 1948–67, that of Jerusalem grew by just 50 percent. To take out a bank loan meant traveling to Amman. Amman had the privilege of hosting the country's first university and the royal family's many residences.

Jerusalem Arabs knew full well what was going on, as evidenced by one notable's complaint about the royal residences: "those palaces should have been built in Jerusalem, but were removed from here, so that Jerusalem would remain not a city, but a kind of village."[52] East Jerusalem's Municipal Counsel twice formally complained of the Jordanian authorities' discrimination against their city. °One observer noted in 1954 that while Israel had made Jerusalem its state capital, in Jordan "we reduced Jerusalem from a position of preeminence to its current place that does not rise above the rank of a village."[53] More broadly, Kimberly Katz of Towson University notes in her book *Jordanian Jerusalem: Holy Places and National Spaces*, "Jerusalem was a source of contention for many Palestinians, who claimed that the Holy City was being discriminated against, while Amman, the capital city, received a disproportionate share of political, economic, and infrastructure attention."[54°]

Perhaps most insulting of all was the decline in Jerusalem's religious standing. Mosques lacked sufficient funds. Jordanian radio broadcast the Friday prayers not from Al-Aqsa Mosque but from an upstart mosque in Amman. (Ironically, Radio Israel began broadcasting services from Al-Aqsa immediately after the Israel victory in 1967.) This was part of a larger pattern, as the Jordanian authorities sought to benefit from the prestige of controlling Jerusalem even as they put the city down: Marshall Breger and Thomas Idinopulos note that although King 'Abdullah "styled himself a protector of the holy sites, he did little to promote the religious importance of Jerusalem to Muslims."[55]

Nor were Jordan's rulers alone in ignoring Jerusalem; the city virtually disappeared from the Arab diplomatic map. Malcolm Kerr's well-known study on inter-Arab relations during this period (*The Arab Cold War*) appears not once to mention the city.[56] No foreign Arab leader came to Jerusalem during the nineteen years when Jordan controlled East Jerusalem, and King Hussein (r. 1952–99) himself only rarely visited. King Faisal of Saudi Arabia spoke often after 1967 of his yearning to pray in Jerusalem, yet he appears never to have bothered to pray there when he had the chance. Perhaps most remarkable is that the PLO's founding document, the Palestinian National Covenant of 1964, does not once mention Jerusalem or even allude to it.

VI. Israeli Rule

This neglect came to an abrupt end when the Old City came under Israeli control in June 1967. Palestinians again made Jerusalem the centerpiece of their political program. The Dome of the Rock turned up in pictures everywhere, from Yasir Arafat's office to the corner grocery. Slogans about Jerusalem proliferated, and the city quickly became the single most emotional issue of the Arab-Israeli conflict. The PLO made up for its 1964 oversight by specifically mentioning Jerusalem in its 1968 constitution as "the seat of the Palestine Liberation Organization."[57]

"As during the era of the Crusaders," Lazarus-Yafeh points out, Muslim leaders "began again to emphasize the sanctity of Jerusalem in Islamic tradition."[58] In the process, they even relied on some of the same arguments (e.g., rejecting the occupying power's religious connections to the city) and some of the same *hadiths* to back up those allegations. Muslims began echoing the Jewish devotion to Jerusalem: Arafat declared that "Al-Quds is in the innermost of our feeling, the feeling of our people and the feeling of all Arabs, Muslims, and Christians in the world."[59] Extravagant statements became the norm (Jerusalem was now said to be "comparable in holiness" to Mecca and Medina; or even "our most sacred place").[60] Jerusalem turned up regularly in Arab League and United Nations resolutions. The Jordanian and Saudi governments now gave as munificently to the Jerusalem religious trust as they had been stingy before 1967.

Nor were Palestinians alone in this emphasis on Jerusalem: the city again served as a powerful vehicle for mobilizing Muslim opinion internationally. This became especially clear in September 1969, when Saudi king Faisal parlayed a fire at Al-Aqsa Mosque into the impetus to convene twenty-five Muslim heads of state and establish the Organization of the Islamic Conference, a United Nations-style institution for Muslims °known since 2011 as the Organization of Islamic Cooperation. His successor, King Abdullah, in 2007 put the Dome of the Rock and Al-Aqsa on the two sides of a 50-riyal banknote.° In Lebanon, the Islamist group Hezbollah depicts the Dome of the Rock on everything from wall posters to scarves and under the picture often repeats its slogan: "We are advancing." Lebanon's leading Shi'i authority, Muhammad Hussein Fadlallah, regularly exploits the theme of liberating Jerusalem from Israeli control to inspire his own people; he does so, explains his biographer Martin Kramer, not for pie-in-the-sky reasons but "to mobilize a movement to liberate Lebanon for Islam."[61]

Similarly, the Islamic Republic of Iran has made Jerusalem a central issue, following the dictate of its founder, Ayatollah Khomeini, who remarked that "Jerusalem is the property of Muslims and must return to them."[62] Since shortly after the regime's founding, its 1-rial coin and 1000-rial banknote have featured the Dome of the Rock (though, embarrassingly, the latter initially was mislabeled "Al-Aqsa Mosque"). Iranian soldiers at war with Saddam Hussein's forces in the 1980s received simple maps showing their sweep through Iraq and onto Jerusalem. Ayatollah Khomeini decreed the last Friday of Ramadan as Jerusalem Day, and this commemoration has served as a major occasion for anti-Israel harangues in many countries, including Turkey, Tunisia, and Morocco. The Islamic Republic of Iran celebrates the holiday with stamps and posters featuring scenes of Jerusalem accompanied by exhortative slogans. In February 1997, a crowd of some three hundred thousand celebrated Jerusalem Day in the presence of dignitaries such as President Hashemi Rafsanjani. Jerusalem Day is celebrated (complete with a roster of speeches, an art exhibit, a folkloric show, and a youth program) as far off as Dearborn, Michigan.

As it has become common for Muslims to claim passionate attachment to Jerusalem, Muslim pilgrimages to the city have multiplied four-fold in recent years. A new "virtues of Jerusalem" literature has developed.[63] So emotional has Jerusalem become to Muslims that they write books of poetry about it (especially in Western languages).[64] And in the political realm, Jerusalem has become a uniquely unifying issue for Arabic-speakers. "Jerusalem is the only issue that seems to unite the Arabs. It is the rallying cry," a senior Arab diplomat noted in late 2000.[65]

The fervor for Jerusalem at times challenges even the centrality of Mecca. No less a personage than then-Crown Prince 'Abdullah of Saudi Arabia has been said repeatedly to say that for him, "Jerusalem is just like the holy city of Mecca."[66] Hasan Nasrallah, the leader of Hezbollah goes further yet, declaring in a major speech: "We won't give up on Palestine, all of Palestine, and Jerusalem will remain the place to which all jihad warriors will direct their prayers."[67]

Dubious Claims

Along with these high emotions, four historically dubious claims promoting the Islamic claim to Jerusalem have emerged.

1. *The Islamic connection to Jerusalem is older than the Jewish.* The Palestinian "minister" of religious endowments asserts that Jerusalem has "always" been under Muslim sovereignty.[68] Likewise, Ghada Talhami, a polemicist, asserts that "There are other holy cities in Islam, but Jerusalem holds a special place in the hearts and minds of Muslims because its fate has always been intertwined with theirs."[69] Always? Jerusalem's founding antedated Islam by about two millennia, so how can that be? Ibrahim Hooper of the Washington-based Council on American-Islamic Relations explains this anachronism: "the Muslim attachment to Jerusalem does not begin with the prophet Muhammad, it begins with the prophets Abraham, David, Solomon and Jesus, who are also prophets in Islam."[70] In other words, the central figures of Judaism and Christianity were really proto-Muslims. This accounts for the Palestinian man-in-the-street declaring that "Jerusalem was Arab from the day of creation."[71] There has even been some scholarship, from 'Ayn Shams University in Egypt, alleging to show that Al-Aqsa Mosque predates the Jewish antiquities in Jerusalem—by no less than two thousand years.[72]

2. *The Koran mentions Jerusalem.* So complete is the identification of the Night Journey with Jerusalem that it is found in many publications of the Koran, and especially in translations. Some state

in a footnote that the "furthest mosque" "must" refer to Jerusalem.[73] Others take the (blasphemous?) step of inserting Jerusalem right into the text after "furthest mosque." This is done in a variety of ways. The Sale translation[74] uses italics:

> from the sacred temple *of Mecca* to the farther temple *of Jerusalem*

the Asad translation[75] relies on square brackets:

> from the Inviolable House of Worship [at Mecca] to the Remote House of Worship [at Jerusalem]

and the Behbudi-Turner version[76] places it right in the text without any distinction at all:

> from the Holy Mosque in Mecca to the Al-Aqsa Mosque in Palestine.

If the Koran in translation now has Jerusalem in its text, it cannot be surprising to find that those who rely on those translations believe that Jerusalem "is mentioned in the Koran"; and this is precisely what a consortium of American Muslim institutions claimed in 2000.[77] One of their number went yet further; according to Hooper, "the Koran refers to Jerusalem by its Islamic centerpiece, al-Aqsa Mosque."[78]

°Whole books are devoted to this topic, such as Imran N. Hosein's *Jerusalem in the Qur'an* a book-length study on a nonexistant topic— despite the author's acknowledgment that "the word 'Jerusalem' does not explicitly occur in the Qur'an."[79°] This errroneous claim has practical consequences: for example, Ahmad 'Abd ar-Rahman, secretary-general of the PA "cabinet," rested his claim to Palestinian sovereignty on this basis: "Jerusalem is above tampering, it is inviolable, and nobody can tamper with it since it is a Koranic text."[80]

3. *Muhammad actually visited Jerusalem.* The Islamic biography of the Prophet Muhammad's life is very detailed and it very clearly does not mention his leaving the Arabian Peninsula, much less voyaging to Jerusalem. Therefore, when Karen Armstrong, a specialist on Islam, writes that "Muslim texts make it clear that . . . the story of Muhammad's mystical Night Journey to Jerusalem . . . was not a physical experience but a visionary one," she is merely stating the obvious. Indeed, this phrase is contained in an article titled, "Islam's Stake: Why Jerusalem Was Central to Muhammad" which posits that "Jerusalem was central to the spiritual identity of Muslims from the very beginning of their

faith."[81] Not good enough. Armstrong found herself under attack for a "shameless misrepresentation" of Islam and claiming that "Muslims themselves do not believe the miracle of their own prophet."[82]

4. *Jerusalem has no importance to Jews.* The first step is to deny a Jewish connection to the Western (or Wailing) Wall, the only portion of the ancient Temple that still stands. In 1967, a top Islamic official of the Temple Mount portrayed Jewish attachment to the wall as an act of "aggression against al-Aqsa mosque."[83] The late King Faisal of Saudi Arabia spoke on this subject with undisguised scorn: "The Wailing Wall is a structure they weep against, and they have no historic right to it. Another wall can be built for them to weep against."[84] 'Abd al-Malik Dahamsha, a Muslim member of Israel's parliament, has flatly stated that "the Western Wall is not associated with the remains of the Jewish Temple."[85] The Palestinian Authority's website states about the Western Wall that "Some Orthodox religious Jews consider it as a holy place for them, and claim that the wall is part of their temple which all historic studies and archeological excavations have failed to find any proof for such a claim." The PA's mufti describes the Western Wall as "just a fence belonging to the Muslim holy site" and declares that "There is not a single stone in the Wailing-Wall relating to Jewish history."[86] He also makes light of the Jewish connection, dismissively telling an Israeli interviewer, "I heard that your Temple was in Nablus or perhaps Bethlehem."[87] Likewise, Arafat announced that Jews "consider Hebron to be holier than Jerusalem."[88] The head of Al-Azhar University in Cairo, Mohammed Sayyed Tantawi, announced that "the temple is not to be found underneath Al-Aqsa mosque as the Jews claim."[89]

In this spirit, Muslim institutions pressure the Western media to call the Temple Mount and the Western Wall by their Islamic names (*Al-Haram ash-Sharif, Al-Buraq*), and not their much older Jewish names. (*Al-Haram ash-Sharif*, for example, dates only from the Ottoman era.) When Western journalists did not comply, Arafat responded with outrage, with his news agency portraying this as part of a "constant conspiracy against our sanctities in Palestine" and his mufti deeming this contrary to Islamic law.[90]

The second step is to deny Jews access to the wall. "It's prohibited for Jews to pray at the Western Wall," asserts an Islamist leader living in Israel.[91] The director of the Al-Aqsa Mosque asserts that "This is a place for Muslims, only Muslims. There is no temple here, only Al-Aqsa Mosque and the Dome of the Rock."[92] The Voice of Palestine radio station demands that Israeli politicians not be allowed even to touch the wall.[93] 'Ikrima Sabri, the Palestinian Authority's mufti, prohibits Jews from making repairs to the wall and extends Islamic claims further: "All the buildings surrounding the Al-Aqsa mosque are an Islamic waqf."[94]

The third step is to reject any form of Jewish control in Jerusalem, as Arafat did in mid-2000: "I will not agree to any Israeli sovereign presence in Jerusalem."[95] He was echoed by Saudi Arabia's Crown Prince Abdullah, who stated that "There is nothing to negotiate about and compromise on when it comes to Jerusalem."[96] Even Oman's Minister of State for Foreign Affairs Yusuf bin 'Alawi bin 'Abdullah told the Israeli prime minister that sovereignty in Jerusalem should be exclusively Palestinian "to ensure security and stability."[97]

The final step is to deny Jews access to Jerusalem at all. Toward this end, a body of literature has blossomed that insists on an exclusive Islamic claim to all of Jerusalem.[98] School textbooks allude to the city's role in Christianity and Islam, but ignore Judaism. An American affiliate of Hamas claims Jerusalem as "an Arab, Palestinian and Islamic holy city."[99] A banner carried in a street protest puts it succinctly: "Jerusalem is Arab."[100] No place for Jews here.

Anti-Jerusalem Views

This Muslim love of Zion notwithstanding, Islam contains a recessive but persistent strain of anti-Jerusalem sentiment, premised on the idea that emphasizing Jerusalem is non-Islamic and can undermine the special sanctity of Mecca.

In the early period of Islam, Princeton historian Bernard Lewis notes, "there was strong resistance among many theologians and jurists" to the notion of Jerusalem as a holy city. They viewed this as a "Judaizing error—as one more among many attempts by Jewish converts to infiltrate Jewish ideas into Islam."[101] Anti-Jerusalem stalwarts circulated stories to show that the idea of Jerusalem's holiness is a Jewish practice. In the most important of them, a converted Jew named Ka'b al-Ahbar suggested to Caliph 'Umar that Al-Aqsa Mosque be built by the Dome of the Rock. The caliph responded by accusing him of reversion to his Jewish roots:

> 'Umar asked him: "Where do you think we should put the place of prayer?"
>
> "By the [Temple Mount] rock," answered Ka'b.
>
> By God, Ka'b," said 'Umar, "you are following after Judaism. I saw you take off your sandals [following Jewish practice]."

"I wanted to feel the touch of it with my bare feet," said Ka'b.

"I saw you," said 'Umar. "But no . . . Go along! We were not commanded concerning the Rock, but we were commanded concerning the Ka'ba [in Mecca]."[102]

Another version of this anecdote makes the Jewish content even more explicit: "in this one, Ka'b al-Ahbar tries to induce Caliph 'Umar to pray north of the Holy Rock, pointing out the advantage of this: "Then the entire Al-Quds, that is, Al-Masjid al-Haram will be before you."[103] In other words, the convert from Judaism is saying, the Rock and Mecca will be in a straight line and Muslims can pray toward both of them at the same time.

That Muslims for almost a year and a half during Muhammad's lifetime directed prayers toward Jerusalem has had a permanently contradictory effect on that city's standing in Islam. The incident partially imbued Jerusalem with prestige and sanctity, but it also made the city a place uniquely rejected by God. Some early *hadith*s have Muslims expressing this rejection by purposefully praying with their back sides to Jerusalem,[104] a custom that still survives in vestigial form; he who prays in Al-Aqsa Mosque not coincidentally turns his back precisely to the Temple area toward which Jews pray. Or, in Prime Minister Ariel Sharon's sharp formulation: when a Muslim prays in Al-Aqsa, "his back is to it. Also some of his lower parts."[105]

Ibn Taymiya (1263–1328), one of Islam's strictest and most influential religious thinkers, is perhaps the outstanding spokesman of the anti-Jerusalem view.[106] In his wide-ranging attempt to purify Islam of accretions and impieties, he dismissed the sacredness of Jerusalem as a notion deriving from Jews and Christians, and also from the long-ago Umayyad rivalry with Mecca. Ibn Taymiya's student, Ibn Qayyim al-Jawziya (1292–1350), went further and rejected *hadith*s about Jerusalem as false. More broadly, learned Muslims living after the Crusades knew that the great publicity given to *hadith*s extolling Jerusalem's sanctity resulted from the Countercrusade—from political exigency, that is—and therefore treated them warily.

There are other signs too of Jerusalem's relatively low standing in the ladder of sanctity: Eva Baer, a historian of art finds that, "in contrast to representations of Mecca, Medina, and the Ka'ba, depictions of Jerusalem are scanty."[107] The belief that the Last Judgment would take place in Jerusalem was said by some medieval authors to be a forgery to induce Muslims to visit the city.

Modern writers sometimes take exception to the envelope of piety that has surrounded Jerusalem. Muhammad Abu Zayd wrote a book in Egypt in 1930 that was so radical that it was withdrawn from circulation and appears no longer even to be extant. In it, among many other points, he

> dismissed the notion of the Prophet's heavenly journey via Jerusalem, claiming that the Koranic rendition actually refers to his Hijra from Mecca to Madina; "the more remote mosque" (*al-masjid al-aqsa*) thus had nothing to do with Jerusalem, but was in fact the mosque in Madina.[108]

That this viewpoint is banned shows the nearly complete victory in Islam of the pro-Jerusalem viewpoint. Still, an occasional expression still filters through. At a summit meeting of Arab leaders in March 2001, Mu'ammar al-Qaddafi made fun of his colleagues' obsession with Al-Aqsa Mosque. "The hell with it," delegates quoted him saying, "you solve it or you don't, it's just a mosque and I can pray anywhere."[109]

Conclusion

Politics, not religious sensibility, has fueled the Muslim attachment to Jerusalem for nearly fourteen centuries; what the historian Bernard Wasserstein has written about the growth of Muslim feeling in the course of the Countercrusade applies through the centuries: "often in the history of Jerusalem, heightened religious fervour may be explained in large part by political necessity."[110] This pattern has three main implications. First, Jerusalem will never be more than a secondary city for Muslims; "belief in the sanctity of Jerusalem," Sivan rightly concludes, "cannot be said to have been widely diffused nor deeply rooted in Islam."[111] Second, the Muslim interest lies not so much in controlling Jerusalem as it does in denying control over the city to anyone else. Third, the Islamic connection to the city is weaker than the Jewish one because it arises as much from transitory and mundane considerations as from the immutable claims of faith.

Mecca, by contrast, is the eternal city of Islam, the place from which non-Muslims are strictly forbidden. Very roughly speaking, what Jerusalem is to Jews, Mecca is to Muslims—a point made in the Koran itself (2:145) in recognizing that Muslims have one *qibla* and "the people of the Book" another one. The parallel was noted by medieval Muslims; the geographer Yaqut (1179–1229) wrote, for example, that "Mecca is holy to Muslims and Jerusalem to the Jews."[112] In modern times, some scholars have come to the same conclusion: "Jerusalem plays for the Jewish people the same role that Mecca has for Muslims," writes Abdul Hadi Palazzi, director of the Cultural Institute of the Italian Islamic Community.[113]

The similarities are striking. Jews pray thrice daily to Jerusalem and Muslims five times to Mecca. Muslims see Mecca as the navel of the world, just as Jews see Jerusalem. Whereas Jews believe Abraham nearly sacrificed his son Isaac in Jerusalem, Muslims believe this episode (involving Abraham's other son, Ishmael) took place in Mecca. The Ka'ba in Mecca has similar functions for Muslims as the Temple in Jerusalem for Jews (such as serving as a destination for pilgrimage). The Temple and Ka'ba are both said to be inimitable structures. The supplicant takes off his shoes and goes barefoot in both their precincts. Solomon's Temple was inaugurated on Yom Kippur, the tenth day of the year, and the Ka'ba receives its new cover also on the tenth day of each year.[114] If Jerusalem is for Jews a place so holy that not just its soil but even its air is deemed sacred, Mecca is the place whose "very mention reverberates awe in Muslims' hearts," according to Abad Ahmad of the Islamic Society of Central Jersey.[115]

This parallelism of Mecca and Jerusalem offers the basis of a solution, as Sheikh Palazzi wisely writes:

> separation in directions of prayer is a mean to decrease possible rivalries in management of Holy Places. For those who receive from Allah the gift of equilibrium and the attitude to reconciliation, it should not be difficult to conclude that, as no one is willing to deny Muslims a complete sovereignty over Mecca, from an Islamic point of view—notwithstanding opposite, groundless propagandistic claims—there is not any sound theological reason to deny an equal right of Jews over Jerusalem.[116]

To back up this view, Palazzi notes several striking and oft-neglected passages in the Koran. One of them (5:22–23) quotes Moses instructing the Jews to "enter the Holy Land (al-ard al-muqaddisa) which God has assigned unto you." Another verse (17:104) has God Himself making the same point: "We said to the Children of Israel: 'Dwell securely in the Land.'" Koran 2:145 states that the Jews "would not follow your qibla; nor are you going to follow their qibla," indicating a recognition of the Temple Mount as the Jews' direction of prayer. "God himself is saying that Jerusalem is as important to Jews as Mecca is to Moslems,"[117] Palazzi concludes.

His analysis has a clear and sensible implication: just as Muslims rule an undivided Mecca, Jews should rule an undivided Jerusalem.

Notes

1. Ehud Olmert, "I Am the Most Privileged Jew in the Universe," *Middle East Quarterly*, Dec. 1997, p. 65.
2. It bears noting that "Mecca" appears just once in the Koran.
3. *The Jerusalem Post*, Aug. 23, 2000.
4. Associated Press, Aug. 11, 2000; Reuters, Aug. 25, 2000.
5. Reuters, Aug. 12, 2000.
6. American Muslim Council, "American Muslims Identify Top Ten Issues," Feb. 29, 2000; Council on American-Islamic Relations, "New Survey Reiterates American Muslim Concern for Jerusalem," July 6, 2000.
7. At-Tabari, *Jami' al-Bayan fi Tafsir al-Qur'an* (Cairo, 1321/1903), quoted in F. E. Peters, *Jerusalem* (Princeton, N.J.: Princeton University Press, 1985), p. 181.
8. W. Montgomery Watt, *Muhammad in Medina* (Oxford: Oxford University Press, 1956), p. 200.
9. Quoted in Peters, *Jerusalem*, pp. 195–96.
10. Its holiness in the monotheistic traditions gave it a special standing. For example, while the word for *Zion* in Arabic is *Sihyawn* (or *Sahyun*), and it historically refers to Jerusalem (or sometimes to Byzantium), on rare occasions it has referred to Mecca, possibly "an early tendency to enhance the holiness of Mecca by attributing to it holy merits of Biblical places and persons." *The Encyclopaedia of Islam*, 2nd edition, c.v. "Sihyawn."
11. Amikam Elad, "Why Did 'Abd al-Malik Build the Dome of the Rock?" *Bayt al-Maqdis: 'Abd al-Malik's Jerusalem*, ed. Julian Raby and Jeremy Johns (Oxford: Oxford University Press, 1992), vol. 1, p. 48.
12. Ibid.; Izhak Hasson, "The Muslim View of Jerusalem: The Qur'an and Hadith," *The History of Jerusalem: The Early Muslim Period, 638–1099*, ed. Joshua Prawer and Haggai Ben-Shammai (New York: New York University Press, 1996), p. 358.
13. For a revisionist account, which interprets the construction of the Dome of the Rock as the beginning of Islam, see Moshe Sharon, "The Birth of Islam in the Holy Land," *The Holy Land in History and Thought*, ed. Moshe Sharon (Leiden: E J. Brill, 1988), pp. 225–35.
14. B. Schreike, "Die Himmelreise Muhammeds," *Der Islam* 6 (1915–16): 1–30; J. Horovitz, "Muhammeds Himmelfahrt," *Der Islam* 9 (1919): 159–83; Heribert Busse, "Jerusalem in the Story of Muhammad's Night Journey and Ascension," *Jerusalem Studies in Arabic and Islam* 14 (1991): 1–40. See also Heribert Busse and Georg Kretschmar, *Jerusalemer Heiligstumstraditionen* (Weisbaden: Otto Harrassowitz, 1987).
15. Arthur Jeffrey, "The Suppressed Qur'an Commentary of Muhammad Abu Zaid," *Der Islam*, 20 (1932): 306.
16. Alfred Guillaume, "Where Was Al-Masjid Al-Aqsa?" *Al-Andalus*, (18) 1953: 323–36.

17. Quoted in Joseph van Ess, "'Abd al-Malik and the Dome of the Rock," *Bayt al-Maqdis: 'Abd al-Malik's Jerusalem*, ed. Julian Raby and Jeremy Johns (Oxford: Oxford University Press, 1992), vol. 1, p. 93.

18. Ibn al-Rawandi, "Origins of Islam: A Critical Look at the Sources," *The Quest for the Historical Muhammad*, ed. Ibn Warraq (New York: Prometheus, 2000), p. 101.

19. A. L. Tibawi, *Jerusalem: Its Place in Islam and Arab History* (Beirut: Institute for Palestine Studies, 1969), p. 9.

20. Examples are in Hasson, "The Muslim View of Jerusalem," p. 353.

21. R. J. Zwi Werblowsky, "The Meaning of Jerusalem to Jews, Christians, and Muslims," *Jerusalem in the Mind of the Western World, 1800–1948*, vol. 5 of *With Eyes toward Zion*, ed. Yehoshua Ben-Arieh and Moshe Davis (Westport, Conn.: Praeger, 1997), p. 10. The "virtues of Jerusalem" literature was once thought to date from centuries later, but recent research has established its Umayyad origins.

22. Ignaz Goldziher, *Muhammadanische Studien*, vol. 2 (Halle: Max Niemeyer, 1889–90), pp. 34–37.

23. Abdul Aziz Duri, "Jerusalem in the Early Islamic Period, 7th–11th Centuries AD," in *Jerusalem in History: 3,000 B.C. to the Present Day*, rev. ed., ed. Kamil J. Asali (London: Kegan Paul International, 1997), p. 112.

24. Hasson, "The Muslim View of Jerusalem," p. 377.

25. Paul Wheatley, *The Places Where Men Pray Together: Cities in Islamic Lands, Seventh through the Tenth Centuries* (Chicago: University of Chicago Press, 2001), p. 297.

26. F. E. Peters, *The Distant Shrine: The Islamic Centuries in Jerusalem* (New York: AMS, 1993), p. 71.

27. Shams ad-Din al-Muqaddasi, *Ahsan at-Taqasim fi Ma' rifat at-Taqalim*, ed. M. J. de Goeje (Leiden: E. J. Brill, 1877). Quoted in Guy Le Strange, *Palestine under the Moslems* (Boston: Houghton Mifflin, 1890), p. 86.

28. Mutahhar b. Tahir al-Maqdisi, *Kitab al-Bad' wa't-Ta'rikh*, vol. 4, ed. Clément Huart (Paris: Ernest Leroux, 1907), p. 72.

29. Amikam Elad, *Medieval Jerusalem and Islamic Worship* (Leiden: E. J. Brill, 1995), p. 1.

30. S. D. Goitein, "Al-Kuds," *The Encyclopaedia of Islam*, 2d edition, vol. 5, pp. 329, 322.

31. Peters, *Jerusalem*, p. 214.

32. Robert Irwin, "Muslim Responses to the Crusades," *History Today*, Apr. 1997, p. 44.

33. Emmanuel Sivan, *Interpretations of Islam: Past and Present* (Princeton, N.J.: Darwin Press, 1985), p. 76.

34. Ibid., pp. 83, 87.

35. Ibn Shaddad, *An-Nawadir as-Sultaniya wa'l-Mahasin al-Yusufiya*, vol. 3 (Paris, 1884), p. 265; quoted in Donald P. Little, "Jerusalem under the Ayyubids and Mamluks, 1187–1516 AD," in *Jerusalem in History*, p. 179.

36. Oleg Grabar, *The Shape of the Holy* (Princeton, N.J.: Princeton University Press, 1996), p. 157. See also p. 113.

37. Little, "Jerusalem under the Ayyubids and Mamluks," p. 181.

38. Hans I. Gottschalk, *Al-Malik al-Kamil von Ägypten und seine Zeit* (Wiesbaden: O. Harrassowitz, 1958), p. 88.

39. R.J.C. Broadhurst, *A History of the Ayyubid Sultans of Egypt Translated from the Arabic of al-Maqrizi* (Boston: Twayne, 1980), p. 26.

40. Ibid., p. 26.

41. Ibid., p. 207.

42. Quoted in Claude Cahen and Ibrahim Chabbouh, "Le testament d'al-Malik as-Salih Ayyub," *Bulletin d'Etudes Orientales*, 29 (1977): 100.

43. Sivan, *Interpretations of Islam*, p. 100.

44. 'Ali b. 'Abd al-Kafi as-Subki, *Shifa' as-Saqam fi Ziyarat Khayr al-Anam* (Cairo, 1318), p. 49. Referenced in Moshe Gil, *A History of Palestine, 634–1099*, trans. from Hebrew (Cambridge, Eng.: Cambridge University Press, 1992), p. 99.

45. James Parkes, *Whose Land? A History of the Peoples of Palestine*, rev. ed. (Harmondsworth, Eng.: Penguin, 1970), p. 171.

46. Henry McMahon to John Shuckburgh, Mar. 12, 1922, in Martin Gilbert, *Winston S. Churchill*, vol. 4, companion document volume, part 3, p. 1805. The author thanks Sir Martin for this reference.

47. Quoted in Pierre van Paasen, *Days of Our Years* (New York: Hillman-Curl, 1939), p. 379. Although van Paasen's credibility has sometimes been called into doubt, his biographers H. David Kirk and Beverly Tansey have checked out "his often colorful pronouncements against the sober realities" and found him reliable ("Pierre van Paasen's Unheeded Warnings of a Coming Holocaust," *Midstream*, July/Aug. 2000), p. 10.

48. Hava Lazarus-Yafeh, "The Sanctity of Jerusalem in Islam," *Some Religious Aspects of Islam: A Collection of Articles* (Leiden: E. J. Brill, 1981), p. 70.

49. *Milhemet Ha-Meqomot Ha-Qedoshim* (Jerusalem: Makhon Yerushalayim Le-Heker Yisrael, 2000).

50. *The Palestine Post*, Nov. 20, 1949.

51. Kimberly Katz, *Jordanian Jerusalem: Holy Places and National Spaces* (Gainesville, Flor.: University Press of Florida, 2005), p. 87.

52. Quoted in Meron Benvenisti, *Jerusalem: The Torn City* (Minneapolis: University of Minnesota Press, 1976), p. 28.

53. Yusuf Hanna, quoted in Katz, *Jordanian Jerusalem*, p. 85.

54. Ibid., p. 81.

55. Marshall J. Breger and Thomas A. Idinopulos, *Jerusalem's Holy Places and the Peace Process* (Washington: Washington Institute for Near East Policy, 1998), p. 15.

56. Malcolm H. Kerr, *The Arab Cold War: Gamal 'Abd al-Nasir and His Rivals, 1958–70*, 3d ed. (London: Oxford University Press, 1971).

57. Text in Y. Harkabi, *The Palestinian Covenant and its Meaning* (London: Valentine, Mitchell, 1979), p. 126.

58. Lazarus-Yafeh, "The Sanctity of Jerusalem in Islam," p. 223.

59. *The Jerusalem Post*, Aug. 29, 2000. The inclusion of Christians (and the absence of Jews) makes Arafat's political purposes particularly obvious.

60. PA Mufti 'Ikrama Sabri quoted in Khalid Amayreh, "Mufti of Palestine: Alqods is the Sister of Mecca and Madina," Islamic Association for Palestine,

Aug. 6, 2000; Hasan Abu 'Ali, a stone throwing teenager, quoted in Associated Press, Sept. 30, 2000.

61. Martin Kramer, "Redeeming Jerusalem: The Pan-Islamic Premise of Hizballah," *The Iranian Revolution and the Muslim World*, ed. David Menashri (Boulder, Colo.: Westview, 1990), p. 125.

62. Cited in Peter Chelkowski and Hamid Dabashi, *Staging a Revolution: The Art of Persuasion in the Islamic Republic of Iran* (New York: New York University Press, 1999), p. 23.

63. Examples in English include Tibawi, *Jerusalem: Its Place in Islam and Arab History*; M. A. Aamiri, *Jerusalem: Arab Origins and Heritage* (London: Longman, 1978); Islamic Council of Europe, *Jerusalem: The Key to World Peace* (London: Islamic Council of Europe, 1980).

64. Such as Imad Saleh, *Entre mon rêve et Jérusalem: Poèmes* (Paris: L'Harmattan, 1999).

65. Reuters, Oct. 21, 2000.

66. Reuters, June 14, 2001.

67. *Ha'aretz*, June 11, 2001.

68. *Al-Quds*, Nov. 14, 1997.

69. Ghada Talhami, "Jerusalem in the Muslim Consciousness," *The Muslim World*, 86 (1996): 229.

70. Ibrahim Hooper, "Jerusalem Belongs to All Faiths," *The Washington Post*, Oct. 16, 1996.

71. Yunis Yusuf, a seventy-eight-year old Palestinian who sells vegetables in the Dheisheh refugee camp, in Christine Hauser, "Jerusalem is explosive issue at U.S. peace summit," Reuters, July 10, 2000.

72. As described in "Recent study reveals: Al-Haram Al-Sharif's western wall is not the Wailing," ArabicNews.com, Mar. 5, 2001.

73. English examples: *The Holy Qur-an: Text, Translation and Commentary by Abdullah Yusuf Ali*, fn. 2168 and *The Meaning of the Glorious Koran by Mohammed Marmeduke Pickthall*, fn. 2.

74. *The Korân: Translated into English from the Original Arabic by Reverend George Sale* (first published in 1734).

75. *The Message of the Qur'ân: Translated and explained by Muhammad Asad.*

76. *The Quran: A New Interpretation, Textual Exegesis by Muhammad Baqir Behbudi*, trans. Colin Turner.

77. "American Muslim Organizations Emphasize Muslim Rights in Jerusalem," July 10, 2000, a statement endorsed by American Muslim Council, American Muslim Foundation, American Muslims for Jerusalem, Council on American-Islamic Relations, Islamic Association for Palestine, Islamic Circle of North America, Islamic Society of North America, Muslim Public Affairs Council.

78. Hooper, "Jerusalem Belongs to All Faiths."

79. °2d ed. Abridged. Long Island, New York: Masjid Dar-Al-Qur'an, 2003.°

80. The Palestinian Information Center, Sept. 21, 2000.

81. Time.com, Apr. 10, 2001.

82. al-awda.org, May 16, 2001.

83. 'Abd al-Hamid as-Sa'ih, Radio Amman, Sept. 23, 1967, quoted in *Middle East Record*, 3 (1967): 294.

84. Quoted in David Holden and Richard Johns, *The House of Saud: The Rise and Rule of the Most Powerful Dynasty in the Arab World* (New York: Holt, Rinehart and Winston, 1981), p. 344.

85. Interviewed by Aaron Lerner of the Independent Media Review & Analysis, Mar. 24, 1997.

86. *Makor Rishon*, May 22, 1998; *Die Welt*, Jan. 17, 2001.

87. *Makor Rishon*, May 22, 1998. Curiously, *A Brief Guide to al-Haram al-Sharif* (Jerusalem: Supreme Moslem Council, 1930), a nine-page English-language tourist guide, tells otherwise: "The site is one of the oldest in the world. Its sanctity dates from the earliest times. Its identity with the site of Solomon's Temple is beyond dispute. This, too, is the spot, according to universal belief, on which David built there an altar unto the Lord, and offered burnt offerings and peace offerings." A footnote refers to 2 Samuel 26:25. *The Jerusalem Post*, Jan. 26, 2001, reports on this booklet.

88. Al- Jazira Television, June 28, 1998.

89. Agence France Press, Aug. 3, 2001.

90. Wikalat al-Anba' al-Falastiniya, Oct. 25, 1990; PA Mufti 'Ikrama Sabri, Reuters, Feb. 20, 2001. Two days later, the Egyptian mufti endorsed this *fatwa* (Reuters, Feb. 22, 2001).

91. *The Jerusalem Report*, Apr. 3, 1997. A. L. Tibawi, *Jerusalem: Its Place in Islamic and Arab History* (Beirut: The Institute for Palestine Studies, 1969) argues against any Jewish connection to the Temple Mount in general and to the Western Wall in particular, which Tibawi in one place (p. 34) disrespectfully refers to as "the Wailing place."

92. Sheikh Muhammad Husayn, *The New York Times*, Oct. 27, 1996.

93. Voice of Palestine, Feb. 23, 2001.

94. *Sawt Al-Haqq wa'l-Hurriya*, Aug. 25, 2000. Nonetheless, out of "respect to Judaism," the Palestinian Authority is willing to permit Jews to pray at the Western Wall—on condition Jews have no sovereign rights there; as PA Mufti 'Ikrima Sabri puts it, "granting free access to the wall does not mean that the wall will belong to them. The wall is ours." (*Kull al-Arab*, Aug. 16, 2000). All quotations from Middle East Media and Research Institute (MEMRI), "The Debate at Camp David over Jerusalem's Holy Places," Aug. 28, 2000.

95. *Al-Hayat al-Jadida* (Gaza), Aug. 10, 2000. Cited in "The Debate at Camp David over Jerusalem's Holy Places."

96. Associated Press, Sept. 14, 2000.

97. Reuters, Sept. 19, 2000.

98. For example, in English: Mohammed Abdul Hameed Al-Khateeb, *Al-Quds: The Place of Jerusalem in Classical Judaic and Islamic Traditions* (London: Ta-Ha, 1419/1998); Ghada Hashem Talhami, "Academic Myths and Propaganda," *Middle East Policy*, Feb. 2000, pp. 113–29.

99. Islamic Association for Palestine, "Camp David II Must Address the Historical Injustices against the Palestinian People," July 12, 2000.

100. *The New York Times*, Mar. 1, 1997.

101. Bernard Lewis, *The Jews of Islam* (Princeton, N.J.: Princeton University Press, 1987), pp. 70–71.

102. At-Tabari, *Ta'rikh ar-Rusul wa'l-Muluk*, vol. 1, ed. M.J. de Goeje, et al. (Leiden: E.J. Brill, 1879–1901), pp. 2408–09; text in Bernard Lewis, *Islam*

from the Prophet Muhammad to the Capture of Constantinople, vol. 2 of *Religion and Society* (New York: Harper & Row, 1974), p. 3.

103. As-Suyuti, "Ithaf al-Akhissa," manuscript, Hebrew University Library, fol. 81a, l.8, quoted in "al-Kuds" in *Encyclopaedia of Islam*, 2nd ed. The curious term Al-Masjid al-Haram ("Mosque of the Sanctuary") is not in use among Muslims.

104. On which, Gil, *A History of Palestine*, pp. 67 (note 90), 102.

105. Quoted in Jeffrey Goldberg, "Arafat's Gift: The Return of Ariel Sharon," *The New Yorker*, Jan. 29, 2001, p. 55.

106. °See Charles D. Matthews, "A Muslim Iconoclast (Ibn Taymīyyeh) on the 'Merits' of Jerusalem and Palestine," *Journal of the American Oriental Society*, 56 (1936), pp. 1–21.°

107. Eva Baer, "Visual Representations of Jerusalem's Holy Islamic Sites," *The Real and Ideal Jerusalem in Jewish, Christian and Islamic Art*, published as *Journal of the Center of Jewish Art*, The Hebrew University of Jerusalem, vol. 23–24, ed. Bianca Kühnel, (1997–98): 392.

108. Ami Ayalon, *Egypt's Quest for Cultural Orientation* (Tel Aviv: Tel Aviv University, 1999), p. 7. Reference to Arthur Jeffrey, "The Suppressed Qur'an Commentary of Muhammad Abu Zaid," *Der Islam* 20 (1932), p. 306.

109. Reuters, Mar. 28, 2001.

110. Bernard Wasserstein, *Divided Jerusalem: The Struggle for the Holy City* (London, Profile, 2001), p. 11. On p. 13, Wasserstein notes that "political considerations have played a significant part" in all three of the major monotheistic traditions' focus on Jerusalem.

111. Sivan, *Interpretations of Islam*, p. 79.

112. Moshe Kohn, *The Jerusalem Post*, June 2, 2000.

113. Abdul Hadi Palazzi, "Antizionism and Antisemitism in the Contemporary Islamic Milieu" (undated).

114. Heribert Busse, "Jerusalem and Mecca, the Temple and the Kaaba," *The Holy Land in History and Thought*, pp. 236–46, provides a fuller list of comparisons and connections between the two cities and concludes that the many similarities are not a coincidence: the Prophet Muhammad, he finds, apparently "made use of elements from Jewish sources" in transforming the Ka'ba from a local, pagan temple into a universal, monotheistic sanctuary (p. 244).

115. *The Wall Street Journal*, Jan. 31, 1997.

116. Abdul Hadi Palazzi, "Antizionism and Antisemitism." Palazzi notes the curious fact that those Islamists who closely follow Ibn Taymiya's ideas about politics are also the ones leading the fight for an Islamic Jerusalem; they choose entirely to ignore the fact that Ibn Taymiya himself saw no special role for Jerusalem in Islam.

117. *The Jerusalem Post*, Feb. 28, 1997.

3

The Hell of Israel Is Better than the Paradise of Arafat

In the Palestinian Authority's (PA) elections that took place in January 2005, a significant percentage of Arab Jerusalemites stayed away from the polls out of concern that voting in them might jeopardize their status as residents of Israel. For example, the Associated Press quoted a twenty-eight-year-old truck driver who expressed strong support for Mahmoud Abbas but said he had no plans to vote: "I can't vote. I'm afraid I'll get into trouble. I don't want to take any chances."[1] A taxi driver, asked if he would vote, responded with indignation, "Are you kidding? To bring a corrupt [Palestinian] Authority here. This is just what we are missing."[2]

This reluctance—as well as administrative incompetence—helped explain why, in the words of the *Jerusalem Post*, "at several balloting locations in the city [of Jerusalem], there were more foreign election observers, journalists, and police forces out than voters."[3] It also explains why, in the previous PA election in 1996, a mere 10 percent of Jerusalem's eligible population voted, far lower than proportions elsewhere.

At first blush surprising, the worry about jeopardizing Israeli residency turns out to be widespread among the Palestinians in Israel. When given a choice of living under Zionist or Palestinian rule, they decidedly prefer the former. More than that, there is a body of pro-Israel sentiments from which they draw. No opinion surveys cover this delicate subject, but a substantial record of statements and actions suggest that, despite their anti-Zionist swagger, Israel's most fervid enemies do perceive its political virtues. Even Palestinian leaders, between their fulminations, sometimes let down their guard and acknowledge Israel's virtues. This undercurrent of Palestinian appreciation of the Jewish state has hopeful and potentially significant implications.

Pro-Israel expressions fall into two main categories:[4] preferring to remain under Israel rule and praising Israel as better than Arab regimes.

No Thank You, Palestinian Authority

Palestinians already living in Israel, especially in Jerusalem and the "Galilee Triangle" area, tell, sometimes volubly, how they prefer to remain in Israel.

Jerusalem. In mid-2000, when it appeared that some Arab-majority parts of Jerusalem would be transferred to Palestinian Authority control, Muslim Jerusalemites expressed less than delight at the prospect. Peering over at Arafat's PA, they saw power monopolized by domineering and corrupt autocrats, a thug-like police force, and a stagnant economy. Arafat's bloated, nonsensical claims ("We are the one true democratic oasis in the Arab region")[5] only exacerbated their apprehensions.

'Abd ar-Razzaq 'Abid of Jerusalem's Silwan neighborhood pointed dubiously to "what's happening in Ramallah, Hebron, and the Gaza Strip" and asked if the residents there were well off. A doctor applying for Israeli papers explained:

> The whole world seems to be talking about the future of the Arabs of Jerusalem, but no one has bothered asking us. The international community and the Israeli Left seem to take it for granted that we want to live under Mr. Arafat's control. We don't. Most of us despise Mr. Arafat and the cronies around him, and we want to stay in Israel. At least here I can speak my mind freely without being dumped in prison, as well as having a chance to earn an honest day's wage.[6]

In the colorful words of one Jerusalem resident, "The hell of Israel is better than the paradise of Arafat. We know Israeli rule stinks, but sometimes we feel like Palestinian rule would be worse."[7]

In the view of Fadal Tahabub, a member of the Palestinian National Council, an estimated 70 percent of the two hundred thousand Arab residents of Jerusalem preferred to remain under Israeli sovereignty.[8] A social worker living in Ras al-'Amud, one of the areas possibly falling under PA control, said: "If a secret poll was conducted, I am sure an overwhelming majority of Jerusalem Arabs would say they would prefer to stay in Israel."[9]

Indeed, precisely when Palestinian rule seemed most likely, in 2000, the Israeli Interior Ministry reported a substantial increase in citizenship applications from Arabs in eastern Jerusalem.[10] A Jerusalem city councilor, Roni Aloni, heard from many Arab residents about their not wanting to live under PA control. "They tell me—we are not like Gaza or the West Bank. We hold Israeli IDs. We are used to a higher standard of living. Even if Israeli rule is not so good, it is still better than that of the PA."[11] Shalom Goldstein, an adviser on Arab affairs to the Jerusalem mayor, found likewise: "People look at what is happening inside the Palestinian-controlled areas today and say to themselves, 'Thank God we have Israeli ID cards.' In fact, most of the Arabs in the city prefer to live under Israeli rule than under a corrupt and tyrannical regime like Yasser Arafat's."[12]

So many Jerusalem Arabs considered taking out Israeli papers in 2000 that the ranking Islamic official in Jerusalem issued an edict prohibiting his flock from holding Israeli citizenship (because this implies recognizing Israeli sovereignty over the holy city). Faisal al-Husseini, the Palestine Liberation Organization's man in charge of Jerusalem affairs, went further: "Taking Israeli citizenship is something that can only be defined as treason," and he threatened such people with exclusion from the Palestinian state.[13] Finding his threat ineffective, Husseini upped the ante, announcing that Jerusalem Arabs who take Israeli citizenship would have their homes confiscated.[14] The PA's radio station confirmed this, calling such persons "traitors" and threatening that they would be "tracked down."[15] Many Palestinians were duly intimidated, fearing the authority's security forces.[16]

But some spoke out. Hisham Gol of the Mount of Olives community council put it simply: "I prefer Israeli control."[17] An affluent West Bank woman called a friend in Gaza to ask about life under the PA. She heard an ear-full: "I can only tell you to pray that the Israelis don't leave your town," because "the Jews are more human" than Palestinians.[18]

One individual willing publicly to oppose Arafat was Zohair Hamdan of Sur Bahir, a village in the south of metropolitan Jerusalem; he organized a petition of Jerusalem Arabs demanding that a referendum be held before Israel lets the Palestinian Authority take power in Jerusalem. "For 33 years, we have been part of the State of Israel. But now our rights have been forgotten." Over a year and a half, he collected more than twelve thousand signatures (out of an estimated Jerusalem Arab population of two hundred thousand). "We won't accept a situation where we are led like sheep to the slaughterhouse."[19] Hamdan also expressed a personal preference that Sur Bahir remain part of Israel[20] and estimated that the majority of Palestinians reject "Arafat's corrupt and tyrannical rule. Look what he's done in Lebanon, Jordan, and now in the West Bank and Gaza Strip. He has brought one disaster after another on his people."[21]

The Galilee Triangle. Nor are such pro-Israeli sentiments limited to residents of Jerusalem. When Prime Minister Ariel Sharon's government released a trial balloon in *February* 2004 about giving the Palestinian Authority control over the Galilee Triangle, a predominantly Arab part of Israel, the response came strong and hard. As Mahmoud Mahajnah, 25, told Agence France-Presse, "Yasir Arafat runs a dictatorship, not a democracy. No one here would accept to live under that regime. I've done my [Israeli] national service; I am a student here and a member of the Israeli Football Association. Why would they transfer me? Is that logical or legitimate?"[22] One resident quoted what he called a local saying, that "the 'evil' of Israel is better than the 'heaven' of the West Bank." (A Jerusalem resident used similar words, so it could not be all that local.) Shu'a Sa'd, 22, explained why: "Here you can say whatever you like and do whatever you want—so long as you don't touch the security of Israel. Over there, if you talk about Arafat, they can arrest you and beat you up." Another young man, 'Isam Abu 'Alu, 29, put it differently: "Mr. Sharon seems to want us to join an unknown state that doesn't have a parliament, or a democracy, or even decent universities. We have close family ties in the West Bank, but we prefer to demand our full rights inside Israel."[23]

The entrance to Umm al-Fahm, the largest Muslim town in Israel, sports the green flags of the Islamic Movement Party that rules the town, along with a billboard denouncing Israel's rule over Jerusalem. That said, Hashim 'Abd ar-Rahman, mayor and local leader of the Islamic Movement, has no time for Sharon's suggestion: "Despite the discrimination and injustice faced by Arab citizens, the democracy and justice in Israel is better than the democracy and justice in Arab and Islamic countries."[24] Nor does Ahmed Tibi, an Israeli Arab member of parliament and advisor to Arafat, care for the idea of PA control, which he calls "a dangerous, antidemocratic suggestion."[25]

Just 30 percent of Israel's Arab population, a May 2001 survey found, would agree to the Galilee Triangle being annexed to a future Palestinian state, meaning that a large majority prefers to remain in Israel.[26] By *February* 2004, according to the Haifa-based Arab Center for Applied Social Research, that number had jumped to 90 percent preferring to remain in Israel. No less startling, 73 percent of Triangle Arabs said they would resort to violence to prevent changes in the border. Their reasons divided fairly evenly between those claiming Israel as their homeland (43 percent) and those cherishing Israel's higher standard of living (33 percent).[27] So intense was the Arab opposition to ceding the Galilee Triangle to the Palestinian Authority that Sharon quickly gave the idea up.

The issue arose a bit later, in 2004, as Israel built its security fence. Some Palestinians, like Umm al-Fahm's Ahmed Jabrin, sixty-seven, faced a choice on which side of the fence to live. He had no doubts. "We fought [the Israeli authorities so as] to be inside of the fence, and they moved it so we are still in Israel. We have many links to Israel. What have we to do with the Palestinian Authority?"[28] His relative, Hisham Jabrin, thirty-one, added: "We are an integral part of Israel and will never be part of a Palestinian state. We have always lived in Israel and there is absolutely no chance that that will change."[29]

Preferring Israel to the Arab Regimes

Palestinians—from the lowest level to the highest ranking—sometimes acknowledge how they prefer Israel to Arab countries. As one PLO official observed, "We no longer fear the Israelis or the Americans, regardless of their hostility, but we now fear our Arab 'brothers.'"[30] Or, in the general observation of a Gazan, "The Arabs say they're our friends, and treat us worse than the Israelis do."[31] Here are examples of attitudes toward three states:

- *Syria*. Salah Khalaf (a.k.a. Abu Iyad), one of the PLO's top figures, declared in 1983 that crimes committed by the Hafez al-Assad regime against the Palestinian people "surpassed those of the Israeli enemy."[32] In like spirit, Yasir Arafat addressed a PLO figure murdered at Syrian instigation at his funeral: "The Zionists in the occupied territories tried to kill you, and when they failed, they deported you. However, the Arab Zionists represented by the rulers of Damascus thought this was insufficient, so you fell as a martyr."[33]

- *Jordan*. Victor, a Jordanian who once worked as advance man for a senior Saudi government minister, observed in 1994 that Israel was the only Middle Eastern country he admires. "I wish Israel would just take over Jordan," he said, his brother nodding in vigorous agreement. "The Israelis are the only people around here who are organized, who know how to get things done. And they're not bad people. They're straight. They keep their word. The Arabs can't do anything right. Look at this so-called democracy in Jordan. It's a complete joke."[34]

- *Kuwait*. Palestinians collaborated with Iraqi forces occupying Kuwait in 1990–91, so when the country was liberated, they came in for some rough treatment. One Palestinian newspaper found that in Kuwait, "Palestinians are receiving treatment even worse than they have had at the hands of their enemies, the Israelis."[35] After surviving the Kuwaiti experience, another Palestinian minced no words: "Now I feel Israel is paradise. I love the Israelis now. I know they treat us like humans. The West Bank [still then under Israeli control] is better [than Kuwait]. At least before the Israelis arrest you, they bring you a paper."[36] With less exuberance, Arafat himself concurred: "What Kuwait did to the Palestinian people is worse than what has been done by Israel to Palestinians in the occupied territories."[37]

Palestinians living in the West who visit the Palestinian Authority are vividly aware of its drawbacks compared to Israel. "There is a difference between the Israeli and the PA occupation," wrote Daoud Abu Naim, a medical researcher in Philadelphia, while visiting family in Shuafat:

> The Israelis whom I met with over the years have been diverse. Some have been insensitive to our needs, and some have not been. On the other hand, the Arafat/Rajoub regime is more than simply "corrupt." It is exclusively interested in setting up a dictatorship in which Palestinian citizens will have no civil liberties whatsoever.[38]

Rewadah Edais, a high school student who lives most of the year in San Francisco and visits Jerusalem regularly, added, "The Israelis took our land, but when it comes to governing, they know what they're doing."[39]

Many Palestinians already understood the virtues of Israeli political life decades ago. As one man from Ramallah explained, "I'll never forget that day during the Lebanon war [of 1982], when an Arab Knesset member got up and called [Prime Minister Menachem] Begin a murderer. Begin didn't do a thing [in response]. If you did that to Arafat, I don't think you'd make it home that night."[40] Before the Palestinian Authority came into existence in 1994, most Palestinians dreamt of autonomy without worrying much about the details. After Arafat's return to Gaza, they could make a direct comparison between his rule and Israel's, something they frequently do. They have many reasons for preferring life in Israel:

Restraints on violence. After the PA police raided the house of a Hamas supporter in an after-midnight operation and roughed up both him and his seventy–year-old father, the father yelled at the police, "Even the Jews did not behave like you cowards." And the son, when he came out of the PA prison, declared his experience there much worse than in the Israeli jails.[41] An opponent of Arafat's pointed out how Israeli soldiers "would first fire tear gas, and then fire rubber bullets, and only then shoot live ammunition. They never shot at us without a direct order to shoot, and then they only shot a few bullets. But these Palestinian police started shooting immediately, and they shot everywhere."[42]

Freedom of expression. 'Adnan Khatib, owner and editor of *Al-Umma,* a Jerusalem weekly whose printing plant was burned down by PA police in 1995, bemoaned the troubles he'd had since the Palestinian Authority's heavy-handed leaders got power over him: "The measures they are taking against the Palestinian media, including the arrest of journalists and the closure of newspapers, are much worse than those taken by the Israelis against the Palestinian press."[43] In an ironic turn of events, Na'im Salama, a lawyer living in Gaza, was arrested by the PA on charges he slandered it by writing that Palestinians should adopt Israeli standards of democracy. Specifically, he referred to charges of fraud and breach of trust against then-prime minister Binyamin Netanyahu. Salama noted how the system in Israel allowed police to investigate a sitting prime minister and wondered when the same might apply to the PA chieftain. For this audacity, he spent time in jail.[44] Hanan Ashrawi, an obsessive anti-Israel critic, reluctantly acknowledged that the Jewish state has something to teach the nascent Palestinian polity: "freedom would have to be mentioned although it has only been implemented in a selective way, for example, the freedom of speech."[45] 'Iyad as-Sarraj, a prominent psychiatrist and director of the Gaza Community Mental Health Program, confesses that "during the Israeli occupation, I was 100 times freer [than under the Palestinian Authority]."[46]

Democracy. Israel's May 1999 elections, which Netanyahu lost, impressed many Palestinian observers. Columnists cited in a Middle East Media and Research Institute (MEMRI) study remarked on the smooth transition in Israel and wanted the same for themselves; as one put it, he envies the Israelis and wants "a similar regime in my future state."[47] Even one of Arafat's employees, Hasan al-Kashif, director-general of the PA's Information Ministry, contrasted Netanyahu's immediate and graceful exit from office with the perpetual power of "several names in our leadership" who go on ruling indefinitely.[48] Nayif Hawatma, leader of the terrorist Democratic Front for the Liberation of Palestine, wished the Palestinian Authority made decisions more like Israel:

> We want the PNC [Palestine National Council] to discuss the developments since 1991, particularly the Oslo accords, which were concluded behind the back of the PNC contrary to what happened in Israel, for example, where the accords were presented to the Knesset and public opinion for voting.[49]

His facts might not be completely accurate, but they do make his point.

Rule of law. As the *intifada* of 1987 degenerated into fratricidal murder and became known as the "intrafada," PLO leaders increasingly appreciated Israeli fairness. Haydar 'Abd ash-Shafi, head of the Palestinian delegation to the Washington peace talks, made a remarkable observation in 1992, according to a transcript published in a Beirut newspaper: "Can anyone imagine that a family would be happy to hear a knock at the door in the middle of the night from the Israeli army?" He continued: "When the infighting began in Gaza, the people were happy because the Israeli army imposed a curfew."[50] Likewise, Musa Abu Marzouk, a high-ranking Hamas official, scored points against Arafat in 2000 by comparing him unfavorably with the Jewish state: "We saw representatives of the Israeli opposition criticize [Israeli prime minister Ehud] Barak and they were not arrested . . . but in our case, the Palestinian Authority arrests people as the first order of business."[51]

Protection of minorities. Christians and secular Muslims particularly appreciate Israel's protection at a time when Palestinian politics has taken an increasingly Islamist cast. The French weekly *L'Express* quotes a Christian Palestinian to the effect that when the Palestinian state comes into existence, "the sacred union against the Zionist enemy will die. It will be time to settle accounts. We will undergo the same as our Lebanese brothers or the Copts in Egypt. It saddens me to say so, but Israeli laws protect us."[52] His fear is in many ways too late, as the Palestinian Christian population has precipitously declined in recent decades, to the point that one analyst asks if Christian life is "to be reduced to empty church buildings and a congregation-less hierarchy with no flock in the birthplace of Christianity?"[53]

Economic benefits. Palestinians who live in Israel (including Jerusalem) appreciate Israel's economic success, social services, and many benefits. Salaries in Israel are about five times higher than in the West Bank and Gaza Strip, and Israel's social security system has no parallel on the Palestinian side. The director of the Bayt Hanina community council in northern Jerusalem, Husam Watad, found that the prospect of finding themselves living under Arafat's control had people "in a panic. More than 50 percent of east Jerusalem residents live below the poverty line, and you can imagine how the situation would look if residents did not receive [Israeli] National Insurance Institute payments." Palestinians living outside of Israel want economically in; when the Israeli government announced the completion of an eighty-five-mile-long section of a security fence to protect the country from

Palestinian terrorists, one resident of Qalqiliya, a West Bank border town, reacted with a revealing outrage: "We are living in a big prison."[54]

Tolerance of homosexuals. In the West Bank and Gaza, conviction for sodomy brings a three- to ten-year jail term, and gay men tell of being tortured by the PA police. Some of them head for Israel where one estimate finds three hundred mostly male gay Palestinians living. Donatella Rovera of Amnesty International comments, "Going to Israel is a one-way ticket, and once there their biggest problem is possibly being sent back."[55]

Conclusion

Several themes emerge from this history. First, for all the overheated rhetoric about Israel's "vicious" and "brutal" occupation, Palestinians are alive to the benefits of its liberal democracy. They appreciate the elections, rule of law, freedom of speech and religion, minority rights, orderly political structures, and the other benefits of a decent polity. There is, in short, a constituency for normality among the Palestinians, difficult as that may be to perceive in the hate-filled crowds that so dominate news coverage. Second, many of those who have tasted Israel's economic benefits are loath to forego them; however impervious Palestinians may seem to economics, they know a good deal when they have one. Third, the percentage of Palestinians who would prefer to live under Israeli control cited in the estimates noted above—an overwhelming majority of 70 to 90 percent—point to this being more than a rarity among Palestinians. This has obvious implications for Israeli concessions on the "right to return," suggesting that Palestinians will move to Israel in large numbers. Fourth, it implies that some of the more imaginative final status solutions that involve the redrawing of borders will be hard to implement; Palestinians appear no more eager to live under Palestinian Authority rule than are Israelis.

In word and deed, then, even Palestinians acknowledge Israel as the most civilized state in the Middle East. Amid the gloom of today's political extremism and terrorism, this fact offers wisps of hope.

Notes

1. Associated Press, Jan. 6, 2005.
2. *The Jerusalem Post*, Jan. 9, 2005.
3. Ibid.
4. There is a third expression, of equal importance but very complex and not covered here, namely the in-migration to Israel by Palestinian and other Middle Easterners.

5. *Sawt al-Jabal* (Shanayh), Mar. 6, 1993.

6. *The Daily Telegraph* (London), Jan. 28, 2001.

7. 'Abd as-Samiya Abu Subayh, quoted in *The Washington Post*, July 25, 2000.

8. *The Washington Post*, July 25, 2000.

9. *The Daily Telegraph*, Jan. 28, 2001.

10. Ibid.

11. *The Jerusalem Post*, Nov. 8, 2000.

12. *The Jerusalem Report*, Sept. 9, 2002.

13. Reuters, Aug. 17, 2000.

14. Israel Wire Service, Sept. 4, 2000.

15. Reuters, Aug. 17, 2000.

16. *The Jerusalem Report*, Sept. 9, 2002.

17. *Ha'aretz* (Tel Aviv), Dec. 29, 2000.

18. *The Forward*, Aug. 11, 1995.

19. *The Jerusalem Post*, Dec. 22, 2002.

20. Ibid., Nov. 8, 2002. For his efforts, he was threatened by the PA with his effigy on an electric pole, declared an enemy on Hezbollah television, and finally gunned down, taking five bullets in the abdomen, shoulder, and leg. (Joseph Farah, "My New Muslim Hero," *WorldNetDaily.com*, Nov. 28, 2001.)

21. *The Jerusalem Post*, Dec. 22, 2002.

22. Agence France-Presse, Feb. 3, 2003.

23. *The Washington Times*, Feb. 17, 2004.

24. *Newsday*, Mar. 7, 2004.

25. Associated Press, Feb. 3, 2004.

26. Conducted by the Peace Research Institute at Givat Haviva, *The Jerusalem Post*, May 21, 2001.

27. Quoted in *Newsday*, Mar. 7, 2004.

28. *Newsday*, Mar. 7, 2004.

29. Agence France-Presse, Feb. 3, 2003.

30. *Ar-Ra'y* (Amman), Nov. 5, 1991.

31. Quoted in Milton Viorst, *Sandcastles: The Arabs in Search of the Modern World* (New York: Alfred A. Knopf, 1994), p. 370.

32. *Al-Majalla* (London), Nov. 26, 1983.

33. *The Washington Post*, Jan. 1, 1985.

34. Ethan Bronner, "The Arab Paradox," *The Boston Globe Magazine*, May 8, 1994.

35. *Al-Fajr* (Jerusalem), June 3, 1991.

36. Quoted in Deborah Amos, *Lines in the Sand: Desert Storm and the Remaking of the Arab World* (New York: Simon and Schuster, 1992), p. 180.

37. *Al-Musawwar* (Cairo), Nov. 15, 1991.

38. "Encounter-EMEM-for Middle East Peace Activists," July 16, 2001.

39. *The Washington Post*, July 25, 2000.

40. Peter Hirschberg, "The Dark Side of Arafat's Regime," *The Jerusalem Report*, Aug. 22, 1997, p. 25.

41. *The Jerusalem Report*, Feb. 23, 1995.

42. *Los Angeles Times*, Nov. 19, 1994

43.   *The Jerusalem Report*, June 15, 1995.

44.   *The Washington Post*, May 2, 1997.

45.   *Neues Deutschland* (Berlin), June 16, 1994.

46.   Anthony Lewis, "Darkness in Gaza," *The New York Times*, May 6, 1996.

47.   *Al-Quds* (Jerusalem), May 24, 1999, in MEMRI, June 4, 1999.

48.   *Al-Ayyam* (Ramallah), May 22, 1999, in MEMRI, June 4, 1999.

49.   *Ad-Dustur* (Amman), Feb. 3, 1996.

50.   *As-Safir* (Beirut), Oct. 22, 1992.

51.   Islamic Association for Palestine, Aug. 16, 2000.

52.   *L'Express* (Paris), Dec. 24, 1992.

53.   Daphne Tsimhoni, "Israel and the Territories—Disappearance," *Middle East Quarterly*, Winter 2001. p. 31.

54.   *The New York Times*, July 31, 2003.

55.   Reuters, Sept. 17, 2003. For details of one case, see Molly Moore, "Down and Out in Israel: A Gay Arab From the West Bank Finds He Can't Go Home Again," *The Washington Post*, Feb. 8, 2004.

4

The Year the Arabs Discovered Palestine

News reports give the impression that an Arab "Palestine" long existed at the eastern edge of the Mediterranean Sea, and that somehow Zionism is responsible for its disappearance. Similarly, outsiders are inclined to accept the oft-stated insistence that "Palestinians" constitute an ancient ethnicity. In fact, both of these assertions are wrong.

Rather, the idea of an Arab state resting between the Jordan River and the Mediterranean Sea is a twentieth-century concept whose origins can be traced with surprising precision to a single year—1920. In January 1920, the notion of Palestine hardly existed; by December of that critical year, it had been born.

The events of 1920 encapsulate the current successes and tribulations of the Palestinian nationalist movement. They also foreshadow some abiding themes, such as the potential for rapid change and the major role of the Western powers. For these reasons, studying what happened in 1920 offers insight into the most widely supported but possibly the least successful nationalist cause of the past century.

No Historic Muslim Concept of Palestine

Palestinian nationalism cannot be age-old.

To begin with, the nationalist idea itself originated only in late eighteenth-century Europe, and only later took hold among Muslims. Until modern times, the ancestors of those who today call themselves Palestinians thought of themselves mainly in terms of religion. Islam emphasizes bonds between fellow-believers, allowing little scope for territorially bound loyalties. Coreligionists shared strong bonds, but they had few ties outside their own community. Religious lines became residence lines; except for specific commercial or political purposes, little intermingling took place, for adherents of other religions also found primarily identifying along religious lines. A sense of common political identity based on geography barely existed.

When nationalism reached the Middle East from Europe, it captivated Middle Easterners as it did much of the world. The dream of governments embodying the spirit of their people may have been alien, but it attracted many adherents. The difficulty in the Middle East, as in most places, was exactly how to apply the national ideal. Where would the boundaries be placed? For example, do Maronite Christians constitute a nation of their own, or do the Christians of the Levant collectively form one? Who is Syrian or Arab?

Theorists spun grandiose plans for their favorite nation. But no one imagined a Palestinian nation, and for good reason. Palestine had always been a Jewish and Christian concept, meaningless and alien to Muslims. *Eretz Yisrael* and *Terra Sancta* have no analogue in Islam. Muslims look to the Hijaz, not Palestine, for their most sacred landmarks. Further, there has never been an independent state in Palestine ruled by Muslims; either Jews or Christians created such states that did exist there. As the historian Bernard Lewis writes, for Muslims the name *Filastin* "had never meant more than an administrative sub-district and [after the Crusades] it had been forgotten even in that limited sense."[1]

The British Creation of Palestine

Muslim distaste for the notion of Palestine was evident in April 1920, when the British authorities carved out a Palestinian entity; they responded with extreme suspicion, seeing the delineation of this territory as a victory for the Zionists. In part, Muslims perceived lingering Crusader impulses among the British, °a fear encouraged by the response to this taking of Palestine in 1917. (For example, note the New York newspaper headline that read "Jerusalem Rescued by British after 673 Years of Moslem Rule: Great Rejoicing in the Christian World.")[2]°

In part, they worried about the Zionist accomplishment of a formal definition of Palestine, correctly seeing this as a major step on the road to Theodor Herzl's *Judenstaat*. (In other words, the term "Palestine," which today symbolizes the Arab rejection of Israel, served the Jews not so long ago as a symbol of Jewish nationalism.)

This point cannot be overemphasized. Palestine was brought into existence by British imperial authorities, not by Arabs; further, Muslims felt defeated by the British carving out of a distinct Palestinian entity. I know of no Palestinian endorsing this act when it took place in 1920. To the contrary, every recorded opinion suggests intense opposition.

Early 1920: The Heyday of Pan-Syrianism

What, then, was the objective of the Arabs living between the Jordan and the Mediterranean? What political unit did they endorse? To the extent that there was any proto-national unit to the east of the Mediterranean Sea, it was not called *Filastin* but Sham, the historic region of Syria which included the modern states of Syria, Lebanon, Israel, and Jordan. This choice reflected a basic fact about the Levant, now often forgotten: *Sham*, usually translated as "Greater Syria," was a truly age-old ecological and cultural (but not political) unit.

Like Egypt, Arabia, Yemen, and the other large traditional units of the Middle East, it had geographic boundaries and ecological characteristics that made it distinct from adjoining areas. It constituted the western part of the Fertile Crescent, a dry region that supports life when—and only when—tended with great care. Residents of this area share a physical typology and an extended family structure. They speak Arabic with a distinctive lilt and prepare foods in a similar fashion. Just after World War I, a meeting of Arabs called for a united Syria on the basis that "the people speak Arabic; they are intermarried and have many links of kinship; and commerce has for ages moved freely between them."[3]

Even so, Pan-Syrian sentiment was extremely weak before World War II; Greater Syria was but only a proto-nationalist unit. Europeans and Westernized Syrians often remarked on the absence of national solidarity. Testimony on this subject is unanimous. The well-informed author of a British travel guide to Greater Syria noted in the mid-nineteenth century that "patriotism is unknown. There is not a man in the country, whether Turk or Arab, Mohammedan or Christian, who would give a para [penny] to save the empire from ruin; that is, if he be not in government pay. . . . The patriotism of the Syrian is confined to the four walls of his own house; anything beyond them does not concern him."[4] Gertrude Bell, a knowledgeable British observer, wrote in 1907 that "Syria is merely a geographical term corresponding to no national sentiment in the breasts of the inhabitants."[5] K. T. Khaïrallah found in 1912 that "Syrian society did not exist in the past. There was nothing but distinct and often hostile groups. . . . Society was based on a despotism of brutal force modeled on that of the ruler."[6]

By the end of World War I in November 1918, however, the notion of a Syrian nation had made considerable headway among the Arabs of Palestine. They agreed almost unanimously on the existence of a

Syrian nation. With few exceptions, they identified with the Syrian Arab government in Damascus, headed by Prince Faisal, a member of the Hashemite family.

Palestinian enthusiasm for Pan-Syrian unity steadily increased through mid-1920. There is ample evidence for this enthusiasm. Three major Palestinian organizations propounded Pan-Syrian ideas in the immediate aftermath of World War I: the Arab Club, the Literary Club, and the Muslim-Christian Association. (Note that none of these names makes any mention of Palestine.) The first two groups went furthest, calling outright for unity with Syria under Faisal. Even the Muslim-Christian Association, an organization of traditional leaders—men who would expect to rule if Palestine became independent—demanded incorporation in Greater Syria.

The Muslim-Christian Association held a congress in January–February 1919 to draw up demands to submit to the Paris Peace Conference. Representatives of fourteen Palestinian cities and towns presented a petition calling for Southern Syria to be "inseparable from the independent Arab Syrian government."[7] The congress declared Palestine "nothing but part of Arab Syria and it has never been separated from it at any stage." The delegates saw Palestine tied to Syria by "national, religious, linguistic, moral, economic, and geographic bonds." On the basis of this view, they called for a Palestine that would remain "undetached from the independent Arab Syrian Government."[8]

Musa Kazim al-Husseini, head of the Jerusalem Town Council (in effect, mayor) told a Zionist interlocutor in October 1919: "We demand no separation from Syria."[9] According to Ahmad ash-Shuqayri (the man who headed the PLO in the 1960s), the ubiquitous slogan of 1918–19 was "Unity, Unity, From the Taurus [Mountains] to Rafah [in Gaza], Unity, Unity."[10] The same appeal echoed from all corners. A singer in Ramla encouraged her "enraptured listeners" to join Faisal's forces.[11] From San Salvador, of all places, a protest in March 1919 went out from the "Syrian Palestinians" to international leaders calling for "no separation between Syria and Palestine" and expressing hope that "Syria and Palestine remain united." The Salvadorans declared: "We trust that if Syria and Palestine remain united, we will never be enslaved by the Jewish yoke."[12]

A congress of Palestinians met in Damascus in February 1920 and strongly advocated Pan-Syrian unity. One speaker suggested that

Palestine stood in the same relationship to Syria as Alsace-Lorraine did to France. According to a contemporary newspaper report,

> 'Izzat Darwaza spoke about Palestine and [the need for] Syrian unity, then he submitted a statement for general opinion. No one disagreed with him. The discussion proceeded further on this matter; some participants wanted not to mention Palestine but to use the expression Greater Syria for all the regions of Syria, and they were applauded.

The Congress passed four resolutions. The first of them noted that "it never occurred to the peoples of Northern and Coastal Syria that Southern Syria (or Palestine) is anything but a part of Syria." The second called for an economic boycott of the Zionists in "all three parts of Syria" (meaning the whole of Greater Syria). The third and fourth resolutions called for Palestine "not to be divided from Syria" and for "the independence of Syria within its natural borders."[13]

The crowning of Faisal as King of Syria in March 1920 elicited strong Pan-Syrian reactions among the Arabs of Palestine. The British military governor of Palestine received a petition (bearing Amin al-Husseini's signature) that demanded the eradication of borders with Syria and the inclusion of Palestine in a Syrian union. Musa Kazim al-Husseini broke his promise not to engage in politics and spoke from the municipality building's balcony in praise of Faisal. 'Arif al-'Arif led a mass demonstration in Jerusalem in which the participants carried pictures of Faisal and called for unity with Syria.

Then, in April, came the sobering news from San Remo that the British and French governments had decided to separate Palestine from Syria and to keep both territories under their control. This precipitated protests from all parts of Palestine. New calls went out for the independence of a united Syria stretching from Turkey to the Sinai.

These and many other indications point to two indisputable facts: until July 1920, the Palestinian goal was to join in a union with Syria, while the aspiration of an independent Palestinian state barely existed. Matters changed quickly in the next few months, however.

Palestinian-Syrian Tensions

Despite the apparent solidity of Palestinian interest in union with Syria, the sentiment was always precarious. In large part, this has to do with the two sides, Syrian and Palestinian, having had different expectations. Prince Faisal, who, along with many Syrians in 1918–20, saw the Zionists as a less pressing danger than the Maronites of Lebanon, was willing to work with the Jews if they could help him achieve his Greater Syrian goal. In January 1919, for example, he reached an agreement with the Zionists. In return for Faisal's promise "to encourage and stimulate immigration of Jews into Palestine on a large scale," he won Zionist backing for his campaign against the French.[14] (But this agreement was contingent on Britain keeping France out of Syria; and since this was not done, the accord did not take effect.) Soon after, in a letter to Felix Frankfurter, Faisal noted that "there is room in Syria for both of us."[15]

Palestinian leaders, in contrast, saw Zionism as the preeminent problem. In their eyes, Faisal's standing depended almost exclusively on his ability to help them against the Zionists. In late 1918, the Palestinians considered Faisal (in the words of a French diplomat) the only Arab leader "capable of resisting the Jewish flood" into Palestine.[16] Faisal's subsequent willingness to deal with the Zionists diminished Palestinian backing for him.

This divergence in outlook created tensions between Syrian and Palestinian leaders from the moment World War I ended in November 1918. Signs of disaffection were apparent within three months of Faisal's arrival in Damascus, and they grew with time. Already in early 1919, the Muslim-Christian Association resolved that Palestine "should be part of Southern Syria, provided the latter is not under foreign control."[17] The Association's Jerusalem branch went farther, calling for an independent government in Palestine to be only "politically associated" with Syria. It authorized Faisal "to represent Palestine and defend it at the Paris Conference," on the understanding that Palestine would enjoy full autonomy within a Syrian union.[18] And while 'Arif Pasha ad-Dajjani, president of the Muslim-Christian Association, insisted that "Palestine or Southern Syria—an integral part of the one and indivisible Syria—must not in any case or for any pretext be detached,"[19] he also had doubts about rule from Damascus.

Arguments against connections to Damascus appeared in the press as early as 1919. The Arab Club was the first nationalist institution to abandon Faisal's leadership. Despite its name, the newspaper *Suriya al-Janubiya* ("Southern Syria") led the campaign away from Pan-Syrianism, arguing that Syrians had become too absorbed in their conflict with France to pay enough attention to the Zionist challenge. In January 1920, when Faisal returned empty-handed from his second trip to Europe, some top Palestinians began to see him as not essential to their cause, an impression reinforced by the lack of Syrian response to the Jerusalem riots of April 1920.

But these strains had only limited importance. Syrian and Palestinian leaders, who both had an interest in Prince Faisal's success, effectively minimized their differences until July 1920.

Late 1920: The Rise of Palestinian Nationalism

The French conquered Damascus and scuttled the Arab kingdom ruled over by Faisal in July 1920. One result was that Syrians came to devote almost all their attention to the issue of French rule, leaving very little time or concern for Palestine. Another was that, for Palestinians, the attractiveness of a Syrian connection faded away. Why be joined to Damascus, the Palestinians felt, if this meant rule by Paris? Palestinian leaders came to recognize that they were on their own against the British and the Zionists. From that point on, they sought to establish an autonomous Arab government in Palestine which would be ruled by themselves, not by politicians in Damascus. Herein lay the origins of Palestinian nationalism.

This reorientation was made formal by the Third Palestinian Congress, meeting in December 1920. Delegates decided to drop the appellation Southern Syria and to stop demanding the joining of Palestine with Syria. At this moment, Palestine became acceptable to the Muslims; and it would not be long before they would actually find it appealing and later inspirational.

Subsequent meetings confirmed this new identity. When the Syrian Congress (the main exile organization dedicated to building Greater Syria) met in August 1921, Palestinians would no longer endorse the unity of Greater Syria. They even compelled the organization to rename itself *The Syro-Palestinian Congress* and to issue a statement calling for the "independence of Syria and of Palestine."[20] A year later, Palestinians withdrew altogether from this Congress.

What accounts for the extremely rapid collapse of Pan-Syrian sentiment in Palestine? Yehoshua Porath, the leading historian of Palestinian nationalism, argues in his 1974 book, *The Emergence of the Palestinian-Arab National Movement, 1918–1929*, that Palestinians supported Pan-Syrianism only as long as it served them but abandoned it when it no longer had utility. In contrast to Syrians, who tended to see Pan-Syrianism as an end in itself, he says, Palestinians saw it as a means, a weapon in the battle against Zionism; it was a weak support because it only served an ulterior purpose.

Being treated as part of Syria had had three advantages in the years 1918–20.[21] A joint Anglo-French declaration of November 1918 promised "to encourage and assist the establishment of native governments and administrations in Syria and Mesopotamia"—not Palestine.[22] This declaration made it desirable for Palestine to be seen as part of Syria. Also, associating with the larger Muslim population of Greater Syria offered a way to overwhelm the Jews demographically. And alliance with Faisal gave Palestinians a relatively powerful protector. According to Porath, the French conquest of Damascus caused all three advantages to disappear:

> Disappointment over the moderation of the Syrians toward Zionism cooled the Palestinians' enthusiasm for the idea of Pan-Syrian unity. . . . The orientation towards Damascus was based less on the growth of nationalism around this area [i.e., Greater Syria] than upon a given political situation. When this situation changed, the foundations of the Pan-Syrian movement collapsed.[23]

All these points are correct, but not the implication that Pan-Syrian nationalism was merely a tactic, while Palestinian nationalism appealed to deep sentiments. The reverse is closer to the truth. Existing sentiments fitted better within Greater Syria than Palestine. Palestinians abandoned Pan-Syrianism and replaced it with Palestinian separatism for tactical reasons, not out of heartfelt sentiment. Porath himself quotes one Palestinian leader who openly admitted this; only days after the fall of Faisal's government, Musa Kazim al-Husseini declared, "after the recent events in Damascus, we have to effect a complete change in our plans here. Southern Syria no longer exists. We must defend Palestine."[24] Kamil ad-Dajjani explained many years after the event that "the collapse of Faisal's rule in Syria and the disappointment of the hopes which were pinned upon that rule, made Palestinians feel that the orientation toward a Greater Syria bore no fruit."[25] Palestinian nationalism originated not in spontaneous feelings but in calculated politics, and a long time passed before the emotional appeal of this premeditated and novel allegiance matched that of Pan-Syrian nationalism.

In short, the Palestine concept served better than that of Greater Syria. It allowed the Arab leaders of Palestine to speak the same political language as the Zionists and the British. Rather than refer to some outside source of authority, they could claim sovereignty for themselves. In the process, they evolved from provincial notables into independent actors. Thus, tactical considerations caused the rapid rise of Palestinian nationalism.

Ultimately, Palestinian nationalism originated in Zionism; were it not for the existence of another people who saw British Palestine as their national home, the Arabs would have continued to view this area as a province of Greater Syria. Zionism turned Palestine into something worthy in itself; if not for the Jewish aspirations, Sunni Arab attitudes toward Palestine would no doubt have resembled those toward the territory of Transjordan—an indifference only slowly eroded by many years of governmental effort. Palestinian nationalism promised the most direct way to deal with the challenge presented by Zionist settlers—a challenge never directly felt on the East Bank.

Amin al-Husseini

The career of Al-Hajj Muhammad Amin al-Husseini (1895–1974), the longtime mufti of Jerusalem, dramatizes the switch from Pan-Syrianism to Palestinian nationalism.

Husseini began as a partisan of Greater Syria. He wrote sentimentally about ties between Syrians and Palestinians during World War I. When the Hashemites launched the Arab revolt, breaking the Ottoman Empire's four centuries' control over the Levant, Husseini saw this as a more effective way to block the Zionists. As Philip Mattar, a biographer of the mufti, writes: "Since it appeared futile for the Arabs to oppose British rule, Amin believed the only practical approach was to attempt to change the British Balfour policy by organizing mass support for reuniting Syria and Palestine, which would then work together against Zionism."[26]

Husseini therefore deserted the Ottoman army and joined the Hashemites. He then became a leading agent of the Hashemites (an ironic development in light of his later mortal enmity with this family), recruiting about two thousand military volunteers in 1918 and working actively on Faisal's behalf in 1919. At the Palestinian congress in January–February 1919, Husseini called for unity between Palestine and Syria. A British diplomatic report noted that Husseini's activities were directed "in favor of union with Sharifian [i.e., Faisal's] Syria."[27]

Husseini served as president of the Arab Club, which was especially eager for union with Syria. Toward the end of 1919, this group tent a letter to the British military governor of Jerusalem declaring that "Southern Syria forms a part of the United Syria beginning from Taures [and extending to] Rafa, the separation of which we do not tolerate under any circumstances, and we are as well prepared to sacrifice ourselves towards its defense with all our power."[28]

Returning from Damascus on April 1, 1920, Husseini introduced a new element into an already tense atmosphere in Palestine by reporting (wrongly) that the British government would be willing to recognize Faisal as ruler of Palestine as well as Syria. This report raised Pan-Syrian expectations to a fever pitch. Then came the Nabi Musa riots in Jerusalem on April 4, when Arab mobs attacked Jews; according to Horace B. Samuel (and the British police report corroborates his account), these disturbances were initiated by two young men who shouted "Long live our King—King Feisul."[29] Taysir Jbara, a historian, believes that Amin al-Husseini was one of these two.[30] The police sought Husseini, but he fled to Damascus, where he again worked to spread the influence of King Faisal. Although a Palestine court had sentenced Husseini in absentia to ten years in jail, the high commissioner of Palestine, Sir Herbert Samuel, pardoned him less than five months after the Jerusalem disturbances had occurred. This permitted Husseini to make his way back to Palestine after the fall of Damascus.

Faisal's defeat caused Husseini, like the other leaders, to change ideologies without missing a beat, turning into an unbending Palestinian nationalist. He became mufti of Jerusalem in 1921, president of the Supreme Muslim Council in 1922, and president of the Arab Higher Committee in 1936. Each of these positions gave him new power; by the mid-1930s he had become the outstanding political leader of the Palestinians, the symbol and the bulwark of Palestinian nationalism.

Conclusion

Four major events occurred in 1920. In March, Faisal was crowned king of Syria, raising expectations that Palestine would join his independent state. In April, the British put Palestine on the map, dashing those hopes. In July, French forces captured Damascus, ending the Palestinian tie with Syria. And in December, responding to these events, the Palestinian leadership adopted the goal of an independent Palestinian state.

Having thus originated out of political calculus, not spontaneous feelings, Palestinian nationalism had to wait for many years to pass before acquiring real force. Still, what Palestinian nationalism lacked by way of natural origin, it soon made up for with passionate identification. How did a premeditated and novel allegiance come to exert so strong an emotional appeal? The logic of need caused Palestinian nationalism to flourish, and it became a popular cause.

So thoroughly has it come to dominate the current scene that its recent and utilitarian origins have been forgotten by all but a handful of scholars. Distorting matters more, an informal campaign seems to be underway to suppress the fact that Pan-Syrianism predominated for two critical years. A number of otherwise solidly researched academic books of recent years[31] wave this whole phenomenon aside in an effort retroactively to enhance the stature of the Palestinian nationalism of those years.

This rewriting of history serves to emphasize the abiding importance of 1920. A review of the events of that year points, first, to the fact that Palestinian nationalism is just one variant of anti-Zionism; in turn, others are always nipping at its own heels. The PLO leadership and its followers can never rest easy, for they always have to contend with not only their Israeli enemy but also their Arab rivals.

Second, 1920 demonstrates the extreme fickleness of the Arabs' nationalist loyalties. Only superficially grounded in nationalist sentiments, they found it easy to bounce from one formulation to another. Palestinian leaders supported the Greater Syria goal so long as it served their purposes; then, after the French capture of Damascus changed the premises, the leadership seamlessly adopted a new approach. During the 1950s, when Gamal Abdel Nasser and Arab nationalism were flying high, many of the Palestinian leaders moved into his camp. °In the 1990s, they adopted Islamism.° This could happen again. Were circumstances to call for another switch, say, to federation with Jordan, many of those who now fervently espouse an independent Palestinian state might take up this new aspiration.

While it is true that the flexibility of 1920 occurred at a moment of special fluidity, and positions have since hardened, the Middle East remains the world's most politically volatile area, where major realignments persistently take observers by surprise. Given that today's constellation of forces is unlikely to last into the distant future and that an independent Palestinian state does seem forthcoming, the primacy of Palestinian nationalism could eventually come to an end, perhaps as quickly as it got started.

Notes

1. Bernard Lewis, "Palestine: On the History and Geography of a Name," *The International History Review*, January 1980, p. 6.
2. *The New York Herald*, Dec. 11, 1917.
3. *Al-Mufid* [Damascus], 1924, Arabic text in Georg Kampffmeyer. "Urkunden and Berichte zur Gegenwartsgeschichte des arabischen Orients," *Mitteilungen des Seminars für Orientalische Sprachen an der Friedrich-Wilhelms-Universität zu Berlin*, vols. 26 and 27 (1924): 88.

4. *A Handbook for Travellers in Syria and Palestine* (London: John Murray, 1858), vol. 1, p. xlvi.

5. Gertrude Lowthian Bell. *Syria: The Desert & the Sown*, new ed. (London: William Heinemann, 1919), p. 228.

6. K.T. Khaïrallah, "La Syrie," *Revue du monde musulman* 19 (1912): 104.

7. Akram Zu'aytir papers, File A/Manuscript 16, Feb. 5, 1919, Institute for Palestine Studies. Quoted in Muhammad Y. Muslih, *The Origins of Palestinian Nationalism* (New York: Columbia University Press, 1988), p. 177.

8. Akram Zu'aytir papers, File A/Manuscript 16, Institute for Palestine Studies. Quoted in Muslih, *op. cit.*, pp. 181–82.

9. Text in Neil Caplan, *Futile Diplomacy:* vol. 1, *Early Arab-Zionist Negotiation Attempts, 1913–1931* (London: Frank Cass, 1983), p. 157.

10. Ahmad ash-Shuqayri, *Hiwar wa-Asrar ma'a'lMuluk wa'r-Ru'asa* (Beirut: Dar al-'Awda, [1970?]), pp. 15, 24.

11. Muslih, *op. cit.*, p. 199.

12. Texts in Bayan al-Hut, ed., *Watha'iq al-Haraka al-Wataniya al-Filastiniya, 1918–1939: Min Awraq Akram Zu'aytar* (Beirut: Mu'assasa ad-Dirasat al-Filastiniya, 1979), pp. 9–11.

13. Text in *Al-Mufid*, February 1920, pp. 35–36. In a letter to the author (dated June 30, 1986), Yeshoshua Porath suggests that this meeting was not a real congress but rather "a meeting of some representatives who were members of the General Syrian Congress." Muslih (*Origins of Palestinian Nationalism*, p. 199) believes it was a group of what he calls "Younger Politicians" who convened their own meeting.

14. Agreement of Jan. 3, 1919. Text in Neil Caplan, *op. cit.*, p. 146.

15. Letter of Mar. 1, 1919. For text see Caplan, *op. cit.*, p. 150.

16. Paul-Marie Durieux to Georges Picot, Dec. 4, 1918, Ministère des Affaires Étrangères, Levant, 1918–1929, Palestine, vol. 11. fols. 250–51. Quoted in Jan Karl Tanenbaum, *France and the Arab Middle East, 1914–1920* (Philadelphia: The American Philosophical Society, 1978), p. 26.

17. J.N. Camp report, Foreign Office 371/4153/41476, Feb. 2, 1919. Quoted in Simha Flappan, *Zionism and the Palestinians* (London: Croom Helm, 1979), p. 59.

18. Jerusalem Muslim-Christian Association to the Governor of Jerusalem, Feb. 11, 1919; "Copy of the Power of Attorney given to Prince Faysal," Feb. 10, 1919. Both documents are in the Israel State Archives, Chief Secretary, 156 and quoted in Yeshoshua Porath, *The Emergence of the Palestinian-Arab National Movement, 1918–1929* (London: Frank Cass, 1974), p. 85–86.

19. Quoted in Benoit Aboussouan, *Le Problème politique syrien* (Paris: Librairie de Jurisprudence Ancienne et Moderne, 1925), p. 247.

20. Archives diplomatiques, Paris, E, Turkey, vol. 274, Aug. 26, 1921. Quoted in Marie-Renée Moutoun, "Le congrès syrio-palestinien de Genève (1921)," *Relations internationales* 19 (1979): 322.

21. Porath, *op. cit.*, Chapter 2.

22. *Papers Relating to the Foreign Relations of the United States: The Paris Peace Conference, 1919* (Washington: Government Printing Office, 1942–47), vol. 5, p. 3.

23. Porath, *op cit.*, pp. 114, 103.
24. Zionist Archives, Z/4, 2800 II, Report No. 138. Aug. 5, 1920. Quoted in *ibid.*, p. 107.
25. Interview with Dajjani by Muhammad Y. Muslih on Mar. 11, 1979. Quoted in Muslih, *op. cit.*, p. 203.
26. Philip Mattar, *The Mufti of Jerusalem: Al-Hajj Amin al-Husayni and the Palestinian National Movement* (New York: Columbia University Press, 1988), p. 14.
27. J.N. Camp's letter to the Foreign Office. 371/4153/41476/f275. Quoted in Taysir Jbara, *Palestinian Leader Hajj Amin al-Husayni, Mufti of Jerusalem* (Princeton, NJ: Kingston Press, 1985), p. 29.
28. Letter dated Dec. 8, 1919, in Israel State Archives, Pol. 2095. Quoted in Aaron S. Klieman, *Foundations of British Policy in the Arab World: The Cairo Conference of 1921* (Baltimore: Johns Hopkins Press, 1970), p. 62.
29. Horace B. Samuel, *Unholy Memories of the Holy Land* (London: The Hogarth Press, 1930), p. 57.
30. Jbara, *op. cit.*, p. 33.
31. Most notably, Muhammad Y. Muslih, *op. cit.*

5

Mirror Image: How the PLO Mimics Zionism

At Basel I founded the Jewish State.
—Theodor Herzl, writing in his diary about the First Zionist
Conference of 1897

In Madrid, we founded the Palestinian state.
—A Palestinian, talking about the 1991 international conference

The Palestine Liberation Organization (PLO) is Israel's most intimate and permanent enemy, so it is especially paradoxical to realize just how deeply it has been shaped by Zionism, the Jewish national movement.

To start with, the very delineation of a territory called "Palestine" in 1920 was a Zionist achievement; had Jews not pressed the British government to create such a unit, Arabic-speakers of the area would have continued to see themselves living in a Greater Syria or in an Arab or Muslim nation; there simply would have been no Arab feeling for *Filastin*. The PLO exists, in other words, only because Israel exists.

Second, had the PLO's enemy not been Israel, it would not have enjoyed the extraordinary international prominence that it actually does. Imagine that Yasir Arafat headed an organization fighting for the liberation of East Timor from Indonesia; would you ever have heard of him? Israel's renown provided celebrity, money, and political support for its enemy too.

Third—my subject here—Palestinian nationalists[1] have time and again modeled their institutions, ideas, and practices on the Zionist movement. This ironic tribute means that the peculiar nature of the PLO can be understood only with reference to its Zionist inspiration. More: imitation offers possible insights into the PLO's future course.

Carbon Copies . . .

Like the World Zionist Organization (founded in 1897), the Palestine Liberation Organization (founded in 1964) is an umbrella organization under which factions simultaneously cooperate and compete. Like the WZO, the PLO comprises affiliated institutions such as labor unions, health organizations, and vocational training schools.

Palestinian agencies copy their Zionist precursors so closely, Sadik J. Al-Azm, a Syrian analyst, calls them "carbon copies."[2] The Arab lobby In the United States, the National Association of Arab-Americans, for example, tried to replicate the form and function of its Jewish precursor, the American Israel Public Affairs Committee. Other Palestinian groups even mimic the names of Jewish organizations: the Arabs' Anti-Discrimination Committee (which gets its name from the Anti-Defamation League), the Holy Land Fund (the Jewish National Fund), °the National Council of Presidents of Arab-American Organizations (the Conference of Presidents of Major American Jewish Organizations),° and the United Palestinian Appeal (the United Jewish Appeal). Just as the Zionist agencies collected for tree-planting, so now Plant-a-Tree calls on Palestinians to reforest Palestine. °Birthright Israel has spawned a Birthright Palestine. Today's Israel Philharmonic Orchestra began life in 1936 as the Palestine Symphony Orchestra; in 2010, a Palestine National Orchestra debuted, using almost the identical name.°

Al-Azm makes an interesting case for seeing Yasir Arafat as a latter-day version of one of the great figures of early Zionism. Arafat, he writes,

> with his paternalistic attitude towards the whole Palestinian Resistance Movement, his constant traveling between international and Arab capitals, his unceasing dealings with a curious assortment of heads of state, Prime Ministers et al., his constantly open channels with each and every party with some interest in the Palestinian problem, plus his renowned political flexibility, diplomatic expertise and pragmatic tactics, is a kind of Palestinian Chaim Weizmann.[3]

Also anticipating Arafat, Weizmann served as its chief interlocutor with the outside world and the main arbiter of its factions.

When the PLO declared the establishment of a Palestinian state in November 1988, its words brought Israel's 1948 Proclamation of Independence to mind. The PLO statement echoed the Israeli prototype in its subject matter, organization, and even in specific phrasing. For example, both appealed to their ethnic brethren and proclaimed equal rights for all in the new state. The words of Israel's proclamation echo throughout the PLO document of forty years later. David Ben-Gurion called on "the Jewish people all over the world to rally to our side" and Arafat called on "Arab compatriots to consolidate and enhance the emergence and reality of our state." Both called for immigration, with Ben-Gurion announcing that "The State of Israel will be open to the immigration of Jews from all countries of their dispersion," and Arafat declaring the same: "The State of Palestine is the state of Palestinians wherever they may be."[4]

. . . and Mirror Images

Palestinians have adopted a vision of their own history that in many ways recapitulates the Jewish experience. Calling themselves the "Jews of the Middle East," they often point to their diaspora as a parallel and a successor to the Jewish one. Like the Jews, they note, Palestinians are more educated and mobile than the majority populations among which they live, yet they suffer prejudice, dispossession, and expulsion. In particular, just as medieval Jews got thrown out of one country after another, the Palestinians had to leave three countries (Jordan, Lebanon, Kuwait) in twenty years.

The PLO takes this analogy yet further: Just as Jews suffered a Holocaust at Nazi hands, it says, Palestinians suffered a holocaust at Israeli hands. However outrageous, this analogy has captured the imagination of many Arabs, for in one stroke it both reduces the moral stature of the Israelis and elevates that of Palestinians. Kanan Makiya, the Iraqi analyst, observes that "the hallowed status of Palestinian dispossession in 1948 . . . has become for Arab politics what the Holocaust is for Israeli politics: mirror images of one another."[5]

The Palestinians closely emulate other Zionist concepts. The "Law of Return," the notion that every Jew has an inalienable right to live in Israel, underpins the whole venture of colonizing Palestine and creating a Jewish national home there. Similarly, Palestinian nationalists proclaim a "Right of Return" which asserts that every Palestinian refugee, or his descendants, has the prerogative to repossess lands left in 1948–49.

The pattern of imitation extends even to the smallest particulars: Zionists famously tried to land the *Exodus*, a freighter with 4,500 desperate displaced persons seeking refuge from the Nazi concentration camps, on the beaches of Palestine in 1947. When British authorities forbade the Jews to disembark, the ship returned its miserable passengers to Germany, thereby dramatizing the need for a Jewish state.

In 1988, the PLO self-consciously attempted to stage a repeat version of this event to publicize the Palestinian plight. It bought a Greek car ferry, the *Sol Phryne*, renamed it *Al-'Awda* ("The Return"), and worked out the plans for a landing of exiled Palestinians, with plenty of journalists in attendance, on the beaches of Israel. (The scheme might have worked but for the fact that someone, presumably the Israelis, blew up the ship before it took on any passengers.)

Looking to the future, the PLO portrays the creation of a Palestinian state much as Zionists saw the establishment of Israel—as a quasi-messianic event imbued with world-historical importance. Palestine's sovereignty, it holds, will mark the resurgence of Arab dignity and the rebirth of Muslim power. It will also signal the reestablishment of Third World power and the ending of hegemonic imperialism. These are not modest movements.

Sacred Geography

Jerusalem is the only capital of a Jewish state, as well as a unique city in Jewish history, religion, and emotions. In contrast, the city is so minor in Islam, it is not even once mentioned in the Koran. Nor did it ever serve as a political capital or cultural center. Because of the centrality of Jerusalem in Judaism boosts the Zionist claim to that city, Palestinian in the twentieth century have retroactively enhanced Jerusalem's religious and historical stature in Islam. They came up with the by-now universally accepted notion of Jerusalem being the third most holy city of Islam (after Mecca and Medina) and they deemed it the Palestinians' "eternal capital."

Palestine has undergone an even more dramatic transformation. While Jews have the concept of *Eretz Yisrael* ("the Land of Israel") and Christians have *Terra Sancta* ("Holy Land"), Muslims have no parallel concept, for Palestine historically had no special status in the Islamic tradition. Further, it did not even exist as a political or cultural unit during their centuries of rule over the area. The only time Palestine existed as a polity was either under the rule of Christians (Crusader kingdoms, the British empire) or Jews (Judea, Israel). As late as the beginning of 1920, "Palestine" had no resonance among Muslims.

From these inauspicious beginnings, the romance of Palestine grew into today's powerful nationalist force that rivals its Jewish precursor. To build up such feelings, Palestinian nationalists drew heavily on the Zionist storehouse of longing for the Land of Israel. For example, Arafat adopted such Zionist terminology as referring to Palestine as "the promised land."[6] At the very moment that establishing the State of Israel achieved the Jews' two-millennia old dream of returning to the land of milk and honey, Palestinians initiated a parallel longing for the lost orange groves of Jaffa and gardens of Ramla. Palestinians have in effect inherited the unrequited Jewish longing for Eretz Yisrael.

The Zionist venture sees itself reestablishing Jewish sovereignty after an interregnum of two thousand years. Palestinians can't claim quite such a long period, but they do insist that they too are rebuilding: "after one hundred years we are again on the geographical map" said Arafat.[7] (In fact, the only thing on the map back then was an administrative unit, the Mutasarrifiya of Jerusalem, but never mind.)[8]

So far has the process of Zionizing Islam's notions of holy space progressed, Arafat sometimes looks to the Bible for authentication of Palestinian nationalism. One interesting example dates from 1991, when an assertive Brazilian journalist, Jordan Jose Arbex, told him: "You are struggling for an entity—the Palestine state—that, from a historic and geographical viewpoint, has never existed because Palestine historically corresponds to a region in southern Syria." To this (completely accurate) statement, Arafat replied by pointing to a Zionist authentication: "You must read the Bible, because it contains abundant historic references that demonstrate the existence of a cultural and geopolitical Palestinian identity for many thousands of years."[9] A Muslim politician justifying his ideology with references to Jewish scripture? Only if he is a Palestinian Zionist.

When Palestinians reach the point that they justify their anti-Israel ideology with reference to the Bible, they have truly become the Zionists' double, or what the Germans call a *Doppelgänger*—an evil twin and nemesis. Indeed, Palestinians sometimes take an odd delight in the similarity of their politics with those of Israel. Yasir Arafat likes to declare, "We are like our cousins, the Jews." Bassam Abu Sharif says that sometimes, when he reads or listens to Israeli officials' reactions, he laughs, "because they are exactly like us, the way they react, the way they stick to things."[10]

Dependence on Great Powers

Both the Jewish and Palestinian national movements have to a highly unusual extent looked to international backing in general and to the United Nations in particular. Israel came into existence as the result of a UN General Assembly vote. As for Yasir Arafat, Harris Shoenberg writes that his "long-term success derived from his ability to use the

UN to elevate the PLO, and himself as Chairman, to a level of significance they might otherwise not deserve."[11] Israeli governments bound themselves to a great power patron, the United States, by faithfully serving its interests abroad; the PLO tried to do likewise for the Soviet Union. Non-Palestinian Arabs took on a role for the PLO akin to that of non-Israeli Jews for Israel.

Palestinians, like Zionists, rely heavily on foreign funds. Zionists looked initially to fellow Jews for support, then for larger amounts to states (West Germany for reparations, the United States for aid). Palestinians also began by depending on coreligionists (Arab authorities), then expanded to foreign governments (the Soviet Union, then the Western states). Palestinian dependence on foreign sources became so deep that Arafat announced in 1994 that "if no one pays for this peace [with Israel] . . . it cannot be achieved."[12]

Strangely too, leaders of both movements openly express resentment of their donors. An Israeli minister of finance in 1984 railed against US economic advice even as his country accepted $3 billion dollars in aid: "The High Commissioner sent us a note from Washington and gave us a negative term report!"[13] In a similar spirit, Yasir Arafat in 1994 addressed a meeting of Palestinian contractors and (according to an Egyptian news account) "criticized the donor nations because they allocated just $2.2. billion for the West Bank and Gaza Strip over five years at the rate of $440 million a year."[14] He later became even more annoyed, denouncing World Bank and Western government conditions for aid: "We didn't finish military occupation to get economic occupation!"[15]

Origins of the Imitation

Although some aspects of Palestinian Zionism (such as the notion of Jerusalem as the third most holy site of Islam) go back earlier in the twentieth century, most of them date from after 1967. Before that year, not only did Palestinians not know much about Israel, but to show too much interest in the Jewish state made one suspect, and even vulnerable to charges of treason. Only after Israel's astounding victory in June 1967 did two processes begin.

First, residents of Jerusalem, the West Bank, and Gaza Strip came under Israel's direct control. Despite rhetorical insistence about the ugliness of military occupation, Palestinians in these areas learned a great deal from Israelis about politics, and especially democracy and human rights. In some ways, Palestinians have become more like Israelis than like their fellow Arabs. For example, Hanan Ashrawi in 1994 turned down a position in Arafat's Palestine Authority in favor of setting up the Palestinian Independent Commission for Citizens' Rights, an organization she hopes will acquire the powers of ombudsman and state controller. Ashrawi herself termed the creation of such an institution "an unusual precedent in the Arab world";[16] she did not point out, however, that it derives directly from Israeli, not Arab political culture.

Second, the 1967 war caused Palestinians to give up on the Arab states. The destruction of three conventional armies in six days made them realize that only Palestinian self-help could eliminate Israel and lead to the creation of their independent state. This led to the further recognition that they would have to put together the nuts and bolts of administration well before attaining sovereign power. The PLO made a first attempt at this in Jordan (1968–70) and a second in Lebanon (1970–82) before finally trying it in the West Bank and Gaza in 1988. During the third of these efforts, it recognized that it was recapitulating the Zionist enterprise during the Mandatory period, 1918–48. Accordingly, Palestinians belatedly took the Zionist "state in the making" as their model.

The Jewish accomplishment during the Mandatory period was indeed impressive: by developing the Jewish Agency into a proto-state institution, Zionists created the bases for the full-fledged government that emerged in 1948. They already had a political authority, a military wing, an educational system, a mechanism to distribute welfare, and so forth. In contrast, Palestinians failed to match these institutions, and so found themselves disorganized when the British withdrew from Palestine in 1948. One historian, Benny Morris, describes the Palestinian Arabs of the late 1940s as "backward, disunited, and often apathetic, a community only just entering the modern age politically and administratively." Another historian, Ilan Pappé, dismisses the Palestinian leadership as "an élite in confusion" and argues that it failed to use the Mandatory period to prepare for the war that came in 1948.[17] In effect, the Palestinians are trying decades later to make up for their mistakes of the Mandatory period.

Emulating the Zionists means learning from them, and a hunger for information has spawned many studies about the enemy. Palestinians now research the Zionist experience in minute detail, hoping to glean ideas on ways to repeat the Israeli accomplishment. Books appear in Arabic bearing titles such as *Israel from the Inside* and *The Political System in Israel*.[18] Even radicals take up this study. Luyis 'Abduh, a terrorist in his twenties, learned Hebrew in an Israeli jail and went on to translate books on Zionist history and politics from that language into Arabic. He became a leading advocate of building institutions along the lines of the Jewish Agency.[19]

The notion of a state-in-the-making distinguishes these two movements from virtually all other anticolonial efforts. With the rarest of exceptions (the Americans who founded the United States, the Muslims in India who founded Pakistan), liberation movements inherit the colonial state. From the Canadians in 1867 to Nelson Mandela in 1994, they wait for existing institutions to fall into their hands. Zionists and Palestinians are set apart by building their institutions from scratch.

Sensing this similarity, even some Israelis have come explicitly to see the Palestinian future in terms of the Zionist past. Discussing the prospect of Palestinian autonomy, Prime Minister Yitzhak Rabin in April 1993 foresaw that "a Palestinian entity, which is not a state, will come into being. It will be an entity similar to the Jewish community here at the time of the British Mandate, which ran its own affairs."[20] A Palestinian *yishuv*?

The Coattail Effect

Of course, not everything about the PLO and its Zionist precursor is similar. Jewish nationalism derives from a millennial-old love of Zion, whereas its Palestinian counterpart dates back no further than the second half of 1920. Zionists had only intermittent help from foreign states and basically had to create Israel on their own; the PLO benefited from state aid more than any other irredentist group in history. Zionists sought to create an island of Western civilization, the PLO has a thoroughly Middle Eastern outlook. And while mainstream Zionist groups rejected the terrorist instrument, the PLO wholeheartedly embraced it over a period of decades. Still, one expects the differences; it's the similarities that surprise.

Do those similarities have significance? For some Zionists, the weirdly imitative pattern of the PLO renders suspect the very claim of a Palestinian nation. Ruth Wisse of Harvard sums up this outlook:

> For some time now, and with ever greater forcefulness, Palestinian Arabs have been representing themselves as the real "Jews," systematically usurping all the symbols and terms of Jewish history and national consciousness. . . . It may not be for us to question the Palestinian Arabs' claim that they are a distinct Arab people, but if they are a people, why do they represent themselves as Jews?[21]

To answer Wisse's question: like a child imitates its parents, so do Palestinians imitate Israelis—to learn from their closest role model. From the Palestinian viewpoint, it is a merely practical way to find methods and ideas that work. Copying does not in itself obviate the validity of Palestinian nationhood. The remarkable thing is not that Palestinians copy, but that they do it so thoroughly.

The real question is, rather, how copying affects the Palestinian enterprise. In the short run, the Zionist model has clearly propelled the Palestinians ahead by providing institutions, ideas, and practices. The latter hardly had to invent, for copying proved easier and more expedient. "On the coattails of the victors the Palestinians hitched a heady ride," as the late Fouad Ajami put it.[22]

But coattails are in the back; and imitation is likely to keep Palestinians always trailing Israel. Just as the Soviet dependence on technology stolen from the West condemned the USSR perpetually to lag behind the West, so following the Zionist example handicaps the PLO. How can it defeat the Jews at their own game? Zionists have mastered the practices they first invented and implemented; if in the near term, borrowing from Zion strengthens the Palestinians, ultimately it limits their capabilities.

This limitation has become especially evident after Israel and the PLO signed the Oslo Accord in September 1993, when the Palestinian Authority tried to put together the essential elements of a government. Its weak institutional development, ruinous finances, and a strong inclination toward authoritarianism exposed the shallowness of its Zionist imitation.

Notes

1. The following observations apply to Palestinian nationalists, not to their ideological foes such as Islamists, communists, Pan-Arab nationalists, pan-Syrian nationalists, or pro-Jordanians.
2. Sadik J. Al-Azm, "Palestinian Zionism," *Die Welt des Islams* 28 (1988): 93.
3. Al-Azm, "Palestinian Zionism," p. 97.
4. For a comparison of the two texts, see Daniel Pipes, "Declaring Statehood: Israel and the PLO." *Orbis* 33 (1989): 247–59. Reprinted in *Sandstorm: Middle East Conflicts and America*, edited by Daniel Pipes, (Lanham, MD.: University Press of America, 1993), pp. 197–216.
5. Kanan Makiya, *Cruelty and Silence: War, Tyranny, Uprising, and the Arab World* (New York: W. W. Norton, 1993), p. 260.
6. For example, on ORF Television (Vienna), June 18, 1991.
7. Middle East News Agency, May 31, 1994.
8. 'Abd al-'Aziz Muhammad 'Awwad, *Al-Idara al-'Uthmaniya fi Wilayat Suriya, 1864–1914* (Cairo: Dar al-Ma'arif, 1969), pp. 71–72.

9. *Folha de São Paulo* (São Paulo), Feb. 18, 1991. At other times, Arafat posited the Covenant of 'Umar, written at the time of the Muslim conquest of Jerusalem in AD 637, as the Muslim equivalent of the Torah (e.g., *Al-Quds*, June 8, 1994).

10. Quoted in Janet Wallach and John Wallach, *Arafat: In the Eyes of the Beholder* (New York: Lyle Stuart, 1990), pp. 34–35.

11. Harris Okun Shoenberg, *Mandate for Terror: The United Nations and the PLO* (New York: Shapolsky, 1989), p. 449.

12. *The New York Times*, July 7, 1994.

13. Gad Ya'acobi, *Ma'ariv*, Dec. 26, 1984.

14. Middle East News Agency, May 31, 1994.

15. *The Washington Post*, July 3, 1994.

16. *Los Angeles Times*, June 9, 1994.

17. Benny Morris, *The Birth of the Palestinian Refugee Problem, 1947–1949* (Cambridge, Eng.: Cambridge University Press, 1987), p. 17; Ilan Pappé, *The Making of the Arab-Israeli Conflict, 1947–51* (New York: I. B. Tauris, 1992), p. 56. For an opposing interpretation, see Baruch Kimmerling and Joel S. Migdal, *Palestinians: The Making of a People* (New York: Free Press, 1993), pp. 136–37.

18. Diya Hajri, *Isra'il min ad-Dakhil* (Cairo: Maktabat Ibn Sina', 1992); Fawzi Muhammad Tayil, *An-Nizam as-Siyasi fi Isra'il* (Cairo: Ma'had al-Buhuth wa'd-Dirasat al-'Arabiya, 1989).

19. Barry Rubin, *Revolution Until Victory? The Politics and History of the PLO* (Cambridge, Mass.: Harvard University Press, 1994), p. 94.

20. *Yedi'ot Aharonot*, April 25, 1993.

21. Ruth Wisse, "The Big Lie: Reinventing the Middle East," in *The Middle East: Uncovering the Myths*, edited by Cynthia Ozick (New York: Anti-Defamation League, 1991), p. 19.

22. *U.S. News & World Report*, Sept. 11, 1993.

6

The Road to Damascus: What Netanyahu Almost Gave Away in 1998

The most dramatic moment of the Israeli election campaign in 1999 was not a clash between Prime Minister Benjamin Netanyahu and his main challenger, Ehud Barak. Rather, it was a TV debate in mid-April between Netanyahu and Yitzhak Mordechai, Netanyahu's own former defense minister who had quit to challenge his old boss on a minor-party ticket. In a discussion of Syria, Netanyahu declared that he would not "give [Syrian President Hafez al-]Assad what Barak is willing to give Assad." Mordechai stunned the Israeli electorate with his dramatic reply. He coldly dared Netanyahu to repeat his claim. "Look me in the eye, Bibi . . . look me in the eye," he demanded. Netanyahu did not repeat his statement.

Just what was Mordechai talking about? Israeli political circles buzzed about the exchange. Then, in late May, government sources gave the Israeli press a sketchy story about back-channel talks between Jerusalem and Damascus during Netanyahu's tenure. Now, however, the full story can be told.

Based on information from several sources with firsthand knowledge of the talks, it is clear that, during 1998, Netanyahu became deeply involved in a secret negotiation with Assad over the terms and conditions under which Israel would transfer the Golan Heights, taken from Syria in the 1967 Six Day War, back to Syrian control. Even more astonishing, some of those involved in the talks make the assertion—hotly disputed by Netanyahu and his supporters—that the prime minister, in contrast to both his hard-line image and his promises to supporters, was ready to make big concessions to Assad for a peace agreement from which Israel would get diplomatic recognition, trade, and other attributes of peace.

Background

The American-encouraged negotiating track between Syria and Israel had stalled when Netanyahu came to office in May 1996. Assad insisted that negotiations resume where they had left off with the previous Labor government—namely, at an agreement in principle that Israel return the Golan Heights. Netanyahu saw no reason to concede this in advance. Although both the US government and Israel's Labor Party agreed with Netanyahu on this point, Assad would not budge, and diplomacy shuddered to a halt.

For the next two years, Assad continued to refuse direct or official negotiations, but, in the two-month period of August and September 1998, he did agree to what one high-level Israeli calls "very intensive and very unofficial" talks. These negotiations took place completely outside any governmental framework. Rather, private American citizens went back and forth between the two countries. Ronald Lauder, a New York-based businessman and friend of the prime minister's, along with his aide Allen Roth, forwarded Netanyahu's ideas to Assad. George Nader, publisher of the Washington-based *Middle East Insight*, presented Syrian views. While there may have been other negotiating tracks, this was the only one that Netanyahu saw as possibly leading to a breakthrough; as an aide of his puts it, this was the "most serious and credible channel" because it involved discussions with top officials in both countries.

The Israeli team included Netanyahu; Mordechai; Uzi Arad, the prime minister's diplomatic adviser; and Danny Naveh, the Cabinet secretary. Others involved included Yaakov Amidror, an aide to Mordechai, and Brigadier General Shimon Shappira, military secretary to the prime minister. On the Syrian side, Assad depended primarily on Foreign Minister Faruq ash-Shar and Walid Mualem, his ambassador in Washington.

Syrians and Israelis never had direct contact; instead, the talks took place in classic shuttle-diplomacy style. All told, the Americans visited Damascus nine times, meeting with Assad on each occasion, and made a similar number of trips to Israel. All the participants made great efforts to keep the negotiations secret; for example, the American go-betweens only traveled on their own plane, always stopping in Cyprus between Jerusalem and Damascus. Not even the US government was informed.

But, beyond these basic facts, almost everything about the talks—why they happened, which side made what concessions, and why nothing ultimately came of them—is a matter of contention among the participants.

The Critics' Version

Netanyahu's critics, including some former members of his inner circle, maintain that Netanyahu started the talks for two reasons. First, he feared that the Americans would ram a deal with the Palestinians down his throat (as indeed happened at Wye in October 1998) unless he could produce a deal with Syria. Second, his government was reeling from a succession of crises, domestic and foreign, mostly of its own making. Netanyahu wanted to reestablish himself with a major, world-shaking event. Yet drama on the Egyptian, Jordanian, and Palestinian tracks had been used up; the only neighbors left were Syria and its satrapy, Lebanon. The sight of Netanyahu, the tough-talking Israeli, flying to Damascus to sign a peace treaty with an archenemy would revitalize his prime ministry. A highly favorable world reaction would be accompanied by howls of rage from Netanyahu's own coalition, which would promptly collapse. But the breakthrough with Syria would win Netanyahu a stunning endorsement at the polls and a second term as prime minister.

Netanyahu's critics profess astonishment at the security price they say he was willing to pay Assad in each one of the four main areas under discussion: the extent of an Israeli withdrawal, its timing, demilitarized zones, and early warning stations.

Rabin had informally agreed to hand the Golan Heights to Syria, pulling Israeli troops back to an international boundary delineated between Syria and Palestine in 1923. Shimon Peres went a step further and, in April 1995, publicly agreed to this line as the border. But neither of these Labor Party prime ministers, condemned as reckless doves by Netanyahu, ever accepted the Syrian demand that Israel go back even farther, to the lines in place on June 4, 1967, before war broke out.

Although the 1967 lines give Syria only twenty-five additional square miles beyond the 1923 ones, they include land with both symbolic and hydraulic significance: were Syria to get them, it would have much greater leverage over the Banyas, Yarmuk, and Jordan rivers, as well as over Lake Tiberias—affecting nearly half of Israel's water supplies. Sources critical of Netanyahu say he began the talks by picking up where his Labor predecessors left off: Israel would return the territory on the Golan, accepting the international border but not the cease-fire lines. Yet, faced with Assad's steadfast rejection of these terms, he capitulated and, in a stunning reversal, agreed that Israel would, indeed, return to the 1967 lines. Also, having initially demanded that the Israeli withdrawal take place over a ten- to fifteen-year period, he ultimately settled on sixteen to twenty-four months. "The years kept flying by real fast," notes one Netanyahu confidant.

To prevent a repetition of the surprise attack from Syria in 1973, Netanyahu demanded an extensive demilitarization of Syrian territory near the Golan and an early warning station. This was to include no fewer than three demilitarized zones in Syria: the one closest to Israel completely empty of troops, a second with only lightly armed troops, and the third with troops bearing only defensive weapons, aides say. The third of these zones would extend well beyond Damascus, a prospect that upset the Syrians more than anything else. According to the critics, Assad simply refused the suggestion, insisting that Israel would never determine how many troops he would deploy around his capital city. Netanyahu backed off on this point, too; by the end of the negotiations, a "semi-agreement" lacking specifics was reached that each side would somewhat demilitarize a single zone ten kilometers wide along its border.

As for the final issue, Netanyahu demanded that Israel maintain in perpetuity a high-tech early warning station atop Mount Hermon, the nine-thousand–foot mountain that dominates the Syrian-Israeli border. When Assad balked at this, Netanyahu was said to have offered Assad a deal under which the two sides would share control over the warning station. No, again, Assad said—though he did agree to a U.N. team manning the station. If "United Nations" meant US and French nationals, Netanyahu said, he could accept it. There the matter was left, with Israelis looking at the prospect of access only to the information that the American or French governments wished them to have.

If Netanyahu was willing to give so much, why, in the end, was there no deal? His critics say it was not because he had any reservations about these terms—he was eager to sign—but because he personally lacked the credibility to make such far-reaching concessions that so starkly contradicted the principles of both his party and his cabinet. He needed a defense heavyweight to endorse the deal. During the active period of negotiations, that would have to have been Mordechai, an ex-general. Netanyahu twisted Mordechai's arm, but Mordechai would not (in his own words) "jeopardize Israel's security." Mordechai's reluctance, one close observer told me, "frustrated the hell out of Bibi." So, when Ariel Sharon was appointed foreign minister on October 9, 1998, Netanyahu asked for his blessing. Sharon also balked. Lacking an endorsement from Mordechai or Sharon, Netanyahu could not go it alone. As a result, the agreement was stillborn.

The Loyalists' Version

A Netanyahu supporter calls all of this "the opposite of the truth" and "an effort to rewrite history." The Netanyahu camp insists that his political ambitions had nothing to do with the talks. Rather, they say, Netanyahu signaled the Syrians shortly upon taking office that he wanted to talk but that he needed more security concessions than Labor had required. In 1997, he sent what an aide characterizes as a "barrage of messages" to Damascus to reinforce this point. The talks began in mid-'98, when an emissary came from Damascus to Israel saying that Assad was ready.

While Netanyahu's camp concedes that he did show flexibility on the issue of a timetable for Israeli withdrawal, it insists that he took a hard line on the three other issues. According to Netanyahu and his aides, the Syrians time and again demanded that Israel accept the 1967 borders but Netanyahu said no. Until it was clear where and how the Syrian military forces would redeploy, he insisted, Israel could not commit itself to specific lines. "Never" did he agree to a borderline, an aide says.

Netanyahu supporters say Assad accepted the idea of three demilitarized zones but wanted them to be less than ten kilometers wide. Netanyahu said no, and the Syrians acknowledged the need to make them wider. At that point, the talks broke off. As for a high-tech listening and watching post on Mount Hermon, Assad balked at this but did concede that Israelis would remain on the Golan Heights for some years. Netanyahu aides uniformly characterize this as "progress."

Indeed, Netanyahu's supporters claim much was achieved from Israel's point of view, despite the ultimate collapse of the talks. They say Netanyahu forced Assad to improve his offer over what he had given the Labor Party on such matters; thus the talks left his successor, Barak, in an enhanced position. There was no deal on his watch, Netanyahu told his Cabinet, because "Israel did not consent to Syria's territorial demands."

The Netanyahu faction seems especially incensed at the claim that Netanyahu was willing to cut a deal and was only stopped by Mordechai and Sharon. Uzi Arad, for example, says flatly that "Mordechai supported Netanyahu's position." Admittedly, he was "slow in acting but at no point opposed." As for Sharon, one participant says, he did effectively block the deal by not pursuing it—perhaps because it was not his own idea.

Adjudicating the Two Versions

Netanyahu's critics contend that things really ended much earlier, when Mordechai and Arad were tasked with drawing up a map to give to the Syrians but Mordechai stopped the process by never providing one. The negotiations "died because no map was produced," says a critic. For their parts, both Mordechai and Sharon have lent credence to the critics by publicly confirming their role in stopping the deal. Mordechai declared in his TV debate with Netanyahu: "More than once . . . I acted as a responsible defense minister of this country and prevented what had to be prevented. You know things would have looked very different otherwise." *Ha'aretz* reports that Sharon "told fellow Likud members . . . that he torpedoed the third-party efforts with Syria." It also quotes "government sources" saying that, when Sharon learned about the talks in September 1998, he confronted Netanyahu and said there was "not enough of a basis for Israel to put forward any withdrawal map."

Other circumstantial factors seem to support the critics' case. For all its emphatic certainty, the Netanyahu camp has seemed inconsistent and devious ever since Mordechai's "look me in the eye" challenge. For example, right after that dramatic confrontation, a senior official at the prime minister's office announced that "Mordechai does not know anything about" the talks between Jerusalem and Damascus—a clearly preposterous claim that even other pro-Netanyahu types have contradicted. One of them told me, for example, that Mordechai was "in the picture throughout."

And, while Netanyahu called Sharon's claim to have "torpedoed" the talks "nonsense" and "a false charge," the only support he offered for this statement was the legalistic and irrelevant point that Sharon "was appointed foreign minister only after the secret contacts ended." Netanyahu's argument also begs the question: If the prime minister was not doing anything contrary to his own party platform, why does he now claim to have kept the negotiations a complete secret from even his defense and foreign ministers?

°A handwritten English-language draft dated August 29, 1998, and titled "Treaty of Peace between Israel and Syria" that emerged publicly in April 2001 does not help decide between the two versions. It refers to "a commonly agreed border based on the international line of 1923"; it sketches a three-phase withdrawal but lacks a specific period of time; it provides no specifics about demilitarized zones; and it indicates that Israeli, Syrian, American, and French personnel will staff the early-warning station. Ronald Lauder subsequently indicated that this draft was rejected by Netanyahu.

The publication of a vague assertion in Bill Clinton's June 2004 memoir that Netanyahu would "give up the Golan" for a security treaty with Syria prompted much debate in Israel. Netanyahu and his successor at prime minister, Ehud Barak both denied Clinton's account but Uri Saguy, Barak's chief negotiator with the Syrians, confirmed it. Dennis Ross published his own memoir right after Clinton and he confirmed that Netanyahu was willing to withdraw to the 1967 lines.°

Anyone who has followed Netanyahu's career will instantly recognize in this episode the man's well-established pattern of speaking loudly but carrying a small stick. For example, Netanyahu's trademark issue throughout his career was a policy of tough antiterrorism—he founded an institute dedicated to this goal, wrote a book on the topic, and made it the subject of innumerable public appearances. But, when the US government offered to extradite to Israel a suspected Hamas terrorist, Musa Abu Marzook, Netanyahu took a bye (seemingly scared of the trouble this would cause). Released, Abu Marzook went on to live as a free man and a high Hamas official.

Thus does the evidence point heavily to the unhappy likelihood that Netanyahu's version is not true. More precisely, he appears to be boasting of his earlier, tougher positions with the Syrians but hiding the concessions he made as the talks went on. In fact, Netanyahu gave more to the Syrians than did either of the predecessors he so deeply scorned, Yitzhak Rabin and Shimon Peres. It was also more than his successors would concede.

Conclusion

This extraordinary episode reveals nothing new about the Syrian side, which merely confirmed its well-established pattern, going back twenty-five years, of attempting to draw maximum leverage from a position of weakness. As in the past, Assad gave the absolute minimum in negotiations and doled out concessions in the slowest and most incremental manner.

But the story of the secret Netanyahu-Assad channel has important implications in two areas: Israeli politics and the future of Syrian-Israeli relations. The negotiations reveal that Netanyahu is a leader who would do almost anything to stay in power. And Netanyahu's having discussed major concessions to Damascus weakened the negotiating position of his successors. Advantage, Syria.

Part II

Middle Eastern Politics

7

Understanding Middle Eastern Conspiracy Theories

The conspiracy mentality in the Middle East is so commonplace, few can resist its impact.[1] It engulfs whole societies. Conspiracy theories in the Middle East are espoused by leading politicians, religious figures, intellectuals, and journalists, and have a home at the heart of the political spectrum.

Conspiracy theories change history. The Organization of Islamic °Cooperation° was born of a conspiracy theory. That Shah Mohammad Reza Pahlavi saw the Iranian opposition made up not of patriotic Iranians but of Soviet, British, and American stooges contributed to his profound misreading of the situation and left him unprepared for Khomeini's challenge. Ayatollah Khomeini's conspiratorial mindset encouraged him to ignore the growing evidence of an Iraqi attack in September 1980. Anti-Semitism and fears of Israeli expansionism perpetuate the Arab-Israeli conflict.

Beyond specific examples, conspiracy theories spawn their own discourse, complete in itself and virtually immune to rational argument. Individuals or societies vulnerable to this way of thinking imbue imaginary creations with real properties and then respond to them.

Their Nature

Assumptions. Five assumptions distinguish the conspiracy theorist from conventional patterns of thought.

1. *Appearances deceive.* Things are never what they seem to be; there must be more to this than what we know. Killers are victims and victims are perpetrators. When Israelis appear to be massacred by PLO terrorists, the Israeli government is in fact murdering its own citizens in an elaborate ruse to discredit the Palestinians. Enemies are really allies; Qaddafi and Khomeini toil for the US government, while Zionists cooperate with

anti-Semites worldwide. Allies really are pawns, to be discarded when no longer useful; the British and Israeli governments are controlled by Washington. Skewed relationships replace the interplay of interests, the give and take of daily life, and normal reciprocal bonds. When everyone is exploiter or exploited, friendship is illusory.

2.   *Conspiracies drive history.* For the conspiracy theorist, change results from efforts by small, clandestine, and evil cliques unconstrained by morality or by means. Anonymous forces ("they") devised industrial techniques to undermine the cotton industry, to overthrow the king of France, to undermine the Arab nation, and are plotting terrible deeds even now. On a personal level, "they" caused my business to fail or insects to eat my harvest. If cabals determine history, the rest of the world consists of dupes and agents. The masses, always manipulated, count for nothing. Economic conditions lose importance, social forces become irrelevant, and intellectual debates are meaningless. Mobilizing ideologies such as nationalism and socialism delude people into thinking they have a role to play.

3.   *Nothing is haphazard.* The conspiracy theorist's obsessively orderly mind has no room for errors, accidents, or coincidences. The inadvertent is transformed into volitional, benign into malevolent, and weak into powerful. Random events turn into carefully plotted sequences; patterns of surreptitious association are triumphantly exposed. A sequence of events must be deliberately planned, the theorist assumes, and probably portends a full-blown plot.

4.   *The enemy always gains.* Whatever the event, the conspiracy theorist responds by asking, "How did my opponent profit?" He then seizes on any benefit, no matter how trivial or speculative, to explain why the event took place. The conspiracy theorist typically keys in on some minor dimension of an event and moves it to the center. Because every cloud has a silver lining, this means that any event can be interpreted to mean its opposite.

5.   *Always ask qui bono.* The conspiracy theorist has a dreary view of mankind: Power, fame, money, or sex account for all. Everyone is always competing. Competition and the gain of one party at the expense of another is universal. Invariably, the issue is seen in terms of status, wealth, or erotic reward.

Why So Many Conspiracy Theories? The most common explanation for the abundance of conspiracy theories in the Middle East concerns Islam—the nature of the Koranic message, the alleged fatalism of Muslims, or the Shi'i practice of *taqiya.* But Islam cannot be the reason because the Middle East hosted extremely few conspiracy theories before the year 1800. To the contrary, when analyzing problems, Muslims tended very much to hold themselves responsible for their circumstances. Or, as one writer neatly phrased it: "Our forefathers gave praise to God for their successes, and laid the blame for their failures on their sins and shortcomings. . . . We thank ourselves for our successes, and lay the blame for our failures on others."[2] Bearing in mind the principle that static phenomena do not cause change, conspiracy theories cannot be ascribed to Islam.

Instead, four factors explain the prevalent fear of conspiracy in the Middle East:

1. *The trauma of modern Islam.* The Muslim dilemma lies not in the Koran or Islam, but in the acute failures of the past two centuries. The Middle East has been consumed by an extended crisis lasting since Napoleon's invasion of Egypt in 1798. Middle Eastern attempts to cope with these tribulations have often been expressed via conspiracy theories. The conspirators are ascribed motives ranging from economic domination to genocide, much of it based on a deep hostility to Islam.

2. *The impact of Western ideas.* Surprising at it may seem, the major themes of conspiracy theories found in the Middle East derive almost without exception from the West. And the West, in its ebullient self-confidence, cannot imagine any mortal danger coming anywhere but from within itself. Accordingly, both of the Muslims' two main fears—Zionism and imperialism—are European in origin.

3. *Actual conspiracies.* Conspiracy theories and (actual) conspiracies reinforce each other and are more closely related than they may at first appear. The connection is mutual: imaginary plots generate actual ones, actual ones generate imaginary ones. Entering the mental world of a conspiracy theorist usually implies engaging in the actions of a conspirator. Fears generated by actual conspiracies create an opening for conspiracy theories. Vulnerability to the conspiracist mentality tends not to be entirely irrational, but results from witnessing many actual conspiracies.

   The Middle East has hosted an exceptional number of actual conspiracies in the past two centuries, and they have done much to foster conspiracy theories. Time and again, Western governments have relied on devious means to influence Middle East politics; Israelis have resorted to unconventional methods; and locals have indeed sold out to foreign interests.

4. *Political structures.* The failure to establish humane or democratic political structures also accounts for the inordinate Middle East fear of conspiracies. Three problems stand out: the Arab state system, autocracy, and mirror-imaging. The Arab system creates a strange brotherhood at once fraternal and fratricidal that breeds conspiracy theories. Autocratic regimes—such as those, other than in Israel, which predominate throughout the Middle East—disproportionately generate conspiracy theories. Middle East politicians incessantly plot and scheme against their rivals, so they naturally expect others to do the same to them.

Key themes. Almost every Middle East speculation about the hidden hand ultimately refers back to two grand conspirators: Zionists on the one hand, imperialists—specifically meaning Britons and Americans—on the other. It is striking how little the rest of the world worries Middle Easterners: not the French, Germans, Russians, Indians, Chinese, or Japanese, not the Fascists or Communists. These tend to come into consideration only to the extent that they ally with Zionists and imperialists.

Indeed, the connection is yet more precise. While the love of Zion and the impulse to military expansion both originated in the distant past, Zionism and imperialism took on their modern form only in the late nineteenth century. And it is the ideas of that era which remain potent to Arabs, °Turks,° and Iranians. In a sense, the Middle East presents a time warp, a place where Europe's phobias of a century back are preserved with few changes. Just as Marxists are still mired in the British economic battles of the nineteenth century, so the Middle East is yet entangled in European political debates over Jews and colonialism.

The practice of turning the tables on the victim and blaming him for what has befallen him is a very common theme; and so is accusing governments of sponsoring their most antagonistic enemies. Together, these sometimes make the Middle East nearly indecipherable to the outsider.

Who Believes?

Are those who claim to find conspirators under every bed as scared as they would have us think? Publics in the Middle East are genuinely as frightened as they seem to be. Leaders are a different story. While they clearly share some of the public's fears, they are also in a position to manipulate a gullible public for their own ends. The record shows a perplexing mixture of fear and manipulation; the same individual will alternately be sensible and then indulge in the paranoid style. It is hard for the outsider to explain how he can switch from one to the other; it is even harder to say which view represents his true thoughts.

The Public. Every indication suggests that the public in the Muslim Middle East truly believes in conspiracy theories.

To begin with, rumors circulate broadly through the region, and very many of them concern conspiracy theories. Jonathan Raban captures the wild spirit of these notions:

> Radio, television and newspapers tell one little or nothing; real news is still passed by word of mouth. Traveling businessmen and flight

crews are seized on and questioned; impressions of impressions of impressions ripple through the cities in widening and increasingly distorted circles. One hears strange things. During my trip, I heard that the Israelis had sacked Cairo; also that Palestinian guerrillas had taken control of Jerusalem. This dependence on whispers and rumors gives all news a particularly extremist flavor—everything turns into either a victory or a catastrophe. . . . I had the uneasy feeling that it would not be beyond the capacity of a mad cabin steward to provoke a full-scale war.[3]

On occasion, conspiracy theories begin at the grassroots level and then are adopted by the leadership. The campaign against Salman Rushdie began on the streets of Great Britain and Pakistan; only later did the Saudi and Iranian governments pick it up and make an international incident of it.

Public displays of things-aren't-what-they-appear-to-be attitude can take the breath away. In February 1954, the residents of Damascus initially dismissed the declaration by the military leaders of a *coup d'état* when they announced over the radio that they had taken power. Amazingly, they did so on the grounds that the declaration was merely an Israeli effort to provoke troubles in Syria.

The evidence points to the masses of Muslim Middle Easterners spontaneously and sincerely believing in conspiracy theories.

Rulers. Leaders' attitudes toward conspiracy theories are far more complex. When heads of government, foreign ministers, or editorial writers accuse Israel or the United States of plotting, it is not clear that they believe what they are saying. At times, they seem to believe in conspiracy theories as much as anyone else, but they also display a cynicism about using these to further their own goals. How can one distinguish sincerity from opportunism? What is the ratio of one to the other? The record is mixed and difficult to interpret. We begin by reviewing the evidence for manipulation and for sincerity.

1. *Manipulation.* There are good reasons to think that cynical leaders use conspiracy theories, and that their programmed efforts to encourage hidden hand explanations promote paranoid thinking. They know better, but knowingly exploit the gullibility of their listeners for any of a great range of reasons.

Conspiracies delegitimate opposition. When the old-guard Arab Higher Council, unhappy about the creation in 1964 of the rival Palestine Liberation Organization, sought to undermine this new institution, it called it "a colonialist, Zionist conspiracy aiming at the liquidation of the Palestinian cause."[4] The point of this transparently insincere calumny was to keep the PLO from usurping the Arab Higher Council's role.

They demonize the enemy. When the Jordanian government attempted to curb the country's phenomenal birth rate, an Islamist party in parliament denounced birth control as "a conspiracy serving Zionist plans to deprive Arab lands . . . of much needed manpower."[5]

They create bogeymen. Discovering evidence of plots by dispossessed landlords or disgruntled intellectuals is especially valuable to shaky governments seeking to rally the population behind them. Egypt's President Gamal Abdel Nasser created widespread concern about a powerless group of people when he fabricated evidence about the dispossessed upper classes collaborating with foreign elements to topple his regime.

They create a climate of fear. In January 1980, the Iranian government conveniently discovered a plot against United Nations Secretary General Kurt Waldheim during his visit to Tehran. Out of ostensible concern for his safety, it could keep him away from public view.

They justify inconsistencies. For over ten years, the Syrian government viciously assailed Cairo for its 1979 peace treaty with Israel. When the time came to renew relations on Egyptian terms, Syrian spokesmen explained the action as a result of the need to combat conspiracies surrounding the Arab nation.

They dispose of awkward news. When the news came from Romania about Arab commandos fighting with forces loyal to the deposed dictator, Nicolae Ceausescu, the PLO reaction was facile: blame "Zionist elements" working at Radio Free Europe[6] and pray the problem goes away.

They rewrite history. The Iraqi claim to Kuwait of 1961—an event recorded in countless documents, newspapers, and memoirs[7]—has been deemed a "phony story" put forward by British intelligence as "a pretext to wave the flag."[8]

They keep the faithful in line. The PLO has long excelled at finding intrigues, especially Israeli assassination attempts, which its heroic fighters constantly defeat; these burnish the organization's heroic posture and therefore its political standing. In Nasser's case, the constant stress on the imperialist bogeyman kept the Egyptians united against a common foe.

They exclude foreigners. Accusing foreign media of engaging in conspiracies against the homeland provides a mechanism to prohibit, even criminalize listening to their programs. Saddam Hussein instructed that Iraqi children be taught to "beware foreigners, for they are the eyes of their country and some of them seek to destroy the revolution."[9]

Perhaps most important, conspiracy theories turn anger outward and justify aggressive actions against a foreign state. When Saddam Hussein wanted to bully Kuwait into ceding territory and reducing its oil output, he concocted an elaborate plot by which tiny Kuwait (whose entire citizenry was smaller than Iraq's armed forces) was steadily taking over Iraqi territory in league with the "imperialist-Zionist plan against Iraq."[10]

2. *Sincerity.* The fact that leaders bring up conspiracy theories in private as well as public suggests sincere belief. Nasser told American officials in private what he said publicly: that he was convinced the US government "was trying to keep Egypt weak and that this resulted from Jewish influence."[11] As Husni Za'im, the first military dictator of Syria, was in the process of being overthrown by a military coup, he tried desperately and unsuccessfully to escape execution by bribing his guard. Once Za'im realized he was done for, however, he muttered, "This is a plot by the British to destroy the independence of the country."[12] This statement, made at so critical a moment, no doubt reflected Za'im's deepest feelings.

Westerners who met alone with Iranian leaders at the time of the Islamic Revolution were convinced of their sincerity. The US ambassador, William H. Sullivan, had frequent interviews with the shah, writes that the conspiracy mentality extends "from the lowliest peasant all the way up to the shah himself."[13] The British ambassador, Anthony Parsons, reached precisely the same conclusion.

At times, the conspiracy mentality degenerates into a naked fear of being surrounded, and this certainly appears sincere. Mu'ammar al-Qaddafi, who worried that the whole world was out to get him, sometimes imagined that diametrically opposed elements—such as communists and Muslim Brethren—joined together to work "in the same alliance against the [Libyan] revolution."[14]

There is good reason for leaders to fall into the same traps as their listeners. Government officials enter office with assumptions and prejudices that reasonably reflect the political culture at large; and if these are permeated with conspiracy theories, so are they. In an atmosphere rife with plots, real and imaginary, rulers are subject to the same fears as others. Nasser's biographer, P. J. Vatikiotis, suggests that "in his suspicious and limited perception of the world about him, Abdel Nasser personified the view of the vast majority of his fellow-countrymen, especially the poor and miserable of Egypt."[15]

When a conspiracy theory wins an enthusiastic reception, the instigator is tempted by his own fabrication. Kamal Jumblatt, then Lebanon's interior minister, blamed a failed *coup d'état* by the Syrian Social Nationalist Party in December 1961 on the British; he even claimed personally to have witnessed Her Majesty's ambassador on the roof of the British Embassy signaling a British warship at sea. In fact, the closest British naval unit at the time was in Gibraltar, but this hardly diminished the enthusiastic reception for Jumblatt's story, which then appears to have convinced him of his own fabrication.

Leaders can be even more susceptible than the populace to their own lies, especially if they are under stress. Surrounded by yes-men, it becomes more difficult to maintain a critical posture. Leaders hear their own incessant propaganda more than most citizens; and they hear their own voice at closer range. The author of a conspiracy theory is especially susceptible to its charms. Rulers have a vested interest in having their statements believed; not to do so means living a lie. Leaders have another reason to believe in the plots they conjure up—what if they turn out to be true, as does sometimes happen?

Assessment. Credulity and manipulation sometimes exist in their pure forms, but a mixture of the two elements is more common. Conspiracy theories appear to combine interests and beliefs in complex ways. What Norman Cohn writes about Hitler applies to others as well:

> It has sometimes been argued that Hitler was simply a super-Machiavellian, a man without convictions or loyalties, an utter cynic for whom the whole aim and value of life consisted in power and more power. There certainly was such a Hitler—but the other Hitler, the haunted man obsessed by fantasies about the Jewish world-conspiracy, was just as real. What one would like to know is just how far the near-lunatic was active even in the calculating opportunist.[16]

Pondering King Faisal's thesis about a joint Zionist-Communist conspiracy, Henry Kissinger showed how the fanatic and the opportunist can comfortably co-exist. He observed that, however bizarre the king's vision, it "was clearly deeply felt. At the same time," Kissinger correctly noted,

> it reflected precisely the tactical necessities of the Kingdom. The strident anti-Communism helped reassure America and established

a claim on protection from outside threats (which were all, in fact, armed by the Soviet Union). The virulent opposition to Zionism reassured radicals and the PLO and thus reduced their incentive to follow any temptation to undermine the monarchy domestically.[17]

The utility of conspiracy theories makes them all the more credible; in keeping with psychological theory, beliefs follow interests. This does not, it should be noted, make them any the less sincere.

Evidence points to several stages in the evolution of an irrational belief: initial sincerity, followed by manipulation, increasing sincerity, and concluded by a weak acknowledgment of fabrication. Judging from information about other leaders (Joseph Goebbels comes to mind), this inconsistent pattern seems more typical than surprising. But how can it be accounted for? How are truth and fabrication both sincere?

The answer lies in the ability of conspiracy theorists to believe in an idea but manipulate its manifestations. Faith in a conspiracy precedes and overrides the need for proof. Documentation is a mechanism for convincing others; conspiracy theorists have a faith that welcomes but does not need verification. They are so convinced of a basic truth that they are willing to bend the rules of evidence and logic to prove their point to others. Parallels are not hard to find in religion and politics. The mental flexibility of conspiracy theorists permits them to stop talking about conspiracy theories when these are counterproductive, and merely to keep their own counsel.

Despite the many reasons suggesting manipulation, real fears seem even more prevalent. This conclusion leads to two rules of thumb. First, rulers appear to act more consistently with the grandiose theories they spin, less so with the very specific ones. The larger and more pervasive the alleged conspiracy, the more likely it is put forward sincerely. Second, unless there are reasons to think otherwise, a leader's resort to the conspiracy explanation should be viewed as sincere.

A Case Study: Iraq and Iran

The governments of Iran and Iraq are two of the most highly attuned to conspiracy theories. Both their constitutions specifically refer to plotting. Eight years of Iraq-Iran war and poor relations between both countries and the West sharpened a general susceptibility to the conspiracy mentality, making it central to the politics of both countries. When looking at the outside world, their thoroughly different ideologies would seem to matter less than a shared vocabulary of fear.

Three events—the Iraq-Iran war, the Rushdie affair, and the invasion of Kuwait—magnified the conspiracy mentality and made it an obsession.

The Iraq-Iran War. As any reasonably well-informed American knew, his government's relations with both Iran and Iraq after 1979 ranged from bad to terrible. These were the years when the Iranian authorities sanctioned the seizure of the US embassy, suicide bombings, hostage-takings, and airline explosions. While relations with Iraq were not quite so hostile before the seizure of Kuwait, the brutal and aggressive regime of Saddam Hussein represented exactly the kind of rule that Americans deplore.

So much for reality; propaganda emanating from Tehran and Baghdad told an entirely different story. In what may have been a historical first, each side blamed the same third party—the US government—for inciting the other to start the war and then keep it going. Uncannily similar accusations resulted from concentrating only on the enemy's bonds to the United States, no matter how meager, and ignoring all the sources of enmity. Further straining the bonds of credulity, each party portrayed the other as Israel's close ally.

Iranians explained that "global arrogance" and "international blasphemy" (i.e., the West, including sometimes the Soviet Union) panicked on seeing Iranians assert Muslim power. To stop the Islamic movement from getting out of hand, the powers planned ways to subvert the Islamic Revolution. "All the West's plots," explained President Khamene'i, "are aimed at stopping Islam and the revolution from becoming a world model."[18] Had the White House and Kremlin not fought Iran, they would forfeit their ill-gotten but favorable positions.

The Iraqi government portrayed the war similarly. Its propaganda depicted a Western world deeply fearful of Iraq attaining its rightful military, industrial, and scientific strength. A fully modern Iraq, Saddam Hussein told his citizens time and again, frightened the many Westerners yet clinging to the illusions of colonialism. It would also deprive the West of control over the oil reserves of the Persian Gulf. This the West could not tolerate: to obstruct Iraq from modernizing, it called in its well-known agent, the Ayatollah Khomeini.

With the end of the war, both Tehran and Baghdad claimed victory over each other and the West. The Americans and Europeans, the conclusion ran in both capitals, realized that brute force would not work; and so they shifted emphasis. Military means having failed, the

Westerners regrouped and thought up a second strategy. The second strategy was a more indirect one, intended to sap the very foundations of the country's strength. Iranians hypothesized Western cultural warfare; Iraqis worried about economic warfare.

The Rushdie Affair. Round two for Iran meant contending with cultural imperialism by Western governments that developed "a comprehensive way to confront Islam."[19] That effort centered on *The Satanic Verses*,[20] ostensibly a novel composed by Salman Rushdie but in fact, Tehran insisted, the culmination of a great plot involving several intelligence services. Rafsanjani even commended the British for choosing Rushdie as a shill, for he provided an ideal front for Iran's enemies.

Although Rushdie had almost nothing then to do with the United States—he was a Muslim of Indian origins living in England—the Iranian government insisted on seeing him as an American agent, part of Great Satan's conspiracy to undo the Islamic Revolution. But Muslims recognized the Western plot for what it was, leading to Ayatollah Khomeini's February 14, 1989, death edict against Rushdie and "all those involved in its publication who were aware of its contents."[21]

The Invasion of Kuwait. For Iraq, round two meant staving off economic imperialism. When the Western powers finally realized that the Iranians could not defeat Iraq on the battlefield, they had no choice but to enter the fray themselves, "playing the game directly."[22] Frustrated and fearful of Iraqi pan-Arabism, the imperialists shifted gears and attacked the bases of Iraqi strength: oil. Iraqi authorities also claimed to have information that the Israelis were about to launch an attack on Iraq.

Saddam Hussein unearthed a "large-scale, premeditated campaign by the official and nonofficial imperialist and Zionist circles against Iraq." Those circles adopted a new method "to cut off livelihood, while the old method, which has already been contained, sought to cut off necks." Saddam pointed a finger at his neighbors, criticizing "the new oil policy which certain rulers of the Gulf states have for some time intentionally been pursuing to reduce oil prices." Saddam also included a threat: "If words fail to afford us protection, then we will have no choice but to resort to effective action to put things right and ensure the restitution of our rights."[23]

Just two weeks and a day after this speech, on August 2, 1990, Iraqi forces entered Kuwait. Plots had a large role in justifying the conquest of Kuwait: just hours after the occupation, the first communiqué of the "Provisional Free Kuwaiti Government" attacked the prior Kuwaiti authorities for a conspiracy in league with imperialism and Zionism "against the steadfast brother, Iraq."[24] A few weeks later, Saddam Hussein put it more bluntly: "The rulers of Kuwait wanted to destroy Iraq."[25]

Iranian and Iraqi perceptions followed parallel paths. Both leaderships portrayed their accomplishments (genuine Islam in Iran, a modern economy in Iraq) as so threatening to American and Europe that Western imperial interests had to overturn their regimes. Rather than do this themselves, they called on a local agent. That agent (read Iraq or Iran) battered itself for eight long years against the unbeatable will of righteousness. Eventually the West acknowledged the futility of the military effort, so it called off its proxy and the war came to an end in 1988. But, still unable to tolerate the example of Iran (or Iraq), the West switched to a second and more subtle way of undermining its revolution. This time the goal was to strike at the heart of its strength; again a Muslim agent did the West's dirty work. Each of these agents (Rushdie, Kuwait) was rewarded with a death sentence.

These closely matching patterns call for an explanation. Did the two governments cue each other? Or was there some underlying structure that they shared and which impelled them down similar paths? The latter seems more likely. The two leaderships shared so much—hostility toward the West, grand ambitions, a repressive government system, an economy tied to oil sales—that they found themselves frustrated by similar developments and responded in similar ways. In the end, systemic similarities outweighed ideological differences in the way they defined challenges and failures.

Credence in conspiracy theories influences the tenor of Middle East political life. The conspiracy mentality makes it harder to face up to reality. Much of the region's anti-Western, anti-Israel, anti-democratic, anti-moderate, and anti-modern behavior results from fears of clandestine forces. Only when Middle Easterners push conspiracy theories aside can they become succeed in the modern world.

Notes

1. Some of these remarks may apply to other regions of the world; the Middle East has no monopoly on conspiracy theories.
2. Quoted in M. Plessner, "Ist der Zionismus gescheitert?" in Weiner Library, London, *Mitteilungsblatt*, Oct. 24, 1952, no. 42. Quoted in Bernard Lewis, *The Middle East and the West* (London: Weidenfeld and Nicolson, 1963), p. 96.

3. Jonathan Raban, *Arabia: A Journey Through the Labyrinth* (New York: Simon & Schuster, 1979), pp. 166–67.

4. *Al-Kitab as-Sanawi li'l-Qadiya al-Filastiniya, 1964*, p. 102. Quoted in Helena Cobban, *The Palestinian Liberation Organization: People, Power and Politics* (Cambridge, Eng.: Cambridge University Press, 1984), p. 31.

5. 'Abd al-Latif 'Arabiyat, spokesman of Islamic Movement deputies in the House of Representatives, *Ad-Dustur*, May 14, 1990.

6. San'a Voice of Palestine, Dec. 27, 1989.

7. For a sampling of evidence, see *Middle East Record* 2 (1961): 117–39.

8. Saïd K. Aburish, *Beirut Spy: The St George Hotel Bar* (London: Bloomsbury, 1989), pp. 47–48. Aburish has this event off by two years, placing it in 1959.

9. Saddam Hussein, *Ad-Dimuqratiya: Masdar Quwwa li'l-Fard wa'l-Mujtama'* (Baghdad: Dar ath-Thawra, 1977), p. 20. The same passage also includes a call for children to report on their parents.

10. Radio Baghdad, July 18, 1990

11. Telegram from George V. Allen, Oct. 1, 1955. Text in *Foreign Relations of the United States, 1955–1957*, volume 14, *Arab-Israeli Dispute 1955*, p. 539.

12. Fadlallah Abu Mansur, *A'asir Dimashq* (Beirut: n.p., 1959). Quoted in Elie Kedourie, *Arabic Political Memoirs and Other Studies* (London: Frank Cass, 1974), p. 183.

13. William H. Sullivan, *Mission to Iran* (New York: W. W. Norton, 1981), p. 47.

14. Tripoli Television, Apr. 7, 1990.

15. P. J. Vatikiotis, *Nasser and His Generation* (New York: St. Martin's Press, 1978), p. 322.

16. Norman Cohn, *Warrant for Genocide: The Myth of the Jewish World Conspiracy and the* Protocols of the Elders of Zion (New York: Harper & Row, 1969), p. 192.

17. Henry Kissinger, *Years of Upheaval* (Boston: Little, Brown, 1982), p. 662.

18. Radio Tehran, Mar. 12, 1989.

19. Radio Tehran, Mar. 1, 1983.

20. New York: Viking, 1989.

21. *Kayhan Havai*, Feb. 22, 1989.

22. "Statement made by President Saddam Hussein," Baghdad, Apr. 2, 1990.

23. Radio Baghdad, July 17, 1990.

24. Baghdad Sawt ash-Sha'b, Aug. 2, 1990.

25. Radio Baghdad, Aug. 30, 1990.

8

Dealing with Middle East Fears of Conspiracy

Don't make the mistake of thinking that the longer you've been here the more you understand Iran. Most of our intelligence reporting has been wrong all along and not just since the revolution. Yours will be too. None of us understands the Iranians.
—An Asian diplomat in Tehran[1]

If you want to confound your enemies, the best technique is to create clandestine sects, wait for dangerous enthusiasms to precipitate, then arrest them all. In other words, if you fear a plot, organize one yourself; that way, all those who join it come under your control.
—Umberto Eco, Foucault's Pendulum[2]

Introduction

A strange event took place in November 1977 as the shah of Iran, Mohammad Reza Pahlavi, was visiting Washington.

Iranians both protesting and supporting the shah's regime (with the former wearing masks to hide their identities from the Iranian secret police, SAVAK) took advantage of his presence to rally in Washington. They confronted each other on the Ellipse near the White House, first trading insults then physical blows. To separate the Iranian factions, the police used tear gas, some of which wafted over the White House grounds at the very moment President Jimmy Carter was formally welcoming the shah. As the gas settled, high-ranking figures cried, wheezed, and coughed. Predictably, pictures of the two heads of state wiping tears from their eyes were widely and prominently distributed.

American officials saw this mishap as embarrassing and amusing, but not as terribly significant. After all, anyone can demonstrate in the Ellipse; and tear gas on the White House resulted from nothing more than a mix of Iranian passions and untoward wind patterns. Not for a moment did American officials connect the botched ceremony in Washington with subsequent disturbances in Iran.

But they should have, for Iranians saw the incident very differently. Pro- and anti-shah elements alike agreed that it marked complete US government abandonment of the shah. When the head of SAVAK saw a videotape of the incident, he reportedly concluded that the shah could not last. Pahlavi himself, in typical Iranian style, suspected the US government of simultaneously welcoming him and supporting his enemies. He focused on the demonstrators' hidden faces, arguing that this proved his opposition was made up of foreigners. "The masks hid non-Iranian demonstrators—professional troublemakers hired on the spot. . . . Most of them were young Americans—blonds, blacks, Puerto Ricans, together with some Arabs. Moreover, there was foreign money involved in paying their bills."[3]

The opposition found the tear gas even more significant. Ibrahim Yazdi, leader of the main Iranian dissident organization in the United States, reported to Khomeini that the Carter administration had abandoned the shah. How did he know this? According to Gary Sick, President Carter's Middle East specialist, the dissidents "reasoned that such an event could have occurred only at the president's behest. Thus they quickly concluded that Carter had abandoned the shah and launched a series of protest demonstrations and meetings [in Iran]." What came to be known as "the Washington tears" undermined the shah's claim to American support and deeply harmed his imperial prestige.[4]

As this episode suggests, Americans and Middle Easterners understand politics in different ways. The event may take place in downtown Washington and concern a key ally; still, Americans responsible for foreign policy miss its implications for the other side. While American officials are nearly blind to conspiracy theories (the terminology used here has a *conspiracy* being real and a *conspiracy theory* imaginary),[5] Iranians discern them in the merest accidents. These discrepancies hobble Americans' understanding of public life in the Middle East. Indeed, neglecting conspiracy theories can lead to a profound misreading of that region.

To overcome this obstacle, I shall show that ignoring conspiracy theories means missing much that makes Middle East politics tick. I then recommend that the US government act with the conspiracist mentality in mind. The final part considers whether or not Washington should exploit opportunities created by the conspiracy mentality.

Pay Close Attention

That the US government is blamed for so much that goes wrong in the Middle East means that conspiracy theories bear many implications for it. They should be integrated into reporting, briefing, and negotiating activities.

Acknowledge conspiracy theories. The paranoid style needs to be accepted as a major force.

It is tempting for the serious analyst or policymaker to dismiss conspiracy theories. They derive from rumors, sensational news items, ephemeral tracts, breezy memoirs, and other suspect sources. Their patently false quality makes them appear unsuitable for discussion in the conference rooms and hallways of sober bureaucracies. Just as fastidious historians usually avoid "this dubious documentation, preferring the seemingly purer evidence of well-written official dispatches or of well-bound books,"[6] fastidious intelligence analysts are inclined to ignore bombastic and scurrilous claims.

Americans especially tend reflexively to dismiss the idea of conspiracy. Living in a political culture ignorant of secret police, a political underground, and coups d'état, they often find it hard to imagine that plots do play a role in other countries. Indeed Middle East paranoia bemuses sophisticated Americans. At a Beirut dinner party once hosted by Malcolm Kerr, then president of the American University of Beirut, the conversation turned to a hail storm the night before, prompting guests to speculate about its possible meteorological causes. Kerr mischievously speculated, "Do you think the Syrians did it?"[7] Fair enough—so long as merriment does not distract from the somber importance of the conspiracy mentality.

It is especially easy to disregard the theories when they pertain to oneself and one knows them to be patently false. Jordanian talk about the worldwide power of the Zionist movement inspires disdainful smiles in Jerusalem; a like reaction is not unknown in Washington. But inaccuracy does not render these conjectures insignificant.

Listen to Middle East informants. The better to comprehend Arab and Iranian views, close attention should be given to the glosses offered by their conationals. As Yehoshafat Harkabi remarked, "Arabs interpret their position copiously, and their elaborations are always superior to foreign, including Israeli, expositions."[8] While this may taking the point a bit far, it is true that there is much to learn from those who understand the conspiracy mentality from the inside.

By similar token, statements to constituents count more than rhetoric vented at the United Nations. Read the local press for insights into the minds of the leadership.

Report conspiracy thinking . . . To protect their own credibility, Western journalists, diplomats, and intelligence agents in the Middle East generally bleach conspiracy theories out of their reporting. The US press devoted massive attention to aspects of the Rushdie affair, but it hardly ever mentioned the conspiratorial interpretation of *The Satanic Verses* that loomed so large for Khomeini and his aides. The sentence of Saddam Hussein's April 2, 1990 speech in which he threatened to burn half of Israel was quoted over and over again; but much longer passages about conspiracies were ignored.

There is a world of difference between Middle East media in the raw and the sanitized news that reaches the West. John B. Kelly highlighted this disparity in a memorable passage published in 1973:

> Distance, the filtering of news through so many intermediate channels, and the habitual tendency to discuss and interpret Middle Eastern politics in the political terminology of the West, have all contrived to impart a certain blandness to the reporting and analysis of Middle Eastern affairs in Western countries. It is highly salutary (and also slightly unnerving) to be reminded . . . of the language, tone and manner in which political debate is customarily carried on in the "progressive" Arab states. To read, for instance, the extracts from the Cairo and Baghdad press and radio . . . is to open a window upon a strange and desolate landscape, strewn with weird, amorphous shapes cryptically inscribed "imperialist plot," "Zionist crime," "Western exploitation," "socialist solidarity," "people's justice," "brotherhood," "nationalism," "liberation," "vile conspiracy," "unending struggle," "immortal leader," "the glorious revolution," "the undefeated revolution," and "the revolution betrayed." Around and among these enigmatic structures, curious figures, like so many mythical beats, caper and cavort—"enemies," "traitors," "stooges," "hyenas," "puppets," "lackeys," "feudalists," "gangsters," "tyrants," "criminals," "oppressors," "plotters" and deviationists." . . . It is all rather like a monstrous playing board for some grotesque and sinister game, in which the snakes are all hydras, the ladders have no rungs, and the dice are blank.[9]

Diplomats also discount this mentality. When US Ambassador William H. Sullivan had to report on a conspiracy-obsessed shah of Iran during the terrible days of late 1978, he dealt with the shah's worries in as delicate and roundabout manner as he could. Returning from a particularly agitated session at the royal palace, Sullivan decided to request a letter from President Jimmy Carter to the shah, "reaffirming policy support for him." But Sullivan would go only so far in that reaffirmation:

> I felt it would be inappropriate for the president in any way to take cognizance of the wild accusations about CIA support for the shah's opponents, but I suggested that the message be so written as to give the lie to any such speculation.[10]

Was Sullivan right to maintain the formal protocol of diplomacy in this incidence? Or would he have done better to have recommended that Carter directly confront the shah's obsessions?

There can be little doubt that the latter course would have been the wiser. True, it falls outside the normal bounds of diplomacy to deny that one's intelligence service is working hand-in-glove with its enemy; but this is no reason to shy away from doing so. Obvious inaccuracy does not reduce the importance of conspiracy theories; nothing is so false that someone will not believe it. Arguably, not reporting on the shah's thinking cost the US government very heavily in Iran, for it deprived Washington of information on which to make a decision. Reticence on the part of the ambassador in Tehran meant willfully obscuring a key actor's thinking.

No matter how bizarre they sound back home, theories about the hidden hand should be carefully accounted for by diplomats and intelligence agents. Ignoring this prominent strain of Middle East thinking means not to understand the way intellectuals, religious leaders, bureaucrats, and politicians see the world. The analyst ignores Kelly's "monstrous playing board" at his peril.

. . . *But with extra care.* Conspiracy theories must be reported with special consideration, lest they be portrayed as the truth. Radio Monte Carlo, a French station, fell into this trap when its correspondent, Mustafa Bakri, reported on the killing of Palestinian workers by a deranged Israeli gunman in May 1990. He related that "important diplomatic sources" in Cairo "revealed new information" to the effect that Prime Minister Yitzhak Shamir of Israel personally ordered not only the murders, but also that soldiers chase and kill Palestinians afterward.[11] Quite the reverse: Shamir unreservedly condemned the killings and the soldiers protected Palestinians. Bakri had every reason to transmit the thinking prevalent in Cairo, but not to endorse it as he did.

All those who deal with conspiracy theories, whether journalists or government employees, must use discretion and judgment to distance themselves from these notions. As with all disinformation, conspiracy theories need to be known for what they are, and not purveyed as plain news. This subject matter demands extra judgment by the reporter of conspiracy theories and his editorial supervisor.

Act Defensively

Anticipate malign interpretations. The Middle Eastern readiness to misread even the most innocuous acts means that anything is likely to be interpreted in a hostile way. The worthiest impulses quickly become deathly plots. Miles Copeland, an American with years of experience in intelligence, put it well: "In the Arab world, even the most innocent, high sounding statement . . . is examined microscopically for and can be given the most sinister implications by a clever opponent bent on doing so."[12] The wrong timing or the wrong wording can make Westerners an unwitting party to the political hallucinations of others. Once this happens, they find themselves caught in a vortex of illusion that is nearly impossible to escape.

Innocent of the Middle East's paranoid style, Americans during the 1960s and 1970s inadvertently did just about everything to confirm Iranian fears of plots. The huge size of the official American presence and its proximity to the central institutions of power, economics, and culture eased the way for the opposition to direct populist rage against Americans. American arrogance grated on Iranians. Worst of all, US citizens in Iran won immunity from Iranian laws, a privileged position that smacked of the old capitulations (and gave Ayatollah Khomeini his first public issue). Awareness of the conspiracy mentality could have done much to prevent this hostility from forming in the first place.

The US Senate's vote in the spring of 1979 to condemn Tehran's execution of a Jewish merchant who had been accused of being a Zionist agent had an unintended impact in Iran. Rather than showing America's humanitarian concern, it was perceived as a proof of a Zionist-imperialist alliance, and thus undercut the possibility of improved relation with Washington. It specifically led to the ambassador-designate to Iran, Robert Cutler, being rejected. More generally, as the Iranian specialist William O. Beeman, notes: "the American government, without specifically intending to do so, continued to behave throughout the revolution in ways that could be shown by skillful rhetoricians in the mosques and the streets in Iran to be characteristic of The Great Satan."

Israelis also find their actions get interpreted in ways they not only never intended but never imagined. Take two incidents: In 1956, Israeli forces avenged a terrorist incident from Egyptian soil by striking hard against an Egyptian target, intending to make sure that there would be no repetition. Instead, the disproportionate use of force led Egyptians to see Israel as an American agent. One Egyptian told an Israeli interlocutor, "You frequently do things that give the impression that you are the tool of an alien policy in the Middle East." The outbreak of the intifada in December 1987 resulted from the widespread conviction in Gaza that a traffic accident (in which an Israel truck driver struck a car, killing four Palestinian laborers) was a purposeful act of revenge by a relative of the Israeli who had been stabbed to death in Gaza two days earlier. The resulting fury took Israelis completely by surprise.

Avoid steps that can be seen as confirming conspiracy theories. Even routine greetings on the occasion of a holiday—the sort of thing that goes on all the time in diplomatic exchanges—can arouse suspicions; this was the case in September 1978, when the US government congratulated the shah on the occasion of the end of the Ramadan fast. The opposition interpreted this as an declaration of renewed support for the shah. A memo from the State Department in May 1990 instructed its diplomats to warn participants in an Arab League summit that their anti-American rhetoric harm relations with the US government; Saddam Hussein portrayed this routine message as proof of a conspiracy against himself.

In 1962, Richard Murphy recounts, the US Embassy in Damascus distributed pictures of Astronaut John Glenn "to a fascinated Syrian public." This seemingly innocent act came to be interpreted as the first step in a far-reaching political realignment:

> We did not foresee that distribution of our colonel's smiling face would take place only a few days before the countercoup aimed at helping Colonel [Gamal Abdel] Nasser return to Syria. For years afterwards we were credited with having planned that coup attempt. I personally and our Aleppo Consulate General staff in general were widely identified as having led a procession down Aleppo's tram line distributing Nasser's photograph in a determined if vain effort to encourage the rebellion. Those few Syrians who did not actually believe this story hugely enjoyed retelling it.

The political scientist Robert Jervis generalizes: "Because decision makers know that others are not apt to believe in coincidences, they may delay or change their behavior in order to avoid the appearance of being influenced by other events that are happening at the time." In short, think like a conspiracy theorist.

Worry more about quiescence than active support. The real danger of conspiracy theories lies not in how many people believe but in how many refuse to oppose the idea. Obsessive anti-Zionism and anti-imperialism do not win enough support to get a ruler into power, but they do much to facilitate the ruler's imposition of a xenophobic and repressive regime.

Hear yourself as a Middle Easterner would. American politicians often neglect to consider how their words resonate in the Middle East. The Eisenhower Administration exaggerated its role in restoring the shah of Iran in 1953, thereby confirming the worst fears of the Iranian opposition. When Senator J. William Fulbright, chairman of the Senate Foreign Relations Committee, told a television audience in 1973 that the US government bears "a very great share of the responsibility" for violence in the Middle East, he was referring to what he saw as the incompetence of American policy. But Middle Eastern listeners heard something quite different; for them, the statement confirmed their suspicions that the US government had sponsored violence in the region. In this way, Fulbright unintentionally confirmed Middle East paranoia. When Senator Henry Jackson averred in October 1979 that the Iranian revolution was bound to fail, and that Iran would then break up into many smaller states, he was expressing his deep concern. Rather than understand this, Iranians interpreted it as a declaration of American wishes: some took heart and others despaired at the news.

The George H. W. Bush administration's first major policy statement on the Middle East, delivered by Secretary of State James Baker on May 22, 1989, demonstrated American tone deafness. For the most part, Baker used standard phrases and recalled traditional American policies. But one line, his call to Israelis "to lay aside, once and for all, the unrealistic vision of a greater Israel,"[13] was startlingly original. By "greater Israel," Baker meant to refer to the Likud Party's hopes to retain control of the West Bank, an area occupied in 1967. In the Arab world, however, Greater Israel means something much grander, namely Israeli conquest of a huge area stretching from Egypt to Iran.[14]

Thus, the American secretary's call seemed authoritatively to confirm a deeply held and cherished fantasy. As Syrian Vice President 'Abd al-Halim Khaddam put it, "the Zionist call for establishing a state of Greater Israel from the Nile to the Euphrates is no longer a secret."[15] In support of this interpretation, Yasir Arafat concocted an elaborate back story. The notion of a Greater Israel, he said, "did not come from Baker's imagination. He heard about it from the Zionist leadership in the United States and the American Israel Public Affairs Committee, which published maps on this issue.[16]

Timing is important too. Hafez al-Assad chose to consider a US government announcement about the Hama massacre of February 1982 as an effort to encourage the uprising against his regime. When the Red Cross condemned both the Iraqi and Iranian governments for their treatment of prisoners of war, the question arose on both sides, "Why now? Who benefits?"

Speeches, letters, and other forms of communication need to be gone over by specialists with an eye to nuances and misinterpretations. Do the contents contain ambiguities that can be misinterpreted? (Check the dictionary.) Does the timing have some implication in the Middle East? (Check the Islamic calendar.) Does the manner of presentation send an untoward signal? (Check with old hands.)

Remember that official and unofficial words get confused. Baffled by freedom of speech and the freewheeling ways of democratic govern-ments, Middle Eastern leaders cannot always tell the difference between official policy and the views of editorialists and parliamentarians. *New York Times* editorials are assumed to carry official sanction. The US Congress' essentially meaningless gesture in 1990 urging that the US government recognize Jerusalem as Israel's capital was wrongly perceived in the Middle East as a major change in American policy; accordingly, this event, barely reported in the United States, received enormous attention in Arab capitals.

Assure a successful outcome before formal negotiations begin;. When public negotiations fail, they have potential great implications. Not closing a deal is likely to be seen as a sign of insincerity. William R. Brown, an American official who worked for Henry Kissinger, has an interesting perspective on this subject:

> Looking back on a series of negotiations that were not brought to frui-tion many Arabs are not inclined to see a simple and straightforward failure resulting from an inability to achieve an accommodation of interests. Instead, they often suspect that the negotiations were not for the stated purpose at all. Malevolence is attributed to the other side, which is accused of entering into negotiations to cover some hidden objective, generally seen as dividing the Arabs.[17]

In advance of formal negotiations, foreigners should make sure there is a realistic expectation of success; or that even failure has benefits which outweigh the costs of failing.

Listen to public rather than private statements. Middle East leaders often say something different in private from what they hold in public. Which counts more, the confidences vouchsafed in private or the statements issued in press conferences? Diplomats, intelligence agents, journalists, and others with access to the mighty tend to flatter themselves with the assumption that the inside story is the real one. But this is usually incorrect. Even if private remarks more accurately reflect a leader's personal views, they are not policy. Public statements usually reflect policies more accurately than private ones; when they do not, the government is headed for trouble.[18] Were the views expressed in *tête-à-têtes* with Western officials operational, the Arab-Israeli conflict would have been resolved long ago.

Don't bestow the kiss of death. Conspiracy theories foster a widespread suspicion that some Muslim rulers are manipulated by foreign powers; accordingly, even a modicum of overt influence is taken as evidence of huge covert influence. The kiss of death then redounds back to hurt the foreign patron. Overbearing foreign support undermines a Middle East leader's reputation. In Syria, the government did so badly in the elections of 1954 in large part because it was seen as far too pliant to American wishes. Not accidentally, it was replaced by leftist politicians who viewed Washington with hostility, and these latter ruled for decades afterward. The shah of Iran and Anwar as-Sadat both lost their countrymen's respect because they were seen as agents of Washington, even through they were independent allies. Hafez al-Assad and the communist rulers of Afghanistan suffered from their too close association with Moscow.

The merest sign of good will can be blown up into collusion by suspicious Middle Easterners. In 1979, Carter's national security advisor, Zbigniew Brzezinski, met Iranian prime minister Mehdi Bazargan at a celebration in Algeria, and thereby virtually ended Bazargan's political career. The next year, Brzezinski signaled an American interest to improve relations to the Iraqi government. While the Iraqis hardly noted his offer, the Iranians jumped on it as a sign of Iraqi subservience to the US government and responded with threats to kill American hostages in Tehran.

Leaders being no more immune to conspiracy thinking than the citizenry, they too tend to exaggerate the role of the foreigner. The shah of Iran, for example, came to depend deeply on the US government. On the one hand, good relations made him confident: "As long as the Americans support me, we can do and say whatever we want—and

I am immovable." On the other hand, insufficient support rendered him desperate: "If America does not provide military aid, I will have no further responsibility for keeping Iran independent." In general, when a leader is so vilified as an American puppet that he withdraws from his own body politic, and instead seeks approval from abroad, the moment has arrived when foreign kisses threaten his rule.

Target enemy leaders. US government use of force requires special care, especially as Arab and Muslim leaders are likely to perceive its goals as more extensive than is the case. Limited objectives are likely to be interpreted as something much more ambitious and subversive. When great powers dispatch force, Middle Easterners assume that the target regime itself is under attack. Should the regime remain in office, that in itself constitutes a great victory. This was Nasser's response to the Suez operation of 1956, Tehran's to American efforts to spring the US hostages at the Tehran embassy in April 1980, Qaddafi's to the American raid on Tripoli in 1986, and Saddam Hussein's to the war against him in 1991. In each case, Middle Eastern leaders saw their very survival as a great achievement. For the most part, once fighting begins, the enemy leader had better go.

Use conspiracy theories as a window into the accuser's mind. Conspiracy theories provide remarkable insights into the minds of their propagators. Mirror imaging—the projecting of one's own motives and behavior on to others—implies that accusations often reflect the speaker's own intentions. In February 1943, Josef Goebbels instructed Nazi propagandists to stress that if Germany loses the war, the Germans "will all be annihilated by world Jewry. Jewry is firmly decided to exterminate all Germans. International law and international custom will be no protection against the Jewish will for total annihilation."[19] This was, of course total fantasy; but it did closely describe what Nazis were doing to Jews.

Soon after Mehmet Ali Ağca's attempt to assassinate Pope John Paul II in May 1981, Soviet authorities put out stories about Washington having plotted the assassination attempt because of the pope's stand on the Palestinian issue. In reality, it was the Kremlin that arranged for the killing, fearing John Paul's stand on Polish issues. Nasser's belief that Israel planned to eliminate the Arabs corresponded to his own effort to eliminate Israel. Assad's references to Greater Israel confirm his own intent to establish a Greater Syria; indeed, the more active his pursuit of Greater Syria, the more he spoke of Greater Israel. When Iranian leaders accuse the "anti-human inmates" of the George H. W.

Bush White House of not caring "a bit for the people of the United States, not even for the lives of the American hostages,"[20] they betray much about their own attitudes toward Iranian citizens.

Saddam Hussein habitually engaged in a mirror-imaging. In an open letter to George H. W. Bush, he accused the American president of "living in a world you created for yourself through money, threats, and the love of destruction and harm."[21] Saddam's speech of July 17, 1990 (which set off the Kuwait crisis) revealed the US government's detailed plan for world hegemony:

> Now that it has the chance, the United States is determined to become the only superpower, without competition, not only now or in the future, but, as will all dreamers, for a time when it can transform this dream into a boundless reality for years. To achieve this, it is striving to guarantee the flow of oil to it at the cheapest prices. It also works to control oil and those who own it so it can later control the fate of its other consumers, particularly the European states and Japan, and perhaps the Soviet Union if it becomes an oil importer at a later time. . . . The United States and Israel would then be out to start wars whenever they deem it necessary, without worrying about a potential halt to the flow of oil to American and other world markets.[22]

Whereas this fantasy has no connection to American intentions, it does offer startling insights into Saddam Hussein's own ambition. Substitute *Iraq* for *the United States* and *expensive* for *cheap* and his plan is quite exactly laid out.

Iraqi accusations were also revealing in their detail. A Baghdad radio station blamed the CIA for planning to remove the Saudi crown prince, 'Abdallah bin 'Abd al-'Aziz, either through political means or by means of an "accident" that would not arouse suspicion—precisely the way that Saddam had repeatedly disposed of his enemies.

The Iraqi regime that occupied Kuwait, plundered the country, and tried to erase its identity accused the US government of intending not merely "to strip nations of their natural resources but also to strip them of their cultural, historical wealth."[23] An editorial in an Iraqi newspaper was even more revealing and articulate; the consequences of an American victory over Iraq, it said, would

> lead the world into an age of dictatorship in which the US president will be a world dictator and the Third World nations would become slaves. Mankind would then witness a dark age, and the future of humanity would be shrouded in the darkness of a universal domination.[24]

"World dictator" nicely sums up Saddam's own ambitions.

Saddam Hussein's subservient media actually described their own master when describing the king of Saudi Arabia: "This Fahd is no more than a sinful libertine who filled the earth with sins and debauchery before he came to his throne through plotting and treachery. It is easy for such a treacherous libertine to lie, fabricate, and forge facts." Saddam Hussein used foreign hostilities to mobilize support at home, so he assumes democratic leaders do likewise, accusing the Thatcher government in early 1990 of creating a crisis with Iraq "to divert attention" from deteriorating circumstances within Britain. In fact, Saddam accurately described his own actions, for the end of the war with Iran in 1988 created economic and political expectations he could not fulfill.

When Middle Eastern despots rail against enemies, projection often causes them inadvertently to offer candid self-descriptions. "America isn't a nation at all. It's one enormous gang! A gang like Al Capone's!" Thus spoke Yahya Hamuda, Yasir Arafat's predecessor as head of the PLO. This rings false for the United States, but it does accurately describe the PLO of the 1960s. When Arabs accuse Israel of beating prisoners on the head until wounds appear, they are in fact conjuring up their own tortures.

Investigations in most of the Middle East being a sham, they must be fraudulent in Israel too. When the Rabin government put together the Shangar Commission to look into the February 1994 massacre of Arabs in Hebron by an Israeli, Syrian radio saw the whole thing as a hoax and accused the commission of having "fabricated an investigation." Middle Eastern narcotics agents profit from the trade they are supposed to suppress, and so too must their Western counterparts; according to the head of the Iranian anti-drug effort, Reza Sayfollahi, "the international drug smugglers conducted by the US Central Intelligence Agency (CIA) earned billions of dollars for the US annually."

This points to a deeper truth. While the conspiracy theorist sees himself as very different from the conspirators he despises, he actually resembles them closely. In this, he echoes the clinical paranoid's pattern: "the faults he finds in others are usually his own, and his picture of other people is a mirror of himself." While conspiracy theorists see themselves as persecuted and endangered, in the process of defending themselves, they switch roles with their victims and end up as the persecutors and bullies. "Those who fear a Jewish Conspiracy," Tadao Yanaihara rightly observes, "are those who suffer from nightmares of persecutions they themselves inflicted on Jews." Conspiracy theories, in short, provide rare insights to the internal workings of otherwise inaccessible minds.

The Case for Discouraging

By far the most sensitive and risky issue concerns the possible exploitation of conspiracy theories by the US government. Americans (along with Europeans, Russians, and Israelis) have a choice: help wean Middle East Muslims from the conspiratorial obsession; or probe this weakness to further their own policies. Should the US government tamp down the conspiracy mentality or exploit this vulnerability?

In normal circumstances, the US government should counsel Middle East friends against conspiracy theories, for they are pernicious and redound to everyone's harm. There are three main reasons for this.

(1) Reliance on conspiracy theories indicates extremist politics; their absence means improvement. Conspiracy theories make for a heavy, unpleasant political atmosphere, rife with danger and suspicion. The way to improve the atmosphere is not to make such accusations.

(2) The fear of conspiracy has a logic of its own and can easily work against one's interests. King al-Hussein of Jordan believed that Ariel Sharon's notion of "Jordan is Palestine" caused Israeli leaders to favor his overthrow in favor of a Palestinian leader. In response, the king did just what the Israelis least wanted him to do—move close to Saddam Hussein of Iraq.

(3) Throw dirt and you get it thrown back. The more prone a politician is to accuse others of conspiracies, the more likely he will be accused in turn. The paranoid mentality traps its own practioners. There is a subtle dynamic at work here: portraying a conflict in conspiratorial terms often provokes a response in kind by the enemy.

Hitler suffered the posthumous fate of being seen as a pawn of the Elders of Zion; how else could Adolf Eichmann explain his failure to destroy the Jews? Gamal Abdel Nasser was subjected to the same unfriendly scrutiny he applied to others. Thus, when he announced in Moscow a crackdown of the Muslim Brethren, Islamists saw this as a sign of his being in league against them with the communists. Nasser delivered so little of what he promised, those disappointed by him did not blame him for aiming to high, but suspected him of working for Washington.

The more emphatically an Arab proclaims Israeli conspiracies, the more likely he in turn will be accused of serving as an agent for Israel; forty years of anti-Zionism did not protect Yasir Arafat from taunts about being an Israeli agent. Even as the allied ground war against Iraq was in full pitch, the official Kuwaiti newspaper reported that an Iraqi diplomat defected and carried with him "a file on secret contacts" he had made with Israeli officials on the direct orders of Saddam Hussein.[25] In short, you can't be too anti-Israel to be tarred with the brush of Zionist conspiracy.

The Muslim Brethren accused Taha Hussein, the greatest Arab belle-lettrist writing in the twentieth century, of working for French intelligence—which even provided him with a French wife. But then Hasan al-Banna, founder of the Muslim Brethren, was himself accused of being an agent for the Freemasons. Muslim Brethren portray every opponent as a Zionist agent; they in turn are suspected of working for the Central Intelligence Agency.

The way to diminish such accusations is not to make them oneself. A man like President Husni Mubarak of Egypt offers a happy example. Moderate in style, he engages less in conspiracies, accuses others of them less, and is in turn less accused of them himself.

To discourage fears of conspiracy means taking the following steps: *Deny the validity of conspiracy theories;.* The high road—not dignifying the outrageous with a response—does not work. Left alone, conspiracy theories fester. Better to do as Middle Easterners often do: reply promptly and in kind. If the accusations are made privately, reply in private; if publicly, then in public.

When accusations of Syrian complicity in Lebanon with the Maronites and Americans gathered such force, Syrian president Hafez al-Assad eventually responded directly to them. In a April 1976 speech he denied as "groundless" all charges that he was siding with Christians against Muslims.[26] Three months later he explicitly raised and denied the charges of an "American-Syrian plot" in Lebanon. Assad eventually tried to put this issue to rest by reasserting the "firm and principled" Syrian position.[27] "Sick voices" was the Saudi characterization of Iranian efforts to blame the July 1990 deaths of pilgrims in Mecca on the Saudi police.[28] The Kuwaiti foreign minister did not hesitate to call Iraqi accusations against his government "fabrications and unfounded lies."[29]

Egypt's Communications Ministry responded to conspiracy theories about a US firm building the country's telephone system and so being able to tap it at will, even when Mubarak or Arafat were on the phone, by insisting there was "absolutely no truth" to this report. In one of the more colorful and direct efforts to cope with the accusation of conspiracy, Husni Mubarak of Egypt confronted Mu'ammar al-Qaddafi of

Libya at an emergency Arab summit meeting just after the Iraqi invasion of Kuwait. After a morning session, Qaddafi regaled PLO officials with accusations that calling the summit meeting showed Mubarak part of an "imperialist conspiracy against the Arab nation." Hearing of this comment, Mubarak confronted the Libyan: "Mu'ammar, if you think I would be party to such a conspiracy, as you say, then I would long ago have sent a couple of armored divisions to occupy Libya; I had a hundred and one pretexts for doing so, as you know." This apparently left Qaddafi speechless, so Mubarak put a hand on his shoulder and added, "Come, I will buy you lunch."

The Israeli government usually hastens to deny a conspiracy theory. After Yasir Arafat presented X-rays of the Hamas fatalities in November 1994 and noted that the type of bullet was found only in the Israeli arsenal, the reply came quickly: "The IDF today rejected 'Arafat's hints that Israel was involved in some way in the death of demonstrators in Gaza last Friday." Faced with rumors about Israel seeking economic hegemony over the Middle East, Shimon Peres rightly replied, "we are not giving up control over Arab territory in order to win control of the Arab economy." When the PLO spread rumors about Israelis making up part of the American expeditionary force in Saudi Arabia, both immediately denounced the report.

The Russians know what to do. When alarm spread during 1990 about the decline in tensions between Americans and Soviets, and what this would mean for the Middle East, the Soviet ambassador to the United Arab Emirates, Feliks Nikalayevich Fedotov, explicitly denied the existence of a "US-Soviet conspiracy."[30] This sort of denial may not be heeded, but it always needs to be made, repeated, and amplified.

Americans should emulate this practice. Sometimes they do. Post-war suspicion of Jewish power was so strong, recalls Miles Copeland, a CIA operative at the time, that American diplomacy in the Arab world during the period 1947–52 consisted largely of trying "to convince the various Foreign Offices that our Government was not under the control of the Zionists." In October 1989, Secretary of State James A. Baker 3d directly responded to Iraqi accusations about Washington attempting to bring down Saddam Hussein: "the United States is not involved in any effort to weaken or destabilize Iraq."

In a notorious meeting with five US senators in April 1990, Saddam Hussein repeatedly alluded to "a large-scale campaign" in the West against Iraq. After listening to this barrage, Senator Alan Simpson

(Republican of Wyoming) properly replied: "There is no conspiracy by the US government, or in England or Israel, to attack this country."[31]

Of course, denial does not always convince, to put it mildly. When Anthony Parsons, the last British ambassador to the shah's court, denied that his government supported Khomeini against the shah, an Iranian interlocutor responded: "But of course you have to say that. I know. I was educated in your country and am married to an English lady. You cannot deceive me."

Some denials eventually pay off. Anwar as-Sadat credited his own enlightenment to just such persuasion. "My talks with Dr. Kissinger convinced me," he explained, "that he rejects the simplistic notion of some of your strategists who see—or saw—Israel as the American gendarme in this part of the world."[32] Sadat is not likely soon to become a model for other Middle East leaders, but to the extent they realize the excessive quality of their fears, the more likely it will be that they live in peace with their neighbors.

Teach about the wider world. The conspiracy mentality will subside only when Middle Easterners come to understand that not all states— and especially not democracies—engage in conspiracies as much as they do. Only when they develop a greater sense of openness and awareness of the workings of other states will they be able to drop the notion that plots are a central feature of international politics.

Although concepts such as democracy, freedom of speech, freedom of religion, civil rights, and the rule of law were introduced to the Middle East two centuries ago, they have hardly penetrated the region's public life beyond the ranks of a small minority. Not comprehending these fundamentals, Middle Eastern leaders are puzzled by the motives of Western governments. Cultural distance thus encourages credence in conspiracy theories about Europe and America.

Point out that conspiracy theories backfire. "The Shah," Marvin Zonis observes, "despite his attacks on the West and his efforts and those of his officials to foist the failings of their rule onto foreigners, never managed to convince the Iranian people that they were not part of some foreign conspiracy to crush Iranian culture." Sometimes they do real harm to the one who spreads accusations of conspiracy. Anwar as-Sadat's seizure of 1,500 opponents in September 1981 on charges of conspiracy, for example, caused massive disaffection in Egypt.

Do not conspire. Western leaders have to act with special propriety to shed a long-established (and deserved) reputation for deviousness.[33]

This means no back door deals, no major discrepancies between stated policy and actual behavior, and a minimum of clandestine activities. It also means remembering the conspiracy outlook and treading so delicately that suspicions are not raised. This appears to have been a motive of George Allen, the US ambassador in Iran, when he refused to coordinate actions with the British embassy during 1946. For similar reasons, President Lyndon B. Johnson hesitated to meet with Foreign Minister Abba Eban of Israel on the eve of the Six Day War. The British ambassador to Iran, Anthony Parsons, did his best to avoid the appearance of conspiracy during his last meeting with the Mohammad Reza Pahlavi. When the shah pressed him to recommend a course of action, Parsons tried not to answer, noting that the shah would construe whatever he said as a British plot. Only when the Iranian gave his word of honor that Parson's advice would not be misrepresented did the ambassador volunteer his own thinking.[34]

The Case for Exploiting

Yet such model behavior, however laudable, may not work. Suspicions are so deeply ingrained in the Middle East outlook that even saintly activities are bound to arouse doubts. The British ambassador's very reticence vis-à-vis the shah could be seen as part of an especially subtle plot; thus, one author notes that the ambassador's "inordinately defensive stand" confirmed Iranian suspicions about him.

Or take this long-ago example from 1939 concerning King Ghazi of Iraq: Although he formally ruled Iraq, London retained effective control on the country, leading to a tense situation. Ghazi had a weakness for alcohol and fast cars, and on April 4, 1939, he took his roadster for a spin while under the influence of alcohol. Driving at high speed, he smashed into an electric pole, killing both his companions immediately. Taken to his palace with a fractured skull, the king died an hour later. His British physicians were alert enough to understand the danger they were in; to protect themselves against suspicions of murder, they insisted that an Iraqi doctor of Arab nationalist bent witness their actions. As one of the British doctors put it, "I was fearful lest, if no Iraqi doctor was in attendance, Anglophobic mischief-makers might originate canards to the effect that [Noel] Braham and I were responsible for the King's demise."

But this caution did little good. Most Iraqis pointed to the British or to pro-British elements. Salah ad-Din as-Sabbagh, a leading politician, held that "Ghazi was the victim of a conspiracy plotted by Nuri [as-Sa'id] and some of the officers." By similar token, Rashid Ali al-Kilani suspected Nuri as- Sa'id. Rumors swept the country: "One that was persistently repeated," the British ambassador cabled London, "was the story that the English had killed the King. . . . Another story . . . was that Nuri Sa'id had murdered King Ghazi and several groups of mourners were heard chanting the slogan, 'Thou shalt answer for the blood of Ghazi, O Nuri.'"

And "Anglophobic mischief-makers," German and Arab, exploited the incident anyway. Fritz Grobba, the chief Nazi diplomat in Baghdad, recounts how he learned the news from his Iraqi servant, who told him that "the English have killed our king."[35] Within hours, Nazi radio blamed the British for Ghazi's death. Rumors of a secret British plot spread behind the apparent accident spread rapidly through the whole country and British officialdom held German radio broadcasts and local agents primarily responsible for the unrest that followed. The next day, as the British consul in Mosul attempted to calm angry crowd by explaining what had happened, he was murdered from behind with a pickax.

Realistically, then, policymakers must recognize that actions by foreigners will not do much to reduce the conspiratorial mindset. Self-confidence and commonsense are the only true antidotes to this mentality, and there is no basis to think they are waxing. If the conspiratorial outlook is likely long to remain a feature of the Middle East, the other course of action—encouraging one's opponents to believe in selected conspiracy theories—becomes worthy of consideration.

There are several reasons to promote conspiracy theories. They weaken the enemy's camp and enhance his sense of one's power. Co-nationals must worry about being sold out and allies are constrained to eye each other with suspicion. When Bassam al-'Adl, a lone Syrian pilot, decided to defect to Israel in October 1989, Minister of Defense Mustafa Tlas characterized his action as the result of a vast conspiracy by the Israelis.

> They worked in the pitch dark, like blind bats, to find an agent and traitor willing to sell his conscience at the cheapest of prices. They found their lost soul in the traitor Bassam al-'Adl. . . . Their aim is, of course, to influence and affect our people and armed forces psychologically and morally.[36]

The effect of such suspicion is to fill the ranks with agents of the enemy and to spawn an atmosphere of the deepest mistrust. But if the enemy is everywhere, how can he be defeated? Syrians feel surrounded. Defeatism and despair are the natural responses, as is anger against the regime for so poorly protecting the country's interests.

Worrying about foreign intrigue unwittingly imbues the foreigner with power. The more the enemy is hated, the taller he stands. Here is Muhammad al-Ghazali, a prominent Egyptian Islamist, writing in 1951 about the British:

> There is not a single Englishman who commits a mistake on purpose, for he does everything on principle ... making war against you on the principle of nationalism, robbing you on the principle of commerce, enslaving you on the principle of imperialism, threatening you on the principle of pride.[37]

Or Sattareh Farman Farmaian's account of the servants in her family's house: they "believed that the englis-ha [English] were so diabolical that they could even cause floods, droughts, and earthquakes. And it was true that to Iranians, the British seemed almost supernaturally clever. They took nearly all the money from Iran's oil while we stayed poor."

Virtually every major accusation of a conspiracy, from the British having sponsored the Baha'i religion to the Americans messing up Tehran traffic, reflects an assumption of Western omnipotence. The US government is regularly seen as controlling its most avid enemies in the Middle East, including such figures as Yasir Arafat, Mu'ammar al-Qaddafi. Ayatollah Khomeini, and Saddam Hussein. Middle Easterners see bureaucrats sitting in Washington, London, and Jerusalem as awesomely capable.

These fears create opportunities. If the hidden hand clearly offers a useful tool of statecraft for local governments—the Iranian, Iraqi, and Egyptian in particular—why should foreign powers not rely on it too? In fact, they occasionally have done so.

On returning to Iran in 1943, Ziya ad-Din Tabataba'i was widely seen as a British agent, and to build up his base the British authorities did nothing to discourage this assumption. In 1954, the perception that the British government sought a union of Iraq and Syria under Iraqi leadership contributed to the failure of this scheme. In actual fact, London was not enthusiastic about such a union and may have intentionally created this misleading impression as a way to scuttle it. In 1966, when Moscow had not yet embraced the Palestine Liberation Organization (it still referred to Palestinian terrorists as "provocateurs"), the Soviet ambassador to Israel suggested that either Israeli or American intelligence had instigated the Palestinian raids, and was using them to push Israel into war against the Arab states. After being told at a 1979 meeting by Yasir Arafat that the Lebanese crisis resulted from an American conspiracy, Soviet foreign minister Andrei Gromyko then spoke of the situation in almost identical language.[38]

In January 1980, when the American hostages were being held at the US embassy, Americans took advantage of Iranian susceptibilities. Gary Sick, who had been on the National Security Council staff, relates that the escape of six Americans from Tehran with Canadian help threatened to jeopardize delicate negotiations between Washington and Tehran. To minimize their impact, Hamilton Jordan of the White House staff came up with idea of blaming the timing of the escape on the exigencies of the Canadian prime minister's reelection campaign. Of course, "the conspiratorial nature of the explanation had immediate appeal to [Foreign Minister Sadegh] Ghotbzadeh, who added his own distinctive touches to the story."[39] What could be more natural to an Iranian politician than having Canadian domestic politics run Iranian life?

At other times, *without having to do anything at all*, foreign powers benefit from the conspiratorial mentality. Fearful of falling into a trap, Middle Easterners fail to exploit advantages. In late August 1918, on the eve of the British victory over Turkish forces in the Levant, Faisal ibn al-Hussein, military leader of the Arab revolt and T. E. Lawrence's partner, proposed to the Turks that he switch to their side in return for an Ottoman guarantee of Arab independence. His stunning offer was rejected, apparently because it was (wrongly) believed to be a British plot.[40] In 1976, the Syrian government's deep belief in an "imperialist-Zionist" plot caused it to magnify the role of the United States in the Lebanese civil war, and therefore to exercise more caution than circumstances warranted. Khomeini was so confident that Saddam Hussein would not tangle with the power and prestige of the Islamic Republic that he assumed there could be no war with Iraq. Having decided this, according to Egyptian journalist Mohamed Heikal, he suspected that information about Iraqi preparations for war was manufactured by Iranian army intelligence, which hoped thereby to make the revolutionaries dependent on the military.[41] Too much suspicion rendered the Iranian government less capable of responding to a real threat.

Conspiracy theorists sometimes insist on turning an enemy's accidents and failures into victories. So disinclined are the Arabs to accept an Israeli mistake, they find a rationale to explain it. When Jerusalem foolishly held elections in 1976 that enhanced the PLO's standing on the West Bank, anti-PLO elements suspected a clever Israeli maneuver. As they saw it, Jerusalem promoted its most intractable enemy so that it could plausibly announce to the outside world that no reasonable negotiating partner could be located on the West Bank. Thus was an Israeli miscalculation turned into a master stroke of strategic thinking. The inadvertent downing of an Iran Air flight in July 1988 by the US Navy had a profound impact on the leadership in Tehran, which worried what Washington's next step might be. This fear then played a significant role in the decision taken two weeks later to end the war with Iraq. The Iranians' assumption that the US government had acted in a premeditated fashion turned an accident into a major, positive event.

As this suggests, conspiracy theories can be turned against their creators by anyone disposed to make the most of his opponent's foibles. This is making the best of a bad situation. It is also a form of disinformation, and therefore to be engaged in very sparingly and only when the stakes are sufficiently high. Also, the US government must have specific goals before embarking on such a risky undertaking. Exploiting the conspiracy mentality could include the following methodologies:

Deny with a wink. Disclaim the existence of conspiracies; but then add a verbal nudge to make the target audience think twice. This is what Yitzhak Shamir did in August 1990, when King al-Hussein of Jordan was particularly agitated about an Israeli conspiracy to control the world media. Shamir told an interviewer:

> The king has suddenly discovered the Zionist movement and its great strength to influence the international media and policy makers. If it were only true! Nevertheless, perhaps I should call Mr. [Simcha] Dinitz [chairman of the World Zionist Organization, one of the most suspect institutions in Arab eyes] tomorrow and invite him over and ask where he has been and impose several tasks on him.[42]

Formally, Shamir disavowed the notion of a Jewish conspiracy; informally, he signaled to Hussein that worse is to come.

Suggest that your enemies work for you. Middle Easterners are particularly susceptible to the notion that apparent enemies are in fact co-conspirators. Damascus routinely calls Yasir Arafat "a US tool against Palestine and Palestinian rights" and the PLO responds by accusing Assad of participating in a US-Israeli-Syrian conspiracy against the Palestinians. Abo'l-Hasan Bani-Sadr, Khomeini's onetime ally and Iran's first president, accused Khomeini of working hand in glove with

Ronald Reagan, while Iranian leftists theorized that Khomeini was the chosen American instrument to steal the revolution from them. The list goes on and on.

It may be possible to undermine one's opponents by fabricating conspiracies that do not exist. This might include offering praise for a well-known enemy in private conversation or connecting him to the US government in public statements. The inclination will always be to believe the conspiracy, not the denial. There is a danger here, of course: hints that enemies are in the US government pay might spur them, in the effort to prove their credentials, to new heights of anti-Americanism.

Conspire. There is nothing like actual conspiracies to fuel the conspiracy mindset. Learning that the US government is indeed as tricky as everyone worries it is establishes new respect for it. Revelations about the Iran/*contra* affair had meant that, for once, Americans lived up to their reputation. Given prevailing assumptions, a bit of money and few weapons can go a long way.

Keeping this in mind, it may be possible to undermine one's opponents by fabricating conspiracies that do not exist. This might include offering praise for a well-known enemy in private conversation or connecting him to the US government in public statements. Sending unsolicited arms in such a way that third parties become aware of them would convince many in the Middle East that what appears to be enmity toward the US government is in fact a cover for collusion. The inclination will always be to believe the conspiracy, not the denial.

There is a danger here: If hinting that enemies are in Washington's pay is devastating for their reputation, it can also spur them on to even more fervent anti-Americanism to prove their credentials.

Recommendations

The picture is not a simple one. Detaching Middle Easterners from their susceptibilities is a very attractive prospect but also a highly uncertain one. Indeed, there is reason to doubt whether outsiders can affect such deeply held views. In contrast, while the dangers of exploiting the conspiracy mentality are decidedly great, the benefits can be immediate and concrete.

This leads to a twofold recommendation: As a rule, do not play games; but be aware of vulnerabilities created by the conspiracy mentality and, on special occasions, exploit these to the maximum.

Notes

1. Quoted in Robin Wright, *In the Name of God: The Khomeini Decade* (New York: Simon & Schuster, 1989), p. 21.

2. Umberto Eco, *Foucault's Pendulum* (London: Picador, 1990), p. 475.

3. Mohammad Reza Pahlavi, *Answer to History* (New York: Stein and Day, 1980), pp. 151–52.

4. Gary Sick, *All Fall Down: America's Tragic Encounter with Iran* (New York: Random House, 1985), p. 31.

5. Conspiracy theories are not inherently implausible. Indeed, there is no objective way to distinguish between a conspiracy and a conspiracy theory, nor between the sensible and the frenzied search for conspiracies. Nonetheless, I assume that a normal observer can in virtually all cases determine which is which.

6. L. Carl Brown, *International Politics and the Middle East: Old Rules, Dangerous Game* (Princeton, N.J.: Princeton University Press, 1984), p. 234.

7. Thomas L. Friedman, *From Beirut to Jerusalem* (New York: Farrar, Straus and Giroux, 1989), p. 37.

8. Yehoshafat Harkabi, *Palestinians and Israel* (New Brunswick: Transaction, 1974), p. 197.

9. *Middle Eastern Studies*, January 1973, p. 112.

10. Sullivan, *Mission to Iran*, p. 158.

11. Radio Monte Carlo, May 28, 1990.

12. Miles Copeland, *The Game of Nations: The Amorality of Power Politics* (New York: Simon and Schuster, 1969), p. 198.

13. Secretary of State James A. Baker, Jr., "Principles and Pragmatism: American Policy toward the Arab-Israeli Conflict," May 22,1989.

14. °Daniel Pipes, "Imperial Israel: The Nile-to-Euphrates Calumny," *Middle East Quarterly*, March 1994.°

15. Radio Damascus, June 19, 1989. Khaddam had made the same accusation before, but usually without the Greater Israel moniker. Thus, he explained to *Tishrin* (on May 17, 1980) that "the enemy wants all Syria, all Iraq, Saudi Arabia, the Gulf, and Egypt."

16. *Ad-Dustur*, April 17, 1990.

17. William R. Brown, *The Last Crusade: A Negotiator's Middle East Handbook* (Chicago: Nelson-Hall, 1980), pp. 68–69.

18. °Daniel Pipes, "Both Sides of Their Mouths Arab Leaders' Private vs. Public Statements," *The Jerusalem Post*, August 4, 1993.°

19. Quoted in Cohn, *Warrant for Genocide*, p. 207.

20. *Jomhuri-ye Islami*, Apr. 26, 1990.

21. Radio Baghdad, Jan. 17, 1991.

22. Radio Baghdad, July 17, 1990.

23. Radio Baghdad, Feb. 9, 1991.

24. *Ath-Thawra*, Dec. 14, 1990.

25. *Sawt al-Kuwait*, Feb. 26, 1991.

26. Radio Damascus, Apr. 12, 1976.

27. Radio Damascus, July 20, 1976.

28. Saudi Press Agency, July 9, 1990.

29. Kuwaiti News Agency, Oct. 31, 1990.
30. WAKH, Mar. 1, 1990.
31. Radio Baghdad, Apr. 16, 1990.
32. *Newsweek*, Mar. 25, 1974.
33. The list of clandestine activities is a long one: examples that stand out include the Sykes-Picot Agreement of 1916, the Lavon Affair of 1954, the Suez Crisis of 1956, and the Iran/*contra* affair of 1985–86.
34. Anthony Parsons, *The Pride and the Fall: Iran 1974–1979* (London: Jonathan Cape, 1984), pp. 124–25.
35. Fritz Grobba, *Männer und Mächte im Orient: 25 Jahre diplomatischer Tätigkiet im Orient* (Göttingen: Musterschmidt, 1967), p. 176.
36. Damascus Television, Oct. 16, 1989.
37. Muhammad al-Ghazali, *Min Huna Na'lam*, 5th ed. (Cairo: Matba'at as-Sa'ada, 1965), p. 95.
38. Text in Raphael Israeli, ed., *PLO in Lebanon: Selected Documents* (New York: St. Martin's Press, 1983), pp. 39, 49.
39. Sick, *All Fall Down*, pp. 259–60.
40. Liman von Sanders, *Fünf Jahre Türkei* (Berlin: August Scherl, 1920), pp. 330–31.
41. Mohamed Heikal, *Iran: The Untold Story* (New York: Pantheon, 1981), pp. 3–4.
42. Jerusalem Television, Aug. 22, 1990.

9

The Alawi Capture of
Power in Syria

For many centuries, the Alawis were the weakest, poorest, most rural, most despised, and most backward people of Syria. Over the past half-century, however, they transformed themselves into the powerful ruling elite of Damascus who came to dominate the government and armed forces, and enjoy a disproportionate share of the country's resources. How did this dramatic change occur, when did the Alawi manage to escape their traditional confines, and what was the mechanism of their rise?

Contending Theories

Sunnis and others unsympathetic to the Assad regime answer this question by accusing the Alawis of an elaborate and long-term conspiracy to take power in Syria. Annie Laurent suggests that "determined to get their revenge" after the failure of a rebel leader, Suleiman Murshid, "the Alawis put into effect a strategy of setting up cells in the army and the Ba'th Party, and this won them power in Damascus."[1] Adherents of this view date the Alawi ascent to 1959, the year that the Military Committee of the Ba'th Party was formed. Why, they ask, did leaders of this group keep its existence secret from the party authorities? Their furtiveness suggests that the Military Committee from the beginning had a sectarian agenda. Matti Moosa argued that "it is almost certain that the officers were acting not as Baathists, but as Nusayris [Alawis], with the intent of using the Baath and the armed forces to rise to power in Syria. The formation of the military committee was the beginning of their plan for a future takeover of the government."[2]

This speculation finds confirmation in a 1960 clandestine meeting of Alawi religious leaders and officers (including Hafez al-Assad) that reportedly took place in Qardaha, Assad's home town. "The main goal of this meeting was to plan how to forward the Nusayri officers into the ranks of the Ba'th Party. They would then exploit it as a means to arrive at the rule in Syria."[3] Three years later, another Alawi meeting in Homs is said to have followed up the earlier initiatives. Among other steps, it called for the placement of more Alawis in the Ba'th Party and army. Further secret meetings of Alawi leaders appear to have taken place later in the 1960s.[4]

Analysts better disposed to Assad tend to discount not just these meetings and a premeditated drive for power, but the sectarian factor more generally. John F. Devlin, for example, denies that the disproportion of Alawis in the army implies Alawi dominance of Syria. He would resist seeing "every domestic disagreement in terms of a Sunni-Alawi clash." For him, the fact that Alawis are in power is basically accidental: "The Ba'th is a secular party, and it is heavy with minorities."[5] Alasdair Drysdale calls it "reductionist" to focus on ethnicity, arguing that this is one of many factors—geographic, class, age, education, occupation—that define the ruling elite.[6] According to Yahya M. Sadowski, "sectarian loyalties play an insignificant role in the Ba'th, and even confessional bonds are only one among many avenues by which patronage is extended."[7]

The truth lies between conspiracy and accident. The Alawis did not "plan for a future takeover" years in advance, nor was it mere chance that the Ba'th Party was "heavy with minorities." Alawi power resulted from an unplanned but sectarian transformation of public life in Syria. Michael van Dusen explains: "From 1946 to 1963, Syria witnessed the gradual erosion of the national and eventually subnational political power of the traditional elite, not so much through the emergence of new and especially dynamic elites but rather by internal conflict."[8] Translated from the jargon of political science, van Dusen is saying that internal divisions caused non-Ba'th civilian Sunnis to lose power. This provided an opening that Ba'thist officers of Alawi origins exploited.

How these processes occurred is my subject here. First, however, some background on the Alawis and their place in traditional Syrian society, followed by a sketch of their ascent.

THE ALAWI HERESY TO 1920
People and Faith

"Alawi" is the term that Alawis (also called Alawites) usually apply to themselves; but until 1920 they were known to the outside world as Nusayris or Ansaris. The change in name—imposed by the French upon their seizure of control in Syria—has significance. Whereas "Nusayri" emphasizes the group's differences from Islam, "Alawi" suggests an adherent of 'Ali (the son-in-law of Islam's Prophet Muhammad) and accentuates the religion's similarities to Shi'i Islam.[9] Consequently, opponents of the Assad regime habitually use the former term, supporters of the regime use the latter.

Alawis today number approximately 1.3 million, of which about a million live in Syria. They constitute some 12 percent of the Syrian population. Three-quarters of the Syrian Alawis live in Latakia, a province in the northwest of Syria, where they make up almost two-thirds of the population.

Alawi doctrines date from the ninth century AD and derive from the Twelver or Imami branch of Shi'i Islam (the sect that predominates in Iran). In about AD 859, one Ibn Nusayr declared himself the *bab* ("gateway to truth"), a key figure in Shi'i theology. On the basis of this authority, Ibn Nusayr proclaimed a host of new doctrines[10] which, to make a long story short, make Alawism into a separate religion. According to Ibn Kathir (d. 1372), where Muslims proclaim their faith with the phrase "There is no deity but God and Muhammad is His prophet," Alawis assert "There is no deity but 'Ali, no veil but Muhammad, and no *bab* but Salman."[11] Alawis reject Islam's main tenets; by almost any standard they must be considered non-Muslims.

Some Alawi doctrines appear to derive from Phoenician paganism, Mazdakism, and Manicheanism. But by far the greatest affinity is with Christianity. Alawi religious ceremonies involve bread and wine; indeed, wine drinking has a sacred role in Alawism, for it represents God.[12] The religion holds 'Ali, the fourth caliph, to be the (Jesus-like) incarnation of divinity.[13] It has a holy trinity, consisting of Muhammad, 'Ali, and Salman al-Farisi, a freed slave of Muhammad's. Alawis celebrate many Christian festivals, including Christmas, New Year's, Epiphany, Easter, Pentecost, and Palm Sunday. They honor many Christian saints: St. Catherine, St. Barbara, St. George, St. John the Baptist, St. John Chrysostom, and St. Mary Magdalene. The Arabic equivalents of such Christian personal names as Gabriel, John, Matthew, Catherine, and Helen, are in common use. And Alawis tend to show more friendliness to Christians than to Muslims.

For these reasons, many observers—Gospel missionaries especially— have suspected the Alawis of a secret Christian proclivity. Even T. E. Lawrence described them as "those disciples of a cult of fertility, sheer pagan, anti-foreign, distrustful of Islam, drawn at moments to Christianity by common persecution."[14] The Jesuit scholar Henri Lammens unequivocally but gullibly concluded from his research that "the Nusayris were Christians" and their practices combine Christian with Shi'i elements.[15]

Not Muslims

The specifics of the Alawi faith are hidden not just from outsiders but even from the majority of the Alawis themselves. In contrast to Islam, which is premised on direct relations between God and the individual believer, Alawism permits only males born of two Alawi parents to learn the religious doctrines. When deemed trustworthy, these are initiated into some of the rites at sixteen to twenty years of age; other mysteries are revealed later and only gradually. Religious secrecy is strictly maintained, on pain of death and being incarnated into a vile animal. Whether the latter threat is made good, mortals cannot judge; but the first certainly is. Thus, the most renowned apostate from Alawism, Suleiman Efendi al-Adhani, was assassinated for divulging the sect's mysteries. Even more impressive, at a time of sectarian tension in the mid-1960s, the suggestion that the Alawi officers who ran the country publish the secret books of their religion caused Salah Jadid to respond with horror, saying that, were this done, the religious leaders "would crush us."[16]

Women do most of the hard labor; they are prized "precisely because of the work they do that men will not do except grudgingly, finding it incompatible with their dignity."[17] Women are never inducted into the mysteries ("Would you have us teach them whom we use, our holy faith?");[18] indeed, their uncleanliness requires their exclusion from all religious rituals. Females are thought to retain the pagan cult of worshipping trees, meadows, and hills, and to have no souls.[19] In all, females are treated abominably; but one consequence of this disrespect is that they need not be veiled and enjoy greater freedom of movement than Muslim women.

Unveiled women and several other Alawi practices—in particular, that wine drinking is permitted, and that some ceremonies take place at night—long excited Muslim suspicions about Alawi behavior. Then too, the obsessive secrecy inherent to the religion suggested to many Sunnis that the Alawis had something to hide. But what? Over the centuries, the Sunnis' imaginations supplied a highly evocative answer: sexual abandon and perversion. Thus, the theologian al-Ash'ari (874–936) held that Alawism encourages male sodomy and incestuous marriages and the founder of the Druze religious doctrine, Hamza ibn 'Ali (d. 1021), wrote that Alawis consider "the male member entering the female nature to be the emblem of their spiritual doctrine."[20] Accordingly, Alawi men freely share their wives with co-religionists.

These and other accusations survived undiminished through the centuries and even circulated among Europeans.[21] A British traveler of the early 1840s, who was probably repeating local rumors, wrote that "the institution of marriage is unknown. When a young man grows up he buys his wife."[22] Even Alawis believed in the "conjugal communism" of their religious leaders.[23] Such calumnies remain a mainstay of the anti-Alawi propaganda circulating in Syria today.

Although the charges are false, Alawis do reject Islam's sacred law, the Shari'a, and therefore indulge in all manner of activities that Islamic doctrine strictly forbids. Alawis ignore Islamic sanitary practices, dietary restrictions, sexual mores, and religious rituals. Likewise, they pay little attention to the fasting, almsgiving, and pilgrimage ceremonies of Islam; indeed, they consider the pilgrimage to Mecca a form of idol worship. "Spiritual marriages" between young (male) initiates and their religious mentors probably lie at the root of the charges of homosexuality.

Most striking of all, Alawis have no prayers or places of worship; indeed they have no religious structures other than tomb shrines. Prayers take place in private houses, usually those of religious leaders. The fourteenth-century traveler Ibn Battuta described how they responded to a government decree ordering the construction of mosques: "Every village built a mosque far from the houses, which the villagers neither enter nor maintain. They often shelter cattle and asses in it. Often a stranger arrives and goes to the mosque to recite the [Islamic] call to prayer; then they yell to him, 'Stop braying, your fodder is coming.'"[24] Five centuries later another attempt was made to build mosques for the Alawis, this time by the Ottoman authorities; despite official pressure, these were deserted, abandoned even by the religious functionaries, and once again used as barns.

Beyond specific divergences, nonconformity to the Shari'a means that Alawi life follows its own rhythms, fundamentally unlike those of Muslims. Alawis do not act like Sunni Muslims, with only slight differences; rather, they and Muslims pursue wholly distinct ways of life. Matti Moosa notes that, "like the other extremist Shiites ... the Nusayris had total disregard for Muslim religious duties."[25] Ignaz Goldziher put it succinctly: "This religion is Islam only in appearance."[26] It is important to make this point very clear: Alawis have never been Muslims and are not now. Alawis are to Muslims roughly as Christians are to Jews.

Taqiya

Yet, as Ibn Battuta's account suggests, there is a permanent inconsistency in the Alawi wish to be seen as Muslim. In his case, it was mosques built and then neglected; at other times it is some other half-hearted adoption of Islamic ways. Alawis have a long history of claiming Islam when this suits their needs and ignoring it at other times. In short, like other sects of Shi'i origins, Alawis practice *taqiya* (religious dissimulation). This might mean, for example, praying side by side with Sunni Muslims but silently cursing the Sunni caliphs. The apostate Alawi, Suleiman Efendi al-Adhani, recounted having been sworn to dissimulate about his religion's mysteries.[27] An Alawi saying explains the sentiment behind *taqiya*: "We are the body and other sects are but clothing. However a man dresses does not change him. So we remain always Nusayris, even though we externally adopt the practices of our neighbors. Whoever does not dissimulate is a fool, for no intelligent person goes naked in the market."[28] Another Alawi phrase expresses this sentiment succinctly: "Dissimulation is our righteous war!" (*al-kitman jihadna*).[29]

A British traveler observed in 1697 that the Alawis are

> of a strange and singular character. For 'tis their principle to adhere to no certain religion; but camelion-like, they put on the colour of religion, whatever it be, which is reflected upon them from the persons with whom they happen to converse. . . . No body was ever able to discover what shape or standard their consciences are really of. All that is certain concerning them is, that they make much and good wine, and are great drinkers.[30]

A hundred and fifty years later, Benjamin Disraeli described the Alawis in a conversation in the novel *Tancred*:

> "Are they Moslemin?"
>
> "It is very easy to say what they are not, and that is about the extent of any knowledge we have of them; they are not Moslemin, they are not Christian, they are not Druzes, and they are not Jews, and certainly they are not Guebres [Zoroastrians]."[31]

Suleiman Efendi al-Adhani explained this flexibility from within:

> They take on the outward practices of all sects. If they meet [Sunni] Muslims, they swear to them and say, "We are like you, we fast and we pray." But they fast improperly. If they enter a mosque with Muslims,

they do not recite any of the prayers; instead, they lower and raise their bodies like the Muslims, while cursing Abu Bakr, 'Umar, 'Uthman, and other [major figures of the Sunni tradition].[32]

Taqiya permitted Alawis to blow with the wind. When France ruled, they portrayed themselves as lost Christians. When Pan-Arabism was in favor, they became fervent Arabs.[33] Over ten thousand Alawis living in Damascus pretended to be Sunnis in the years before Assad came to power, only revealing their true identities when this became politically useful.[34] The Assad's dynasty found them making concerted efforts to portray Alawis as Twelver Shi'is.

Sunni Hostility toward Alawis

Mainstream Muslims, Sunni and Shi'i alike, traditionally disregarded Alawi efforts at dissimulation; they correctly viewed Alawis as beyond the pale of Islam—as non-Muslims. Hamza ibn 'Ali, who saw the religion's appeal lying in its perversity, articulated this view: "The first thing that promotes the wicked Nusayri is the fact that all things normally prohibited to humans—murder, stealing, lying, calumny, fornication, pederasty—is permitted to he or she who accepts [Alawi doctrines]."[35] Abu Hamid al-Ghazali (1058–1111), sometimes called the Thomas Aquinas of Islam, wrote that the Alawis "apostatize in matters of blood, money, marriage, and butchering, so it is a duty to kill them."[36]

Ahmad ibn Taymiya (1268–1328), the still highly influential Sunni writer of Syrian origins, wrote in a *fatwa* (religious decision) that "the Nusayris are more infidel than Jews or Christians, even more infidel than many polytheists. They have done greater harm to the community of Muhammad than have the warring infidels such as the Franks, the Turks, and others. To ignorant Muslims they pretend to be Shi'is, though in reality they do not believe in God or His prophet or His book." Ibn Taymiya warned of the mischief their enmity can do: "Whenever possible, they spill the blood of Muslims. . . . They are always the worst enemies of the Muslims." In conclusion, he argued that "war and punishment in accordance with Islamic law against them are among the greatest of pious deeds and the most important obligations" for a Muslim.[37] From the fourteenth century on, Sunnis used the term "Nusayri" to mean pariah.

According to Martin Kramer of Shalem College,

Sunni heresiographers excoriated Alawi beliefs and viewed the Alawis as disbelievers (*kuffar*) and idolaters (*mushrikun*). Twelver Shi'i heresiographers were only slightly less vituperative and regarded the Alawis as *ghulat,* "those who exceed" all bounds in their deification of Ali.[38]

Alawis had had no recognized position in the *millet* (sectarian) system of the Ottoman Empire. An Ottoman decree from 1571 notes that "ancient custom" required Alawis to pay extra taxes to the authorities and justified this on the grounds that Alawis "neither practice the fast [of Ramadan] nor the ritual prayers, nor do they observe any precepts of the Islamic religion."[39] Sunnis often saw food produced by Alawis as unclean, and did not eat it. According to Jacques Weulerrse, "no Alawi would dare enter a Muslim mosque. Formerly, not one of their religious leaders was able to go to town on the day of public prayer [Friday] without risk of being stoned. Any public demonstration of the community's separate identity was taken as a challenge [by the Sunnis]."[40] Sunnis were not alone in reading Alawis out of Islam—mainstream Shi'is did likewise.

There was one exception to this consensus that Alawis are not Muslims. Toward the end of the nineteenth century, as Christian missionaries began taking an interest in the Alawis, Ottoman authorities tried to bring them into Islam. The French already had special ties to their fellow Catholics, the Maronites, and the authorities in Istanbul feared a similar bond being created with the Alawis. So they built mosques in the Alawi areas, built schools to teach Islam, pressured Alawi religious leaders to adopt Sunni practices, and generally tried to make the Alawis act like proper Muslims. This isolated case of Sunnis reaching out to Alawism came to an end after a few decades and had very little impact on Alawi behavior.

The Islamic religion reserves a special hostility for Alawis. Like other post-Islamic sects (such as the Baha'is and Qadiani Ahmadis), they are seen to contradict the key Islamic tenet that God's last revelation went to Muhammad, and this Muslims find utterly unacceptable. Islamic law acknowledges the legitimacy of Judaism and Christianity because those religions preceded Islam; accordingly, Jews and Christians may maintain their faiths. But Alawis are denied this privilege. Indeed, the precepts of Islam call for apostates like the Alawis to be sold into slavery or executed. In the nineteenth century, a Sunni shaykh, Ibrahim al-Maghribi, issued a *fatwa* to the effect that Muslims may freely take Alawi property and lives; and a British traveler records being told, "these Ansayrii, it is better to kill one than to pray a whole day."[41]

Frequently persecuted—some twenty thousand were massacred in 1317 and half that number in 1516[42]—the Alawis insulated themselves geographically from the outside world by staying within their own rural regions. Jacques Weulersse explained their predicament:

> Defeated and persecuted, the heterodox sects disappeared or, to survive, renounced proselytism. . . . The Alawis silently entrenched themselves in their mountains. . . . Isolated in rough country, surrounded by a hostile population, henceforth without communications with the outside world, the Alawis began to live out their solitary existence in secrecy and repression. Their doctrine, entirely formed, evolved no further.[43]

Jean Émile Janot described the problem: "Bullied by the Turks, victim of a determined ostracism, fleeced by his Muslim landlord, the Alawi hardly dared leave his mountain region, where isolation and poverty itself protected him."[44] In the late 1920s, less than half of one percent lived in towns: just 771 Alawis out of a population of 176,285.[45] In 1945, just 56 Alawis were recorded living in Damascus[46] (though many others may have been hiding their identity). For good reason, "the name Nusayri became synonymous with peasant."[47] The few Alawis who did live away from their mountain routinely practiced *taqiya*. Even in the 1980s, Alawis dominated the rural areas of Latakia but made up only 11 percent of the residents in that region's capital city.

Alawi Hostility toward Sunnis

Centuries of hostility took their toll on the Alawis' psyche. They viewed both Sunnis and Shi'is as deficient. Alawis praying for the damnation of their Sunni enemies and held Twelver Shi'is to be *muqassira*, "those who fall short" of fathoming Ali's divinity.[48] In addition, they attacked outsiders, acquiring a reputation as fierce and unruly mountain people who resisted paying the taxes they owed the authorities and frequently plundered Sunni villagers on the plains. John Lewis Burckhardt observed in 1812 that those villagers "hold the Anzeyrys [Ansaris] in contempt for their religion, and fear them, because they often descend from the mountains in the night, cross the Aaszy ['Asi, or Orontes River], and steal, or carry off by force, the cattle of the valley."[49]

Matters seemed to be even worse in 1860 when Samuel Lyde added that "nothing is thought of thus killing a Mussulman as a natural enemy, or a Christian as an unclean thing."[50] Writing about the same time, a British travel-guide writer warned of the cool reception to be expected from the Alawis: "They are a wild and somewhat savage race, given to plunder, and even bloodshed, when their passions are excited or suspicion roused." With wonderful understatement, the guide author concluded, "their country must therefore be traversed with caution."[51]

Alawis retreated to the mountains because of persecution; they then remained there, shielded from the world at large, lacking political power beyond their region's confines, isolated from the larger polities around them, almost outside the bounds of historical change. The survival, well into the twentieth century, of archaic practices made the Alawi region (in Jacques Weulersse's turn of phrase) a "fossil country." Little changed in that country because "it is not the Mountain that is humanized; man, rather, is made savage." Alawis suffered as a result: "the refuge they had conquered became a prison; though masters of the Mountain they could not leave."[52]

Governments had difficulty subduing the Alawi territory; indeed, it only came under Ottoman control in the late 1850s. Pacification of the region then led to Sunni economic inroads and the formation of an Alawi underclass. As badly educated peasants lacking in political organization or military strength, Alawis typically worked farms belonging to Sunni Arab landlords, receiving but a fifth of the produce. Ottoman agents would often exact double or triple the taxes due in the Latakia region. According to one well-informed observer, the Alawis cursed Islam and prayed "for the destruction of the Ottoman Empire."[53]

Alawis were so badly off after World War I, many of the youth left their homeland to work elsewhere. Sons left to find menial labor or to join the armed forces. Daughters went off at the age of seven or eight years to work as domestics for urban Sunni Arabs. Because many of them also ended up as mistresses (one estimate holds that a quarter of all Alawi children in the 1930s and 1940s had Sunni fathers),[54] both Muslims and Alawis saw this practice as deeply shameful. In some cases, daughters were even sold. It is no exaggeration to say, as does one indigenous historian, that Alawis "were among the poorest of the East."[55] The Reverend Samuel Lyde went even further, writing in 1860 that "the state of [Alawi] society is a perfect hell upon earth."[56]

The political effects of poverty were exacerbated by the nature of these divisions, which followed geographic and communal lines. Sunnis who lived in the towns enjoyed a much greater wealth and dominated the Alawi peasants. Jacques Weulersse described in 1934 how each community "lives apart with its own customs and its own laws. Not only are they different but they are hostile . . . the idea of mixed marriages appears to be inconceivable."[57] In 1946, he added that "the antagonism between urban and rural people goes so deep that one can almost speak of two different populations co-existing within one political framework."[58] A generation later, Nikolaos van Dam observed, "Urban-rural contrasts were sometimes so great that the cities seemed like settlements of aliens who sponged on the poverty-stricken rural population. . . . In the course of time, the Alawi community developed a strong distrust of the Sunnis who had so often been their oppressors."[59] This Alawi resentment of Sunnis has proven enormously consequential in recent years as, of course, has been the reciprocal Sunni loathing of Alawis.

The Rise of the Alawis, 1920–1970

The Alawis' ascent took place over the course of half a century. In 1920 they were still the lowly minority just described; by 1970, they firmly ruled Syria. This stunning transformation took place in three stages: the French mandate (1920–46), the period of Sunni dominance (1946–63), and the era of Alawi consolidation (1963–70).

The French Mandate, 1920–1946

According to Yusuf al-Hakim, a prominent Syrian politician, the Alawis adopted a pro-French attitude even before the French conquest of Damascus in July 1920. "The Alawis saw themselves in a state of grace after hell; accordingly, they were dedicated to the French mandate."[60] So intensely did they oppose Prince Faisal, the Sunni Arab ruler of Syria in 1918–20 whom they suspected of wanting to dominate them, they launched a rebellion against his rule in 1919, using French arms. General Gouraud received a telegram in late 1919 from 73 Alawi chiefs representing different tribes, who asked for "the establishment of an independent Nusayri union under our absolute protection."[61]

Two years later the Alawis rebelled against French rule under the leadership of Salih al-'Ali, an event that the Assad government proudly points to as an anti-imperialist credential. But a close look,[62] suggests that the revolt had more to do with the fact that the Isma'ilis had sided with France and, given the state of Isma'ili-Alawi relations, this led to hostilities between the Alawis and French. As soon as the French authorities granted autonomy to the Alawis, they won Alawi support.

Indeed, the establishment of French rule after World War I benefited the Alawis more than any other community. French efforts to cooperate with minority populations meant the Alawis gained political autonomy and escaped Sunni control; the state of Latakia was set up on July 1, 1922. They also gained legal autonomy; a 1922 decision to end Sunni control of court cases involving Alawis transferred these cases to Alawi jurists.[63] The Alawi state enjoyed low taxation and a sizeable French subsidy. Not surprisingly, Alawis accepted all these changes with enthusiasm. As Sharaf ad-Din, an anti-Alawi historian later put it, "At the time when resistance movements were mounted against the French mandate, when Damascus, Aleppo, and the Hawran witnessed continuous rebellions on behalf of Syrian unity and independence, the Nusayris were blessing the division of the country into tiny statelets."[64]

In return, Alawis helped maintain French rule. When most Syrians boycotted the French-sponsored elections of January 1926, they turned out in large numbers.[65] They provided a disproportionate number of soldiers to the government, forming about half the eight infantry battalions making up the Troupes Spéciales du Levant,[66] serving as police and supplying intelligence. As late as May 1945, the vast majority of Troupes Spéciales remained loyal to their French commanders. Alawis broke up Sunni demonstrations, shut down strikes, and quelled rebellions. Alawis publicly favored the continuation of French rule, fearing that France's departure would lead to a reassertion of Sunni control over them. Henri de Jouvenel, the French High Commissioner for Syria (1925–27), quoted a leading Alawi politician telling him: "We have succeeded in making more progress in three or four years than we had in three or four centuries. Leave us therefore in our present situation."[67]

Pro-French sentiment was expressed especially clearly in 1936, when the temporary incorporation of the Alawi state into Syria provoked wide protests. A March 1936 petition referred to union with the Sunnis as "slavery."[68] On June 11, 1936, an Alawi leader wrote a letter to Prime Minister Léon Blum of France, reminding him of "the profoundness of the abyss that separates us from the [Sunni] Syrians," and asking him to "imagine the disastrous catastrophe that would follow" incorporation.[69]

Days later, six Alawi notables (including Suleiman Assad, said to be Hafez al-Assad's grandfather)[70] sent another letter to Blum in which they made several points: Alawis differ from Sunnis religiously and historically; Alawis refuse to be joined to Syria, for it is a Sunni state and Sunnis consider them unbelievers (*kafirs*); ending the mandate would expose the Alawis to mortal danger; "the spirit of religious feudalism" makes the country unfit for self-rule; therefore, France should secure the Alawis freedom and independence by remaining in Syria.[71]

An Alawi note to the French government in July 1936 asked: "Are the French today ignorant that the Crusades would have succeeded if their fortresses had been in northeast Syria, in the Land of the Nusayris? . . . We are the people most faithful to France."[72] Even more strongly worded was a petition of September 1936, signed by 450,000 Alawis, Christians, and Druzes, which read:

> The Alawis believe that they are humans, not beasts ready for slaughter. No power in the world can force them to accept the yoke of their traditional and hereditary enemies to be slaves forever. . . . The Alawis would profoundly regret the loss of their friendship and loyal attachment to noble France, which has until now been so loved, admired, and adored by them.[73]

Although Latakia lost its autonomous status in December 1936, the province continued to benefit from a "special administrative and financial regime."[74]

Alawi resistance to Sunni rule took a new turn in 1939 with the launching of an armed rebellion led by Suleiman al-Murshid, the "half-sinister, half-ludicrous, figure of the obese, illiterate, miracle-working 'god.'"[75] Murshid, a bandit who proclaimed himself divine, challenged Sunni rule with French weapons and some five thousand Alawi followers. In the words of a 1944 British consular report: "The local Alaouite leaders, whose conception of the new order in Syria is a Nationalist Government who will treat them after the fashion of the French, upholding their authority and condoning their excesses, are doing their best to combine, and the movement appears to be supported by the French."[76] Murshid succeeded in keeping Damascus' authority out of the Alawi territories.

Right up to the time of independence, Alawi leaders continued to submit petitions to the French in favor of continued French patronage. For example, a manifesto signed by twelve leaders in March 1945 called for all Alawi soldiers to remain under French command and French arbitration of disputes between the Alawi government and Damascus.[77]

Sunni Dominance, 1946–1963

It was the Sunnis, and especially the urban Sunni elite, who inherited the government when the French mandate ended in 1946. Even after independence, Alawis continued to resist submission to the central government. Suleiman al-Murshid led a second revolt in 1946, ending in his execution. A third unsuccessful uprising, led by Murshid's son took place in 1952. The failure of these efforts led Alawis to look into the possibility of attaching Latakia to Lebanon or Transjordan—anything to avoid absorption into Syria. These acts of resistance further tarnished the Alawis' already poor reputation among Sunnis.

When they came to power, the Sunni rulers in Damascus spared no effort to integrate Latakia into Syria (in part because this region offered the only access to the sea). Overcoming armed resistance, they abolished the Alawi state, Alawi military units, Alawi seats in parliament, and courts applying Alawi laws of personal status. These measures had some success; Alawis became reconciled to Syrian citizenship after the crushing of a Druze revolt in 1954 and henceforth gave up the dream of a separate state. This change of outlook, which seemed to be a matter of relatively minor importance at the time, in fact ushered in a new era of Syrian political life: the political ascent of the Alawis.

Once they recognized that their future lay within Syria, the Alawis began a rapid rise to power. Two key institutions, the armed forces and the Ba'th Party, had special importance in their transformation.

Even though the special circumstances which had brought them into the military lapsed with the French departure, Alawis and other minorities continued after independence to be over-represented in the army. Old soldiers remained in service and new ones kept coming in. Given the Sunni attitude toward Alawis, the persistence of large numbers of Alawis in the armed forces is surprising. This anomaly resulted from several factors. First, the military retained its reputation as a place for the minorities. The journalist Patrick Seale observed that Sunni landed families, "being predominantly of nationalist sentiment, despised the army as a profession: to join it between the wars was to serve the French. Homs [Military Academy] to them was a place for the lazy, the rebellious, the academically backward, or the socially undistinguished."[78] For the non-Sunnis, however, Homs was a place of opportunity for the ambitious and talented.

Second, the Sunni rulers virtually ignored the army as a tool of state; fearing its power in domestic politics, they begrudged it funds, kept it small, and rendered military careers unattractive. Third, the dire economic predicament of the Alawis and other rural peoples meant that they could not pay the fee to exempt their children from military service. More positively, those children saw military service as a means to make a decent living.

Accordingly, although the proportion of Alawis entering the Homs Military Academy declined after 1946, Alawis remained over-represented in the officer corps. A report from 1949 stated that "persons originating from the minorities" commanded "all units of any importance" in the Syrian military.[79] (This did not mean just Alawis; for example, the bodyguard of President Husni az-Za'im in 1949 was entirely Circassian.) Alawis formed a plurality among the soldiers and some two-thirds of the noncommissioned officers.

Sunni leaders apparently believed that reserving the top positions for themselves would suffice to control the military forces. Accordingly, minorities filled the lower ranks and for some years tey found it difficult to rise above the company level. Ironically, this discrimination actually served them well; as senior officers engaged in innumerable military coups d'état between 1949 and 1963, each change of government was accompanied by ruinous power struggles among the Sunnis, leading to purges, resignations, and the depletion of Sunni ranks. Wags claimed, with some justice, that there were more officers outside the Syrian army than inside it. Standing apart from these conflicts, the non-Sunnis, and Alawis especially, benefited from the repeated upheavals.[80] As Sunni officers eliminated each other, Alawis inherited their positions. With time, Alawis became increasingly senior; and, as one Alawi rose through the ranks, he brought his kinsmen along.

Purges and counter-purges during the 1946–63 period bred a deep mistrust between the officers. Never knowing who might be plotting against whom, superior officers frequently bypassed the normal hierarchy of command in favor of kinship bonds. As fear of betrayal came to dominate relations between military men, having reliable ethnic ties gave minority officers great advantage. In circumstances of almost universal suspicion, those officers within reliable networks could act far more effectively than those without. Sunnis entered the military as individuals, while Alawis entered as members of a sect; the latter, therefore, prospered. Alawi ethnic solidarity offered a far more enduring basis of cooperation than the shifting alliances formed by Sunni officers.

Secondly, Alawis acquired power through the Ba'th Party. From its earliest years, the Ba'th held special attraction for Syrians of rural and minority backgrounds, including the Alawis, who joined in disproportionately large numbers (especially at the Ba'th Party's Latakia branch). Rural migrants who went to Damascus for educational purposes constituted a majority of the membership in the Ba'th Party. They tended to be students of lower middle-class origins, the sons of ex-peasants newly arrived in the towns. In Aleppo, for example, the Ba'th claimed as members as many as three-quarters of the high school students in some schools. One of the founders of the party was an Alawi, Zaki al-Arsuzi, and he brought along many of his (rural) coreligionists to the Ba'th.

In particular, two doctrines appealed to the Alawis: socialism and secularism. Socialism offered economic opportunities to the country's poorest community. (The Ba'th's socialism until the 1960s, however, was anemic; only when minorities took the party over did this feature became prominent). Secularism—the withdrawal of religion from public life—offered to a despised minority the promise of less prejudice. What could be more attractive to members of a downtrodden religious community than a combination of these two ideologies? Indeed, these aspects drew Alawis (and other poor rural minorities) to the Ba'th more than its Pan-Arab nationalism.

The only rival to the Ba'th was the SSNP, which offered roughly the same attractions. The two competed rather evenly for a decade, until the Ba'th eliminated the SSNP through the Maliki affair in 1955. From then on, especially in Syria, Alawis were associated predominantly with the Ba'th.[81]

Alawi Consolidation, 1963–1970

Three changes in regime marked the Alawi consolidation of power: the Ba'th coup d'état of March 1963, the Alawi coup of February 1966, and the Assad coup of November 1970.

Alawis had a major role in the coup of March 8, 1963 and took many of the key government positions in the Ba'th regime that followed. Between 1963 and 1966, sectarian battles pitting minorities against Sunnis took place within the military and the Ba'th Party.

First the military: to resist President Amin al-Hafez, a Sunni, and to consolidate their new position, Alawi leaders flooded the military with co-sectarians. In this way, minority officers came to dominate the Syrian military establishment. When seven hundred vacancies opened in the army soon after the March 1963 coup, Alawis filled half the positions. So restricted were Sunnis, some graduating cadets were denied their commissions to the officer corps. While Alawis, Druze, and Isma'ilis held politically sensitive positions in the Damascus region, Sunnis were sent to regions distant from the capital. Although communal affiliation did not drive every alliance,[82] it provided the basis for most enduring relationships. Alawi leaders such as Muhammad 'Umran built key units of members from their own religious community. Sunni officers often became figureheads, holding high positions but disposing of little power. In retaliation, Hafez came to see nearly every Alawi as an enemy and pursued blatant sectarian policies, for example, excluding Alawis from some positions solely on the basis of communal affiliation.

Even Alawi officers who resisted confessionalism eventually succumbed to it. Political events solidified ties between Alawis, reducing the tribal, social, and sectarian differences that historically had split them. Itamar Rabinovich, a foremost student of this period, explains how confessionalism acquired a dynamic of its own:

> J'did [Salah Jadid, ruler of Syria 1966–70] was among those who (for political reasons) denounced 'Umran for promoting "sectarianism" (ta'ifiyya) but ironically he inherited the support of many Alawi officers who had been advanced by 'Umran. . . . The Alawi officers promoted by 'Umran realized that their overrepresentation in the upper echelons of the army was resented by the majority, and they seem to have rallied around J'did, by then the most prominent Alawi officer in the Syrian army and the person deemed most likely to preserve their high but precarious position. It was also quite natural for [Amin al-]Hafiz . . . to try to gather Sunni officers around himself by accusing J'did of engaging in "sectarian" politics. . . . The solidarity of [Jadid's] Alawi supporters seems to have been further cemented by the feeling that the issue had assumed a confessional character and that their collective and personal positions were at stake.[83]

The same factors caused Druze officers—also overrepresented in high military offices—to throw in their lot with the Alawis in 1965.

Second, the Ba'th Party, where a similar dynamic occurred: just as Alawis filled more than half of seven hundred military vacancies, so many moved into the party. To make their recruitment possible, ideological requirements for admission were relaxed for two years after March 1963. Many party officials brought in members of their family, tribe, village, or sect. As an internal Ba'th Party document of 1966 explained the problem, "friendship, family relationship and sometimes mere personal acquaintance were the basis" of admission to the party, leading "to the infiltration of elements alien to the party's logic and points of departure."[84] While Alawis brought in other Alawis, many Sunnis were purged. Membership quintupled in the year following its accession to power in 1963, transforming the party from an ideological to a sectarian affiliation. By late 1965, after two and half years in power, the Ba'th had become an entirely different institution.

These changes culminated in Hafez's decision in February 1966 to purge thirty officers of minority background from the army. Hearing of his plan, a group of mainly Alawi Ba'thist officers preempted Hafez and took power on February 23 in Syria's bloodiest-ever change of government. Once in office, they purged rival officers belonging to other religious groups—first the Sunnis and Druze, then the Isma'ilis— further exacerbating communal tensions. Alawi officers received the most important postings, and acquired unprecedented power. During the 1966–70 period, the Regional Command of the Ba'th Party, a key decision-making center, included no representatives at all from the urban Sunni areas of Damascus, Aleppo, and Hama. Two-thirds of its members, however, were recruited from the rural and minority popula-tions in Latakia, the Hawran, and Dayr az-Zur. The skewing was even more apparent among military officers on the Regional Command; during 1966–70, 63 percent came from Latakia alone.

The Alawi hold on power provoked bitter complaints from other communities. A Druze military leader, Salim Hatum, told the press after he fled Syria that Alawis in the army outnumbered the other religious communities by a ratio of five to one. He noted that "the situation in Syria was being threatened by a civil war as a result of the growth of the sectarian and tribal spirit." He also observed that "whenever a Syrian military man is questioned about his free officers, his answer will be that they have been dismissed and driven away, and that only Alawi officers have remained." Playing on the Ba'th slogan, "One Arab nation with an eternal mission," Hatum mocked the rulers in Damascus, saying that they believe in "One Alawi state with an eternal mission."[85]

Alawi domination did not assure stability. Two Alawi leaders, Salah Jadid and Hafez al-Assad, fought each other for supremacy in Syria through the late 1960s, a rivalry that ended only when Assad prevailed in November 1970. In addition to differences in outlook—Jadid was more the ideologue and Assad more the pragmatist—they represented diverse Alawi sects. The September 1970 war between the PLO and the Jordanian government was the decisive event in Assad's rise to power. Jadid sent Syrian ground forces to help the Palestinians but Assad refused to send air cover. The defeat of Syrian armor precipitated Assad's bloodless coup d'état two months later. This, Syria's tenth mili-tary coup d'état in seventeen years, was to be the last for a long time to come. It also virtually ended intra-Alawi fighting.

Hafez al-Assad

The man who won the long contest for control of Syria, Hafiz ibn 'Ali ibn Sulayman al-Asad, was born on 6 October 1930 in Qardaha, a village not far from the Turkish border and the seat of the Alawi religious leader. Hafez was the second of five children (Bayat, Hafez, Jamil, Rif'at, Bahija); in addition, his father had an older son by another wife. The family belongs to the Numaylatiya branch of the Matawira tribe. (This means Assad's ancestors came from Iraq in the 1120s.)

Accounts differ whether his father was a poor peasant, a fairly well off farmer, or a notable. Chances are, the family was well off, for while Qardaha consisted mostly of dried mud houses, the Assads lived in a stone house. In later years, however, Assad cultivated a story of poverty, recounting to visitors, for example, about having to drop out of school until his father found the 16 Syrian pounds to pay for his tuition.[86]

True or not, Hafez was a superior student and, on the strength of his academic record, he moved to the nearby town of Latakia in 1940, where he attended a leading high school, the Collège de Lattaquié. Then, sometime after 1944, it appears that he changed his name from Wahsh, meaning "wild beast" or "monster" to Assad, meaning "lion."[87] In 1948, when only 17 years old, he went to Damascus and volunteered in the Syrian army to help destroy the nascent state of Israel, only to be rejected as under age. Nonetheless, at least according to his own testimony, Assad did fight.[88] He enrolled at the Homs Military Academy in 1950, graduated in 1952, and began attending the Aleppo Air School in 1952. He became a combat pilot in 1954 and distinguished himself in this capacity. (He shot down a British plane during the Suez operation.) Assad studied in Egypt and then, for eleven months in 1958, in the Soviet Union, where he learned how to fly MiG 15s and 17s and picked up a bit of the Russian language. During the UAR years, he commanded a night-fighter squadron near Cairo.

Assad was active in politics as early as 1945, serving first as president of the Students' Committee at the Collège de Lattaquié, then as president of the National Union of Students. While still a student, Assad was jailed by the French authorities for political activities. He joined the Ba'th Party soon after its creation in 1947 (making him one of the party's earliest members). Even as he rose through the military ranks, he remained active in the Ba'th Party. In 1959, during his exile in Egypt, Assad helped found the party's Military Committee and organized its activities. By that time, he had also begun the decade-long process of consolidating his position within the Syrian armed forces.

Assad was a powerful figure in 1961, so the conservative leaders who took power in Damascus late that year (after the dissolution of the UAR) forced him to resign his commission as captain and take up a minor position in the Ministry of Transportation. But Assad continued to participate in Military Committee activities, joining in a failed *putsch* on March 29, 1962, after which he fled to Tripoli, Lebanon, where he was apprehended by the authorities and jailed for nine days, then extradited back to Syria. This misadventure notwithstanding, he played an important role in the 1963 coup and was rewarded with a recall to the army and a meteoric rise through the ranks, going from major in early 1963 to major-general in late 1964 and field marshal in 1968. (He resigned from the military in 1970 or 1971.) Assad took command of the air force in 1963 and made this his power base to take control of the entire armed forces during the subsequent years of turmoil.

Assad's support for the rebellion in February 1966 proved decisive in the coup that brought the Alawis to power; his reward was to be appointed defense minister just twenty minutes after the new regime had been proclaimed. This new position gave Assad an opportunity to extend his authority beyond the air force, especially to the combat forces of the army. Then Assad's coup of November 1970 culminated the Alawi rise to power in Syria.

Conclusion

The manner of the Alawi ascent reveals much about Syria's political culture, pointing to complex connections between the armed forces, the political parties, and ethnic communities. The air force, the Ba'th Party, and the Alawis rose in tandem; but which of these three had the most importance? Were the new rulers Ba'thists who just happened to be Alawi soldiers, or were they soldiers who happened to be Alawi Ba'thists? Actually, a third formulation is most accurate: these were Alawis who happened to be Ba'thists and soldiers.

True, the party and the military were critical, but in the end it was the transfer of authority from Sunnis to Alawis that counted most. Without deprecating the critical roles of party and army, the Alawi affiliation ultimately defined the rulers of Syria. Party and career mattered, but, as is so often the case in Syria, ethnic and religious affiliation ultimately define identity. To see the Assad regime primarily in terms of its Ba'thist or military nature is to ignore the key to Syrian politics. Confessional affiliation remains vitally important; as through the centuries, a person's sect matters more than any other attribute.

The Sunni response to the new rulers, which has taken a predominantly communal form, bears out this view. The widespread opposition of Sunnis—who make up about 69 percent of the Syrian population—to Alawi rulers inspired the Muslim Brotherhood organization to challenge the government in violent, even terroristic ways, on several occasions coming close to toppling the regime °even before the civil war that erupted in early 2011 that, at base, pits Sunni rebels against a Alawi government.°

It appears inevitable that the Alawis—still a small and despised minority, for all their present power—will eventually lose their control over Syria. When this happens, it is likely that conflicts along communal lines will bring them down, with the critical battle taking place between the Alawi rulers and the Sunni majority. In this sense, the Alawis' fall—be it through assassinations of top figures, a palace coup, or a regional revolt—is likely to resemble their rise.

Notes

1. Annie Laurent, « Syrie-Liban: Les faux frères jumeaux, » *Politique étrangère* 48 (1983): 598.

2. Matti Moosa, *Extremist Shiites: The Ghulat Sects* (Syracuse, N. Y.: Syracuse University Press, 1988), p. 297.

3. Anon., *Al-Muslimun fi Suriya wa'l-Irhab an-Nusayri, 1964–1979* (Cairo: n.p., n.d.), p. 46.

4. For the fullest account of these meetings, see Abu Musa al-Hariri, *Al-'Alawiyun - an-Nusayriyun* (Beirut: n.p., 1400/1980), pp. 234–37.

5. John F. Devlin, *The Ba'th Party: A History from Its Origins to 1966* (Stanford: Hoover Institution Press, 1976), pp. 319–20.

6. Alasdair Drysdale, "The Syrian Political Elite, 1966–1976: A Spatial and Social Analysis," *Middle Eastern Studies* 17 (1981): 27.

7. Yahya M. Sadowski, "Ba'thist Ethics and the Spirit of State Capitalism: Patronage and Party in Contemporary Syria," in *Ideology and Power in the Middle East: Studies in Honor of George Lenczowski*, edited by Peter J. Chelkowski and Robert Pranger (Durham: Duke University Press, 1988), p. 168.

8. Michael van Dusen, "Syria: Downfall of a Traditional Elite," in *Political Elites and Political Development in the Middle East*, ed. Frank Tachau (Cambridge, Mass.: Schenkman Publishing, 1975), p. 136.

9. Apologists have constructed an elaborate argument to prove that Alawi was the sect's original name. See 'Ali 'Aziz Ibrahim, *Al-'Alawiyun: Fida'iyu ash-Shi 'a al-Majhulun* (n.p., 1392/1972), pp. 9–14.

10. For accounts of Alawi theology and doctrines, see many of the books cited in the following notes, especially those by Sulayman Efendi al-Adhani, Halm, Lammens, Lyde, Moosa, de Sacy, and Sharaf ad-Din.

11. Ibn Kathir, *Al-Bidaya wa'n-Nihaya* (Cairo: Matba'a as-Sa'ada, 13558/ 1932–39), volume 14, p. 83.

12. See Wolff, "Auszüge aus dem Katechismus der Nossairier," *Zeitschrift der Deutschen morgenländischen Gesellschaft* 3 (1849): 308.

13. And just as Muslims traditionally accused Christians of making Jesus divine, so they accused Alawis of doing the same to 'Ali; the parallel is striking.

14. T. E. Lawrence, *Seven Pillars of Wisdom: A Triumph* (Garden City, N. Y.: Doubleday, Doran & Company, 1935), p. 329.

15. Henri Lammens, "Les Nosairis: Notes sur leur histoire et leur religion," *Etudes* 1899, p. 492.

16. Sami al-Jundi, *Al-Ba'th* (Beirut: Dar an-Nahar li'n-Nashr, 1969), p. 145.

17. Pierre May, *L'Alaouite: ses croyances, ses moeurs, les cheikhs, les lois de la tribu et les chefs* (Beirut: Imprimerie Catholique, 1931?), pp. 4243.

18. Frederick Walpole, *The Ansayrii (or Assassins,) with Travels to the Further East, in 1850–51* (London: Richard Bentley, 1851), vol. 3, p. 64.

19. Heinz Halm, *Die islamische Gnosis: die extreme Schia und dieAlawiten* (Zurich: Artemis, 1982), p. 316.

20. Hamza ibn 'Ali, *Ar-Risala ad-Damigha li'l-Fasiq ar-Radd 'ala an-Nusayri.* Text in Silvestre de Sacy, *Exposé de la religion des Druzes* (Paris: A l'Imprimerie Royale, 1838), vol. 2, pp. 571–73.

21. For a wild novelistic account of Alawi religious orgies, see Jehan Cendrieux, *Al-Ghadir ou le Sexe-Dieu* (Paris: Bibliothèque-Charpentier, 1926), pp. 10–11.

22. "An Oriental Student," *The Modern Syrians: or, Native Society in Damascus, Aleppo, and the Mountains of the Druses* (London: Longman, Brown, Green, and Longmans, 1844), p. 281.

23. Sulayman Efendi al-Adhani, *Kitab al-Bakura as-Sulaymaniya fi Kashf Asrar ad-Diyana an-Nusayriya.* Summary and Arabic extracts in Edward E. Salisbury, "The Book of Sulaiman's First Ripe Fruit: Disclosing the Mysteries of the Nusairian Religion," *Journal of the American Oriental Society* 8 (1866): 285, 306. According to Sulayman Efendi, this practice originates in an esoteric interpretation of the Qur'an, Sura 33, Verse 49.

24. Ibn Battuta, *Ar-Rihla* (Beirut: Dar as-Sadr and Dar Bayrut, 1384/1964), pp. 79–80.

25. Moosa, *Extremist Shiites*, p. 271.

26. Ignaz Goldziher, *Vorlesungen über den Islam* (Heidelberg: C. Winter, 1910); trans. by Andras and Ruth Hamori as *Introduction to Islamic Theology and Law*, (Princeton, N.J.: Princeton University Press, 1981), p. 228.

27. Sulayman Efendi al-Adhani, *Kitab al-Bakura.* Extracts in al-Husayni 'Abdallah, ed., *Al-Judhur at-Ta'rikhiya li'n-Nusayriya al-'Alawiya* (Cairo: Dar al-I'tisam, 1400/1980), p. 55.

28. Sulayman Efendi al-Adhani, *Kitab al-Bakura*, in Salisbury, "The Book of Sulaiman's First Ripe Fruit," p. 298. The third sentence in this quote comes from Henri Lammens, *L'Islam, croyances et institutions*, 2d ed., (Beirut: Imprimerie catholique, 1941), p. 228.

29. Paulo Boneschi, « Une fatwà du Grand Mufti de Jérusalem Muhammad 'Amin al-Husayni sur lesAlawites. » *Revue de l'histoire des religions* 122, 23 (Sep.–Dec. 1940): 152.

30. Henry Maundrell, *A Journey from Aleppo to Jerusalem in 1697* (London: J. White & Co., 1810), pp. 16–17.

31. Benjamin Disraeli, *Tancred, or The New Crusade* (London: Longmans, Green, and Co., 1847), pp. 374–75.

32. Sulayman Efendi al-Adhani, *Kitab al-Bakura*, in Salisbury, "The Book of Sulaiman's First Ripe Fruit," p. 298.

33. Muhammad Rida Shams ad-Din, *Ma'a al-'Alawiyin fi Suriya* (Beirut: Matba'a al-Insaf, 1376), pp. 5–6.

34. Annie Laurent and Antoine Basbous, *Guerres secrètes au Liban* (Paris: Gallimard, 1987), pp. 71–72.

35. Hamza ibn 'Ali, *Ar-Risala ad-Damigha*, vol. 2, p. 570. This accusation resembles those used by medieval Christians to explain the popularity of Islam.

36. Quoted in 'Izz ad-Din al-Farisi and Ahmad Sadiq, "Ath-Thawra al-Islamiya fi Suriya," *Al-Mukhtar al-Islami* [Cairo], October 1980, p. 39.

37. Ahmad ibn Taymiya, "Fatwa fi'n-Nusayriya." Arabic text in M. St. Guyard, "Le Fetwa d'Ibn Taimiyyah sur les Nosairis," *Journal Asiatique*, 6th series, vol. 16, no. 66 (1871): 167, 168, 169, 177. For other premodern Sunni assessments of the Alawis—including al-Ash'ari, 'Abd al-Qadir al-Baghdadi, Ibn Hazm, ash-Shahrastani, and Fakhr ad-Din ar-Razi—see as-Sayyid 'Abd al-Husayn Mahdi al-'Askari, *Al-'Alawiyun aw an-Nusayriya* (N.p., 1400/1980), pp. 49–53.

38. Martin Kramer, "Syria's 'Alawis and Shi'ism," in *Shi'ism, Resistance, and Revolution*, ed. Martin Kramer (Boulder, Colo.: Westview Press, 1987), p. 238.

39. Text in Robert Mantran and Jean Sauvaget, eds., *Règlements fiscaux ottomans: Les provinces syriens* (Paris: Librarie d'Amerique et d'Orient, 1951), p. 76. See also pp. 77, 88, 93.

40. Jacques Weulersse, « Antioche, un type de cité d'Islam, » *Comptes rendus du Congrès international de Géographie, Varsovie 1934* (Warsaw: Kasa Im. Mianowskiego, 1937), vol. 3, p. 258.

41. Samuel Lyde, *The Asian Mystery: Illustrated in the History, Religion, and Present State of the Ansaireeh or Nusairis of Syria* (London: Longman, Green, Longman, and Roberts, 1860), p. 196; Walpole, *The Ansayrii*, vol. 3, p. 115.

42. Ibn Battuta, *Ar-Rihla*, p. 80; Muhammad Amin Ghalib at-Tawil, *Ta'rikh al-'Alawiyin*, 2d. ed. (Beirut: Dar al-Andalus, 1386/1966), p. 342. Tawil, a leading Alawi shaykh, published the first edition of his history in 1924.

43. Jacques Weulersse, *Le pays des Alaouites* (Tours: Arrault & Cie., 1940), vol. 1, p. 54.

44. E. Janot, *Des Croisades au Mandat: Notes sur le peuple Alouïte* (Lyon: Imprimerie L. Bascon, 1934), p. 37.

45. Paul Jacquot, *L'état des Alaouites: Guide* (Beirut: Imprimerie Catholique, 1929), p. 10.

46. R. Strothmann, "Die Nusairi im heutigen Syrien," *Nachrichten der Akademie der Wissenschaften in Göttingen*, phil.-hist. Kl. Nr. 4 (1950): 35.

47. George-Samné, *La Syrie* (Paris: Bossard, 1920), p. 340.

48. Kramer, "Syria's 'Alawis and Shi'ism," p. 238.

49. John Lewis Burckhardt, *Travels in Syria and the Holy Land* (London: John Murray, 1822), p. 141.

50. Lyde, *Asian Mystery*, pp. 219–20.

51. *Handbook for Travellers in Syria and Palestine* (London: John Murray, 1858), p. xli.

52. Weulersse, *Le pays des Alaouites*, vol. 1, pp. 73, 317; idem., *Paysans de Syrie et du Proche Orient* (Paris: Gallimard, 1946), p. 272. Étienne de Vaumas shows the similarities of the Lebanese and Alawi regions, then explains the profound differences of their populations in "Le Djebel Ansarieh: Études de Géographie humaine," *Revue de Géographie alpine* 48 (1960): 267–311.

53. Lammens, *L'Islam*, p. 228.

54. Nawfal Iliyas, a lawyer who worked for the Alawi tribes during those decades; reported by Laurent and Basbous, *Guerres secrètes au Liban*, p. 70. On Iliyas, see Jurj Gharib, *Nawfal Iliyas: Siyasa, Adab, Dhikriyat* (Beirut: Dar ath-Thaqafa, 1975).

55. Tawil, *Ta'rikh al-'Alawiyin*, p. 470.

56. Lyde, *Asian Mystery*, p. 222.

57. Weulersse, "Antioche," p. 258.

58. Weulersse, *Paysans de Syrie*, p. 85.

59. Nikolaos van Dam, *The Struggle for Power in Syria: Sectarianism, Regionalism and Tribalism in Politics, 1961–1978* (New York: St. Martin's Press, 1979), p. 22.

60. Yusuf al-Hakim, *Dhikriyat al-Hakim*, vol. 3, *Suriya wa'l-'Ahd al-Faysali* (Beirut: Al-Matba'a al-Kathulikiya, 1966), p. 94.

61. Gouroud to premier and foreign minister, Dec. 29, 1919, Ministère des Affaires Étrangères, Series E, Levant, Syrie-Liban, volume 20, pp. 226–33. Quoted in Wajih Kawtharani, *Bilad ash-Sham* (Beirut: Ma'had al-Inma' al-'Arabi, 1980), p. 211.

62. Taqi Sharaf ad-Din, *An-Nusayriya: Dirasa Tahliliya* (Beirut: n.p., 1983), pp. 73–75.

63. Arrêté no 623, Sept. 15, 1922. Quoted in E. Rabbath, *L'övolution politique de la Syrie sous mandat* (Paris: Marcel Rivière, 1928), p. 185.

64. Sharaf ad-Din, *An-Nusayriya: Dirasa Tahliliya*, p. 80.

65. 77 percent voted in the Alawi state, 20–25 percent in Aleppo, and so few in Hama that elections were cancelled. League of Nations, Permanent Mandates Commission, *Minutes of the 9th Session*, 16th meeting, June 17, 1926, p. 116.

66. Alawis made up the 1st, 2nd, and much of the 5th battalions; Armenians appear to have made up the 4th; and Christians made up the 8th. The composition of the 3rd, 6th, and 7th battalions is unknown. Alawis had no cavalry role. The 2nd battalion, for example, had 773 soldiers, of which 623 were Alawi, 73 Sunni, 64 Christian, and 13 Isma'ilis. See R. Bayly Winder, "The Modern Military Tradition in Syria," unpublished draft dated 5 March 1959, pp. 14–15; and Jacquot, *L'état des Alaouites*, p. 11.

67. President of the Alawis State Representative Council, League of Nations, Permanent Mandates Commission, *Minutes of the 9th Session*, 16th meeting, June 17, 1926, p. 112.

68. Petition dated Mar. 4, 1936, *Bulletin du Comité de l'Asie Française*, April 1936, p. 131.

69. June 11, 1936, Ministère des Affaires Étrangères, Levant 1918–1930, Syrie-Liban, Doc. E-492, fol. 195. Quoted in Laurent and Basbous, *Guerres secrètes au Liban*, p. 74.

70. It is difficult to ascertain whether this is true. The following factors point to its falsehood. (1) Hafiz al-Asad changed his name from Hafiz al-Wahsh only in the mid-1940s; (2) if the president came from a poor peasant family, as he himself maintained, his grandfather would not have been invited to sign a letter to the French prime minister.

71. Document 3547, dated June 15, 1936, Ministère des Affaires Étrangères. Text in Hariri, *AlAlawiyun - an-Nusayriyun*, pp. 228–31. See also *International Impact*, Mar. 28, 1980; al-Farisi and Sadiq, "Ath-Thawra al-Islamiya fi Suriya," p. 39; *Al-Irhab an-Nusayri*, p. 6; Laurent, "Syrie-Liban," p. 598; Annie Laurent and Antoine Basbous, *Une Proie pour deux Fauves?* (Beirut: Ad-Da'irat, 1983), p. 96. Moosa, *Extremist Shiites*, pp. 287–88 provides a full English translation of the letter.

    Laurent and Basbous report (*Guerres secrètes au Liban*, p. 76) that the letter is missing from the Quai d'Orsay and speculate that its absence has to do with the embarrassment it causes the Asad regime.

    Four other memoranda from theAlawis to the French High Commissioner are quoted extensively in Sharaf ad-Din, *An-Nusayriya: Dirasa Tahliliya*, pp. 87–92.

72. Note dated July 3, 1936, quoted in Sharaf ad-Din, *An-Nusayriya: Dirasa Tahliliya*, p. 57, n. 67.

73. Petition dated Sept. 26, 1936, *Bulletin du Comité de l'Asie Française*, December 1936, p. 340.

74. Arrêté of Dec. 5, 1936, *Échos de Syrie*, 13 December 1936.

75. Stephen Helmsley Longrigg, *Syria and Lebanon Under French Mandate* (London: Oxford University Press, 1958), p. 210. British officials called him a "notorious brigand." See "Weekly Political Summary, Syria and the Lebanon," Feb. 2, 1944, E 1049/23/89, Foreign Office 371/40299/7543. For photographs of this strange figure, see Weulersse, *Pays des Alaouites*, vol. 2, pp. XCI–XCII.

76. "Weekly Political Summary, Syria and the Lebanon," Mar. 22, 1944, E 2211/23/89, Foreign Office 371/40300/7543.

77. "The Present State of Syria and the Lebanon," Supplement II, Mar. 23, 1945, Foreign Office 371/45562/7505.

78. Patrick Seale, *The Struggle for Syria* (London: Oxford University Press, 1965), p. 37.

79. Fadlallah Abu Mansur, *A'asir Dimashq* (Beirut: n.p., 1959), p. 51. The total number of army officers at this time, it should be noted, was less than two hundred.

80. The 'Adnan al-Maliki affair of 1955, which eliminated the SSNP from political power in Syria, was an exception, for the SSNP included manyAlawis (including Sergeant Yusuf 'Abd al-Karim, the man who assassinated Maliki). Alawis in the army laid low for some years after this event.

81. On the Ba'th-SSNP rivalry, see Daniel Pipes, "Radical Politics and the Syrian Social Nationalist Party," *International Journal of Middle East Studies*, 20 (1988): 313–16.

82. The most prominent exception to communal alignment was the cooperation between Amin al-Hafiz, a Sunni, and Salah Jadid and Hafiz al-Asad,

bothAlawis. In subsequent years, as non Alawis increasingly served Alawi purposes, cross-communal ties became imbalanced.

83.   Itamar Rabinovich, *Syria Under the Ba'th 1963–1966: The Army-Party Symbiosis* (Jerusalem: Israel Universities Press, 1972), p. 181.

84.   Syrian Regional Command of the Ba'th Party, *Azmat al-Hizb wa Harakat 23 Shubat* (Damascus, 1966), pp. 20–21. This document was classified as a "secret internal publication exlusively for members."

85.   *Ad-Difa'* [Jerusalem], Sept. 14, 1966; *An-Nahar*, Sept. 15, 1966; *Al-Hayat*, Sept. 29, 1966. Quoted in van Dam, *Struggle for Power*, pp. 75–76. For many more examples of suspicion about Alawis, see ibid., pp. 110–24. Much of my information on the rise of the Alawis derives from van Dam's meticulous study.

86.   According to Ahmad Sulayman al-Ahmad, *Al-Watan al-'Arabi*, 5 August 1988.

87.   Michael Hillegas van Dusen, Intra- and Inter-Generational Conflict in the Syrian Army," unpublished Ph.D. dissertation, Johns Hopkins University, 1971, p. 315; Moshe Ma'oz, "Hafiz al-Asad of Syria," *Orbis* 31 (1987): 208. The meaning of the two names is akin, but the tone is entirely different.

88.   Radio Damascus, May 4, 1985.

10

The Scandal of US-Saudi Relations

When it comes to the Saudi-American relationship, the White House
should be called the "White Tent."
—Mohammed Al-Khilewi, a Saudi diplomat who defected to the
United States

Consider two symbolic moments in the US-Saudi relationship involving a visit by one leader to the other's country. In November 1990, President George H. W. Bush went to the Persian Gulf region with his wife and top congressional leaders at Thanksgiving time to visit the four hundred thousand US troops gathered in Saudi Arabia, whom he had sent there to protect that country from an Iraqi invasion. When the Saudi authorities learned that the president intended to say grace before a festive Thanksgiving dinner, they remonstrated; Saudi Arabia knows only one religion, they said, and that is Islam. Bush acceded, and he and his entourage instead celebrated the holiday on the *U.S.S. Durham*, an amphibious cargo ship sitting in international waters.

In April 2002, as Crown Prince Abdallah of Saudi Arabia, the country's effective ruler, was about to travel across Texas to visit President George W. Bush, an advance group talked to the airport manager in Waco (the airport serving the president's ranch in Crawford) "and told him they did not want any females on the ramp and also said there should not be any females talking to the airplane."[1] The Federal Aviation Administration (FAA) at Waco complied with this request and passed it to three other FAA stations on the crown prince's route, which also complied. Then, when queried about this matter, both the FAA and the State Department joined the Saudi foreign minister in flat-out denying that there ever was a Saudi request for male-only controllers.

The import of these incidents is clear enough: Official Americans in Saudi Arabia bend to Saudi customs, as do official Americans in the United States. And it's not just a matter of travel etiquette; one finds parallel American obsequiousness concerning such issues as energy, security, religion, and personal status. The Saudis routinely set the terms of this bilateral relationship.

For decades, US government agencies have engaged in a consistent pattern of deference to Saudi wishes, making so many unwonted and unnecessary concessions that one gets the impression that a switch has taken place, with both sides forgetting which of them is the great power and which the minor one. I shall first document this claim, then offer an explanation for it, and conclude with a policy recommendation.

Small-Scale Obsequiousness

US government acceptance of Saudi norms is particularly evident as concerns the treatment of women, children, practicing Christians, and Jews.

Women

Washington accepts the unequal treatment of women in connection with Saudi Arabia that it would otherwise never countenance. Two examples tell the story.

Starting in 1991, the US military required its female personnel based in Saudi Arabia to wear black, head-to-foot abayas. (This makes Saudi Arabia the only country in the world where US military personnel are expected to wear a religiously mandated garment.) Further, the women had to ride in the back seat of vehicles and be accompanied by a man when off base.

In 1995, Lt. Col. Martha McSally, the highest-ranking female fighter pilot in the US Air Force, initiated an effort within the system to end this discriminatory treatment. As she put it, "I'm able to be in leadership positions and fly combat sorties into enemy territory, yet when I leave the base, I hand over the keys to my subordinate men, sit in the back, and put on a Muslim outfit that is very demeaning and humiliating."[2] Not succeeding within the system, McSally went public with a law suit in early 2002. Her complaint points to the violation of her free speech, the separation of church and state, and gender discrimination. (Male military personnel not only have no parallel requirements imposed on them but are specifically forbidden from wearing Saudi clothing; also, nonmilitary women working for the US government in Saudi Arabia are not expected to wear an abaya.[3])

After McSally filed her law suit, the Department of Defense responded by changing the requirement that women wear abayas off base; it then rescinded the policies on the other two issues (sitting in the back of a vehicle; having a male escort). Yet these were largely cosmetic changes, for women are still "strongly encouraged" to follow the old rules so as to take "host nation sensitivity" into account. The US government continues to purchase and issue abayas. McSally has argued that the military's "strongly encouraged" abayas effectively continue the old regimen, as women who do not wear the Saudi garb fear harm to their careers; so she continued with her lawsuit. Finally, the House of Representatives in May 2002 voted unanimously to prohibit the Pentagon from "formally or informally" urging servicewomen to wear abayas and forbade the Pentagon from buying abayas for servicewomen.[4] °A month later, the Senate also unanimously to prohibit the DoD from requiring or even formally urging servicewomen in Saudi Arabia to wear the abaya.[5°]

Private American institutions follow suit, perhaps encouraged by the government's policy. American businessmen and diplomats in Riyadh, reports *USA Today*,

> say the biggest U.S. companies in Saudi Arabia—ExxonMobil, ChevronTexaco and Boeing—do not employ any women. Several other U.S. companies, including Citibank, Saks Fifth Avenue, Philip Morris and Procter & Gamble, have women on their payroll, but they work in offices segregated from men, as is the [Saudi] custom. The Saudis do not disclose employment practices of the more than 100 U.S. companies operating in Saudi Arabia, but American businessmen say that to their knowledge, all the companies follow Saudi mores so they don't jeopardize their investments.

°The National Organization for Women found similarly among American companies in the restaurant business:

> At least three major U.S. companies—including McDonald's, Pizza Hut and Starbucks—are reportedly upholding gender apartheid in their franchise stores in Saudi Arabia. The companies have made a number of changes to their business practices in "deference" to Saudi customs, including maintaining segregated seating in their restaurants and having separate entrances for women and men.

Also of note: Starbucks in Saudi Arabia does not show the female figure that normally graces its logo. The president of Starbucks, Peter Maslen, indicated that his company will not budge from its discriminatory practices: "As a guest in any country where we do business, we abstain from interference in local social, cultural and political matters."[6°]

One Western diplomat complains that American businessmen use empty excuses, such as local laws, there being no place for the women to sit, or for them go to the toilet, and concludes that, "It's just like it was in South Africa."[7]

Children

The pattern of Saudi fathers abducting children from the United States to Saudi Arabia, and then keeping them there with the full agreement of the Saudi authorities, affected at least ninety-two children of US mothers and Saudi fathers as of 2002, perhaps many more. In each of these heartbreaking cases, the State Department has behaved with weakness bordering on sycophancy. To be specific, it has accepted the Saudi law that gives the father near-absolute control over the movement and activities of his children and wife (or wives). The department made no real efforts to signal its displeasure to the Saudi authorities over these cases, much less made vigorous efforts to free children held against their American families' wishes.

Here are three cases featured at a June 2002 hearing in the House of Representatives, organized by Representative Dan Burton (Republican of Indiana):

Yasmine Shalhoub (b. 1986), a girl born in the United States, was abducted by her father to Saudi Arabia in 1997. As her mother, Miriam Hernandez, developed plans to extricate Yasmine from her captivity, the American Embassy made it clear that it would provide no help against the father's wishes. Left on her own, Hernandez did find a way to smuggle Yasmine out in 1999, and she is now back in the United States—no thanks to her diplomatic representatives.

Rasheed (b. 1976) and Amjad (b. 1983) Radwan are a boy and girl born in the United States who moved with their parents to Saudi Arabia in 1985. After their father, Nizar Radwan, divorced their mother, Monica Stowers, in 1986, he refused to permit the children to leave the country with her. Stowers left the kingdom for four years, then returned to take back her children in 1990. In December of that year, she did get them and all three took refuge in the American Embassy, where Stowers desperately sought help to take her children out of the country. Instead, the consul general ordered the Marines to evict mother and children from the premises. Shortly after, the children were taken back to the father and the mother was jailed. Rasheed, being male, could leave Saudi Arabia, which he did in 1996; his sister remains confined there as she enters adulthood.

Alia (b. 1979) and Aisha (b. 1982) al-Gheshayan, are two girls born in the United States and abducted to Saudi Arabia in 1986, in defiance of a US court order, by their father, Khalid al-Gheshayan. Until mid-2002, they could not leave Saudi Arabia. Their mother, Pat Roush, had had only a few minutes to visit them over the years. Both children have now reached adulthood and both have been married off; but as females, they cannot leave the country without their male guardian's permission—first, their father, now their husbands. One US ambassador to Saudi Arabia (Walter Cutler) tried to get the children released, only to be instructed by the State Department to "maintain impartiality" in this dispute, after which his efforts to assist came to an end. A second ambassador (Hume Horan) brought the matter up with a ranking Saudi official but soon after found himself recalled due to Saudi complaints. A third (Roy Mabus) devised a plan to put pressure on the Gheshayan family to spring the children but, after his departure, the steps he took were all reversed.

In August 2002, at the precise moment when Representative Burton was leading a congressional delegation to Riyadh to seek the release of abducted Americans, the Gheshayan sisters surfaced in London "on vacation" and met with an American consular official—not in the US embassy, but in a luxury hotel overflowing with high-powered Saudis and their American employees. There they ostensibly renounced the United States and their mother, even as they praised Osama bin Laden. The State Department rejected accusations that the sisters were coerced or under duress during this meeting, or at any time during their stay in London. This was despite the questionable role of the translator, a strong possibility that Saudis were listening in on the conversation (and the likelihood that the sisters knew it), and the failure of US diplomats to inform the two of their rights as American citizens to travel freely, without exit visas or prior permission from anyone.

In all three of these cases—and in the many others like them—the US government has singularly failed to stand up for the rights of its most vulnerable citizens.

Christians

In Saudi Arabia, the US government submits to restrictions on Christian practices that it would find totally unacceptable anywhere else in the world—starting with the US president's not celebrating Thanksgiving at an American military installation on Saudi territory, as mentioned above. Hundreds of thousands of US troops in December 1990 were not permitted to hold formal Christmas services at their bases on Saudi soil; all that was allowed to them were "C-word morale services" held in places where they would be invisible to the outside world, such as tents and mess halls. The goal was for no Saudi to be made to suffer the knowledge that Christians were at prayer.[8]

At least the soldiers in 1990–91 could hold services, a privilege not normally accorded Americans in Saudi Arabia on official business. Timothy Hunter, a State Department employee based in Saudi Arabia during 1992–95 (and a rare source of information from inside the US establishment in Saudi Arabia, one later subjected to reprisals for his whistle-blowing activities), had the job of "monitoring and coordinating the 'Tuesday Lecture' at the Jeddah consulate general—really the Catholic catacomb."[9] (Services in Jeddah, he explains, took place on Tuesday, not Sunday, due to the paucity of clergy and their need to be in other locations on Sundays.) In an article in the *Middle East Quarterly*, Hunter details the methods he was told to use to discourage Catholic worshippers and the even worse options faced by Protestants:

> When Catholic Americans sought permission to worship, I was to receive their telephone inquiries and deflect them by pretending not to know about the "Tuesday Lecture." Only if a person kept calling back and insisting that such a group existed was I to meet with him and get a sense of his trustworthiness. . . . In my time, we never actually admitted anyone. . . . My personal dealings were limited to Catholics. I later learned that others—Protestants, Mormons, and Jews—were denied any sanctuary on the consulate grounds. . . . Non-Catholic Americans were directed to the British Consulate, which both sponsored other religious services and admitted much larger numbers of Catholics. But the UK services were full, leaving most American worshippers only the option of holding services on Saudi territory, thereby exposing themselves to potentially violent attack from the Mutawa [the much-feared Saudi religious police].[10]

Jews

With Jews, the issue is not freedom of religious practice in Saudi Arabia; it is simply gaining entry to the Kingdom. In several instances over many years, agencies of the US government have excluded Jewish Americans from positions in Saudi Arabia. Hunter writes:

> When (in 1993) I worked in the Washington, DC State Department administrative office of the "Near East and South Asia Bureau," it was the duty of the foreign service director of personnel to screen all Foreign Service officers applying for service in KSA [Kingdom of

Saudi Arabia] and to "tick" Jewish officers' names using the letter "J" next to the names so that selection panels would not select Jewish diplomats for service in KSA.

Select senior diplomats of Jewish origin may briefly visit the country on official business but "no low or mid-level Jewish-American diplomat was permitted to be stationed/reside in Kingdom" during Hunter's three-year experience.

> I was instructed that there was a diplomatic protocol between the USA and KSA going back "many years" in which the two governments agreed that no Jewish-American U.S. diplomats would be allowed to be stationed in KSA. The KSA government had expressed its opposition to the stationing of U.S. diplomats who were Jewish because it believed all Jewish people, irrespective of nationality, can be considered Israeli spies. I was told that the U.S. government had not disputed the KSA government's assertion. I explained to the State Department's Office of the Inspector General that the existence of such a protocol was an indication of illegal activity since no treaty provision may be executed without the concurrence of the U.S. Senate.[11]

This US government boycott of Jews has on occasion come to light. Congressional hearings in 1975 exposed the fact that the US Army Corps of Engineers and its subcontractors excluded Jewish (and black) personnel from projects in Saudi Arabia.[12] The Treasury Department issued guidelines in 1976 to help US businesses get around anti-boycott provisions that had just been signed into law.

To prepare its defense in a case brought against it by the Boeing Corporation, the US government hired a Virginia-based contractor, CACI Inc.-Commercial, to send a team to microfilm documents in Saudi Arabia, a task that would take several months. At a November 1991 meeting called by the Air Force, Col. Michael J. Hoover, the chief trial attorney for the Air Force Materiel Command, informed representatives of the Justice Department and CACI Inc.-Commercial that Jews or people with Jewish surnames could not go to Saudi Arabia as part of the microfilming team. On this basis, David Andrew (the senior CACI Inc.-Commercial employee involved in the microfilming project) drafted and Jane Hadden Alperson (Office of Litigation Support, Civil Division, Justice Department, the case manager involved in the microfilming project) edited an "operations plan" in which the "Screening/Selection Process" included the following text:

> No Jews or Jewish surnamed personnel will be sent as part of the Document Acquisition Team because of the cultural differences

between Moslems and Jews in the Region. . . . No Israeli stamped passport, as per Saudi rules.

As the Justice Department and CACI Inc.-Commercial hired the team to go to Saudi Arabia, "At least one U.S. person was refused a place on the team based on religion or national origin."

After hearing a complaint from the Anti-Defamation League, the Office of Antiboycott Compliance at the Department of Commerce conducted a probe lasting (the unusually long period of) one and a half years. The office reached a settlement on February 27, 1997, in which CACI Inc.-Commercial and the key individuals in each institution (Hoover, Alperson, Andrew) agreed to settle the allegations against them. The individuals were assessed suspended fines and CACI-Commercial paid $15,000. Hoover also received a letter of reprimand. For their part, the Air Force and the Department of Justice "agreed to institute measures to prevent a similar event from happening again."[13] To all this, the *New York Daily News* acerbically commented, "The Air Force and Justice apologized and promised to abide by the law. That's comforting, since Justice is supposed to uphold the law."[14]

As in the case of women, where the government leads, private organizations follow. Excluding Jews may be in contravention of US law, which states that "U.S. companies cannot rely on a country's customs or local preferences and stereotypes to justify discrimination against U.S. citizens," but it occurs nonetheless.[15] Until 1959, the Arabian American Oil Co. (ARAMCO) had an exemption from New York State's anti-discrimination laws and was permitted to ask prospective employees if they were Jews, on the grounds that Saudi Arabia refused to admit Jews into the country. When this arrangement was challenged in 1959, the New York State Supreme Court derisively condemned this practice. It told ARAMCO, "Go elsewhere to serve your Arab master—but not in New York State," and instructed the State Commission against Discrimination to enforce the ruling against ARAMCO.[16]

World Airways, which boasts of having "pilgrims from more Muslim countries to the Islamic Holy Land than any other airline in the world," was charged in 1975 with demanding a "letter from a church showing membership, or proof of baptism or marriage in a church" from staff traveling to Saudi Arabia.[17] About that same time, Vinnel Corporation excluded personnel with any "contact or interest" in countries not recognized by the Kingdom.[18]

In 1982, two cardiovascular anesthesiologists (Lawrence Abrams and Stewart Linde) brought charges of discrimination against their employer, the Baylor College of Medicine, for excluding them from an exchange program with the King Faisal Hospital in Saudi Arabia due to their being Jewish. The case went to court, and in 1986 the United States Court of Appeals for the Fifth Circuit agreed with the doctors, finding that "the college intentionally excluded Jews from its beneficial and educational rotation program at Faisal Hospital." The court surmised that Baylor's actions were motivated, at least in part, "by its desire not to 'rock the boat' of its lucrative Saudi contributors."[19]

Other Issues

The Federal government appeases Riyadh when it "meticulously cooperate[s] with Saudi censorship" of mail going to Americans living in the Kingdom:

> Mail to U.S. military and official government personnel enters the Kingdom on U.S. military craft, and American officials in Saudi Arabia follow Saudi wishes by seizing and disposing of Christmas trees and decorations and other symbols of the holiday. They seize and destroy Christmas cards sent to (the mostly non-official) Americans who receive their mail through a Saudi postal box, and even tear from the envelope U.S. stamps portraying religious scenes.

It hardly comes as a surprise, then, to hear from Ron Mayfield, Jr., who worked in Saudi Arabia for eight years with the Army Corps of Engineers, ARAMCO, and Raytheon Corp, that while he was working at Raytheon, the mail censors confiscated a photo of his grandmother on her ninety-fifth birthday, given that this picture contravenes the (episodic) Saudi prohibition of representations of women. More broadly, Mayfield recounts:

> On my first tour of Saudi Arabia, working with the U.S. Army Corps of Engineers, Americans were ordered to remove all decals and photos of the American flag. . . . With my last employer, providing defensive missiles to the Saudis, officers came through on an inspection and ordered removal of all family photos picturing wives and female children. . . . Customs went through a friend's wallet, confiscating a photo of his wife in hot pants.[20]

The Jeddah office of what used to be called the US Information Service, an agency charged with presenting the official American point of view and refuting hostile accounts, was "almost completely staffed by non-US citizens from the Middle East, many of them not friendly to American values and policies," according to Hunter. It "made no effort to counter the systematic, widespread falsehoods in the Saudi media about American society. In some instances, in fact, the USIS actually provided misinformation about US society."[21] The public library at USIS did not stock books critical of the Kingdom or other volumes considered "too sensitive" for Saudi society (such as family health issues). The only books touching on Jews, he reports, were "a small Jewish cookbook" and a great number of antisemitic tomes, including the *Protocols of the Learned Elders of Zion*.[22]

The US government's weak policy can be seen in yet other areas: it does not fight for US scholars or media to get access to the Kingdom; it does not challenge the Saudi refusal to allow American researchers to engage in archaeological excavations; and it provides scant assistance to those unfortunate Americans who get caught up in the Saudi legal system (for something as minor as a fender-bender).

In contrast—and this is a rich subject in its own right—the State Department and other agencies bend over backwards for the kingdom, for example, going to great lengths to keep secret the specifics of its investments in the United States. And when Saudi nationals living in the United States get in trouble with the law (common charges include various forms of rowdiness, sexual harassment, and keeping slaves), they are often granted diplomatic immunity to avoid prosecution, then whisked out of the country. For example, a former US ambassador to Riyadh was dispatched by his Saudi bosses to Miami in April 1982 to keep a Saudi prince our of jail for an altercation with the police; the ambassador won him retroactive diplomatic immunity. Or after Princess Buniah al-Saud, a niece of King Fahd, faced charges of battery for having pushed her Indonesian maid down a flight of stairs in her Orlando, Florida, house, the maid was conveniently denied a visa by the State Department to return to the United States to testify against the princess. More spectacular was the planeload of bin Ladens permitted to leave the United States immediately after September 11, 2001, before US law enforcement officials could question them.

It bears noting, too, that although these examples are limited to individuals and do not touch directly on high policy, they have more than symbolic importance because they set a tone with potentially large implications. In effect, the US government is abetting a profound challenge to American ways by the Islamic mores of Saudi Arabia. McSally, the fighter pilot, explains that putting her in an abaya, requiring that she be escorted and placed in the back seat, has a real psychological effect on military life at US bases in Saudi Arabia, implying that women are inferior and subservient to men.[23]

Large-Scale Obsequiousness

The same obsequiousness that exists on the level of the small-bore and the personal also holds on the grander and better known scale of international politics. Some examples:

- *Oil production and embargo*: Saudi energy policies in 1973–74 helped cause the worst economic decline since the Great Depression; it was met with appeasement and conciliation, without so much as a whisper of bolder action.
- *Lack of cooperation in finding killers of Americans*: American officials meekly accepted in 1995 that the Kingdom executed the (dubious) suspects accused of killing five Americans in Riyadh before US law enforcement officials could interrogate them. A year later, the response was similarly mild about the lack of Saudi cooperation in investigating the murder of American troops at Khobar Towers. After 9/11, it was even worse; as one observer puts it, "The Saudis' cooperation with our efforts to track down the financing of Al-Qaeda appears to be somewhere between minimal and zero."[24]
- *The spread of militant Islam*: "Saudi money—official or not—is behind much of the Islamic-extremist rhetoric and action in the world today," notes Representative Ben Gilman (Republican of New York), then chairman of the House International Relations Committee.[25] The assault on September 11, 2001, was basically Saudi in ideology, personnel, organization and funding—but the US government did not signal a reassessment of policy toward Riyadh, much less raise the idea of suing the Saudis for punitive damages.
- *Islamist institutions in the United States*: US authorities have been lax about the funding of extremist organizations. Only in March 2002, for example, did Federal agents finally get around to raiding sixteen innocuous-looking Saudi-funded institutions such as the Graduate School of Islamic and Social Sciences of Leesburg, Virginia. This problem is widespread and unredressed, as a newspaper editorial from Canada suggests: "[M]any terrorists and terror recruits get their first taste of death-to-the-West Islamic extremism from a Wahhabi imam or centre director in Virginia or London or, presumably, Hamilton or Markham [towns in Canada], whose paycheque is drawn in the Saudi Kingdom. It may not be necessary to add Saudi Arabia to the Axis of Evil, or to invade it. But it will be necessary to engage the Saudi spread of extremism if the war on terrorism is to be won."[26]
- *The Arab-Israeli conflict*: The Bush Administration has pretended that the Abdallah Plan for solving this conflict is a serious proposition, when

it is not just patently ridiculous (demanding that Israel retreat to its 1967 borders) but also offensive (laying out the demographic overwhelming of Israel). Instead of playing unconvincing diplomatic games with Riyadh, the administration should emphasize that the hateful rhetoric and subsidies for suicide bombers must come to an immediate end.

* *Human rights and democracy*: The usual US commitment to these goals seems to wither when Saudi Arabia is involved. The Kingdom's signed commitments to protect the rights of its subjects are virtually ignored, as are such questions as the rule of law, freedom of speech and assembly, the right to travel, women's rights, and religious liberties.

* *Absorbing insults and threats*; A famous case, dating from the 1970s, when Henry Kissinger attended a state dinner in his honor hosted by King Faisal, set the tone. Kissinger recounts how the king informed him that

> Jews and Communists were working now in parallel, now together, to undermine the civilized world as we knew it. Oblivious to my [Jewish] ancestry—or delicately putting me into a special category—Faisal insisted that an end be put once and for all to the dual conspiracy of Jews and Communists. The Middle East outpost of that plot was the State of Israel, put there by Bolshevism for the principal purpose of dividing America from the Arabs.

Kissinger did not confront Faisal but did his best to avoid the whole issue by responding with a question to the king about the palace artwork.[27] Similarly, Crown Prince Abdallah wrote to George W. Bush in August 2001 stating that

> a time comes when peoples and nations part. We are at a crossroads. It is time for the United States and Saudi Arabia to look at their separate interests. Those governments that don't feel the pulse of the people and respond to it will suffer the fate of the Shah of Iran.[28]

This aggressive statement was met not with reproach but with appeasement. And in April 2002, an unnamed but leading Saudi figure warned that to survive, the Kingdom would contemplate joining with America's worst enemies: if reason of state requires that "we move to the right of bin Laden, so be it; to the left of [Libya's ruler Muammar] Qaddafi, so be it; or fly to Baghdad and embrace Saddam like a brother, so be it."[29] The statement appeared prominently in the US press but had no apparent repercussions on policy. More striking yet are the reports from the US-Saudi summit meeting that followed indicating that Abdallah warned Bush that if he won nothing substantive regarding the Arab-Israeli conflict, "our two countries will go their separate ways."[30]

A Matter of Give and Take

What lies behind this pattern of American obsequiousness? Where is the normally robust pursuit of US interests? It is one thing for private companies to bend over backward to please the Saudis, but why does the US government defer to them in so many and in such unique ways?

"Oil" is likely to be the most common explanation proferred, but it does not hold. First, the US government has never cringed before any other major oil supplier as it does to Saudi Arabia. Second, US-Saudi ties have been premised since 1945, when a dying Franklin D. Roosevelt met an aging King Ibn Saud, on an enduring bargain in which Riyadh provides oil and gas and Washington provides security. Because this deal has even more importance for Saudis than Americans—survival versus energy supplies—oil cannot explain why the US side has consistently acted as a supplicant.

Another possible factor is the proclivity of many Americans to strive to tolerate other people's customs and religious beliefs, which in the Saudi case involves such matters as the total covering of women, public executions, and the absence of any pretense of democratic rule. But the lack of reciprocity from the Saudi side, decade after decade, suggests that something else besides an open spirit is at work; no matter how liberal, no one can endure such a one-sided relationship for so long unless there is a payoff.

A hint of that payoff lies in the preemptive quality of some US government measures. Note two cases: The requirement that female military personnel wear the abaya was imposed by Americans, not Saudis; the latter did not even raise the subject. Saudi law only requires Westerners to dress conservatively, not that they wear Saudi garb. Likewise, the investigation of the Air Force-Justice-CACI directive excluding Jews from Saudi Arabia found "no evidence that the restriction was specifically requested by, was required by, or was even known by the Government of Saudi Arabia."[31]

The same preemptive behavior exists among private institutions. Again, note two cases: in the 1959 ARAMCO case, it turned out that the oil company was not compelled by the Saudi government to exclude Jews, but did so anyway as a result of what the court termed "informal statements of State Department underlings."[32] Similarly, the judgment regarding the Baylor College of Medicine found that while college officials informed the two Jewish doctors of problems securing visas for Jews, "Baylor never attempted to substantiate that 'problem,'" leading the court to doubt "the veracity of those assertions." The court also found no evidence supporting the college's contention that the aversion to Jewish doctors in Saudi Arabia "represented the actual position of the Saudi government." To the contrary, it concluded that Michael E. DeBakey, the school's renowned chancellor, failed to obtain "an authoritative statement of the position of the Saudis" until 1983, more than a year after the doctors had initially filed suit. It observed that there was "no evidence that Baylor even attempted to ascertain the official position of the Saudi government on this issue."[33]

In all four cases, Americans in positions of authority over-eagerly imposed regulations they imagined the kingdom would be pleased with—but without checking with it, much less being required by it to take these steps. Why does such a pattern of behavior exist? What could prompt government or hospital staff to run out ahead of the Saudis?

The Saudi ambassador to the United States, Prince Bandar bin Sultan, helpfully hinted in 2002 at an answer in a statement boasting of his success cultivating powerful Americans. "If the reputation . . . builds that the Saudis take care of friends when they leave office," Bandar once observed, "you'd be surprised how much better friends you have who are just coming into office."[34] This admission of effective bribery goes far to explain why the usual laws, regulations and rights do not apply when Saudi Arabia is involved. Hume Horan, himself a former US ambassador to the Kingdom, is the great and noble exception to this pattern. He says this of his former colleagues:

> There have been some people who really do go on the Saudi payroll, and they work as advisers and consultants. Prince Bandar is very good about massaging and promoting relationships like that. Money works wonders, and if you've got an awful lot of it, and a royal title—well, it's amusing to see how some Americans liquefy in front of a foreign potentate, just because he's called a prince.[35]

Over-the-top support of Saudi interests by former ambassador James E. Akins (who criticized Arab governments for not being tougher with Washington and despaired that Arabs did not withdraw their money from US banks) caused him to be described as occasionally appearing "more pro-Arab than the Arab officials."[36]

Several surveys of the post-government careers of ex-US ambassadors to Riyadh all raise eyebrows. Steven Emerson characterizes their behavior as "visceral, overt self-interested sycophancy."[37] The *National Review's* Rod Dreher finds that the number of them "who now push a pro-Saudi line is startling" and concludes that "no other posting pays such rich dividends once one has left it, provided one is willing to become a public and private advocate of Saudi interests."[38] A *National Post* analysis looked at five former ambassadors and found that "they have carved out a fine living insulting their own countrymen while shilling for one of the most corrupt regimes on Earth." If you closed your eyes while listening to their apologies, it goes on, "you would think the person talking held a Saudi passport."[39]

A *Washington Post* account gives some idea of the nature of the "rich dividends" reaped by former officials:

> Americans who have worked with the Saudis in official capacities often remain connected to them when they leave public office, from former president George H. W. Bush, who has given speeches for cash in Saudi Arabia since leaving office, to many previous ambassadors and military officers stationed in the Kingdom. In some cases, these connections have been lucrative. Walter Cutler, who served two tours as the U.S. ambassador in Saudi Arabia, now runs Meridian International Center in Washington, an organization that promotes international understanding through education and exchanges. Saudi donors have been "very supportive" of the center, Cutler said. [Edward] Walker, the former assistant secretary of state for Near Eastern affairs, is president of the Middle East Institute in Washington, which promotes understanding with the Arab world. Its board chairman is former senator Wyche Fowler, ambassador to Riyadh in the second Clinton administration. Saudi contributions covered $200,000 of the institute's $1.5 million budget last year, Walker said.[40]

Nor is this a new problem. Many ex-Washington hands have been paid off by the Kingdom, including not only a bevy of former ambassadors but also such figures as Spiro T. Agnew, Jimmy Carter, Clark Clifford, John B. Connally, and William E. Simon.[41]

The heart of the problem, then, is an all-too-human one: out of personal greed, Americans in positions of authority bend the rules and break with standard policy. In this light, Hunter's report on the three main US government goals in Saudi Arabia begins to make sense: strengthen the Saudi regime, cater to the Saud royal family, and facilitate US exports. All of these fit the rubric of enhancing one's own appeal to the Saudis. So, too, does Hunter's comment that "the U.S. mission is so preoccupied with extraneous duties—entertainment packages for high-level visitors, liquor sales, and handling baggage for VIP visitors" that it has scant time to devote to the proper concerns of an embassy. Likewise, his long list of high-profile ex-officials who visited Saudi

Arabia during his sojourn (Jimmy Carter, George McGovern, Colin Powell, Mack McLarty, Richard Murphy) and "who were feted and presented with medals and gifts at closed ceremonies with the Saudi monarch" also confirms the pattern.[42]

This culture of corruption in the Executive Branch renders it quite incapable of dealing with the Kingdom of Saudi Arabia in the farsighted and disinterested manner that US foreign policy requires. That leaves Congress with the responsibility to fix things. The massive preemptive bribing of American officials requires urgent attention. Steps need to be taken to ensure that the Saudi revolving-door syndrome documented here be made illegal. That might mean that for ten years or more after having extensive contacts with the Kingdom of Saudi Arabia, an official may not receive funds from that source.

Only this way can US citizens regain confidence in those of their officials who deal with one of the world's more important states.

Notes

1. An executive engaged in running the Waco airport, quoted in the *Dallas Morning News*, April 27, 2002.
2. Fox News, March 1, 2002.
3. Cable News Network, April 25, 2002.
4. *Air Force Magazine*, July 2002.
5. Rutherford Institute. June 25, 2002.
6. Nicole Manning, "U.S. Companies Support Gender Segregation in Saudi Arabia," *National NOW Times*, Summer 2002.
7. *USA Today*, May 13, 2002.
8. The State Department remembers the Operation Desert Storm era quite differently—as a time of "U.S. -Saudi cooperation in the areas of cultural accommodation." Here is its idea of balance: "The United States military issued general orders prohibiting the consumption of alcohol and setting guidelines for off-duty behavior and attire. Saudi Arabia accommodated U.S. culture and its military procedures by allowing U.S. servicewomen to serve in their varied roles throughout the Kingdom—a major step for a highly patriarchal society." See "U.S. Department of State Background Note: Saudi Arabia" at http://www.state.gov/outofdate/bgn/saudiarabia/6075.htm.
9. On Hunter, see Martin Edwin Andersen, "Whistle-blowers keep the faith," *Insight*, February 11, 2002.
10. Timothy N. Hunter, "Appeasing the Saudis," *Middle East Quarterly*, Mar. 1996.
11. Letters from Timothy Hunter to the author, June 9, 24, and 25, 2002.
12. Steven Emerson, *The American House of Saud: The Secret Petrodollar Connection* (New York: Franklin Watts, 1985), p. 70.
13. Office of Antiboycott Compliance, Department of Commerce, "CACI/USAF/ DOJ/Hoover/ Alperson/Andrew." For another case that was not litigated, see Journal of Commerce, March 7, 1997.

14. *New York Daily News*, Mar. 10, 1997.
15. Jordan W. Cowman, "U.S. companies doing business abroad must follow U.S. and host country labor and employment laws," *New Jersey Law Journal*, August 4, 1997. Of course, such cases arise in countries other than the United States, too. "A subsidiary of the Manitoba Telephone System, MTS, became embroiled in a controversy in the 1980s when it became known one contract stipulation for upgrading the Saudi telephone system required the exclusion of Jewish MTS employees." *The Gazette* (Montreal), Feb. 7, 2001.
16. 19 Misc. 2d 205; 190 N.Y.S.2d 218; 1959 N.Y. Misc.
17. Emerson, *The American House of Saud*, p. 69.
18. *Ibid.*
19. 805 F.2d 528; 1986 US App.
20. *Roanoke Times*, Feb. 17, 2002.
21. Hunter, "Appeasing the Saudis."
22. Letter from Timothy Hunter to the author, June 24, 2002.
23. *The Washington Post*, Jan. 1, 2002.
24. Michael Barone, *U.S. News & World Report*, June 3, 2002.
25. Associated Press, May 22, 2002.
26. *Edmonton Journal*, May 31, 2002.
27. Henry Kissinger, *Years of Upheaval* (Boston: Little, Brown, 1982), p. 661.
28. *Wall Street Journal*, Oct. 29, 2001.
29. *The New York Times*, Apr. 25, 2002.
30. Confidential sources, Apr. 2002.
31. Office of Antiboycott Compliance, Department of Commerce.
32. 19 Misc. 2d 205; 190 N.Y.S.2d 218; 1959 N.Y. Misc.
33. 805 F.2d 528; 1986 US App.
34. *The Washington Post*, Feb. 11, 2002.
35. Quoted in Rod Dreher, "Their Men in Riyadh," *National Review*, June 17, 2002.
36. Emerson, *The American House of Saud*, p. 250.
37. Emerson, *The American House of Saud*, p. 263.
38. Dreher, "Their Men in Riyadh."
39. Matt Welch, "Shilling for the House of Saud," *The National Post*, Aug. 24, 2002.
40. *The Washington Post*, Feb. 11, 2002.
41. Emerson, *The American House of Saud*, chaps. 7, 13, 19.
42. Hunter, "Appeasing the Saudis."

11

Obituary for Nizar Hamdoon

I first met Nizar Hamdoon in mid-1985, when he was Iraq's immensely popular ambassador in Washington. He promoted the thesis that Iran had started the war with Iraq and bore the onus for its continuation, therefore the US government should help Baghdad. Nizar made these false points with a competence, reasonableness, and self-criticism rare in any diplomat, and extraordinary in one representing a brutal totalitarian thug.

Indeed, Nizar was probably the most skilled diplomat I ever encountered. He never once in my presence praised Saddam Hussein, denigrated the United States, or filibustered his regime's propaganda like the other Iraqi envoys. (What good would that have done with an American audience?) Rather, he granted most his interlocutor's argument and disagreed only at the margins. Thus, he implicitly accepted the virtues of democracy, the existence of Israel, and the horrors of nuclear weapons. He then argued that to achieve these goals meant working with Baghdad, not against it, either by helping it defeat Iran (in the 1980s) or by lifting sanctions (in the 1990s).

Nizar's method brought him great success. During his glory years as Iraqi ambassador in Washington, 1984–87, he had a reach, a public presence, and an impact that fellow ambassadors could only envy.

With me, as with so many others unsympathetic to the regime he represented, Nizar went out of his way to establish a rapport. He telephoned on a regular basis and visited my homes, first in Newport, Rhode Island, then in Philadelphia. When my wife and I traveled to Kuwait in 1987, he arranged a side trip to Baghdad. He invited me to dinner at his Washington residence and in 1992 hosted a bus full of my organization's board members at his mission.

Nizar disappeared from view after he finished his second stint in the United States (as Iraq's United Nations ambassador, from 1992) in 1998. I idly wondered from time to time how he was faring as the US-led war unfolded in March–April 2003; I did not know even if he was still part of the regime. So an e-mail I received on May 15, 2003, just two weeks after major hostilities in Iraq had ended, from "nizarhamdoon@yahoo. com" certainly caught my eye, as did its enigmatic text:

Dear Daniel:

> I have been here in NYC for a while under Chemo treatment. My cell phone if you like to call is 917-325-9252. I will be staying until first week of June.

Thanks, Nizar.

How did he get to the United States and how long had he been in New York? What would he reveal of his career and the regime he worked for now that Saddam Hussein was deposed? I had many questions built up over the nearly twenty years I had known him. Hoping to interview him for the *Middle East Quarterly*, I carried a list of twenty-eight questions and a tape recorder to our meeting on May 21 at (his choice) the Starbucks on the corner of 78th Street and Lexington Avenue in Manhattan.

We talked for nearly one and a half hours. I learned that he had had a medical emergency in March 2003, so he traveled without family to Amman, where after ten days later he received a US medical visa. (°I later learned from the Volcker report investigating corruption in the UN oil-for-food program that Oscar Wyatt Jr., a Texas oil man, covered some of his medical bills.°) He arrived in New York and underwent a chemotherapy treatment, then planned to rejoin his family in Iraq in early June. On arrival in New York, he told me, he moved into the Iraqi ambassador's residence (and his own home during 1992–98) on 80th Street, invited there by the then-Iraqi ambassador to the United Nations, Muhammad ad-Duri. When war broke out and ad-Duri fled the country, Nizar remained, inhabiting just one room, relying on a single local hire to take care of the place.

How could he travel to the United States when his regime was at war with the United States? Nizar said he was not at liberty to speak but would do so in time. The same applied to his experiences in Iraq and his connection to the regime; I had no chance to ask any of the twenty-eight questions burning a hole in my pocket. But he did reply to several of my inquiries in a manner that amplifies the public remarks he made three weeks later to the Middle East Forum.

How could a civilized person like you, I asked him, represent the barbaric regime of Saddam Hussein? He pointed to two factors: fear and loyalty. Fear I understood, but loyalty? Yes, he replied, the ethic of loyalty runs very deep in Iraqi society and even obtains in a case like this. He tried to explain but realized at a certain point I could not understand, and we left it.

Were you tempted to defect? No, he likes the United States but feels rooted in Iraq—the society, the food, the atmosphere—and would not want to live elsewhere.

You took risks in your subtle presentation of the Iraqi case—conceding certain points in order to gain credibility; was this approved by Baghdad? No, and it got him in trouble on occasions. He was constantly instructed to bluster like other ambassadors.

He then told me of a twenty-page personal letter he sent to Saddam Hussein in 1995 in which he told his boss what was on his mind. Why would you send such a letter? Nizar did not offer an explanation. To his surprise, Saddam widely distributed the letter for discussion among the leadership and eventually sent Nizar a personally signed seventy-five-page letter. Why would Saddam Hussein spend a day writing you a letter, I asked incredulously. Nizar shrugged: "That's what he decided to do." In the response, among many other points, Saddam accused Nizar of sending a copy of his letter to the CIA. That should have been the end of your career, at the least, I asked; why wasn't it? Again, Nizar did not convincingly reply; he said that Saddam sensed his loyalty and sincerity, and so did not punish him.

°In 2011, Feisal Amin Rasoul al-Istrabadi, a former Iraqi ambassador to the United Nations, wrote me about this exchange of letters: the head of the secretariat at the Iraqi mission informed him that the gist of Saddam's reply "was that Nizar himself was not entirely innocent of some of the accusations he leveled at Saddam."°

Nizar assured me that he had these letters; and that they and other documents formed an archive he would make public at the right time.

°Nizar Hamdoon was born in Baghdad on May 18, 1944, to a Sunni family with roots in Mosul. He completed Baghdad College (a school run by American Jesuits) in 1960; at the age of fifteen, he joined the Baath party. In 1967 he received his bachelor's degree in architecture and town planning from Baghdad University and did his military service as an air force architect (1968–70). Hamdoon worked at the Baath party headquarters (1970–81), including a stint in Syria, and then served as undersecretary for culture and art in the Ministry of Culture and Information (1981–83).

In November 1983, he was sent to Washington to head the Iraqi interests section. He became Iraq's ambassador to the United States in November 1984 when the two countries resumed full diplomatic relations. (Iraq had severed them in 1967.) In 1988 Hamdoon returned to Baghdad to serve as deputy foreign minister, and in 1992 he was appointed Iraq's ambassador to the United Nations. He was recalled to Baghdad in 1998, and in 1999 became undersecretary of the foreign ministry.°

His career effectively ended in 2001, when a new Iraqi foreign minister pushed him out of the ministry. He was kicked upstairs to the president's office, where he served former foreign minister Tariq Aziz. But it was a purely ceremonial job; Aziz's only foreign portfolio was dealing with the Baath parties abroad and other friendlies. As Nizar oversaw the North American desk, that meant he handled minor-league matters like the anti-sanctions group, Voices in the Wilderness. He spent two hours a day in the office, surfed the Internet there, and went home. But he received his old salary and benefits.

The fact that Saddam Hussein remained on the loose when we met meant that Nizar was both fearful and still burdened with a sense of loyalty to his old patron. In combination, these made him careful about what he said in public. But he raised the idea of giving a talk to the Middle East Forum, which he delivered on June 4, 2003. I believe it was his last public appearance. (An edited text of his presentation and the ensuing discussion was published in the Fall 2003 issue of the *Middle East Quarterly*.)

Nizar Hamdoon died on July 4, 2003, °in New York after a long battle with non-Hodgkin's lymphoma. His remains were returned to Baghdad for burial. He left a wife and two daughters.°

12

What Egypt's President
Sisi Really Thinks

Former air marshal Husni Mubarak, now 86, had ruled Egypt for thirty years when his military colleagues forced him from office in 2011. Three years and many upheavals later, those same colleagues replaced his successor with retired field marshal Abdel Fattah al-Sisi, 59. The country, in short, made a grand round trip, going from military ruler to military ruler, simply dropping down a generation.

This return raises basic questions: After all the hubbub, how much has actually changed? Does Sisi differ from Mubarak, for example, in such crucial matters as attitudes toward democracy and Islam, or is he but a younger clone?

Sisi remains something of a mystery. He plays his cards close to the vest; one observer who watched his presidential inaugural speech on television on June 8 described it as "loaded with platitudes and very long." He left few traces as he zoomed through the ranks in three years, going from director of Military Intelligence and Reconnaissance to become the youngest member of the ruling military council, and then rapidly ascending to chief of staff, defense minister, and president.

Fortunately, a document exists that reveals Sisi's views from well before his presidency: An essay dated March 2006, when he attended the US Army War College in Carlisle Barracks, Pennsylvania. His five-thousand-word English-language term paper, "Democracy in the Middle East," has minimal intrinsic value but holds enormous interest by providing the candid views of an obscure brigadier general soon and unexpectedly to be elected pharaoh of Egypt.

While one cannot discount careerism in a term paper, Sisi's generally assertive and opinionated tone—as well as his negative comments about the United States and the Mubarak regime—suggest that he expressed himself freely.

In the paper, Sisi makes two main arguments: democracy is good for the Middle East; and for it to succeed there many conditions must first be achieved. Sisi discusses other topics as well, which offer valuable insights into his thinking.

Democracy Is Good for the Middle East

Sisi endorses democracy for practical, rather than philosophical, reasons: it just works better than a dictatorship. "Many in the Middle East feel that current and previous autocratic governments have not produced the expected progress." (I have slightly edited his English for the sake of clarity.) Democracy has other benefits, as well: it reduces unhappiness with government and narrows the vast gap between ruler and ruled, both of which he sees contributing to the region's backwardness. In all, democracy can accomplish much for the region and those who promote it "do have an opportunity now in the Middle East."

In parallel, Sisi accepts the free market because it works better than socialism: "many Middle East countries attempted to sustain government-controlled markets instead of free markets and as a result no incentive developed to drive the economy."

It is reasonable, even predictable that General Sisi would view democracy and free markets in terms of their efficacy. But, without a genuine commitment to these systems, will President Sisi carry through with them, even at the expense of his own power and the profits from the socialized military industries run by his former colleagues? His 2006 paper implies only a superficial devotion to democracy; and some of his actions since assuming power (such as returning to appointed rather than elected university deans and chairmen) do not auger well for democracy.

Conditions for Democracy to Succeed in the Middle East

Sisi lays down three requirements for democracy to succeed in the Middle East:

(1) *It must adapt to Islam.* He describes "the religious nature" of the Middle East as "one of the most important factors" affecting the region's politics. Islam makes democracy there so different from its Western prototype that it "may bear little resemblance" to the original. Therefore, it "is not necessarily going to evolve upon a Western template" but "will have its own shape or form coupled with stronger religious ties."

Those religious ties mean that Middle Eastern democracy cannot be secular; separating mosque and state is "unlikely to be favorably received by the vast majority of Middle Easterners," who are devout Muslims. Rather, democracy must be established "upon Islamic beliefs" and "sustain the religious base." The executive, legislative, and judicial branches all must "take Islamic beliefs into consideration when carrying out their duties." Presumably, this translates into the Islamic authorities under President Sisi reviewing proposed laws to safeguard Islamic values, regardless of what the majority of voters wants.

(2) *The West should help, but not interfere.* The West looms large for Sisi, who fears its negative influence even as he seeks its support.

He has many worries: The great powers want a democracy resembling Western institutions rather than accepting a democracy "founded on Islamic beliefs." He interprets the then-named global war on terror as "really just a mask for establishing Western democracy in the Middle East." To meet their energy needs, Westerners "attempt to influence and dominate the region." The wars they started in Iraq and Afghanistan need to be resolved before democracy can take root. Support for Israel raises suspicions about their motives.

Sisi's major concern is US rejection of democracies that "may not be sympathetic to Western interests." He demands that the West not interfere when its adversaries win elections: "The world cannot demand democracy in the Middle East, yet denounce what it looks like because a less than pro-Western party legitimately assumes office." Translation: Do not call President Sisi anti-democratic when he pursues policies Washington dislikes.

But the peoples of the Middle East also need the West. In the economic arena, they are unlikely to succeed "without external support from Western democracies." Accordingly, he pleads for the US government to assist "supportive economic nations in the Middle East, such as Egypt." President Sisi wants American taxpayers to continue footing his bills.

The West is also the answer, in Sisi's view, to the sycophantic and unaccountable Middle East media. "If corruption exists in the government, it is likely to go unreported." Therefore, he wants those in power "to let go of controlling the media." To build a superior press, Sisi looks to the West, specifically to international news organizations and to governments. Inasmuch as President Sisi quickly intimidated the Egyptian media into obsequiousness as soon as he assumed office, it is good to know that, in principle, he appreciates a free press. Westerners who meet with him should unceasingly remind him of this.

(3) *Giving the people more responsibility.* Democracy does not emerge on its own, Sisi asserts, but "needs a good environment—like a reasonable economic situation, educated people, and a moderate understanding of religious issues." The problem in Egypt is that, "the nature of the population has been one of dependence upon and favor from the government." How to break this dependence? "Education and the media are the key enablers toward the establishment of democracy; there must be a shift from state controlled means to population controlled means." General Sisi understood that Egypt needs a politically mature citizenry; but will President Sisi permit it to emerge?

Examining his three preconditions, the first two give Sisi, as ruler, the freedom to act anti-democratically. Only the third component would, in fact, help bring about democracy.

The Middle East as a Unified Region

One unexpected theme that emerges from his paper concerns Sisi's (possibly neo-Nasserist) hope that the Middle East become a single unit: "the Middle East should organize as a region." He wants the Middle East (an area he does not define; one wonders whether Israel would be included) to view itself "much in the same manner as the European Union," implying a customs union, a single currency, freedom of cross-border movement, and a joint foreign policy. He offers this as a goal of free elections: "Democracy in the Middle East . . . must find a unifying theme that draws the Middle East into a unified region."

Clearly, Sisi faces too many pressing domestic issues to try to unify the deeply divided and increasingly anarchic Middle East; should he long remain in power, however, this could become one of his goals and perhaps even take the form of an anti-Muslim Brotherhood alliance under his leadership.

Islamism

Which brings one to the deepest mystery about Sisi: is he an Islamist, someone seeking to apply the Islamic law in all its severity and in its entirety?

Personally pious, he is said to have memorized the Koran. According to the *Financial Times*, "Not only does his wife don the Islamic headscarf now sported by most Egyptian women, but one of his daughters is also said to wear the niqab" (a body and head cover that reveals only the eyes). He became defense minister because the Muslim Brotherhood considered him an ally. Since then, however, he has made himself the mortal enemy of the Muslim Brotherhood while allying with the yet more extreme Salafis, Islamists trying to live as Muhammad did. While Sisi's 2006 essay does not resolve these contradictions, it does offer clues.

Several of his observations about early Islam make it clear that Sisi aligns himself with the Salafis. With them, he recalls the period of Muhammad and the Four Righteous Caliphs (612–660 A.D.) as not only "very special" and "the ideal form of government," but also "the goal for any new form of government." With these early caliphs as models, he envisions Muslims uniting "so that the earliest form of El Kalafa [the caliphate] is reestablished." In passing, he gratuitously denigrates the Shi'is of early Islam (for attempting to offer power "to family members [of Muhammad] rather than to the most qualified leaders").

Other comments of Sisi's, however, criticize Islamists. When an actual caliphate recently declared itself in Syria and Iraq, he responded a week later with unrestrained hostility. Shortly before he submitted his paper in 2006, Hamas, a Muslim Brotherhood offshoot, won a victory in the Palestinian legislative elections, prompting Sisi's mild but critical observation that elected Islamists are likely to face "internal governance challenges down the road." He added that "there is hope that the more moderate religious segments can mitigate extremist measures," although Sisi's current hard line against the Muslim Brotherhood in Egypt suggests that he (along with millions of other Egyptians) has given up any such hope. Sisi even states that Islam as such creates political problems for rulers: "The religious nature of the Middle East creates challenges for the governing authorities."

Anti-Mubarak

Although Sisi represented the Egyptian armed forces at the Army War College, his paper included some brave and accurate statements critical of his country's leadership, even mentioning Mubarak by name:

- *Faux democracy*: "Many autocratic leaders claim to be in favor of democratic ideals and forms of government, but they are leery of relinquishing control to the voting public of their regimes." Also: Middle Eastern governments that claim to be democratic actually "have very tight centralized control and unfairly influence election outcomes through control of the media and outright intimidation."
- *Poor economic policies*: "Excessive government controls and bloated public payrolls stifle individual initiative and tend to solidify the powerbase of ruling political parties. In Egypt under President Sadat, government controls were lifted in an effort to stimulate economic growth; however, these efforts have not blossomed under President Mubarak."

- *Lackey intelligence services*: "The security forces of a nation need to develop a culture that demonstrates commitment to a nation rather than a ruling party."
- *US support for undeserving regimes*: In pursuit of its interests, "America has supported non-democratic regimes and some regimes that were not well respected in the Middle East. Examples include Gulf State regimes, Saudi Arabia, the early Saddam regime, Morocco, Algeria, etc." (One imagines Sisi listing Egypt in a first draft, then—for caution's sake—removing it.)

In addition to showing the courage to criticize his tyrant-boss, if only in an academic term paper, these perceptive comments indicate President Sisi's own deepest aspirations for Egypt—as well as what was *not* on his mind, such as reducing the Islamist threat or the role of the military in Egypt's economy

Conclusion

The pre-political brigadier-general of 2006 anticipated the somewhat contradictory chief of staff, defense minister, and president. Sisi is a pious Muslim ambivalent about Islamists, a fan of the caliphate in theory who rejects it in practice, a critic of Mubarak's who permitted the revival of his political party, a fan of democracy who "wins" 97 percent of the vote, a military officer theorizing on forms of democracy, a fan of independent media who allows journalists to be convicted of terrorism charges, a critic of tyranny who encourages adulation of himself.

Sisi, clearly, remains a work in progress, a fifty-nine-year-old still trying to discover who he is and what he thinks even as he rules a country of eighty-six million. On-the-job training is literal in his case. Amid the political brush fires and exigencies of present-day Egypt, the gist of his eight-year old ideas are likely to emerge as dominant: a heavily conditional form of democracy, at once safe for Islam and from Islam, experiments to loosen controls over the intelligence services, the economy, education and the media, varying tactics toward Islamists, as well as a revived attempt to make the region of the Middle East a world power.

But will he have the time and opportunity to achieve these many goals? Unless he shows a hitherto-unseen competence, his chances are slim.

Outside powers can help by cooperating with Sisi on immediate concerns (arms, counterterrorism, and intelligence) and pressuring him on longer-term issues (military business operations, the rule of law, and human rights).

Part III

Islam in Modern Life

13

Can Islam Be Reformed?

Islam currently represents a backward, aggressive, and violent force. Must it remain this way, or can it be reformed and become moderate, modern, and good-neighborly? Can Islamic authorities formulate an understanding of their religion that grants full rights to women and non-Muslims as well as freedom of conscience to Muslims, that accepts the basic principles of modern finance and jurisprudence, and that does not seek to impose the Shari'a (Islamic law) or establish a caliphate?

A growing body of analysts believe that no, the Muslim faith cannot do these things, that these negative features are inherent to Islam and immutably part of its makeup. Asked if she agrees with my formulation that "radical Islam is the problem, but moderate Islam is the solution," the writer Ayaan Hirsi Ali replied, "He's wrong. Sorry about that." She and I stand in the same trench, fighting for the same goals and against the same opponents, but we disagree on this vital point.

My argument has two parts. First, the essentialist position of these analysts is wrong; and second, that a reformed Islam can emerge.

Arguing against Essentialism

To state that Islam can never change is to assert that the Koran and Hadith, which constitute the religion's core, must always be understood in the same way. But to articulate this position is to reveal its error, for nothing human abides forever. Everything, including the reading of sacred texts, changes over time. Everything has a history. And everything has a future that will be unlike its past.

Only by failing to account for human nature and by ignoring more than a millennium of actual changes in the Koran's interpretation can one claim that the Koran has been understood identically over time. Changes have applied in such matters as jihad, slavery, usury, the principle of "no compulsion in religion," and the role of women. Moreover, the many important interpreters of Islam over the past 1,400 years—ash-Shafi'i, al-Ghazali, Ibn Taymiya, Rumi, Shah Waliullah,

181

and Ruhollah Khomeini come to mind—disagreed deeply among themselves about the content of the message of Islam.

However central the Koran and Hadith may be, they are not the totality of Islam; the accumulated experience of Muslim peoples from Morocco to Indonesia and beyond matters no less. To dwell on Islam's scriptures is akin to interpreting the United States solely through the lens of the Constitution; ignoring the country's history would lead to a distorted understanding.

Put differently, medieval Muslim civilization excelled and today's Muslims lag behind in nearly every index of achievement. But if things can get worse, they can also get better. Likewise, in my own career, I witnessed Islamism rise from minimal beginnings when I entered the field in 1969 to the great powers it enjoys today; if Islamism can thus grow, it can also decline.

How might that happen?

The Medieval Synthesis

The Shari'a's many untenable demands on Muslims makes it key to Islam's role in public life. Running a government with the minimal taxes permitted by Shari'a has proved to be unsustainable; and how can one run a financial system without charging interest? A penal system that requires four men to view an adulterous act *in flagrante delicto* is impractical. Shar'i prohibition on warfare against fellow Muslims is impossible for all to live up to; indeed, I estimate that roughly three-quarters of all warfare waged by Muslims has been directed against other Muslims. Likewise, the insistence on perpetual jihad against non-Muslims demands too much of Muslims.

To get around these and other unrealistic demands, premodern Muslims developed certain legal fig leaves that allowed for the relax-ation of Islamic provisions without directly violating them. Jurists came up with *hiyal* (tricks) and other means by which the letter of the law could be fulfilled while negating its spirit. For example, wars against fellow Muslims were renamed jihad even as the men of religion devised mechanisms to live in harmony with non-Muslim states. The double sale (*bai al-inah*) of an item permits the purchaser to pay a disguised form of interest. Civil codes supplemented the Shari'a so as to maintain order.

This compromise between Shari'a and reality amounted to what I have dubbed Islam's "medieval synthesis." This synthesis translated Islam from a body of abstract, infeasible demands into a workable system.

In practical terms, it toned down the Shari'a and created an operational code of law. Shari'a could now be sufficiently applied without Muslims being subjected to its more stringent demands. Kecia Ali, of Boston University, notes the dramatic contrast between formal and applied law in *Marriage and Slavery in Early Islam*, quoting other specialists:

> One major way in which studies of law have proceeded has been to "compare doctrine with the actual practice of the court." As one scholar discussing scriptural and legal texts notes, "Social patterns were in great contrast to the 'official' picture presented by these 'formal' sources." Studies often juxtapose flexible and relatively fair court outcomes with an undifferentiated and sometimes harshly patriarchal textual tradition of jurisprudence. We are shown proof of "the flexibility within Islamic law that is often portrayed as stagnant and draconian."

While the medieval synthesis worked over the centuries, it never overcame a fundamental weakness: It is not comprehensively rooted in or derived from the foundational, constitutional texts of Islam. Based on compromises and half measures, it always remained vulnerable to challenge by purists. Indeed, premodern Muslim history featured many such challenges, including the Almohad movement in twelfth-century North Africa and the Wahhabi movement in eighteenth-century Arabia. In each case, purist efforts eventually subsided and the medieval synthesis reasserted itself, only to be challenged anew by purists. This alternation between pragmatism and purism characterizes Muslim history, contributing to its instability.

The Challenge of Modernity

This de facto solution broke down with the arrival of modernity imposed by the Europeans, conventionally dated to Napoleon's attack on Egypt in 1798. This challenge pulled Muslims in opposite directions over the next two centuries, to Westernization or Islamization.

Muslims impressed with Western achievements sought to minimize Shari'a and replace it with Western ways in such areas as the nonestablishment of religion and equality of rights for women and non-Muslims. The founder of modern Turkey, Kemal Atatürk (1881–1938), symbolizes this effort. Until about 1970, it appeared to be the inevitable Muslim destiny, with resistance to Westernization looking rearguard and futile.

But that resistance proved deep and ultimately triumphant. Atatürk had few successors and his Republic of Turkey is marching back to Shari'a. Westernization, it turned out, looked stronger than it really was because it tended to attract visible and vocal elites while the masses generally held back and kept silent. Starting around 1930, the reluctant elements began organizing themselves and developing their own positive program, especially in Algeria, Egypt, Iran, and India. Rejecting Westernization and all its works, they argued for the full and robust application of Shari'a such as they imagined had been the case in the earliest days of Islam.

Though rejecting the West, these movements—which are called Islamist—modeled themselves on the surging totalitarian ideologies of their time, Fascism and Communism. Islamists borrowed many assumptions from these ideologies, such as the superiority of the state over the individual, the acceptability of brute force, and the need for a cosmic confrontation with Western civilization. They also quietly borrowed technology, especially military and medical, from the West.

Through creative, hard work, Islamist forces quietly gained strength over the next half century, finally bursting into power and prominence with the Iranian revolution of 1978–79 led by the anti-Atatürk, Ayatollah Khomeini (1902–89). This dramatic event, and its achieved goal of creating an Islamic order, widely inspired Islamists, who in the subsequent thirty-five years have made great progress, transforming societies and applying Shari'a in novel and extreme ways. For example, in Iran, the Shiite regime has hanged homosexuals from cranes and forced Iranians in Western dress to drink from latrine cans, and in Afghanistan, the Taliban regime has torched girls' schools and music stores. The Islamists' influence has reached the West itself, where one finds an increasing number of women wearing hijabs, niqabs, and burqas.

Although spawned as a totalitarian model, Islamism has shown much greater tactical adaptability than either Fascism or Communism. The latter two ideologies rarely managed to go beyond violence and coercion. But Islamism, led by figures such as Turkey's Premier Recep Tayyip Erdoğan (1954–) and his Justice and Development Party (AKP), has explored nonrevolutionary forms of Islamism. Since it was legitimately voted into office in 2002, the AKP gradually has undermined Turkish secularism with remarkable deftness by working within the country's established democratic structures, practicing good government, and excluding the military, long the guardian of Turkish secularism, from politics.

Islamists are on the march today, but their ascendance is recent and offers no guarantees of longevity. Indeed, like other radical utopian ideologies, Islamism will lose its appeal and decline in power. Certainly the 2009 and 2013 revolts against Islamist regimes in Iran and Egypt, respectively, point in that direction, °as do the ferocious battles between Sunni and Shi'i Islamists in the killing fields of Syria and Iraq.°

Toward a Modern Synthesis

If Islamism is to be defeated, anti-Islamist Muslims must develop an alternative vision of Islam and an attractive explanation for what it means to be a Muslim. In doing so, they can draw on the past, especially the reform efforts from the century 1850–1950, to develop a "modern synthesis" comparable to the medieval model. This synthesis would choose among Shar'i precepts and render Islam compatible with modern values. It would accept gender equality, coexist peacefully with unbelievers, and reject the aspiration of a universal caliphate, among other steps.

Here, Islam can profitably be compared with the two other major monotheistic religions. A half millennium ago, Jews, Christians, and Muslims all broadly agreed that enforced labor was acceptable and that paying interest on borrowed money was not. Eventually, after bitter and protracted debates, Jews and Christians changed their minds on these two issues (think of the US civil war); today, no Jewish or Christian voices endorse slavery or condemn the payment of reasonable interest on loans.

Among Muslims, however, these debates have only begun. Even if formally banned in Qatar in 1952, Saudi Arabia in 1962, and Mauritania in 1980, slavery still exists in these and other majority-Muslim countries (especially Sudan and Pakistan). Some Islamic authorities even claim that a pious Muslim must endorse slavery. Vast financial institutions worth possibly as much as $1 trillion have developed over the past forty years to enable observant Muslims to pretend to avoid either paying or receiving interest on money, ("pretend" because the Islamic banks merely disguise interest with subterfuges such as service fees.)

Reformist Muslims must do better than their medieval predecessors and ground their interpretation in both scripture and the sensibilities of the age. For Muslims to modernize their religion they must emulate their fellow monotheists and adapt their religion with regard to slavery and interest, the treatment of women, the right to leave Islam, criminal punishments, and much else. When a reformed, modern Islam emerges it will no longer endorse unequal female rights, the dhimmi status, jihad, or suicide terrorism, nor will it require the death penalty for adultery, breaches of family honor, blasphemy, and apostasy.

Already in this young century, a few positive signs in this direction can be discerned. Note some developments concerning women:

- Saudi Arabia's Shura Council has responded to rising public outrage over child marriages by setting the age of majority at eighteen. Though this doesn't end child marriages, it moves toward abolishing the practice.
- Turkish clerics have agreed to let menstruating women attend mosque and pray next to men.
- The Iranian government has nearly banned the stoning of convicted adulterers.
- Women in Iran have won broader rights to sue their husbands for divorce.
- A conference of Muslim scholars in Egypt deemed clitoridectomies contrary to Islam and, in fact, punishable.
- A key Indian Muslim institution, Darul Uloom Deoband, issued a fatwa against polygamy.

Other notable developments, not specifically about women, include:

- The Saudi government abolished *jizya* (the practice of enforcing a poll tax on non-Muslims).
- An Iranian court ordered the family of a murdered Christian to receive the same compensation as that of a Muslim victim.
- Scholars meeting at the International Islamic Fiqh Academy in Sharjah have started to debate and challenge the call for apostates to be executed.

All the while, individual reformers churn out ideas, if not yet for adoption then to stimulate thought. For example, Nadin al-Badir, a Saudi female journalist, provocatively suggested that Muslim women have the same right as men to marry up to four spouses. She prompted a thunderstorm, including threats of lawsuits and angry denunciations, but she spurred a needed debate, one unimaginable in prior times.

Like its medieval precursor, the modern synthesis will remain vulnerable to attack by purists, who can point to Muhammad's example and insist on no deviation from it. But, having witnessed what Islamism, whether violent or not, has wrought, there is reason to hope that Muslims will reject the dream of reestablishing a medieval order and be open to compromise with modern ways. Islam need not be a fossilized medieval mentality; it is what today's Muslims make of it.

Policy Implications

What can those, Muslim and non-Muslim alike, who oppose Shari'a, the caliphate, and the horrors of jihad, do to advance their aims?

For anti-Islamist Muslims, the great burden is to develop not just an alternative vision to the Islamist one but an alternative movement to Islamism. The Islamists reached their position of power and influence through dedication and hard work, through generosity and selflessness. Anti-Islamists must also labor, probably for decades, to develop an ideology as coherent and compelling as that of the Islamists, and then spread it. Scholars interpreting sacred scriptures and leaders mobilizing followers have central roles in this process.

Non-Muslims can help a modern Islam move forward in two ways: first, by resisting all forms of Islamism—not just the brutal extremism of an Osama bin Laden, but also the stealthy, lawful, political movements such as Turkey's AKP. Erdoğan is less ferocious than Bin Laden, but he is more effective and no less dangerous. Whoever values free speech, equality before the law, and other human rights denied or diminished by Shari'a must consistently oppose any hint of Islamism.

Second, non-Muslims should support moderate and Westernizing anti-Islamists. Such figures are weak and fractured today and face a daunting task, but they do exist, and they represent the only hope for defeating the menace of global jihad and Islamic supremacism, then replacing it with an Islam that does not threaten civilization.

14

You Need Beethoven
to Modernize

It is possible to modernize without Westernizing? This is the dream of despots around the world. Leaders as diverse as Mao on the Left and Khomeini on the Right seek a high-growth economy and a powerful military—without the pesky distractions of democracy, the rule of law, and the whole notion of the pursuit of happiness. They welcome American medical and military technology but reject its political philosophy or popular culture. Technology shorn of cultural baggage is their ideal.

Sadly for them, fully reaping the benefits of Western creativity requires an immersion into the Western culture that produced it. Modernity does not exist by itself, but is inextricably attached to its makers. High rates of economic growth depend not just on the right tax laws, but on a population versed in the basics of punctuality, the work ethic, and delayed gratification. The flight team for an advanced jet bomber cannot be plucked out of a village but needs to be steeped into an entire worldview. Political stability requires a sense of responsibility that only civil society can inculcate. And so forth.

Western classical music proves this point with special clarity, precisely because it is so irrelevant to modernization. Playing the Kreuzer Sonata adds nothing to one's GDP; enjoying an operetta does not enhance one's force projection. And yet, to be fully modern means mastering Western music; competence at Western music, in fact, closely parallels a country's wealth and power, as the experiences of two civilizations, Muslim and Japanese, show. Muslim reluctance to accept Western music foreshadows a general difficulty with modernity; Japanese mastery of every style from classical to jazz helps explain everything from a strong yen to institutional stability.

Muslims

Among Muslims, choice of music represents deep issues of identity.

Secularist Muslims tend to welcome European and American music, seeing it as a badge of liberation and culture. Ziya Gökalp, the leading theorist of Turkish secular nationalism, wrote in the early 1920s that Turks

> face three kinds of music today: Eastern music, Western music, and folk music. Which one of them belongs to our nation? We saw that Eastern music is both deathly and non-national. Folk music is our national culture, Western music is the music of our new civilization. Neither of the latter can be foreign to us.[1]

As Turkish secularists find themselves under siege, sold-out crowds turn out for concerts featuring Western classical music. In the words of a reporter, these have "become a symbolic rallying point for defenders of Turkish secularism."[2] In an event rich with symbolism, the Turkish embassy in Tehran gave a two-hour concert of Western classical music in late December 1997, in tribute to the forthcoming (Christian) new year.[3] Few cultural occasions could quite so sharply delineate the contrasting visions of Atatürk and Khomeini. °Fazıl Say is both one of Turkey's leading classical pianist and composer as well as one of the country's most outspoken secularists.°

In contrast, Islamists, who nurse an abiding suspicion of the West, worry that its music has an insidious effect on Muslims; for them, merely listening to Western music suggests disloyalty to Islam. When Necmettin Erbakan was prime minister of Turkey in 1996–97, he cut back on dance ensembles, symphony orchestras, and other Western-style organizations. Instead, he fought to increase funding for groups upholding traditional musical forms. A speaker at an Islamist rally in Istanbul flattered his audience by telling them, "This is the real Turkey. This is not the aimless crowd that goes out to see [sic] the Ninth Symphony."[4]

An Iranian newspaper published a poem that characterizes the opposite of the downtrodden, faithful Iranians killed by Iraqi troops as an audience of classical music buffs—women with "pushed-back scarves" (i.e., who resist Islamic modesty) and men with "protruding bellies" (i.e., who profit from the black market). The same poem, titled "For Whom do the Violin Bows Move?" argues that concerts of Mozart and Beethoven promote the "worm of monarchic culture."[5] Anyone who listens to *Eine Kleine Nachtmusik*, in other words, must be a traitor to the Islamic republic. Or to Islam itself: naming the very same composers, a Tunisian claims that "the treason of an Arab . . . begins when he enjoys listening to Mozart or Beethoven."[6]

If eighteenth-century composers so rile Islamists, what do they think of rock and rap music? American popular music epitomizes the values that Muslims find most reprehensible about Western culture—the celebration of individualism, youth, hedonism, and unregulated sexuality. The Pakistani Islamist group Hezbollah singled out Michael Jackson and Madonna as cultural "terrorists" who aspire to destroy Islamic civilization. The group's spokesman explained this fear:

> Michael Jackson and Madonna are the torchbearers of American society, their cultural and social values . . . that are destroying humanity. They are ruining the lives of thousands of Muslims and leading them to destruction, away from their religion, ethics and morality.

Hezbollah finished with a call for the two Americans to be brought to trial in Pakistan.[7]

The Hezbollah statement points to the reasons why Islamists mistrust Western music: it demoralizes Muslims and distracts them from the serious requirements of their faith. Ahmad al-Qattan, a Palestinian preacher living in Kuwait, finds that Western music "involves pleasure and ecstasy, similar to drugs" and elaborates:

> I ask a lot of people, "When you listen to Michael Jackson, or Beethoven, or Mozart, what do you feel?"
>
> They tell me: "Oh, I feel my heart torn from the inside."
> I say, "To that extent?"
>
> They tell me: "Yes, by God, to that extent. I fell that all of a sudden I am flying. One moment I am crying, the next moment I am laughing, then dancing, then I am committing suicide."
>
> Our God, we seek refuge with You from singing and its evils.[8]

Ayatollah Khomeini had similar views, as he explained to an Italian journalist:

> *Khomeini*: Music dulls the mind, because it involves pleasure and ecstasy, similar to drugs. Your music I mean. Usually your music has not exalted the spirit, it puts it to sleep. And it destructs [*sic*]

our youth who become poisoned by it, and then they no longer care about their country.

Oriana Fallaci: Even the music of Bach, Beethoven, Verdi?

Khomeini: I do not know these names.

But then, unexpectedly perhaps, Khomeini softens his condemnation: "If their music does not dull the mind, they will not be prohibited. Some of your music is permitted. For example, marches and hymns for marching. . . . Yes, but your marches are permitted."[9] Others join Khomeini in making an exception for marching music. Qattan, for example, distinguishes between degenerate and useful music: "No Mozart and no Michael Jackson, no singing and no instruments, only war drums."[10] Islamists allow the ecstasy that Western music can create only if it helps march youth to their deaths.[11] The author of an advice column in a Los Angeles Muslim weekly concedes that "Music with soft and good tunes, and melodious songs with pure words and concepts are acceptable in Islam," provided that this does not lead to "the mixing of men and women."[12]

(In contrast, the Turkish authorities, marching to a different drummer as is so often the case, rely on classical music to quiet their forces. The so-called "Steel Force" units, the baton-swinging riot police notorious for their tough tactics against street protesters, are forced to listen to Mozart and Beethoven in their buses on the way to operations as a way to calm them down.)[13]

The King Fahd Cultural Center, a magnificent concert hall seating three thousand at the perimeter of Riyadh, Saudi Arabia, symbolizes the Islamist debate on permissible music. Shortly before his death in 1975, King Faisal approved the building of this center as part of the recreational facilities to turn Riyadh, his capital, into a handsome modern city. Completed in 1989 at a cost of $140 million, it boasts such lavish touches as the finest marble and precious woods, not to speak of a state-of-the-art laser lighting system, and a hydraulic stage.

But the hall °did not stage an event for almost two decades.° A foreign diplomat who managed to visit the mothballed facility found that a full-time staff of 180 has for almost a decade maintained the building and its gardens in mint condition. This has meant not just tending the flower beds but air-conditioning the facility all year around so that the delicate woods on the interior not deteriorate. Why was the cultural center not used? Because it offended the strict Islamic sensibilities prevalent in

Saudi Arabia. According to one report, on hearing about Western-style music to be played by mixed casts (meaning men and women) to mixed audiences, the country's religious leaders "went berserk."[14]

°Finally, in May 2008, music was played in the Fahd Center when the German embassy sponsored a free concert by the Artis Piano Quartet. This, the first classical performance held in public in Saudi Arabia, included works by Mozart, Brahms, and Paul Juon and was, not surprisingly, attended by a mostly expatriate audience. Not only was the audience mixed gender, but one couple held hands and a man put his arm around a woman's shoulders—not everyday public occurrences in Saudi Arabia. The quartet's pianist, a woman, considered performing in an abaya but instead wore a long green top with black trousers.[15]

A year later, the French embassy sponsored a women-only concert in Riyadh, with operatic soprano Isabelle Poulenard, a female accompanist, and a female audience. Although canceled two days before the event, the performance took place once the politicians prevailed over the religious authorities.° The saga of Saudi music illustrates the ongoing debate about Western music among Islamists. King Faisal, no slouch in his Islamic faith, thought it a permissible pleasure, but the Saudi religious authorities deemed otherwise.

The Iranian leadership is also inconsistent. Ali Hoseyni Khamene'i, Iran's supreme leader, deems "the promotion of music . . . not compatible with the goals of the Islamic system," so he prohibited "any swing music that is for debauchery," even when played in separate-sex parties.[16] °Nonetheless, some years later, the Tehran Symphony Orchestra went on a tour across Europe, playing bombastic Iranian pseudo-classical music.[17]° Egypt's leading television preacher, Sheikh Muhammad ash-Sha'rawi, went further and condemned Muslims who fall asleep to Western classical music rather than a recording of Koranic recital. Inspired by his words, Islamist hotheads in Upper Egypt stormed a concert and broke musical instruments, leading to their arrest.

With such attitudes prevalent, it is hardly surprising that Muslim practitioners of Western music have achieved little.[18] As the historian Bernard Lewis notes, "Though some talented composers and performers from Muslim countries, especially from Turkey, have been very successful in the Western world, the response to their kind of music at home is still relatively slight."[19] They enjoy neither renown or influence outside of their native countries, and even there remain minor figures.

Japan

How different is Japan! True, the early reactions to Western music were adverse: on hearing a child in song in Hawaii, Norimasa Muragaki, a member of the very first Japanese embassy to the United States in 1860, compared the sound to "a dog howling late at night."[20] Within a few years, however, Japanese heard Western music much more favorably, to the point that the music drew some individuals into Western religion. In 1884, Shoichi Toyama argued that "Christianity ought to be adopted for, first, the benefit of progress in music, second, the development of compassion for fellow men and harmonious cooperation, and third, social relations between men and women."[21] Note that he lists music first.

Before long, some Japanese discovered that Western music expressed their feeling far better than anything in their own tradition. As he left French soil, the leading writer Nagai Kafu (1879–1959) mused wistfully on the beauty of French culture:

> No matter how much I wanted to sing Western songs, they were all very difficult. Had I, born in Japan, no choice but to sing Japanese songs? Was there a Japanese song that expressed my present sentiment—a traveler who had immersed himself in love and the arts in France but was now going back to the extreme end of the Orient where only death would follow monotonous life? . . . I felt totally forsaken. I belonged to a nation that had no music to express swelling emotions and agonized feelings.[22]

Kafu here describes emotions almost entirely unknown to Muslims.

The local musical tradition engages in an intense give and take with Western music. Woodblocks, a traditional Japanese instrument, are a standard of jazz percussion. Traditional Japanese music has influenced many Western composers, John Cage probably the most directly so. The Suzuki Method, which applies the traditional Japanese techniques of rote training (*hiden*) to children learning the violin, has won a substantial following in the West. Yamaha sells over two hundred thousand pianos a year and is the world's largest maker of musical instruments.

Conversely, European classical and American popular music have become part of the Japanese scene. Tokyo has nine professional orchestras and three operas, giving it the highest mass of European classical music talent in the world. Seiji Ozawa, music director of the Boston Symphony Orchestra, rates as the most renowned of Japanese conductors. Classical performers with wide reputations include pianists Aki and Yugi Takahasi and percussionist Stomu Yamashita.

Though Japanese composers are yet little known outside Japan, their pace of activity is considerable. Toru Takemitsu, who makes a specialty of exploring timbre, texture, and everyday sounds in both European and Japanese media, is perhaps the most renowned internationally. Akira Miyoshi composes classic Western music. Toshi Ichiyanagi, Jo Kondo, Teruyaki Noda, and Yuji Takahashi write in an avant-garde manner. Shinichiro Ikebe, Minoru Miki, Makato Moroi, and Katsutoshi Naga-sawa write for traditional Japanese instruments. The marimbist Keiko Abe is the best known of classical Japanese musicians and Toshiko Akiyoshi the best known of jazz players.

European classical music has shed its foreign quality in Japan, becoming fully indigenous. In this, Japan resembles the United States, another country that has imported nearly all of its classical music. Just as Americans have adapted the music to their own tastes and customs—playing the 1812 Overture on the Fourth of July, for example—so have the Japanese. Thus does Beethoven's Ninth Symphony serve as the anthem of the Christmas and New Year's season. Not only do the country's leading orchestras play the symphony over and over again during December, but gigantic choruses (numbering up to ten thousand participants) rehearse for months before bellowing out the *Ode to Joy* in public performances.

As for pop music, the Japanese—like nearly all the world—idolize American pop stars and grow their own local talent. But more interesting is their intense engagement with jazz. So large is the Japanese jazz market that it affects music produced in the United States. Jazz coffee shops (which play music on state-of-the-art equipment) have proliferated, and Japan hosts numerous international jazz festivals each year. *Japanese Swing Journal* sells 400,000 copies a month (compared to only 110,000 copies of the best-known American publication, *Downbeat*) and roughly half of some American jazz albums are bought by Japanese. Indeed, according to one American producer, Michael Cuscuna of Blue Note Records, "Japan almost singlehandedly kept the jazz record business going during the late 1970s. Without the Japanese market, a lot of independent jazz labels probably would have folded, or at least stopped releasing new material."[23] This is too big a market to lose, so American and other artists must increasingly pay attention to Japanese taste.

As for Japanese creativity, the results here have been modest until now—composers and musicians do little more than imitate the styles of foreigners—but the existence of a large and increasingly sophisticated home market offers fertile ground for Japanese musicians to experiment and then to lead. Attempts to combine jazz with traditional Japanese music have begun; these blendings are likely to influence jazz as much as they already have architecture and clothing. It seems safe to predict that the Japanese before long will become a major force in jazz.

The Japanese give musically in other ways too. The *karaoke* machine plays instrumental versions of popular songs and permits a bar patron to accompany the music as though he were an accomplished singer, providing a good time for all. Not only has *karaoke* has become an amusement staple worldwide, but the characteristic Japanese-style bar (with its hostesses, a mama-san, and *karaoke* microphone) has proliferated in the West. *Karaoke* machines are sold in Sears Roebuck stores and have won a large and cheerful, if slightly tipsy following.

Conclusion

°The connection of Beethoven to modernity applies elsewhere too. Lawrence Klepp writes, for example, about Beethoven in China:

> Toward the end of the Chinese Cultural Revolution, in the mid-1970s, the routine attacks on revisionists and running dogs of imperialism were briefly interrupted by a strident anti-Beethoven campaign. A friend of mine who was a schoolgirl in Shanghai at the time remembers that the reeducation sessions demanded particularly resolute striving against the Fifth Symphony, because the dramatic opening chords had been interpreted as fate knocking on the door, and the bourgeois concept of fate was obsolete. The revolutionary will of the people, reinforced by the collective recital of Chairman Mao's thoughts, overcame all inevitability and could accomplish anything.[24°]

Muslim and Japanese responses with Western music symbolize their larger encounters with Western civilization. Muslims have historically approached the West warily, fearful of losing their identity. This prevents them from immersing themselves in Western learning or gaining the needed skills in technology and business. They remain permanently in arrears, coping with one wave of Western influence after another, barely keeping up and exerting virtually no influence over the West.

The Japanese do things very differently. First, they throw themselves wholeheartedly into the new subject, not fearing the loss of their own identity. Second, they acquire skills, matching and even beating the West at its own game; what the Tokyo orchestras are to music, Toyota and Nissan are to cars. Third, Japanese evolve original customs of their own, either based in their traditions (*karaoke*) or an amalgam of cultures (Beethoven's Ninth for New Year's). Finally, they develop techniques that Westerners adopt; the Suzuki Method in music parallels the just-in-time system in car manufacturing (*kanban*). They have absorbed Western civilization in its entirety, discarded what does not interest them, taken what does, and mastered it.

Thus does the response to Western music exemplify the whole of a civilization's experience with modernity. Its lack of utility makes it all the more useful as an indicator of achievement. Why this connection? Because, as Lewis observes, "Music, like science, is part of the inner citadel of Western culture, one of the final secrets to which the newcomer must penetrate."[25] Music represents the challenge of modernity: competence in this arena implies an ability to deal with whatever else the West might serve up. Muslim resistance to accepting music from the West represents its larger unwillingness, whereas the Japanese have truly entered the inner citadel. In short, whoever would flourish must play Beethoven as well as Westerners do.

Notes

1. "Milli Musiki," in Ziya Gökalp, *Türkçülügün Esaslari*, edited by Mehmet Kaplan, 2d ed. (Istanbul: Milli Egitim Basïmevi, 1972), pp. 146–47.
2. *The New York Times*, July 28, 1997.
3. *Turkish Daily News*, Dec. 29, 1997.
4. Ibid.
5. Quoted in Robin Wright, *In the Name of God: The Khomeini Decade* (New York: Simon & Schuster, 1989), p. 192.
6. Al-Wasti, cited by Norman Daniel in *Euro-Arab Dialogue: The Relations Between the Two Cultures*, edited by Derek Hopwood (London: Croom Helm, 1985), p. 88.
7. Ne'matullah Khan, *The Philadelphia Inquirer*, Feb. 13, 1995.
8. Quoted in "Campaign against the Arts," *TransState Islam*, Summer 1995, p. 16.
9. Oriana Fallaci, "An Interview with Khomeini," *The New York Times Magazine*, October 7, 1979.
10. Ahmad al-Qattan, *Hukm al-Islam fi'l-Ghina*, a tape-recorded sermon from a mosque in Kuwait.
11. As an aside, it is interesting to note that marches are the only Western music significantly influenced by the Middle East: Gypsies introduced Turkish—or "Janissary"—music to Europe in the eighteenth century. The Austrian army appears to have been the first to adopt this genre. It involved exotic new uniforms and such new percussion instruments as tambourines, triangles, cymbals, bass drums, and—suggestively—crescents. Accented grace notes added to the exoticism. Soon after, these elements entered the orchestra too; Mozart first used Turkish-style music in a sketch dating from 1772 and "Turkish" effects are especially prominent in his *Abduction from the Seraglio* as well as the finale to Beethoven's Ninth Symphony. In a sense, then, with marching music the Middle East is allowing back in its own innovation.

12.   Muzammil H. Siddiqi, „Shab-e-Barat and Mehndi," *Pakistan Link*, Dec. 22, 1995.

13.   Reuters, Mar. 11, 1998.

14.   *The Washington Post*, Jan. 14, 1997.

15.   Donna Abu-Nasr. Associated Press, May 5, 2008.

16.   *Sobh*, August-September 1996. Text in *Akhbaar Ruz*, Aug. 28, 1996.

17.   *The New York Times*, Feb. 4, 2010

18.   °The one notable exception are the bebop jazz players, black American converts to Islam in the 1950s and 1960s, including Art Blakey, Ahmad Jamal, Yusef Lateef, Dakota Staton, and McCoy Tyner.°

19.   Bernard Lewis, *The Muslim Discovery of Europe* (New York: W. W. Norton, 1982), p. 274.

20.   Text in Donald Keene, *Modern Japanese Diaries: The Japanese at Home and Abroad as Revealed Through Their Diaries* (New York: Henry Holt, 1995).

21.   Quoted in Donald H. Shively, "The Japanization of the Middle Meiji," in Donald H. Shively, ed., *Tradition and Modernization in Japanese Culture* (Princeton, N.J.: Princeton University Press, 1971), p. 92.

22.   Nagai Kafu, *Furansu Monogatori* (Tokyo, 1909), trans. by Mitsoku Iriye and excerpted in William H. McNeill and Mitsuko Iriye, eds., *Modern Asia and Africa* (New York: Oxford University Press, 1971), p. 169.

23.   *The Wall Street Journal*, Jan. 7, 1988.

24.   A review of Harvey Sachs, *The Ninth: Beethoven and the World of 1824* (Random House), *The Weekly Standard*, June 28, 2010. "Spengler" [David P. Goldman], "China's six-to-one advantage over the US," *Asia Times*, Dec. 2, 2008, looks at China in a way complementary to my assessment of Japan and the Muslim world; but whereas I focus here on the cultural dimension, he looks at the mental benefits of mastering this music.

25.   Lewis, *Muslim Discovery*, p. 274.

15

Denying Islam's Role in Terror: Why?

Years after Maj. Nidal Malik Hasan's November 2009 massacre at Ft. Hood, Texas, the classification of his crime remains in dispute. In its wisdom, the Department of Defense, supported by law enforcement, politicians, journalists, and academics, deems the killing of thirteen and wounding of forty-three to be "workplace violence." For example, the eighty-six-page study on preventing a repeat episode, *Protecting the Force: Lessons from Fort Hood*, mentions "workplace violence" sixteen times.[1]

Indeed, were the subject not morbid, one could be amused by the disagreement over what exactly caused the Palestinian-born major to erupt. Speculations included "racism" against him, "harassment he had received as a Muslim," his "sense of not belonging," "mental problems," "emotional problems," "an inordinate amount of stress," the "worst nightmare" of his being deployed to Afghanistan, or something fancifully called "pre-traumatic stress disorder." One newspaper headline, "Mindset of Rogue Major a Mystery," sums up this bogus state of utter confusion.[2]

In contrast, members of congress ridiculed the "workplace violence" characterization and a coalition of 160 victims and family members released a video, "The Truth About Fort Hood," criticizing the administration. On the third anniversary of the massacre, 148 victims and family members sued the US government for avoiding legal and financial responsibility by not acknowledging the incident as terrorism.[3]

The military leadership willfully ignores what stares them in the face, namely Hasan's clear and evident Islamist inspiration; *Protecting the Force* mentions "Muslim" and "jihad" not a single time, and "Islam" only once, in a footnote.[4] The massacre officially still remains unconnected to terrorism or Islam.

This example fits in a larger pattern: The Establishment denies that Islamism—a form of Islam that seeks to make Muslims dominant through an extreme, totalistic, and rigid application of Islamic law, the Shari'a—represents the leading global cause of terrorism when it so clearly does. Islamism reverts to medieval norms in its aspiration to create a caliphate that rules all humanity. "Islam is the solution" summarizes its doctrine. Islam's public law consists of elevating Muslim over non-Muslim, male over female, and endorsing the use of force to spread Muslim rule. In recent decades, Islamists (the adherents of this vision of Islam) have established an unparalleled record of terrorism. To cite one tabulation: TheReligionOfPeace.com counts twenty thousand assaults in the name of Islam since 9/11,[5] or about five a day. In the West, terrorist acts inspired by motives other than Islam hardly register.

It is important to document and explain this denial and explore its implications. The examples come predominantly from the United States, though they could come from virtually any Western country— except Israel.

Documenting Denial

The government, press, and academy routinely deny that Islamist motives play a role in two ways, specific and general. Specific acts of violence perpetrated by Muslims lead the authorities publicly, willfully, and defiantly to close their eyes to Islamist motivations and goals. Instead, they point to a range of trivial, one-time, and individualistic motives, often casting the perpetrator as victim. Examples over the past quarter century include:

- 1990 assassination of Rabbi Meir Kahane in New York: "A prescription drug for . . . depression."[6]
- 1991 murder of Makin Morcos in Sydney: "A robbery gone wrong."
- 1993 murder of Reverend Doug Good in Western Australia: An "unintentional killing."
- 1993 attack on foreigners at a hotel in Cairo, killing ten: Insanity.[7]
- 1994 killing of a Hasidic Jew on the Brooklyn Bridge: "Road rage."[8]
- 1997 shooting murder atop the Empire State Building: "Many, many enemies in his mind."[9]
- 2000 attack on a bus of Jewish schoolchildren near Paris: A traffic incident.
- 2002 plane crash into a Tampa high-rise by an Osama bin Laden–admiring Arab American (but non-Muslim): The acne drug Accutane.[10]
- 2002 double murder at LAX: "A work dispute."[11]
- 2002 Beltway snipers: A "stormy [family] relationship."[12]

- 2003 Hasan Karim Akbar's attack on fellow soldiers, killing two: An "attitude problem."[13]
- 2003 mutilation murder of Sebastian Sellam: Mental illness.[14]
- 2004 explosion in Brescia, Italy outside a McDonald's restaurant: "Loneliness and depression."[15]
- 2005 rampage at a retirement center in Virginia: "A disagreement between the suspect and another staff member."[16]
- 2006 murderous rampage at the Jewish Federation of Greater Seattle: "An animus toward women."[17]
- 2006 killing by SUV in northern California: "His recent, arranged marriage may have made him stressed."[18]

This pattern of denial is all the more striking because it concerns distinctly Islamic forms of violence such as suicide operations, beheadings, honor killings, and the disfiguring of women's faces. For example, when it comes to honor killings, Phyllis Chesler has established that this phenomenon differs from domestic violence and, in Western countries, is almost always perpetrated by Muslims.[19] Such proofs, however, do not convince the Establishment, which tends to filter Islam out of the equation.

The generalized threat inspires more denial. Politicians and others avoid mention of Islam, Islamism, Muslims, Islamists, mujahideen, or jihadists. Instead, they blame evildoers, militants, radical extremists, terrorists, and al-Qaeda. Just one day after 9/11, US Secretary of State Colin Powell set the tone by asserting that the just-committed atrocities "should not be seen as something done by Arabs or Islamics; it is something that was done by terrorists."[20]

Another tactic is to obscure Islamist realities under the fog of verbiage. George W. Bush referred once to "the great struggle against extremism that is now playing out across the broader Middle East"[21] and another time to "the struggle against ideological extremists who do not believe in free societies and who happen to use terror as a weapon to try to shake the conscience of the free world."[22] He went so far as to dismiss any Islamic element by asserting that "Islam is a great religion that preaches peace."[23]

In like spirit, Barack Obama observed that "it is very important for us to recognize that we have a battle or a war against some terrorist organizations, but that those organizations aren't representative of a broader Arab community, Muslim community."[24] Obama's attorney general, Eric Holder, engaged in the following exchange with Lamar Smith (Republican of Texas) during congressional testimony in

May 2010, repeatedly resisting a connection between Islamist motives and a spate of terrorist attacks:

> *Smith:* In the case of all three [terrorist] attempts in the last year, . . . one of which was successful, those individuals have had ties to radical Islam. Do you feel that these individuals might have been incited to take the actions that they did because of radical Islam?
>
> *Holder:* Because of?
>
> *Smith:* Radical Islam.
>
> *Holder:* There are a variety of reasons why I think people have taken these actions. It's one, I think you have to look at each individual case. I mean, we are in the process now of talking to Mr. [Feisal] Shahzad to try to understand what it is that drove him to take the action.
>
> *Smith:* Yes, but radical Islam could have been one of the reasons?
>
> *Holder:* There are a variety of reasons why people . . .
>
> *Smith:* But was radical Islam one of them?
>
> *Holder:* There are a variety of reasons why people do things. Some of them are potentially religious. . . .[25]

And on and on Holder persisted, until Smith eventually gave up. And this was not exceptional: An almost identical denial took place in December 2011 by a senior official from the Department of Defense.[26]

Or one can simply ignore the Islamist element; a study issued by the Department of Homeland Security, *Evolution of the Terrorist Threat to the United States,* mentions Islam just one time. In September 2010, Obama spoke at the United Nations and, using a passive construction, avoided all mention of Islam in reference to 9/11: "Nine years ago, the destruction of the World Trade Center signaled a threat that respected no boundary of dignity or decency."[27] About the same time, Janet Napolitano, the secretary of homeland security, stated that the profiles of Americans engaged in terrorism indicate that "there is no 'typical' profile of a homegrown terrorist."[28]

Newt Gingrich, the former speaker of the US House of Representatives, rightly condemns this mentality as "two plus two must equal something other than four."[29]

Exceptions to Denial

Exceptions to this pattern do exist; Establishment figures on occasion drop their guard and acknowledge the Islamist threat to the civilized world. Gingrich himself delivered a uniquely well-informed speech on Shari'a (Islamic law) in 2010, noting that "This is not a war on terrorism. Terrorism is an activity. This is a struggle with radical Islamists in both their militant and their stealth form."[30]

British Prime Minister Tony Blair offered a stirring and eloquent analysis in 2006:

> This is war, but of a completely unconventional kind. . . . What are the values that govern the future of the world? Are they those of tolerance, freedom, respect for difference and diversity or those of reaction, division and hatred? . . . It is in part a struggle between what I will call Reactionary Islam and Moderate, Mainstream Islam. But its implications go far wider. We are fighting a war, but not just against terrorism but about how the world should govern itself in the early 21st century, about global values.[31]

The current British prime minister, David Cameron, gave a fine analysis in 2005, long before he reached his current office:

> The driving force behind today's terrorist threat is Islamist fundamentalism. The struggle we are engaged in is, at root, ideological. During the last century a strain of Islamist thinking has developed which, like other totalitarianisms, such as Nazism and Communism, offers its followers a form of redemption through violence.[32]

In 2011, as prime minister, Cameron returned to this theme: "we need to be absolutely clear on where the origins of where these terrorist attacks lie. That is the existence of an ideology, Islamist extremism."[33]

The former foreign minister of the Czech Republic, Alexandr Vondra, spoke his mind with remarkable frankness:

> Radical Islamists challenge practically everything that our society claims to stand for, no matter what the Western policies were or are. These challenges include the concept of universal human rights and freedom of speech.[34]

George W. Bush spoke in the period after October 2005 about "Islamo-fascism" and "Islamic fascists." Joseph Lieberman, the US senator from Connecticut, criticized those who refuse "to identify our enemy in this war as what it is: violent Islamist extremism"[35] and sponsored an excellent Senate study on Maj. Hasan. Rick Santorum, then a US senator from Pennsylvania, gave a notable analysis:

> In World War II we fought Naziism and Japanese imperialism. Today, we are fighting against Islamic fascists. They attacked us on September 11th because we are the greatest obstacle to their openly declared mission of subjecting the entire world to their fanatical rule. I believe that the threat of Islamic fascism is just as menacing as the threat from Nazism and Soviet Communism. Now, as then, we face fanatics who will stop at nothing to dominate us. Now, as then, there is no way out; we will either win or lose.[36]

Antonin Scalia, an associate justice of the Supreme Court of the United States, observed in an opinion that "America is at war with radical Islamists."[37] A New York Police Department study, *Radicalization in the West: The Homegrown Threat*, discusses "Islamic-based terrorism" in its first line and never lets up. It contains explicit references to Islamism such as "Ultimately, the jihadist envisions a world in which jihadi-Salafi Islam is dominant and is the basis of government."[38]

So, reality does on occasion poke through the fog of denial and verbiage.

The Mystery of Denial

These exceptions aside, what accounts for the persistent denial of Islamic motives? Why the pretense that no elephant fills the room? An unwillingness to face the truth invariably smacks of euphemism, cowardice, political correctness, and appeasement. In this spirit, Gingrich argues that "the Obama Administration is willfully blind to the nature of our enemies and the forces which threaten America. . . . [I]t's not ignorance; it's determined effort to avoid [reality]."[39]

These problems definitely contribute to denial, but something more basic and more legitimate goes further to explain this reluctance. One hint comes from a 2007 PhD dissertation in politics submitted by Gaetano Ilardi to Monash University in Melbourne. Titled "From the IRA to Al Qa'eda: Intelligence as a Measure of Rational Action in Terrorist Operations," it refers frequently to Islam and related topics; Ilardi has also been quoted in the press on the topic of radicalization. Yet in 2009, as acting senior sergeant of the Victoria police, he was the most vociferous of his twenty law enforcement colleagues insisting to me that the police not publicly mention Islam in any fashion when discussing terrorism. In other words, wanting not to refer to Islam can come from someone who knows full well the role of Islam.

Confirming this point, Daniel Benjamin, the Obama administration's coordinator for counterterrorism in the US State Department, explicitly refutes the idea that silence about Islam means being unaware of it:

> Policy makers fully recognize how al Qaeda's ideologues have appropriated Islamic texts and concepts and fashioned them into a mantle of religious legitimacy for their bloodshed. As someone who has written at length about how al Qaeda and the radical groups that preceded it have picked and chosen from sacred texts, often out of all context, I have no doubt my colleagues understand the nature of the threat.[40]

Ilardi and Benjamin know their stuff; they avoid discussing Islam in connection with terrorism for reasons deeper than political correctness, ignorance, or appeasement. What are those reasons? Two factors have key importance: wanting not to alienate Muslims or to re-order society.

Explaining Denial

Not wanting to offend Muslims, a sincere and reasonable goal, is the reason most often publicly cited. Muslims protest that focusing on Islam, Islamism, or jihad increases Muslim fears that the West is engaged in a "war against Islam." Joseph Lieberman, for example, notes that the Obama administration prefers not to use the term "violent Islamist extremists" when referring to the enemy because using such explicit words "bolsters our enemy's propaganda claim that the West is at war with Islam."[41]

Questioned in an interview about his having only once used the term "war on terror," Barack Obama confirmed this point: "words matter in this situation because one of the ways we're going to win this struggle is through the battle of hearts and minds." Asked, "So that's not a term you're going to be using much in the future?" he replied:

> You know, what I want to do is make sure that I'm constantly talking about al Qaeda and other affiliated organizations because we, I believe, can win over moderate Muslims to recognize that that kind of destruction and nihilism ultimately leads to a dead end, and that we should be working together to make sure that everybody has got a better life.[42]

Daniel Benjamin makes the same point more lucidly:

> Putting the emphasis on "Islamist" instead of on "violent extremist" undercuts our efforts, since it falsely roots the core problem in the faith of more than one billion people who abhor violence. As one internal government study after another has shown, such statements invariably wind up being distorted in the global media, alienating Muslim moderates.[43]

This concern actually has sub-parts for two types of Muslims: Those who would otherwise help fight terrorism feel insulted ("a true Muslim can never be a terrorist") and so do not step forward while those who would be uninvolved become radicalized, some even becoming terrorists.

The second reason to inhibit one's talk about Islam concerns the apprehension that this implies a large and undesirable shift away from how secular Western societies are ordered. Blaming terrorist attacks on prescription drugs gone awry, road rage, an arranged marriage, mental cases going berserk, or freak industrial accidents permits Westerners not to confront issues concerning Islam. If the jihad explanation is vastly more persuasive, it is also far more troubling.

When one notes that Islamist terrorism is almost exclusively the work of Muslims acting out of Islamic convictions, the implication follows that Muslims must be singled out for special scrutiny, perhaps along the following lines this author suggested in 2003:

> Muslim government employees in law enforcement, the military and the diplomatic corps need to be watched for connections to terrorism, as do Muslim chaplains in prisons and the armed forces. Muslim visitors and immigrants must undergo additional background checks. Mosques require a scrutiny beyond that applied to churches and temples.[44]

Implementing such a policy means focusing law enforcement attention on a community that is defined by its religion. This flies in the face of liberal, multicultural, and politically correct values; it also will be portrayed as illegal and perhaps unconstitutional. It means distinguishing on the basis of a person's group characteristics. It involves profiling. These changes have unsettling implications which will be condemned as "racist" and "Islamophobic," accusations that can ruin careers in today's public environment.

Islam-related explanations may offer a more persuasive accounting than turning perpetrators into victims, but the imperative not to tamper with existing social mores trumps counterterrorism. This accounts for police, prosecutors, politicians, and professors avoiding the actual factors behind Islamist attacks and instead finding miscellaneous mundane motives. Those soothing and inaccurate bromides have the advantage of implying no changes other than vigilance against weapons. Dealing with unpleasant realities can be deferred.

Finally, denial appears to work. Just because law enforcement, the military, and intelligence agencies tiptoe around the twin topics of Islamic motivation and the disproportionate Islamist terrorism when addressing the public does not stop these same institutions in practice from focusing quietly on Islam and Muslims. Indeed, there is plenty of evidence that they do just this, and it has led to an effective counterterrorism effort since 9/11 with close scrutiny on everything from mosques to *hawalas* (informal Muslim financial exchanges). As a result, with rare exceptions (such as the Ft. Hood shooter), Islamist terrorist networks tend to be stymied and successful assaults tend to come out of nowhere from perpetrators characterized by sudden jihad syndrome.

Arguing against Denial

While respecting the urge not to aggravate Muslim sensibilities and acknowledging that the frank discussion of Islam can have major consequences for ordering society, this author insists on the need to mention Islam. First, it is not clear how much harm talking about Islam actually does. Genuine anti-Islamist Muslims insist on Islam being discussed; Islamists posing as moderates tend to be those who feign upset about a "war on Islam" and the like.

Second, little evidence points to Muslims being radicalized by mere discussion of Islamism. Quite the contrary, it is usually something specific that turns a Muslim in that direction, from the way American women dress to drone attacks in Somalia, Yemen, and Pakistan.

Third, while conceding that discussion of Islam has costs, ignoring it costs more. The need to define the enemy, not just within the counsels of war but for the public, trumps all other considerations. As the ancient Chinese strategist Sun Tzu observed, "Know your enemy and know yourself and you can fight a hundred battles." Karl von Clausewitz's entire theory of war assumes an accurate assessment of the enemy. Just as a medical doctor must identify and name a disease before treating it, so must politicians and generals identify and name the enemy to defeat it.

To censor oneself limits one's ability to wage war. Avoiding mention of the enemy's identity sows confusion, harms morale, and squanders strengths. In brief, it offers a recipe for defeat. Indeed, the annals of history record no war won when the enemy's very name and identity may not be uttered; this is all the more so in modern times when defining the enemy must precede and undergird military victory. If you cannot name the enemy, you cannot defeat him.

Fourth, even though law enforcement et al. find that saying one thing in public while doing another in private works, this dishonesty comes at the high price of creating a disconnect between the high-flying words of politicians and the sometimes sordid realities of counterterrorism:

- *Government employees at risk*: On the one hand, out of fear of being exposed, public servants must hide or lie about their activities. On the other, to do their work effectively, they must run afoul of studiously impartial government regulations, or even break the law.
- *A confused public*: Policy statements piously reject any link between Islam and terrorism even as counterterrorism implicitly makes just such a connection, leaving the public baffled.
- *Advantage Islamists*: They (1) point out that government declarations are mere puffery hiding what is really a war against Islam; and (2) win Muslim recruits by asking them whom they believe, straight-talking Islamists or insincere politicians.
- *"Security theater" and other pantomimes*: To convince observers that Muslims are not specifically targeted, others are hauled in for show purposes, wasting finite time and resources.[45]
- *An increase in resentments and prejudices*: People keep their mouths shut, but their minds are working. An open public discussion, in which one could condemn Islamists while supporting moderate Muslims, would lead to a better understanding of the problem.
- *Vigilance discouraged*: The campaign of "If You See Something, Say Something" is fine, but what are the costs of reporting dubious behavior by a neighbor or a passenger who turns out to be innocent? Although vigilant neighbors have been an important source of counterterrorism leads, anyone who reports his worries opens himself up to vilification as a racist or "Islamophobe," damage to one's career, or even a lawsuit.[46]

Thus does the unwillingness to acknowledge the Islamist motives behind most terrorism obstruct effective counterterrorism and render further atrocities more likely.

When Denial Will End

Denial is likely to continue until the price gets too steep. The three thousand victims of 9/11, it turns out, did not suffice to shake Western complacency. Thirty thousand dead, in all likelihood, will also not suffice. Perhaps three hundred thousand will. For sure, three million will. At that point, worries about Muslim sensibilities and fear of being called an "Islamophobe" will fade into irrelevance, replaced by a single-minded determination to protect lives. Should the existing order someday be in evident danger, today's relaxed approach will instantly go out the window. The popular support for such measures exists; as early as 2004, a Cornell University poll showed that 44 percent of Americans "believe that some curtailment of civil liberties is necessary for Muslim Americans."[47]

Israel offers a control case. Because it faces so many threats, the body politic lacks patience with liberal pieties when it comes to security. While aspiring to treat everyone fairly, the government clearly targets the most violent-prone elements of society. Should other Western countries face a comparable danger, circumstances will likely compel them to adopt this same approach.

Conversely, should such mass dangers not arise, this shift will probably never take place. Until and unless disaster on a large scale strikes, denial will continue. Western tactics, in other words, depend entirely on the brutality and competence of the Islamist enemy. Ironically, the West permits terrorists to drive its approach to counterterrorism. No less ironically, it will take a huge terrorist atrocity to enable effective counterterrorism.

Addressing Denial

In the meantime, those who wish to strengthen counterterrorism by acknowledging the role of Islam have three tasks.

First, intellectually to prepare themselves and their arguments so when calamity occurs they possess a fully elaborated, careful, and just program that focuses on Muslims without doing injustice to them.

Second, continue to convince those averse to mentioning Islam that discussing it is worth the price; this means addressing their concerns, not bludgeoning them with insults. Accept the legitimacy of their hesitance, use sweet reason, and let the barrage of Islamist attacks have their effect.

Third, prove that talking about Islamism does not lead to perdition by establishing the costs of not naming the enemy and of not identifying Islamism as a factor: note that Muslim governments, including the Saudi one, acknowledge that Islamism leads to terrorism; stress that moderate Muslims who oppose Islamism want Islamism openly discussed; address the fear that frank talk about Islam alienates Muslims and spurs violence; and demonstrate that profiling can be done in a constitutionally approved way.

In brief, even without an expectation of effecting a change in policy, there is much work to be done.

Notes

1. *Protecting the Force: Lessons from Fort Hood*, Department of Defense, Washington, DC, Jan. 2010.
2. *The Australian*, Nov. 7, 2009.
3. Associated Press, Nov. 5, 2012.
4. *Protecting the Force: Lessons from Fort Hood*, p. 18, fn. 22.
5. "List of Islamic Terror Attacks," TheReligionOfPeace.com, accessed Dec. 19, 2012.
6. *The New York Times*, Nov. 9. 1990.
7. *The Independent* (London), Sept. 19, 1997.
8. Uriel Heilman, "Murder on the Brooklyn Bridge," *Middle East Quarterly*, Summer 2001, pp. 29–37.
9. *The Houston Chronicle*, Feb. 26, 1997.
10. *Time Magazine*, Jan. 21, 2002.
11. "Terror in LA?" *Honest Reporting* (Toronto), July 8, 2002.
12. *Los Angeles Times*, Oct. 26, 2002.
13. Daniel Pipes, "Murder in the 101st Airborne," *New York Post*, Mar. 25, 2003.
14. Brett Kline, "Two Sons of France," *The Jerusalem Post Magazine*, Jan. 21, 2010.
15. "Italy: McDonald's Jihad Foiled," Jihad Watch, Mar. 30, 2004.
16. *The Washington Post*, Jan. 11, 2005.
17. *Los Angeles Times*, July 30, 2006.
18. *The San Francisco Chronicle*, Aug. 30, 2006.
19. Phyllis Chesler, "Are Honor Killings Simply Domestic Violence?" *Middle East Quarterly*, Spring 2009, pp. 61–9.
20. *Dateline*, NBC, Sept. 21, 2001.
21. "Remarks," The Islamic Center of Washington, DC, June 27, 2007.
22. "Remarks," UNITY 2004 Conference, Washington DC, Aug. 6, 2004.
23. Al-Arabiya News Channel (Dubai) Oct. 5, 2007.
24. Anderson Cooper 360 Degrees, Feb. 3, 2009.
25. Testimony before the US House Judiciary Committee, May 13, 2010.
26. Testimony before the US House Committee for Homeland Security, Dec. 13, 2011.
27. Remarks, U.N. General Assembly, New York, Sept. 23, 2010.

28. "Nine Years after 9/11: Confronting the Terrorist Threat to the Homeland," statement to the US Senate Committee on Homeland Security and Governmental Affairs, Sept. 22, 2010.

29. Newt Gingrich, "America Is at Risk," American Enterprise Institute, Washington, DC, July 29, 2010.

30. Ibid.

31. Speech to the Los Angeles World Affairs Council, Aug. 1, 2006.

32. Speech at the Foreign Policy Centre, London, Aug. 25, 2005.

33. Munich Security Conference, Feb. 5, 2011.

34. Alexandr Vondra, "Radical Islam Poses a Major Challenge to Europe," *Middle East Quarterly*, Summer 2007, pp. 66–8.

35. Joseph Lieberman, "Who's the Enemy in the War on Terror?" *The Wall Street Journal*, June 15, 2010.

36. "The Great Test of This Generation," speech to the National Press Club, Washington, DC, *National Review Online*, July 20, 2006.

37. *Scalia J., dissenting, Lakhdar Boumediene, et al., Petitioners, Supreme Court of the United States v. George W. Bush, President of the United States, et al.; Khaled A. F. Al Odah, next friend of Fawzikhalid Abdullah Fahad Al Odah, et al., Petitioners v. United States, et al.,* June 12, 2008.

38. New York: 2007, p. 8,

39. Newt Gingrich, "America Is at Risk," American Enterprise Institute, Washington, DC, July 29, 2010.

40. Daniel Benjamin, "Name It and Claim It, or Name It and Inflame It?" *The Wall Street Journal*, June 24, 2010.

41. Lieberman, "Who's the Enemy in the War on Terror?"

42. *Anderson Cooper 360 Degrees*, Feb. 3, 2009.

43. Benjamin, "Name It and Claim It, or Name It and Inflame It?"

44. Daniel Pipes, "The Enemy Within and the Need for Profiling," *New York Post*, Jan. 24, 2003.

45. Daniel Pipes, "Security Theater Now Playing at Your Airport," *The Jerusalem Post*, Jan. 6, 2010.

46. M. Zuhdi Jasser, "Exposing the 'Flying Imams,'" *Middle East Quarterly*, Winter 2008, pp. 3–11.

47. "Fear Factor," Dec. 17, 2004.

16

The Rushdie Rules Ascendant

From a novel by Salman Rushdie published in 1989 to an American civil protest called "Everyone Draw Muhammad Day" in 2010, a familiar three-step pattern has evolved. Westerners say or do something critical of Islam. Islamists respond with name-calling, outrage, demands for retraction, threats of lawsuits and violence, and actual violence. Westerners hem and haw, prevaricate, and finally fold. Along the way, each controversy prompts a debate focusing on the issue of free speech.

I shall argue two points about this sequence. First, that the right of Westerners to discuss, criticize, and even ridicule Islam and Muslims has eroded over the years. Second, that free speech is a minor part of the problem; at stake is something much deeper—indeed, a defining question of our time: will Westerners maintain their own historic civilization in the face of assault by Islamists, or will they cede to Islamic culture and law and submit to a form of second-class citizenship?

The Rushdie Edict

The era of Islamist uproar began abruptly on February 14, 1989, when Ayatollah Ruhollah Khomeini, Iran's supreme leader, watched television reports of Pakistanis responding with violence to a new novel by Salman Rushdie, the famous Muslim-born author of South Asian Muslim origins. The book's title, *The Satanic Verses*, refers to the Koran and poses a direct challenge to Islamic sensibilities; its sarcastic contents further exacerbate the problem. Outraged by what he considered Rushdie's blasphemous portrait of Islam, Khomeini issued an edict whose continued impact makes it worthy of quotation at length:

> I inform all zealous Muslims of the world that the author of the book entitled *The Satanic Verses*—which has been compiled, printed, and published in opposition to Islam, the Prophet, and the Koran—and all those involved in the publication who were aware of its contents, are sentenced to death.

This unprecedented edict—no head of government had ever called for the execution of a novelist living in another country—came out of the blue and surprised everyone, from Iranian government officials to Rushdie himself. No one had imagined that a magical realist novel, replete with people falling out of the sky and animals that talk, might incur the wrath of the ruler of Iran, a country to which Rushdie had few connections.

The edict led to physical attacks on bookstores in Italy, Norway, and the United States and on translators of *The Satanic* Verses in Norway, Japan, and Turkey; in the last case, the translator and thirty-six others perished in an arson attack on a hotel. Other violence in Muslim-majority countries led to more than twenty fatalities, mostly in South Asia. Then, just as the furor wound down, in June 1989, Khomeini died; his death made the edict, sometimes inaccurately called a *fatwa*, immutable.

The edict contains four important elements. First, by noting "opposition to Islam, the Prophet, and the Koran," Khomeini delineated the wide range of sacred topics that may not be treated disrespectfully without invoking a death sentence.

Second, by targeting "all those involved in the publication who were aware of its contents," he declared war not just on the artist but also on an entire cultural infrastructure—including the thousands of employees of publishing houses, advertisers, distribution companies, and bookstores.

Third, by ordering Rushdie's execution "so that no one else will dare to insult the Muslim sanctities," Khomeini made clear his purpose not only to punish one writer but also to prevent further instances of ridicule.

Finally, by demanding that those unable to execute Rushdie "report him," Khomeini called on every Muslim worldwide to become part of an informal intelligence network dedicated to upholding Islamic sanctities.

These four features together constitute what I call the Rushdie Rules. Decades later, they remain very much in place.

Setting Precedents

The edict set several precedents in the West. A foreign political leader successfully ignored conventional limits on state powers. A religious leader intervened directly, with little cost or resistance, in Western cultural affairs. And a Muslim leader established the precedent of applying an aspect of Islamic law, the Shari'a, in an overwhelmingly non-Muslim country. On this last point: Western states have, at times, served as Khomeini's effective agents. The government of Austria imposed a suspended prison sentence on a person who defied the Rushdie Rules, while the governments of France and Australia brought charges that could have meant jail time. Most strikingly, authorities in Canada, Great Britain, the Netherlands, Finland, and Israel actually jailed Rushdie Rule trespassers. It takes effort to recall the innocent days before 1989, when Westerners freely spoke and wrote about Islam and related subjects.

The Rushdie Rules had an immediate impact on Muslims living in the West, whose outbursts of insults and violence generated a newfound sense of power. From Sweden to New Zealand, Islamists responded with joy that, after centuries on the defensive, Muslims had found their voice and, from the belly of the beast, could challenge the West. Most of the violence that followed was of the indiscriminate sort, on the model of 9/11, Bali, Madrid, Beslan, and London, in which jihadists killed whoever happened to cross their paths; TheReligionOfPeace.com documents on average five indiscriminate Islamist terrorist attacks per day around the world.

Less common but more intimidating is the violence that targets those who defy the Rushdie Rules. Let us limit examples of this phenomenon to one country, Denmark. In October 2004, an instructor at the Carsten Niebuhr Institute at the University of Copenhagen was kicked and hit by several strangers as he left the university; they informed him that he had read from the Koran, which as an infidel (*kafir*) he had no right to do. In October 2005, *Jyllands-Posten* editor Flemming Rose was threatened for having commissioned cartoons depicting Muhammad. Two of the cartoonists had to go into hiding; one of them, Kurt Westergaard, subsequently narrowly escaped physical attack inside his home. In March 2006, Naser Khader, an anti-Islamist politician, was threatened by an Islamist who warned that if Khader became a government minister, he and his ministry would be blown up.

The Danish experience is typical. According to the *Wall Street Journal*, "Across Europe, dozens of people are now in hiding or under police protection because of threats from Muslim extremists." Even Pope Benedict XVI received a flurry of threats in the aftermath of his quoting a Byzantine emperor on the subject of Islam. In the Netherlands alone, politicians reported 121 death threats against them in just one year. The November 2004 execution on an Amsterdam street of Theo van Gogh—a well known libertarian, filmmaker, talk show host, newspaper columnist, and mischief-maker who had ridiculed Islam—traumatized his country and led to a brief state of insurrection.

Three Islamist Goals

Westerners generally perceive this violence as a challenge to their right to self-expression. But if freedom of speech is the battlefield, the greater war concerns the foundational principles of Western civilization. The recurrent pattern of Islamist uproar exists to achieve three goals—not always articulated—that go well beyond prohibiting criticism of Islam.

A first goal consists of establishing a superior status for Islam. Khomeini's demands for the sacred trinity of "Islam, the Prophet, and the Koran" imply special privileges for one religion, an exclusion from the hurly-burly of the marketplace of ideas. Islam would benefit from unique rules unavailable to other religions. Jesus may be sacrilegiously lampooned in Monty Python's *Life of Brian* or Terry McNally's *Corpus Christi*, but, as one book's title puts it, "be careful with Muhammad!"

This segues to a second goal—Muslim supremacy and Western inferiority. Islamists routinely say and do things more offensive to Westerners than anything Westerners do vis-à-vis Muslims. They openly despise Western culture; in the words of an Algerian Islamist, it's not a civilization, but a "syphilization." Their mainstream media publishes coarser, viler, and more violent cartoons than anything commissioned by Flemming Rose. They freely insult Judaism, Christianity, Hinduism, and Buddhism. They murder Jews just for being Jews, like Daniel Pearl in Pakistan, Sébastian Sellam and Ilan Halimi in France, and Pamela Waechter and Ariel Sellouk in the United States. Whether because of fear or inattention, Westerners assent to an imbalance whereby Muslims may offend and attack while they themselves are shielded from any such indignities or pains.

Should Westerners accept this imbalance, the *dhimmi* status will follow. This Islamic concept permits "people of the book," monotheists such as Christians and Jews, to continue to practice their religion under Muslim rule, subject to many restrictions. For its time, the *dhimmi* status offered certain benefits (until as recently as 1945, Jews generally had better lives in Islamdom than in Christendom), but it is intended to insult and humiliate non-Muslims, even as it exalts Muslims' superiority. *Dhimmi*s pay additional taxes, may not join the military or the government, and suffer from encompassing legal disabilities. In some times and places, *dhimmi*s could ride on a donkey but not on a horse, wore distinctive clothing, and an elderly *dhimmi* on the street was required to jump out of the way of a Muslim child. Elements of the *dhimmi* status have recently been applied in such varied places as Gaza, the West Bank, Saudi Arabia, Iraq, Iran, Afghanistan, Pakistan, Malaysia, and the Philippines. Clearly, Londonistan and beyond are also in their sights.

In turn, reestablishing the *dhimmi* status is one step toward the Islamist's third and ultimate ambition, applying full Shari'a law. Closing down discussion of Islam paves the way toward this end. Conversely, retaining free speech about Islam represents a critical defense against the imposition of an Islamic order. Keeping our civilization requires open discussion of Islam.

The Shari'a regulates both private and public life. The private dimension includes such intensely personal matters as bodily cleanliness, sexuality, childbearing, family relations, clothing, and diet. In the public realm, the Shari'a regulates social relations, commercial transactions, criminal penalties, the status of women and minorities, slavery, the identity of the ruler, the judiciary, taxation, and warfare. In brief, Islamic law includes everything from toilet etiquette to the conduct of warfare.

Yet the Shari'a contradicts the deepest premises of Western civilization. The unequal relations of male and female, of Muslim and *kafir*, of owner and slave cannot be reconciled with equality of rights. The harem cannot be reconciled with a monogamous order. Islamic supremacism contradicts freedom of religion. A sovereign God cannot allow democracy.

Islamists all concur on the goal of applying Islamic law globally. But they differ on whether to achieve this through violence (the preference of bin Laden), totalitarian rule (Khomeini), or by politically gaming the system (the Swiss intellectual Tariq Ramadan). However done, were Islamists to achieve a Shar'ia order, they would effectively replace Western civilization with Islamic civilization. In American terms, allowing the Koran to trump the Constitution ends the United States as it has existed for more than two centuries.

A Changed West

Accepting the Rushdie Rules, in other words, implies a process that culminates with full application of the Shari'a. Were Khomeini to have his way, those of us who value Western civilization could not argue against Shari'a. To understand the consequences of closing the debate about Islam, note what appears to be an innocuous report published in 2007 by the Muslim Council of Britain (MCB), a leading Islamist institution in the United Kingdom. Titled *Towards Greater Understanding*, it advises British authorities on how to deal with Muslim students in taxpayer-funded schools.

The MCB seeks to create an environment in schools in which Muslim children do not make "inappropriate assumptions" that "to progress in society they will have to compromise or give up aspects of who they are, and their religious beliefs and values." Toward this end, the MCB proposes a jaw-dropping list of changes that would fundamentally alter the nature of British schools, transforming them, in effect, into Saudi-like institutions. Some of its suggestions:

- *Prayers:* Provide (1) extra "water cans or bottles" for washing before the prayers and (2) prayer facilities, ideally separate ones for boys and girls.
- *Friday communal* prayer: Schools should make available "a suitable external visitor, a teacher or an older pupil" to lead the Friday prayers and preach a sermon.
- *Toilets*: Water must be available in water cans or bottles for cleansing purposes.
- *Social customs*: No pressure to shake hands with members of the opposite sex, whether students or teachers.
- *Scheduling*: Vacation days for all on the two major Muslim holidays, the Eids.
- *Holiday celebrations*: Involve non-Muslim students and their parents in Islamic holiday rituals. During Ramadan, for instance, all children, not just Muslim ones, should celebrate "the spirit and values of Ramadan through collective worship or assembly themes and communal Iftar (the breaking of the fast)."
- *Ramadan*: (1) No examinations during this month, "since the combination of preparing for exams and fasting may prove challenging for some pupils" and (2) no sex education, to respect strictures against sex during that month.
- *Food*: Provide halal meals. Permit students to eat with their right hands.
- *Clothing*: Accede to the wearing of hijabs and even jilbabs (a long outer garment down to the ankles). In swimming pools, Muslim children should wear modest swimwear (e.g., for girls, full leotards and leggings). Islamic amulets must be permitted.
- *Beards*: A right for male students.
- *Sports*: Sex segregation where there is physical contact with other team players, as in basketball and football, or when exposed, as in swimming.
- *Shower rooms*: Separate stalls needed, so Muslims are not subject to the "profound indignity" of seeing or being seen in the nude.
- *Music*: Should be limited to "the human voice and non-tunable percussion instruments such as drums."

- *Dancing*: Excluded, unless it is done in a single-sex environment and does not "involve sexual connotations and messages."
- *Teacher and administrator training*: Staff should undergo Islamic "awareness training" so that schools are "better informed and have greater and more accurate appreciation of their Muslim pupils' needs."
- *Art*: Exempt Muslim pupils from producing "three dimensional figurative imagery of humans."
- *Religious instruction*: Pictures of any prophets (including Jesus) prohibited.
- *Language instruction*: Arabic should be made available to all Muslim students.
- *Islamic civilization*: (1) Study the contribution of Muslims to Europe in history, art, mathematics, and science classes and (2) emphasize common aspects of European and Islamic heritage.

The imposition, explicit or implicit, of Rushdie Rules would render impossible any criticism of a program such as the MCB's. I could not write this article, Transaction could not publish it, and you could not read it.

Overhauling schools is just one of a myriad of planned changes. Step by step, piece by piece, Islamists wish to trump the premises of Western life by infusing its education, cultural life, and institutions with a concurrent Islamic system that in time overrides secular institutions, until an Islamic order comes operationally into being. Some changes are already in place and extend to many aspects of life. A few pungent examples:

Polygamous marriages are valid under certain circumstances in the United Kingdom, the Netherlands, Belgium, Italy, Australia, and the Canadian province of Ontario. Muslim women-only swimming sessions exist in municipal pools in Washington State. Women-only classes are being offered at Virginia Tech, a taxpayer-supported university. Women can have their drivers license photographs taken wearing hijabs in three US states. If they work at IKEA or for the London police, women can wear branded hijabs provided by their employers.

Piggy banks have been banned as a symbol of saving at two major British banks. "Any matter containing religious materials contrary to Islamic faith" may not be sent via the US postal system to soldiers serving in the Middle East. Medical personnel may not eat or drink in the presence of Muslim patients or colleagues during the month of Ramadan in a Scottish hospital. The City of Boston sold public land at a discount price to build an Islamic institution.

These steps, large and small, toward Islamization undermine Western values and mores. They are unacceptable: Muslims are entitled to equal rights and responsibilities but not to special privileges. They must fit into the existing order, not remake Western societies in the Islamist mold. Increasing freedom is welcome, regressing to the medieval norms of the Shari'a is not.

Changes since 1989

In retrospect, responses to the Rushdie edict among intellectuals and politicians in 1989 were noteworthy for the support for the imperiled novelist, especially on the left. Leftist intellectuals were more likely to stand by him (Susan Sontag: "our integrity as a nation is as endangered by an attack on a writer as on an oil tanker") than were those on the right (Patrick Buchanan: "we should shove his blasphemous little novel out into the cold"). But times have changed: Paul Berman recently published a book, *The Flight of the Intellectuals*, that excoriates his fellow liberals for (as the dust jacket puts it) having "fumbled badly in their effort to grapple with Islamist ideas and violence."

At the time, François Mitterrand, the socialist president of France, called the threat to Rushdie an "absolute evil." The Green Party in Germany sought to break all economic agreements with Iran. Hans-Dietrich Genscher, the German foreign minister, endorsed a European Union resolution supporting Rushdie as "a signal to assure the preservation of civilization and human values." The US Senate unanimously passed a resolution that declared its commitment "to protect the right of any person to write, publish, sell, buy, and read books without fear of intimidation and violence" and condemned Khomeini's threat as "state-sponsored terrorism." Such governmental responses are inconceivable a quarter century later.

For every exercise in free speech since 1989, such as the Danish Muhammad cartoons or the no-holds-barred studies of Islam published by Prometheus Books, uncountable legions of writers, publishers, and illustrators have shied away from expressing themselves. Two examples: Paramount Pictures replaced the Hamas-like terrorists of Tom Clancy's novel *The Sum of All Fears* with European neo-Nazis in its movie version of the story. And Yale University Press published a book on the Danish cartoon crisis without permitting the cartoons to be reproduced in the study.

The reasoning of those who capitulate is as unexceptional as it is dismal: "This decision was based solely on concern for public safety";

"the safety and security of our customers and employees is a top priority"; "I feel real fear that someone will slit my throat"; "If I would have said what I actually think about Islam, I wouldn't be in this world for long"; and "'If this goes down badly, I'm writing my own death warrant."

Changes since 1989 result mainly from the growth of three isms: multiculturalism, left-fascism, and Islamism. The multicultural impulse regards no way of life, belief system, or political philosophy better or worse than any other. Just as Italian and Japanese food are both delicious and filling, so environmentalism or Wicca offer equally valid alternatives to Judeo-Christian civilization. Why fight for one's way of life when it has no claim to superiority over any other?

But perhaps one way is worse: if Western imperialism and the white race pollute the world, who wants Western civilization? A sizable movement of left-fascists, led by Hugo Chávez, sees Western power, which they call "Empire," as the world's main threat, with the United States and Israel viewed as the chief offenders.

Islamism has grown spectacularly since 1989, becoming the most powerful form of radical utopianism, forming an alliance with the left, dominating civil societies, challenging many governments and taking over others, establishing a beachhead in the West, and smartly advancing its agenda in international institutions.

The yin of Western weakness, in short, has met with the yang of Islamist assertion. Defenders of Western civilization must fight not just Islamists but also the multiculturalists who enable them and the leftists who ally with them.

Part IV

Islam in the West

17

Muslim Immigrants in the United States

Our bookshelves groan under the weight of books bearing titles like *Islam and the West*, *The Future of Islam and the West*, and *The Islamic World and the West*. What is striking about these books—all quite recently written and published—is the anachronism of their geographic premise. With millions of Muslims now living in North America and Western Europe, the old dichotomy of Islam and the West exists no more. This presence of Muslims in the West has profound significance for both civilizations involved, Western and Islamic, and it has a potential for both good and ill. Indeed, looking ahead, it is hard to see any other cultural interaction quite so fraught with implications.

This analysis focuses in on just one portion of Western Islam, namely those Muslims who live in the United States and who are either immigrants or their descendants (hereafter referred to as "Muslim immigrants"). It does not deal with the other major component, the converts; nor does it deal with other Western countries.

Demography and Geography

The first challenge in studying Muslim immigrants in the United States is counting them. By law, the US Census Bureau cannot count adherents of a religion, and Muslims are too few to show up reliably in most survey research. In addition, there are questions about whom to count; do Ahmadis, legally not considered Muslims in Pakistan, count as Muslims in the United States?

Taking these and other complications into account, a statistical picture is emerging that points to a total Muslim population in the United States of about three million, of which immigrants make up two-thirds to three-quarters. Accepting that this number is necessarily rough, it does point to somewhat over two million Muslim immigrants, or slightly less than one percent of the US national population.

Immigrant Muslims are ethnically extremely varied, coming from virtually every country where Muslims live, or well over one hundred countries in all. Symbolic of this diversity, Los Angeles alone boasts such exotic food fare as the Chinese Islamic Restaurant and the Thai Halal Cuisine. The largest numbers of immigrants derive from three main sources: South Asia, Iran, and the Arabic-speaking countries. The single largest group of Muslim immigrants is from South Asia (meaning Bangladesh, India, and Pakistan). They are followed by perhaps three hundred thousand Iranians and six hundred thousand from the Arab countries. Shi'is, who make up about 10 percent of the worldwide Muslim population, probably make up about the same percentage of the US Muslim population.

Like most immigrant communities, Muslims are considerably younger than the national average and heavily weighted toward males. Indeed, Islam is the most male religion in the United States, with roughly two men for every woman. There are many reasons for this imbalance, some of them concerning the mostly African American convert population, others having to do with the general immigrant pattern of men moving to an area before women follow them. There are many other reasons having to do with the specifics of Muslim immigration; for example, thousands of former soldiers of the Iraqi army who defected were settled in the United States. Birth rates for immigrant Muslims start very high, then drop as they Westernize.

Muslims tend to live in the major metropolitan areas where immigrants historically have congregated, including the country's largest cities (New York, Los Angeles, Chicago). More broadly, the Islamic map of the United States features four major regions, all urban: the New York to Washington area; California, especially Los Angeles and San Francisco; a triangle stretching from Chicago to Cleveland to Detroit; and Texas, especially the Houston and Dallas-Fort Worth areas. The southeast and northwest portions of the country have the fewest Muslim immigrants, with the exceptions of southern Florida and the Seattle area.

Many of these centers have a specific ethnic quality. California has especially many Iranians. Los Angeles may have the second-largest Iranian population of any city after Tehran. Texas has a majority of South Asians. The Midwestern triangle has mostly Arabs and American blacks, though Chicago has a near-plurality of East Europeans (Albanians, Bosnians, Turks). Detroit has the country's largest concentration of Arabs (mostly Lebanese, Iraqis, Palestinians, and Yemenis), a legacy of the days when Henry Ford employed Lebanese laborers.

Unlike the Muslim immigrants in Europe who live in ghetto-like areas, Muslim immigrants to the United States are highly dispersed. The only town in the country with a substantial concentration of Muslim immigrants is Dearborn, Michigan, where they make up perhaps 30 percent of the population; and one part of Dearborn, called Southend, is about 97 percent Muslim. In contrast, efforts at Muslim-only towns (such as Baladullah, a Muslim enclave in the Sierra Nevada foothills of California) consist mainly of African American converts to Islam.

Immigration History

The earliest Muslim immigrants came as slaves from Africa beginning perhaps as early as 1501. Their absolute numbers are open to substantial disagreement, with one foremost scholar, Allan D. Austin, putting their number at forty thousand[1] (for the United States alone) and another, Sylviane Diouf, estimating 2.25 and 3 million (for the Americas as a whole).[2] The slave-owners sometimes appreciated and rewarded their literate Muslim slaves, but they despised the religion of Islam and did what they could to prevent it from passing from one generation to the next. As a result, except in vestigial forms (one group of Trinidadian Baptists engage in practices to the present that recall Islamic ritual), the religion disappeared by the 1860s, or two generations after the import of slaves ceased in 1808.

The first free Muslim immigrants may date back to the later sixteenth century, when captured Muslim soldiers were deposited on the coast of North Carolina and elsewhere in the South; if so, then the Melungeons, swarthy whites living on the Cumberland Plateau in remote parts of the southeastern United States, from Virginia to Kentucky, may be their descendants.

The modern history of Muslim immigration to the United States began a decade or so after the Civil War, consisting mostly of Levantines but also a few from Yemen, South Asia, Indonesia, and elsewhere. For example, some seven hundred Punjabi farmers, some of them Muslims, emigrated from India to California. This second wave of immigration lasted, with numerical ups and downs, until 1924, when the door to non-European immigration clanged nearly shut. Over the next forty years, the few Muslim immigrants tended to be Soviet-bloc refugees who arrived in the aftermath of World War II. By the time of the landmark 1965 change in the immigration law, about 100,000 to 150,000 Muslims lived in the United States.

That 1965 legislation imitated the third wave of immigration, which continues to the present. Opening the doors to immigrants from the entire world, it put a premium more on skills and family ties than on provenance. Indeed, with time, making the US population more diverse became a goal in itself, as symbolized by the lotteries, starting in 1989, which gave a chance to anyone around the world to come to the United States with his immediate family.

Accordingly, the numbers of Muslim immigrants began to increase rapidly starting in the late 1960s. An analysis of the 2000 census by the Center for Immigration Studies shows that, among countries with large Muslim populations, Pakistan is by far the leading sending country of immigrants over the last decade, followed by Bangladesh, Iran, Iraq, Turkey, and Egypt.[3]

Once in the United States, temporary sojourns often turn into permanent residence. Workers get accustomed to higher incomes, students stay on beyond their schooling, and intellectuals appreciate the freedom of expression. In general, families stay more than singles, women more than men, educated and skilled individuals more than those who are not, rich ones more than poor ones, and economic refugees more than political ones. There is a growing sense among immigrant Muslims that the home countries are fated to remain politically unfree and economically backward; not surprisingly, they see the United States as a permanent abode.

Reasons for Immigrating

Muslims since 1965 have arrived in the United States for three main reasons:

(1) *Refuge.* Tragic events in predominantly Muslim countries often lead directly to the emergence of a Muslim ethnic community in the United States; Afghanistan and Iraq offer particularly stark examples. The fact that Muslim countries are disproportionately dominated by dictators means that tyranny, persecution, poverty, violent regime changes, civil strife, and wars have driven some of the most talented and wealthy from Muslim countries in the Middle East, South Asia, and beyond. Some examples by category:

- *Ethnic persecution.* Expulsion of Asians from Uganda, followed by smaller numbers from Tanzania and Kenya, led to some six thousand Muslims arriving in North America. Saddam Hussein's extermination campaign against the Kurds led to mass exoduses in 1989, 1991, and 1996.

- *Religious persecution.* Hindu-Muslim clashes in India cause a steady stream of Muslims to seek safety in America, even as members of the country's elite leave due to job discrimination. Even a French Muslim sought religious asylum in the United States.
- *Islamism.* Members of the Ahmadi sect fled Pakistan when their faith was deemed not Islamic in 1974, as did many other Muslims running from the Islamist dictatorship of General Zia ul-Haq. The Iranian revolution of 1979 targeted the sort of person most likely to seek refuge in the United States. Persecuted by Islamists, members of anti-Islamist movements such as the Republican Brothers of the Sudan and the Association of Islamic Charitable Projects of Lebanon, left for America.
- *Anti-Islamism.* Conversely, Islamists flee repression from countries such as Algeria, Egypt, Lebanon, and India by moving to the land of the infidel, where (ironically) they find the freedom to express their views.
- *Civil wars.* Waves of immigrants arrived as a consequence of the lengthy civil war in Sudan, the 1971 Pakistani civil war, the 1975–90 Lebanese civil war, the 1990s anarchy in both Somalia and the former Yugoslavia.
- *International wars.* The Israeli victories in 1948–49 and 1967 caused waves of emigration. The Soviet invasion of Afghanistan in December 1979 and the decade of warfare that followed prompted the educated to flee. The Iraqi invasion of Kuwait in 1990 brought not only Kuwaiti citizens and residents, but also ten thousand Iraqis, one-third of them soldiers (and their family members) who surrendered to the Allied troops and could not be sent back without imperiling their lives.

With the Muslim world dominated by dictators, it seems unlikely that this flow will end or even lessen any time soon.

(2) *Education.* By the 1990s, US colleges and universities attracted over half a million foreign students, many of whom chose to remain in the United States, where facilities for their profession are superior, political freedoms wider, and economic rewards greater. Among medical students, more than 75 percent—and perhaps as many as 90 percent—end up staying in the United States. Female students are also particularly inclined to stay; they appreciate the independence, self-sufficiency, and opportunities for assertiveness the United States offers them and know that to return means having to conform to restrictive ways, demure behavior, and family dictates.

(3) *Islamist Ambitions.* Although the numbers in this category are smaller than refugees or students (and indeed, some Islamists also fit in those two capacities), Islamists have particular importance, for they harbor religious and political ambitions that are in a potential collision course with the majority population.

Islamists arrive in the United States despising the country and what it represents, intending to make converts, exploit the freedoms and rights granted them, and build a movement that will effect basic changes in the country's way of life and its government. The superpower status of the United States makes it especially attractive to those who wish to change the world order; what better place to start? Islamists want to change it into a majority Muslim country where the Koran replaces the Constitution. "Our plan is, we are going to conquer America," is how a missionary put it already in the 1920s.[4] His latter-day successors are no less ambitious. They have two alternate strategies, nonviolent (i.e., conversion of the Christian majority) and violent (i.e., jihad), to accomplish this.

Islamists also find several other advantages to a US residency: Freedom of expression that permits them to write or broadcast whatever they wish. Good communications and transportation allow the Islamists to stay in constant touch with their movements. There is no country as open to outside actors or influences as the United States. Also, American affluence offers many opportunities to raise funds.

But it's not a complete paradise, especially if the Islamists engage in illegal activities. Omar Abdel Rahman, the blind sheikh spending the rest of his life in a US jail for his part in attempting to blow up New York City landmarks, finds things less than ideal in the United States: "I came here to smell freedom; I found it to be suffocating here."[5] Since September 2001, groups (such as the Global Relief Foundation) and individuals (such as Enaan Arnaout, head of the Benevolence International Foundation) who hitherto found the US a playground for dubious behavior have suddenly found themselves caught up with the law.

Religious Practice

Do immigrants become more religious or less so on arrival in the United States? Both. Those who embrace the freedoms America offers and become religiously less observant (or even convert out of Islam), are acting out what they could not fully express in the home countries. In contrast, about one-third of Muslim immigrants say they have become more religious in the United States. Their increased piety has two main sources, cultural and moral. On the cultural level, immigrants respond to the strangeness of a new land by emphasizing familiar rituals and spending time at the mosque. On the moral level, they respond to the radical openness of American life by emphasizing their hitherto neglected faith: "When I came to America, I really became a Muslim. Back home, I took it for granted."[6]

Survey research indicates that the numbers of those who live in some fashion by the laws of Islam are about equal in numbers to those who do not.[7] Such numbers may be deceptive, however, for Muslims tend to overstate their piety. Perhaps half of the Muslims restrict themselves to halal meat. A third of the women obey the injunction against wearing makeup in public, and roughly the same number avoid shaking hands with a member of the opposite sex not related to them. A smaller number of schoolgirls, 20 to 25 percent, cover their hair. Prayers are less common; no more than 10 percent of those with access to mosques attend Friday prayer services. The consumption of alcohol is widespread. The prohibition of extramarital sex is commonly violated, especially by young men who tend to see non-Muslim women as fair game.

Socio-Economic Status

Muslim immigrants of recent years boast exceptionally high levels of education. A 1999 survey found that 52 percent of them have a graduate degree.[8] South Asians appear to the best educated of all. Exceptions to this pattern do exist, of course: Yemeni farmers, Iraqi soldiers, and most illegal immigrants are far less educated. The relatively high level of education results in part from thia Muslim community drawing disproportionately from the elites; often, the best-educated come to settle in the United States or Canada.

Immigrant Muslims tend to concentrate in the professional and entrepreneurial vocations, especially engineering and medicine, which jointly employ about one-third of Muslims in the United States. With such high educational levels, it comes as no surprise that many members of this community have done well; average income for Muslims appears to be higher than the national norm. Although new, the community boasts a significant number of millionaires as well as many other accomplished individuals including one Nobel Prize winner in chemistry, Ahmed H. Zewail, and such notables as the movie actor Omar Sharif, the professional basketball player Hakeem Olajuwon, and the model Iman. Muslim Americans proudly say that theirs is "the richest Muslim society on Earth,"[9] and they are right (well, with the exception of Qatar and perhaps other oil sheikhdoms); more than that, it may be the most accomplished.

Intra-Muslim Tensions

America constitutes a microcosm of the Muslim world, with multiple nationalities present as well as elements of Islam's entire cultural, racial, and sectarian diversity. Thrown together, these peoples discover the differences that lie below the surface of their common faith. Much of this is due to differences in custom. Turks put up gravestones and decorate them with laminated photographs of the deceased; Saudis see gravestones (even without photographs) as a form of idolatry. Because they speak the language of the Koran, Arabs sometimes display an impatience bordering on arrogance toward the Islamic practices of non-Arabs. The result is intra-Muslim bias.

"Muslim parents do not mind their son marrying a white American girl, but they would object if he married a Muslim girl of a different school of thought (Shi'i/Sunni), or different tribe, like Punjabi, Sindhi, Pathan, Arab vs. non-Arab, Afro-American vs. immigrant, or different class, Syed vs. non-Syed," observes a writer in *Pakistan Link*.[10]

Politics fuels animosities. Iranians and Iraqis have not forgotten their long and bloody war from 1980 to 1988, nor have Kuwaitis forgiven Iraq's 1990–91 occupation of their country. Saudis and other Gulf Arabs are disliked for the way they treat Muslim workers in their countries.

Religiosity is another issue. Are mosques to be moderate or Islamist? Many institutions are roiled with confrontations along these lines. The most public such dispute has taken place weekly for nearly decades in front of the Islamic Center in Washington, on the sidewalk of a major avenue. The conflict between Sunnis and Shi'is, which goes back to the first years of the Islamic religion, still has great force. Shi'is have their own mosques and rarely socialize with Sunnis.

Then there are the enduring tensions with American converts to Islam, who are overwhelmingly African American. Immigrants often look down upon converts, especially African Americans. Their enormously different backgrounds cause the two groups—immigrants and natives, foreigners and Americans, Muslims born and reborn—not always to get along well. As one convert puts it, "proselytes almost always complain of the terrible frustration they endure as they struggle to adjust to their new religious community."[11]

Children

Muslim immigrants widely see a range of American customs touching on family relations and the position of women as morally corrupt and endangering their way of life. Their worries include family honor, divorce, abandonment of faith, and intermarriage.

To Muslim parents, children must be respectful, honest, modest, and hard working. In contrast, they see American children as disrespectful, indulgent, proud, and unwilling to work. Many Muslim parents send their children to Islamic schools to control the moral tone of the classroom. Some students find Islamic schools attractive, for they no longer stick out. And yet, Islamic schools do not always isolate Muslim children from the rest of society or solve the problem of peer pressure.

Muslim students are known to hide their families' religious values: Ramadan fasting becomes a diet to lose weight, while not going to the mall is a matter of babysitting duties. Some girls leave home wearing the loose-fitting clothes their parents require but carry something tighter to change into on reaching school. The daughter of a Palestinian family attends an Islamic school, where she wears long dresses and *hijab* (head scarf) and sits separate from the boys. But the *hijab* comes off as soon as she's out of school.

The opposite pattern also exists. In recent years, during the revival of Islam, children of unobservant parents found a range of attractions in Islam—morality, discipline, even plain old-fashionedness. The younger generation rediscovers Islam as the religion of its heritage and takes it up with various degrees of strictness. It's not a simple duality, with parents on one side and children on the other.

Sexual Activity and Tensions

Separation of the sexes follows from the Islamic assumption that if men and women are allowed to mingle, they will indiscriminately engage in sex, thereby disrupting society. Only in the "modern and enlightened" Muslim family do man and woman meet each other before marriage.[12] Fortunately, the two styles can coexist, though with difficulty, and American Muslims are evolving a compromise between arranged and love marriages.

Just when Muslim girls traditionally would be separated from boys, taken out of school, and perhaps start wearing a head covering, their American counterparts begin to discover and experiment with their sexuality. To prevent such experimentation, Muslim parents seek to enforce the traditional rules and sometimes cloister their daughters. But the family lacks aunts and uncles to stand guard; by law, girls must go to school until sixteen or so; and at eighteen, they acquire additional rights. Worse, at times the parents' insistence that their children live as though back in Egypt or Pakistan leads to deep tensions and even, when girls and sex are involved, to violence and death, in honor killings.

Restrictions on meeting young Muslim women leads their male counterparts to look outside the community for companionship and sex, which leads inevitably to their getting involved with non-Muslim women and eventually marrying them. This diminishes the pool of Muslim men, leading Muslim women in turn to go out and find Christian men. Muslim women being forbidden to marry out, their taking Christian husbands is an act of defiance that effectively expels them from her community and sometimes even from their own family, prompting more than a few of them to convert to Christianity.

To encourage the young to marry within the faith, American Muslims are developing a number of novel solutions, including summer camps, socials for singles, and marriage advertisements. But even these Muslim institutions have a difficult time keeping the boys and girls initially apart and later together.

Institutions

One scholar dates to 1982 and the founding of the Islamic Society of North America the "shift from self-imposed alienation from US culture to tentative experiments at political participation."[13] As late as 1991, an analyst wrote that "Muslims have an inordinately small number of political organizations in contrast to other ethnic and religious groups of comparable size."[14] Since that time, a whole infrastructure of Muslim organizations have developed in the United States. They cover a wide range of concerns—religious, social, political, professional, ethnic, doctrinal.

From the outside, the major Islamic organizations resemble their Jewish counterparts, and to some extent are modeled on them. Both take up such issues as religious discrimination, intercommunal relations, and Middle Eastern policy; they sponsor testimonial dinners, conferences, and trips to Capitol Hill in Washington, DC; and they issue press releases, launch direct mail campaigns, take out newspaper ads, and publish periodicals.

Below the surface, however, a profound difference separates the two: whereas the Jewish institutions are conventional ethnic organizations anchored to the mainstream of American political life, the Muslim ones overwhelmingly pursue an Islamist agenda far outside that mainstream. As one moderate Muslim leader, Muhammad Hisham Kabbani, has warned, extremists have "taken over 80 percent of the mosques" in the United States;[15] another moderate refers to the Islamist leaders as "swindlers" and "radicals." The main institutions of American Islam do not represent the interests and views of the moderate Muslims who are good American citizens.

The most visible among the many Muslim organizations are those that claim to represent Muslim political interests, and especially the duo of the Council on American-Islamic Relations and the Muslim Public Affairs Committee. It is striking to note that both organizations are Islamist, and so seek to forward goals deeply at variance with mainstream American principles—as well as the aspirations and concerns of a majority in the Muslim community.[16]

They aspire to achieve four general goals:

- Win special privileges for Islam (e.g., call for the creation of a White House Muslim advisory board);
- Intimidate and silence the opponents of radical Islam (e.g., have death edicts brought down on them, as happened to one co-author of this analysis, Khalid Durán);
- Raise funds for, apologize for, and otherwise forward the cause of Islamist groups abroad, including those that engage in violence (e.g., the Holy Land Foundation, closed down for raising money "used to support the Hamas terror organization.");[17] and
- Sanitize Islamism (e.g., promote the notion that jihad is not warfare but a form of moral self-improvement).

Which brings us to the subject of terrorism: Since the November 1990 assassination of Rabbi Meir Kahane by an Egyptian, i.e., well before the atrocities on September 11, 2001, the immigrant Muslim community has been associated with a great number of violent incidents.[18] In its long history of immigration, the United States has never encountered so violent-prone and radicalized a community as the Muslims who arrived after 1965.

Conclusion

Because the immigrant Muslim community is so new, it is still very much in formation. Which way will the first generation of immigrant children turn? Will their dual identities as Americans and Muslims be complementary or contradictory? Will they accept or reject the Islamist program of changing the United States? Will they control the urge toward violence? More broadly, will they insist on adapting the United States to Islam, or will they agree to adapt Islam to the United States? Much depends on the answer.

A few things are clear. However numerous the American converts to Islam, the immigrant community will set the tone. Fashioning a separate American Islam, away from such historic centers as Egypt and Pakistan, will be a great challenge. And both the United States and Islam are likely to be deeply affected by their mutual encounter.

(Co-authored with Khalid Durán)

Notes

1. Private communication, September 3, 1998. Austin reaches this number as follows: "From the total of 11,000,000+ imports of Africans in the Americas, approximately 6 percent arrived in what would become the United States (700,000+), a little more than half of these (380,000) were from West African ports from whence Muslims might have been shipped. Perhaps something more than 10 percent were Muslims hence +/−40,000."

2. Diouf, Sylviane A. *Servants of Allah: African Muslims Enslaved in the Americas* (New York: New York University Press, 1998), p. 48.

3. Center for Immigration Studies analysis of public use file of Census 2000 supplemental survey.

4. Quoted in Andrew T. Hoffert, "The Moslem Movement in America," *The Moslem World*, 20 (1930): 309.

5. *Time Magazine*, October 9, 1995.

6. "Man From Trinidad," *New York Times*, May 4, 1993.

7. Haddad, Yvonne Yazbeck and Adair T. Lummis. *Islamic Values in the United States* (New York: Oxford University Press, 1987), p. 25 shows 46 percent of a sample of 347. That number has probably risen in the intervening years.

8. Council on American-Islamic Relations. "Report Outlines Political Attitudes of American Muslims: 96 Percent Believe Muslims Should Get Involved in Local and National Politics," Dec. 22, 1999.

9. Khan, Muqtedar. "The Missing Dimension," *The Message*, Dec. 1995.

10. Athar, Shahid. "Marriage of Muslim Girls in the U.S.A.," *Pakistan Link*, Aug. 18, 1995. Syeds (or Sayyids) are descendants of Islam's prophet Muhammad.

11. Lang, Jeffrey. *Even Angels Ask: A Journey to Islam in America*, (Beltsville, Md.: Amana, 1418/1997), p. 38.

12. Khan, Badruddin (pseud.). *Sex Longing and Not Belonging: A Gay Muslim's Quest for Love and Meaning* (Oakland, Calif.: Floating Lotus, 1997), p. 160.

13. Haddad, Yvonne Yazbeck. "Maintaining the Faith of the Fathers," in *The Development of Arab-American Identity*, Ernest McCarus, ed. (Ann Arbor: University of Michigan Press, 1994), p. 75.

14. Johnson, Steve A. "Political Activities of Muslims in America," in Yvonne Yazbeck Haddad, ed., *The Muslims of America* (New York: Oxford University Press, 1991), p. 117.

15. Speaking at the Department of State's Open Forum, Jan. 7, 1999.

16. See Daniel Pipes, "CAIR: 'Moderate' Friends of Terror," *New York Post*, Apr. 22, 2002; and Investigative Project on Terrorism, "Behind the Façade: The Muslim Public Affairs Council," Mar. 16, 2010.

17. "Remarks by the President on Financial Fight against Terror," The White House, Dec. 4, 2001.

18. Others include: the February 1991 murder of Mustafa Shalabi in Brooklyn, NY; the January 1993 attack on CIA personnel, killing two; the February 1993 World Trade Center bombing; the March 1994 shooting at a van of Orthodox Jewish boys, killing one; the February 1997 murder atop the Empire State Building of a Danish tourist; the October 1999 crash of an EgyptAir flight near New York City, killing 217; and the July 2002 attack on the El Al counter at Los Angeles International Airport, killing two.

18

CAIR: Islamists Fooling the Establishment

The Council on American-Islamic Relations (CAIR), headquartered in Washington, is perhaps the best-known and most controversial Muslim organization in North America. CAIR presents itself as an advocate for Muslims' civil rights and the spokesman for American Muslims. "We are similar to a Muslim NAACP," says its communications director, Ibrahim Hooper.[1] Its official mission—"to enhance understanding of Islam, encourage dialogue, protect civil liberties, empower American Muslims, and build coalitions that promote justice and mutual understanding"—suggests nothing problematic.

Starting with a single office in 1994, CAIR now claims over thirty, including a branch in Canada, with more steadily being added. In addition to its grand national headquarters in Washington, it has impressive offices in other cities; the New York office, for example, is housed in the nineteen-story Interchurch Center located on Manhattan's Riverside Drive.

But there is another side to CAIR that has alarmed many people in positions to know. The Department of Homeland Security refuses to deal with it. Senator Charles Schumer (Democrat, New York) describes it as an organization "which we know has ties to terrorism."[2] Senator Dick Durbin (Democrat, Illinois) observes that CAIR is "unusual in its extreme rhetoric and its associations with groups that are suspect." Steven Pomerantz, the FBI's former chief of counterterrorism, notes that "CAIR, its leaders, and its activities effectively give aid to international terrorist groups." The family of John P. O'Neill, Sr., the former FBI counterterrorism chief who perished at the World Trade Center, named CAIR in a lawsuit as having "been part of the criminal conspiracy of radical Islamic terrorism" responsible for the September 11 atrocities. Counterterrorism expert Steven Emerson calls it "a radical fundamentalist front group for Hamas."[3]

Of particular note are the American Muslims who reject CAIR's claim to speak on their behalf. The late Seifeldin Ashmawy, publisher of the New Jersey-based *Voice of Peace*, called CAIR the champion of "extremists whose views do not represent Islam."[4] Jamal Hasan of the Council for Democracy and Tolerance explains that CAIR's goal is to spread "Islamic hegemony the world over by hook or by crook."[5] Kamal Nawash, head of Free Muslims Against Terrorism, finds that CAIR and similar groups condemn terrorism on the surface while endorsing an ideology that helps foster extremism, adding that "almost all of their members are theocratic Muslims who reject secularism and want to establish Islamic states." Tashbih Sayyed of the Council for Democracy and Tolerance calls CAIR "the most accomplished fifth column" in the United States. And Stephen Schwartz of the Center on Islamic Pluralism writes that "CAIR should be considered a foreign-based subversive organization, comparable in the Islamist field to the Soviet-controlled Communist Party, USA."

CAIR, for its part, dismisses all criticism, blaming negative comments on "Muslim bashers" who "can never point to something CAIR has done in its ten-year history that is objectionable." Actually, there is much about the organization's history that is objectionable—and it is readily apparent to anyone who bothers to look.

Part of the Establishment

When President George W. Bush visited the Islamic Center of Washington several days after September 11, 2001, to signal that he would not tolerate a backlash against Muslims, he invited CAIR's executive director, Nihad Awad, to join him at the podium. Two months later, when Secretary of State Colin Powell hosted a Ramadan dinner, he, too, called upon CAIR as representative of Islam in America. More broadly, when the State Department seeks out Muslims to welcome foreign dignitaries, journalists, and academics, it calls upon CAIR. The organization has represented American Muslims before Congress. The National Aeronautics and Space Agency hosted CAIR's "Sensitivity and Diversity Workshop" in an effort to harmonize space research with Muslim sensibilities.

Law-enforcement agencies in Florida, Maryland, Ohio, Michigan, New York, Arizona, California, Missouri, Texas, and Kentucky have attended CAIR's sensitivity-training sessions. The organization boasts such tight relations with law enforcement that it claims to have even been invited to monitor police raids. In July 2004, as agents from the

FBI, Internal Revenue Service, and Homeland Security descended on the Institute of Islamic and Arabic Sciences in America, a Saudi-created school in Merrifield, Virginia, a local paper reported that the FBI had informed CAIR's legal director, Arsalan Iftikhar, that morning that the raid was going to take place.

CAIR is also a media darling. It claims to log five thousand annual mentions on newspapers, television, and radio, including some of the most prestigious media in the United States. The press dutifully quotes CAIR's statistics, publishes its theological views, reports its opinions, rehashes its press releases, invites its staff on television, and generally dignifies its existence as a routine part of the American and Canadian political scenes.

CAIR regularly participates in seminars on Islamic cultural issues for corporations and has been invited to speak at many of America's leading universities, including Harvard, Stanford, Johns Hopkins, and Columbia. American high schools have invited CAIR to promote its agenda, as have educationally minded senior citizens.

Terrorists in Its Midst

Perhaps the most obvious problem with CAIR is the fact that at least five of its employees and board members have been arrested, convicted, deported, or otherwise linked to terrorism-related charges and activities.

Randall ("Ismail") Royer, an American convert to Islam, served as CAIR's communications specialist and civil rights coordinator; today he sits in jail on terrorism-related charges. In June 2003, Royer and ten other young men, ages twenty-three to thirty-five, known as the "Virginia jihad group," were indicted on forty-one counts of "conspiracy to train for and participate in a violent jihad overseas." The defendants, nine of them US citizens, were accused of association with Lashkar-e-Taiba, a radical Islamic group designated as a foreign terrorist organization by the US Department of State in 2001. They were also accused of meeting covertly in private homes and at the Islamic Center in Falls Church to prepare themselves for battle by listening to lectures and watching videotapes. As the prosecutor noted, "Ten miles from Capitol Hill in the streets of northern Virginia, American citizens allegedly met, plotted, and recruited for violent jihad." According to Matthew Epstein of the Investigative Project, Royer helped recruit the others to the jihad effort while he was working for CAIR. The group trained at firing ranges in Virginia and Pennsylvania; in addition, it practiced "small-unit military tactics" at a paintball war-games facility in Virginia, earning it the moniker, the "paintball jihadis." Eventually members of the group traveled to Pakistan.

Five of the men indicted, including CAIR's Royer, were found to have had in their possession, according to the indictment, "AK-47-style rifles, telescopic lenses, hundreds of rounds of ammunition and tracer rounds, documents on undertaking jihad and martyrdom, [and] a copy of the terrorist handbook containing instructions on how to manufacture and use explosives and chemicals as weapons."[6]

After four of the eleven defendants pleaded guilty, the remaining seven, including Royer, were accused in a new, thirty-two-count indictment of yet more serious charges: conspiring to help Al-Qaeda and the Taliban battle American troops in Afghanistan. Royer admitted in his grand jury testimony that he had already waged jihad in Bosnia under a commander acting on orders from Osama bin Laden. Prosecutors also presented evidence that his father, Ramon Royer, had rented a room in his St. Louis–area home in 2000 to Ziyad Khaleel, the student who purchased the satellite phone used by Al-Qaeda in planning the two US embassy bombings in East Africa in August 1998. Royer eventually pleaded guilty to lesser firearms-related charges, and the former CAIR staffer was sentenced to twenty years in prison.

A coda to the "Virginia jihad network" came in 2005 when a Federal court convicted another Virginia man, Ahmed Omar Abu Ali, of plotting to kill President Bush. Prosecutors alleged that Abu Ali participated in the Virginia jihad network's paintball games and perhaps supplied one of his fellow jihadists with an assault rifle. Royer's possible role in Abu Ali's plans are unclear.

Ghassan Elashi, the founder of CAIR's Texas chapter, has a long history of funding terrorism. First, he was convicted in July 2004, with his four brothers, of having illegally shipped computers from their Dallas-area business, InfoCom Corporation, to two designated state-sponsors of terrorism, Libya and Syria. Second, he and two brothers were convicted in April 2005 of knowingly doing business with Mousa Abu Marzook, a senior Hamas leader, whom the US State Department had in 1995 declared a "specially designated terrorist." Elashi was convicted of all twenty-one counts with which he was charged, including conspiracy, money laundering, and dealing in the property of a designated terrorist. Third, he was charged in July 2004 with providing more than $12.4 million to Hamas while he was running the Holy

Land Foundation for Relief and Development, America's largest Islamic charity. When the US government shuttered Holy Land Foundation in late 2001, CAIR characterized this move as "unjust" and "disturbing."

Bassem Khafagi, an Egyptian native and CAIR's onetime community relations director, pleaded guilty in September 2003 to lying on his visa application and passing bad checks for substantial amounts in early 2001, for which he was deported. CAIR claimed Khafagi was hired only after he had committed his crimes and that the organization was unaware of his wrongdoing. But that is unconvincing, for a cursory background check reveals that Khafagi was a founding member and president of the Islamic Assembly of North America (IANA), an organization under investigation by the US Department of Justice for terrorism-related activities. CAIR surely knew that IANA under Khafagi was in the business of, as prosecutors stated in Idaho court papers, disseminating "radical Islamic ideology, the purpose of which was indoctrination, recruitment of members, and the instigation of acts of violence and terrorism."

For example, IANA websites promoted the views of two Saudi preachers, Salman al-Awdah and Safar al-Hawali, well-known in Islamist circles for having been spiritual advisors to Osama bin Laden. Under Khafagi's leadership, Matthew Epstein has testified, IANA hosted a conference at which a senior Al-Qaeda recruiter, Abdelrahman al-Dosari, was a speaker. IANA disseminated publications advocating suicide attacks against the United States, according to federal investigators.

Also, Khafagi was co-owner of a Sir Speedy printing franchise until 1998 with Rafil Dhafir, who was a former vice president of IANA and a Syracuse-area oncologist convicted in February 2005 of illegally sending money to Iraq during the Saddam Hussein regime as well as defrauding donors by using contributions to his "Help the Needy" charitable fund to avoid taxes and to purchase personal assets for himself. Dhafir was sentenced to twenty-two years in prison.

Rabih Haddad, a CAIR fundraiser, was arrested in December 2001 on terrorism-related charges and deported from the United States due to his subsequent work as executive director of the Global Relief Foundation, a charity he cofounded which was designated by the US Treasury Department in October 2002 for financing Al-Qaeda and other terrorist organizations.

Siraj Wahhaj, a CAIR advisory board member, was named in 1995 by US attorney Mary Jo White as a possible unindicted coconspirator in the plot to blow up New York City landmarks led by the blind sheikh, Omar Abdel Rahman. In defense of having Wahhaj on its advisory board, CAIR described him as "one of the most respected Muslim leaders in America." In October 2004, he spoke at a CAIR dinner.

This roster of employees and board members connected to terrorism makes one wonder how CAIR remains an acceptable guest at US government events—and even more so, how US law enforcement agencies continue to associate with it.

Links to Hamas

CAIR has a number of links to the terror organization Hamas, starting with the founder of its Texas chapter, Ghassan Elashi, as noted above.

Secondly, Elashi and another CAIR founder, Omar Ahmad, attended a key meeting in Philadelphia in 1993. An FBI memo characterizes this meeting as a planning session for Hamas, Holy Land Foundation, and Islamic Association of Palestine to find ways to disrupt Israeli-Palestinian diplomacy and raise money for Hamas in the United States. The Philadelphia meeting was deemed such strong proof of Islamic Association of Palestine's relation to Hamas that a federal judge in Chicago in December 2004 ruled the Islamic Association of Palestine partially liable for $156 million in damages (along with the Holy Land Foundation and Mohammad Salah, a Hamas operative)[7] for having aided and abetted the Hamas murder of David Boim, an American citizen.

Third, CAIR's founding personnel were closely linked to the Islamic Association of Palestine, which was founded by Ibrahim Abu Marzook, a senior Hamas operative and husband of Elashi's cousin; according to Epstein, the Islamic Association of Palestine functions as Hamas's public relations and recruitment arm in the United States. The two individuals who established CAIR, Ahmad and Nihad Awad, had been, respectively, the president and public relations director of the Islamic Association of Palestine. Hooper, CAIR's director of communications, had been an employee of the Islamic Association of Palestine. Rafeeq Jabar, president of the Islamic Association of Palestine, was a founding director of CAIR.

Fourth, the Holy Land Foundation, which the US government has charged with funneling funds to Hamas, provided CAIR with some of its startup funding in 1994. In the other direction, according to Joe Kaufman, CAIR sent potential donors to the Holy Land Foundation's website when they clicked on their post-September 11 weblink, "Donate to the NY/DC Disaster Relief Fund."

Fifth, Awad publicly declared his enthusiasm for Hamas at Barry University in Florida in 1994: "I'm in support of Hamas movement more than the PLO." As an attorney pointed out in the course of deposing Awad for the Boim case, Awad both supported Hamas and acknowledged an awareness of its involvement in violence.[8]

Impeding Counterterrorism

A class-action lawsuit brought by the estate of John P. O'Neill, Sr. charges CAIR and its Canadian branch of being, since their inception, "part of the criminal conspiracy of radical Islamic terrorism" with a unique role in the terrorist network:

> both organizations have actively sought to hamper governmental anti-terrorism efforts by direct propaganda activities aimed at police, first-responders, and intelligence agencies through so-called sensitivity training. Their goal is to create as much self-doubt, hesitation, fear of name-calling, and litigation within police departments and intelligence agencies as possible so as to render such authorities ineffective in pursuing international and domestic terrorist entities.

It would be hard to improve on this characterization; under the guise of participating in counterterrorism, CAIR does its best to impede these efforts.

CAIR encourages law enforcement in its work—so long as it does not involve counterterrorism. Wissam Nasr, the head of CAIR's New York office, explains: "The Muslim community in New York wants to play a positive role in protecting our nation's security, but that role is made more difficult if the FBI is perceived as pursuing suspects much more actively than it is searching for community partners." Nasr would have the FBI get out of the unpleasant business of "pursuing suspects" and instead devote itself to building social good will—through CAIR, naturally.

Likewise, on the eve of the US war with Iraq in March 2003, CAIR distributed a "Muslim community safety kit" that advised Muslims to "Know your rights if contacted by the FBI." It tells them specifically, "You have no obligation to talk to the FBI, even if you are not a citizen. . . . You do not have to permit them to enter your home. . . . ALWAYS have an attorney present when answering questions." On the other hand, when it comes to protecting Muslims, CAIR wants an active FBI. The same "Muslim community safety kit" advised: "If you believe you have been the victim of an anti-Muslim hate crime or discrimination, you should: 1. Report the incident to your local police station and FBI office IMMEDIATELY." In January 2006, CAIR joined a lawsuit against the National Security Agency demanding that the US intelligence agency cease monitoring communications with suspected Islamist terrorists. Part of its complaints concerned a belief that the US government monitored its communications with Rabih Haddad, the suspected Al-Qaeda financier who has since moved to Lebanon. Upon learning that CAIR was a fellow plaintiff in the suit, political writer Christopher Hitchens said, "I was revolted to see who I was in company with. CAIR is a lot to swallow."

Finally, CAIR discourages Americans from improving their counter-terrorism skills. Deedra Abboud, CAIR's Arizona director, approves of police learning the Arabic language if that lowers the chances of cultural and linguistic misunderstandings. "However, if they're learning it in order to better fight terrorism, that concerns me. Only because that assumes that the only fighting we have to do is among Arabic speakers. That's not a long-term strategy."[9]

Apologizing for Islamist Terrorism

CAIR has consistently shown itself to be on the wrong side of the war on terrorism, protecting, defending, and supporting both accused and even convicted Muslim terrorists.

In October 1998—months after Osama bin Laden had issued his first declaration of war against the United States and had been named as the chief suspect in the bombings of two US embassies in Africa—CAIR demanded the removal of a Los Angeles billboard calling him as "the sworn enemy," calling this depiction offensive to Muslims. CAIR also leapt to bin Laden's defense, denying his responsibility for the twin East African embassy bombings but instead, in the words of CAIR's Hooper, these explosions resulted from "misunderstandings of both sides." Even after the September 11 atrocity, CAIR continued to protect bin Laden, stating only that "if [note the "if"] Osama bin Laden was behind it, we condemn him by name." Not until December 2001, when bin Laden on videotape boasted of his involvement in the attack, did CAIR finally acknowledge his role.

CAIR has also consistently defended other radical Islamic terror-ists. Rather than praise the conviction of the perpetrators of the 1993 World Trade Center bombing, it deemed this "a travesty of justice."[10] It labeled the extradition order for suspected Hamas terrorist Mousa Abu Marzook "anti-Islamic" and "anti-American."[11] CAIR co-sponsored

Yvonne Ridley, the British convert to Islam who became a Taliban enthusiast and someone who denied that Al-Qaeda was involved in 9/11. When four US civilian contractors in Falluja were (in CAIR's words) "ambushed in their SUV's, burned, mutilated, dragged through the streets, and then hung from a bridge spanning the Euphrates River," CAIR issued a press release that condemned the mutilation of the corpses but stayed conspicuously silent on the actual killings.

During the 2005 trial of Sami Al-Arian, accused of heading Palestinian Islamic Jihad in the United States, Ahmed Bedier of CAIR's Florida branch emerged as Al-Arian's informal spokesman, providing sound bytes to the media, trying to get his trial moved out of Tampa, commenting on the jury selection, and so on.

More broadly, TheReligionofPeace.com website pointed out in 2005 that "of the more than 3100 fatal Islamic terror attacks committed in the last four years, we have only seen CAIR specifically condemn 18."

Ties to Extremists, Left and Right

The Council on American-Islamic Relations has affinities to extremists of both the left and right, sharing features with both. Its extensive ties to far-left groups include funding from the Tides Foundation for its "Interfaith Coalition against Hate Crimes"; endorsing a statement issued by Refuse & Resist and a "National Day of Protest . . . to Stop Police Brutality, Repression and the Criminalization of a Generation." CAIR supported the "Civil Liberties Restoration Act," legislation drafted by Open Society Policy Center, an organization founded by George Soros that would obstruct US law enforcement from prosecuting the "War on Extremism." Far-left members of Congress such as Dennis Kucinich (Democrat, Ohio) and Jim McDermott (Democrat, Washington) have turned up as featured speakers at CAIR fundraising events.

Its neo-Nazi side came out most clearly in CAIR's early years. In 1996, according to testimony by Steven Emerson, Yusuf Islam—the Muslim convert formerly known as the singer Cat Stevens—gave a keynote speech at a CAIR event. The contents of the speech itself are not known but Yusuf Islam wrote a pamphlet published by the Islamic Association of Palestine, CAIR's stepparent, which included these sentences:

> The Jews seem neither to respect God nor his Creation. Their own holy books contain the curse of God brought upon them by their prophets on account of their disobedience to Him and mischief in the earth. We have seen the disrespect for religion displayed by those who consider themselves to be "God's Chosen People."

In 1998, CAIR cohosted an event at which an Egyptian Islamist leader, Wagdi Ghunaym, declared Jews to be the "descendants of the apes."

CAIR continues to expose its fascistic side by its repeated activities with William W. Baker, exposed as a neo-Nazi in March 2002. Even after that date, CAIR invited Baker to speak at several events, for example in Florida on August 12, 2003 and New Jersey on October 18, 2003. CAIR liked Baker's work so much, it used the title of his book, *More in Common Than You Think*, in one of its ad campaigns in March 2004 and as the title of an Elderhostel lecture.

Foreign Funding

According to filed copies of its annual Internal Revenue Service Form 990, CAIR's US chapters have more than doubled their combined revenues from the $2.5 million they recorded in 2000 to $5.6 million in 2002, though the number dipped slightly to $5.3 million in 2003, the most recent year for which figures are available. That CAIR has recorded at least $3.1 million on its year-end combined balance sheets since 2001, combined with its minimal grant-making ($27,525 was the total that all CAIR chapters granted in 2003), suggests that CAIR is building an endowment and planning for the long term.

The Internal Revenue Service filings claim that the bulk of its funds come from "direct public support"[12] and its website explicitly denies that CAIR receives support from foreign sources: "We do not support directly or indirectly, or receive support from, any overseas group or government." However, this denial is flatly untrue, for CAIR has accepted foreign funding, and from many sources.

A press release from the Saudi Arabian embassy in Washington indicates that in August 1999, the Islamic Development Bank—a bank headquartered in Jeddah, Saudi Arabia—gave CAIR $250,000 to purchase land for its Washington, DC, headquarters. CAIR's decision to accept Islamic Development Bank funding is unfortunate, given the bank's role as fund manager of the Al-Quds and the Al-Aqsa Funds, established by twelve Arab countries in order to fund the Palestinian *intifada* and provide financial support to the families of Palestinian "martyrs."

According to records made public by Paul Sperry, CAIR purchased its national headquarters in 1999 through an unusual lease-purchase transaction with the United Bank of Kuwait. The bank was the deed holder and leased the building to CAIR; yet despite not owning the building, CAIR recorded the property on its balance sheet as a property asset valued at $2.6 million. This arrangement changed in September 2002 when CAIR bought out the Kuwaiti bank with funds provided, at least in part, by Al-Maktoum Foundation, based in Dubai and headed by Dubai's crown prince and defense minister, Sheikh Mohammed bin Rashid al-Maktoum. The markings on the deed indicate that the foundation provided "purchase money to the extent of $978,031.34" to CAIR, or roughly one-third the value of the property. One only wonders what a more complete investigation of its real estate transactions would turn up.

In December 1999, the World Assembly of Muslim Youth (WAMY), an organization benefiting from Saudi patronage,[13] announced at a press conference in Saudi Arabia that it "was extending both moral and financial support to CAIR"[14] to help it construct its $3.5 million headquarters in Washington, DC. WAMY also agreed to "introduce CAIR to Saudi philanthropists and recommend their financial support for the headquarters project."[15] In 2002, CAIR and WAMY announced, again from Saudi Arabia, their cooperation on a $1 million public relations campaign. The *Saudi Gazette*, which reported the story, said that CAIR's leader, Nihad Awad, "had already met leading Saudi businessmen" in order to "brief them about the projects and raise funds."

Later that week on the same fundraising trip through the Middle East, CAIR reportedly received $500,000 from Saudi prince Al-Waleed bin Talal, reputed to be one of the world's richest men. Waleed also, in May 2005, stated that he is "more than prepared" to work with organizations such as CAIR, "and to provide needed support" to them.

CAIR has received at least $12,000 from the International Relief Organization (also called the International Islamic Relief Organization, or IIRO), which itself was the recipient of some $10 million from its parent organization in Saudi Arabia. The International Institute of Islamic Thought (IIIT) gave CAIR's Washington office $14,000 in 2003. According to a court-filed affidavit, David Kane of the US Customs Service determined that the IIIT receives donations from overseas via its related entities. Law enforcement is looking at the IIIT connection with Operation Green Quest, the major investigation into the activities of individuals and organizations believed to be "ardent supporters" of the Palestinian Islamic Jihad, Hamas, and Al-Qaeda. CAIR, not surprisingly, criticized the probe of its donor, telling the *Financial Times* of London that the investigation is an attack on "respected Islamic institutions."[16]

Despite these many foreign sources, CAIR still claims to receive no funds from outside the United States.

An Integral Part of the Wahhabi Lobby

CAIR has a key role in the "Wahhabi lobby"—the network of organizations, usually supported by donations from Saudi Arabia, whose aim is to propagate the especially extreme version of Islam practiced in Saudi Arabia. For one, it sends money to other parts of the lobby. According to CAIR's Form 990 filings for 2003, its California offices invested $325,000 with the North American Islamic Trust (NAIT). The NAIT was established in 1971 by the Muslim Student Association of the US and Canada, which bills itself as the precursor to the Islamic Society of North America, now the largest member of the Wahhabi lobby. According to *Newsweek*, authorities say that over the years "NAIT money has helped the Saudi Arabian sect of Wahhabism—or Salafism, as the broader, pan-Islamic movement is called—to seize control of hundreds of mosques in US Muslim communities." J. Michael Waller, a terrorism expert, testified before the Senate Judiciary Committee that NAIT is believed to own 50 to 79 percent of the mosques in North America. According to Waller, NAIT was raided as part of Operation Green Quest in 2002, on suspicions of involvement in terrorist financing.

CAIR affiliates regularly speak at events sponsored by the Islamic Society of North America (ISNA), an umbrella organization of the Wahhabi lobby. Nabil Sadoun, a director of CAIR-DC, spoke at the ISNA's regional conference in 2003. Hussam Ayloush, executive director of CAIR's Southern California chapter, and Fouad Khatib, the CAIR-California chairman, spoke at an ISNA-sponsored event. Safaa Zarzour, president of CAIR-Chicago, was also an ISNA speaker, as was Azhar Azeez, a board member of CAIR-Dallas, who has spoken at several ISNA conferences.

In January 2003, the Saudi newspaper *Ar-Riyadh* reported that Nihad Awad appeared on a panel along with 'Aqil ibn 'Abd al-'Aziz al-'Aqil, secretary-general of the Saudi charity Al-Haramain Foundation—despite that organization's well-known ties to terrorism and the fact that already in March 2002, long before Awad's visit with Al-Haramain, the US and Saudi governments had jointly designated eleven of its branches "financial supporter[s] of terrorism." The US-based branch of the organization was also subsequently designated in September 2004.

To fully appreciate what it means that more than half of US mosques are promoting Saudi-style Islam, we refer to the Freedom House report,

"Saudi Publications on Hate Ideology Invade American Mosques." It explains that Saudi documents disseminated at US mosques are telling America's Muslims that it is a religious obligation for them to hate Christians and Jews and warning that Muslims should not have Christians and Jews as friends, nor should they help them.

The Freedom House report indicates that Saudi publications disseminated by US mosques say it is lawful for Muslims to physically harm and steal from adulterers and homosexuals; condemn interpretations of Islam other than the strict "Wahhabi" version preached in Saudi Arabia; advocate the killing of those who convert out of Islam; assert that it is a Muslim's duty to eliminate the State of Israel; and promote the idea that women should be segregated and veiled and, of course, barred from some employment and activities. But not to worry; CAIR's spokesman, Ibrahim Hooper, tells us, "The majority of the stuff they picked is in Arabic, a language that most people in mosques don't read."[17]

Muslim Supremacism

CAIR's personnel are normally tight-lipped about the organization's agenda but sometimes let their ambitions slip out. CAIR's long-serving chairman, Omar Ahmad, reportedly told a crowd of California Muslims in July 1998, "Islam isn't in America to be equal to any other faith, but to become dominant. The Koran . . . should be the highest authority in America, and Islam the only accepted religion on earth." Five years later, Ahmad denied having said this and issued a press release saying he was seeking a retraction. But the reporter stood behind her story, and the newspaper that reported Ahmad's remarks told *WorldNetDaily* it had "not been contacted by CAIR."

In 1993, before CAIR existed, Ibrahim Hooper told a reporter: "I wouldn't want to create the impression that I wouldn't like the government of the United States to be Islamic sometime in the future."[18] On the Michael Medved radio show in 2003, Hooper made the same point more positively: if Muslims ever become a majority in the United States, it would be safe to assume that they would want to replace the US Constitution with Islamic law, as most Muslims believe that God's law is superior to man-made law.[19]

Other CAIR personnel also express their contempt for the United States. Ihsan Bagby of CAIR's Washington office has said that Muslims "can never be full citizens of this country," referring to the United States, "because there is no way we can be fully committed to the institutions and ideologies of this country."[20] Ayloush said that the war on terror has become a "war on Muslims" with the US government the "new Saddam." He concluded: "So let's end this hypocrisy, this hypocrisy that we are better than the other dictator."

In a bizarre coda, Parvez Ahmed, a CAIR chairman, touted the virtues of Islamic democracy in 2004 by portraying the Afghan constitutional process as superior to the US one:

> The new Afghan constitution shows that the constitution of a Muslim nation can be democratic and yet not contradict the essence of Islam. During my meeting with a high-ranking Afghan delegation during their recent visit to the United States, I was told that the Afghan constitutional convention included Hindu delegates despite Hindus accounting for only 1 percent of the population. Contrast this with our own constitutional convention that excluded women and blacks.[21]

Intimidation

CAIR attempts to close down public debate about itself and Islam in several ways, starting with a string of lawsuits against public and private individuals and several publications. CAIR's Rabiah Ahmed has openly acknowledged that lawsuits are increasingly an "instrument" for it to use.

In addition, CAIR has resorted to financial pressure in an effort to silence critics. One such case concerns ABC radio personality Paul Harvey, who on December 4, 2003, described the vicious nature of cockfighting in Iraq, then commented: "Add to the [Iraqi] thirst for blood, a religion which encourages killing, and it is entirely understandable if Americans came to this bloody party unprepared." CAIR responded a day later with a demand for "an on-air apology." CAIR then issued a call to its supporters to contact Harvey's advertising sponsors to press them to pull their ads "until Harvey responds to Muslim concerns." Although Harvey quickly and publicly retracted his remarks, CAIR continued its campaign against him.

Another case of financial intimidation took place in March 2005, when CAIR campaigned to have *National Review* remove two books from its online bookstore—Serge Trifkovic's *The Sword of the Prophet* and J. L. Menezes's *The Life and Religion of Mohammed*—as well as the positive reviews of those books. CAIR claimed the books defame Islam and the Prophet Muhammad. When it did not get immediate satisfaction from *National Review*, it instructed its partisans to pressure the Boeing Corporation to withdraw its advertisements from the magazine. *National Review* briefly took down both books but then quickly reposted the one by Trifkovic. Trifkovic himself argued that CAIR's success here "will only whet Islamist appetites and encourage their hope that the end-result will be a crescent on the Capitol a generation or two from now."

CAIR resorted to another form of intimidation versus Florida radio show host and Baptist pastor Mike Frazier. Frazier had criticized local and state officials in September 2004 for attending a CAIR awards dinner because, as he put it, "If these people would have bothered to check CAIR out beforehand they would have seen that it is a radical group." He termed what followed "absolutely unbelievable." Within a month, he says he received six death threats and forty-seven threatening phone calls, was accosted by strangers, was labeled an "extremist" and a "fundamentalist zealot," and accused of "propagating fear, terror and disunity" by the *St. Petersburg Times*. Several members of his church fled his congregation because, according to Frazier, "they were afraid."

Other CAIR targets of intimidation have included the Simon Wiesenthal Center for juxtaposing a picture of the Ayatollah Khomeini next to Adolf Hitler, and the *Reader's Digest* for an article, "The Global War on Christians," which CAIR found "smears Islam" by citing well-documented cases of Christian persecution. CAIR's Nihad Awad faulted the *Reader's Digest* for leaving the impression that "Islam somehow encourages or permits rape, kidnapping, torture, and forced conversion."

In December 2003, CAIR ruined the career of an army officer and nurse, Captain Edwina McCall, who had treated American soldiers wounded in Iraq and Afghanistan but ended up resigning under a cloud of suspicion. Her crime? Using her military e-mail address on an Internet discussion board concerning the Islamist agenda. CAIR sent the comments to the secretary of defense, calling attention to her allegedly "bigoted anti-Muslim comments" and demanding that her "extremist and Islamophobic views" be investigated and then followed by "appropriate action." The army immediately cast the officer under suspicion, leading her to resign from a career she had loved.

At times, CAIR inspires its attack dogs to make threats and sits back when they follow through. After Daniel Pipes published an article in July 1999 explaining the difference between moderate and radical Islam, CAIR launched fifteen separate attacks on him in the space of two months, attacks widely reprinted in Muslim publications. Dozens of letters followed to the newspapers that carried Pipes's articles, some calling him harsh names ("bigot and racist"), others comparing him to the Ku Klux Klan and the neo-Nazis, or characterizing his writings as an "atrocity" filled with "pure poison" and "outright lies." More alarmingly, the letter writers accused the author of perpetrating a hate crime against Muslims or of promoting and abetting such crimes. One threatened: "Is Pipes ready to answer the Creator for his hatred or is he a secular humanist . . .? He will soon find out."

CAIR metes out even worse treatment to Muslim opponents, as the case of Khalid Durán shows. Durán taught at leading universities and wrote about Islam for think tanks; he was commissioned by the American Jewish Committee to write *Children of Abraham: An Introduction to Islam for Jews.* Fourteen scholars of Islam endorsed the manuscript prior to publication; it won glowing reviews from such authoritative figures as Cardinal William Keeler of Baltimore, the eminent church historian Martin Marty, and Prince Hassan of Jordan. Then, before the book was even released, CAIR issued two press releases insulting Durán personally and demanding that the *Children of Abraham* be withheld until a group of CAIR-approved academics could review the book to correct what it assumed (without having read the manuscript) would be its "stereotypical or inaccurate content."

Islamist publications quickly picked up CAIR's message, with Cairo's *Al-Wafd* newspaper announcing that Durán's book "spreads anti-Muslim propaganda" through its "distortions of Islamic concepts." A weekly in Jordan reported that 'Abd al-Mun'im Abu Zant—one of that country's most powerful Islamist leaders—had declared that Durán "should be regarded as an apostate," and on this basis called for an Islamic ruling to condone Durán's death. Days later, Durán's car was broken into, and a dead squirrel and excrement were thrown inside. CAIR, far from apologizing for the evil results of its handiwork, accused the American Jewish Committee of fabricating the death edict as a "cheap publicity stunt to boost book sales."

Deceit

CAIR has a long record of unreliability and deceit even in relatively minor matters. To begin with, it has the audacity to claim to be "America's largest civil rights group," ignoring much larger groups by far, such as the National Association for the Advancement of Colored People and the Anti-Defamation League.

In May 2005, CAIR published its annual report on the violations of Muslim civil rights in America which purported to document a significant rise in the number of hate crimes directed at Muslims. According to the report, "anti-Muslim hate crimes in the United States" have gone up dramatically: from 42 cases in 2002, to 93 cases in 2003, to 141 in 2004. The mainstream media dutifully recycled CAIR's press release, effectively endorsing this study by reporting it as a serious piece of research.[22] But closer inspection shows that of twenty "anti-Muslim hate crimes" for which CAIR gives information, at least six are invalid.

David Skinner points out a further problem with the 2004 report: its credulity in reporting any incident, no matter how trivial, subjective or unsubstantiated. One anecdote concerns a Muslim college student who encountered "flyers and posters with false and degrading statements about the Qur'an and the prophet Muhammad"; another concerns a student at Roger Williams University in Rhode Island who wrote that "a true Muslim is taught to slay infidels." Also, any reluctance to accommodate Muslim women wearing a headscarf or veil was tallied as a bias incident, even in the case of genuine quandaries (such as veiled athletes or drivers applying for their licenses).

Nor is this the first unreliable CAIR study. Referring to the 1996 version, Steven Emerson noted in congressional testimony that "a large proportion of the complaints have been found to be fabricated, manufactured, distorted, or outside standard definitions of hate crimes." Jorge Martinez of the US Department of Justice dismissed CAIR's 2003 report, *Guilt by Association*, as "unfair criticism based on a lot of misinformation and propaganda."

CAIR's manipulative habits assert themselves even in petty ways. For example, CAIR is not above conducting straw polls in an effort to forward its political agenda and may even be willing to exaggerate its own outreach efforts. This seems to be the case in CAIR's library project, where it claims to have sent thousands of packages of books and tapes to American libraries. An inquiry turned up the curious fact that while CAIR claimed the District of Columbia had received thirty-seven such packages, records showed only one such copy being recorded. Maybe the mailmen lost the remaining thirty-six?

In September 2005, CAIR indulged in some Stalinist revisionism: as Robert Spencer revealed, CAIR doctored a photo on its website to make it more Islamically correct by manually adding a *hijab* onto a Muslim woman. Despite all this, CAIR's statements continue to gain the respectful attention of uncritical media outlets.

The Establishment's Failure

The few hard-hitting media analyses of CAIR generally turn up in the conservative press.[23] Otherwise, it generally wins a pass from news organizations, as Erick Stakelbeck has documented. The mainstream media treat CAIR respectfully, as a legitimate organization, avoiding the less salutary topics explored here, even the multiple connections to terrorism.

One telling example of the media's negligence in investigating CAIR occurred when Ghassan Elashi—a founding board member of CAIR's Texas chapter—was indicted and convicted of supporting terrorism by sending money to Hamas and Mousa Abu Marzook. Reporting on this, not one single mainstream media source mentioned Elashi's CAIR connection. Worse, the media went to CAIR and quoted it on Elashi's arrest, without noting their close affiliation.[24]

The Washington Post seems particularly loath to expose CAIR's unsavory aspects. For example, on January 20, 2005, it ran a story about the opening of CAIR's new Virginia office on Grove Street in Herndon. The article not only passed up the opportunity to consider CAIR's presence in a town notorious for Islamist organizational connections to Al-Qaeda and to the Wahhabi network, but it was also remarkably similar in tone and style to CAIR's own press release on the same subject. (A later *Washington Post* article did mention that the new CAIR offices are located on the very street where federal agents had conducted a major raid in March 2002.)

There is much else for the press to look into. One example: CAIR-DC lists the Zahara Investment Corporation as a "related organization" on its IRS Form 990. Curiously, Zahara Investment Corporation was listed as a tax-exempt entity in 2002; in 2003, it became a non-tax-exempt entity.[25] This prompts several questions: how is a tax-exempt like CAIR related to an investment company, much less a corporation? How does an investment corporation become a tax-exempt? And how does it change itself into a non-exempt? And why did CAIR-DC invest $40,000 of the public's money in 1998 in securities that it would have to write off less than three years later? Whose securities were these? The usual databases have nothing on Zahara Investment Corporation; all this took place under the radar screen.

That the US government, the mainstream media, educational institutions, and others have given CAIR a free pass amounts to a dereliction of duty. Yet, there appear to be no signs of change. How long will it be until the Establishment finally recognizes CAIR for what it is and denies it mainstream legitimacy?

(Co-authored with Sharon Chadha)

Notes

1. *Columbus Dispatch* (Ohio), Jan. 1, 2002.
2. *FDCH Political Transcripts*, Sept. 10, 2003.
3. Steven Emerson, "Re: Terrorism and the Middle East Peace Process," prepared testimony before the US Senate Foreign Relations Committee, Subcommittee on Near East and South Asia, Mar. 19, 1996.
4. *The Jerusalem Post*, Mar. 5, 1999.
5. Personal communication from Jamal Hasan to Daniel Pipes, July 25, 2003.
6. *FDCH Political Transcripts*, June 27, 2003.
7. Mohammad Salah also appears to be the uncle of Abdullah Salah, vice president of CAIR's Chicago chapter.
8. Steven Emerson, *American Jihad: The Terrorists Living Among Us* (New York: Free Press, 2003); *Deposition of Nihad Awad, Oct. 22, 2003, In the Matter of: Stanley Boim, et al. v. Quranic Literacy Institute, et. al*, p. 58.
9. *The Arizona Republic* (Phoenix), Mar. 25, 2004.
10. Jake Tapper, "Islam's Flawed Spokesmen," *Salon*, Sept. 26, 2001.
11. *Newsletter of the Marzuk Legal Fund*, June 1996.
12. The IRS offers several choices under the item "Revenues," including direct public support, indirect public support, government contributions (grants), membership dues and assessments, and net income or (loss) from special events or rental properties—the categories in which CAIR has classified its revenues.
13. WAMY's relationship to Saudi Arabia was described this way by its secretary general: "The Kingdom provides us with a supportive environment that allows us to work openly within the society to collect funds and spread activities. It also provides us with protection abroad through Saudi embassies and consulates, in addition to financial support." "WAMY Team in Afghanistan Risks Life to Deliver Aid," Middle East Newsfile, Nov. 20, 2001.
14. "WAMY Spends SR12m on New Mosques," Middle East Newsfile, Dec. 23, 1999.
15. *Arab News*, Dec. 23, 1999.
16. *Financial Times* (London), Mar. 28, 2002.
17. *Dallas Morning News*, Feb. 5, 2005.
18. *Star Tribune* (Minneapolis), Apr. 4, 1993.
19. Personal communication from Michael Medved, Oct. 21, 2004.
20. Quoted in Steve A. Johnson, "Political Activities of Muslims in America," in Yvonne Yazbeck Haddad, ed., *The Muslims of America* (New York: Oxford University Press, 1991), p. 115.
21. *Orlando Sentinel*, Feb. 23, 2004.
22. See, for example, *The New York Times*, May 12, 2005; *The Washington Post*, May 12, 2005; and *Los Angeles Times*, May 12, 2005.

23. Zev Chafets, "Beware the Wolves Among Us," *The New York Daily News*, Sept. 28, 2001; editorial, "CAIR and Terrorism," *The Washington Times*, July 24, 2004; David Frum, "The Question of CAIR," *The National Post*, Nov. 23, 2004; Eli Lake, "Me Rethinks a CAIR Event," *The New York Sun*, Nov. 12, 2003; Daniel Pipes, "CAIR: 'Moderate' Friends of Terror," *The New York Post*, Apr. 22, 2002; Michael Putney, "Pressure May Smother Dialogue," *The Miami Herald*, Sept. 10, 2003; Stephen Schwartz, "Not So Holy after All; The Bush Administration Takes on a Hamas Front Group," *The Weekly Standard*, Dec. 17, 2001; and Glenn Sheller, "Muslim Group's Conflict with Discrimination Is Uphill Fight," *The Columbus Dispatch*, Aug. 31, 2004.

24. "4 Indicted in Texas Terror Probe," *The Boston Globe*, Dec. 19, 2002; "5 Brothers Charged with Aiding Hamas," *The New York Times*, Dec. 19, 2002; "Hamas Arrests Called Unfair," *Fort Worth Star-Telegram*, Dec. 20, 2002; "Aid Sought for 5 Suspected of Terror Ties," Associated Press, Feb. 15, 2003; "Muslim Leader Criticizes Prosecution," United Press International, July 9, 2004; "Muslim Leaders Blast Brothers' Convictions," *The Dallas Morning News*, July 10, 2004.

25. CAIR's DC office is required to make its Form 990 available to the public upon request.

19

Barack Obama's Muslim Childhood

Barack Obama has come out swinging against his Republican rival, sponsoring television advertisements that ask, "What is Mitt Romney hiding?" The allusion is to such relatively minor matters as Romney's prior tax returns, the date he stopped working for Bain Capital, and the non-public records from his service heading the Salt Lake City Olympics and as governor of Massachusetts. Obama defended his demands that Romney release more information about himself, declaring in August 2012 that "The American people have assumed that if you want to be president of the United States that your life's an open book when it comes to things like your finances." Liberals like Paul Krugman of the *New York Times* enthusiastically endorse this focus on Mitt Romney's personal history.

If Obama and his supporters wish to focus on biography, of course, this is a game two can play. Already, the temperate, mild-mannered Romney criticized Obama's reelection campaign as "based on falsehood and dishonesty" and a television ad went further, asserting that Obama "doesn't tell the truth."

A focus on openness and honesty are likely to hurt Obama far more than Romney. Obama remains the mystery candidate with an autobiography full of gaps and even fabrications. For example, to sell his autobiography in 1991, Obama falsely claimed that he "was born in Kenya." He lied about never having been a member and candidate of the 1990s Chicago socialist New Party; and when Stanley Kurtz produced evidence to establish that he was a member, Obama's flacks smeared and dismissed Kurtz. Obama's 1995 autobiography, *Dreams from My Father*, contains a torrent of inaccuracies and falsehoods about his maternal grandfather, his father, his mother, his parents' wedding, his stepfather's father, his high school friend, his girlfriend, Bill Ayers and Bernardine Dohrn, and the Rev. Jeremiah Wright. As historian

Victor Davis Hanson puts it, "If a writer will fabricate the details about his own mother's terminal illness and quest for insurance, then he will probably fudge on anything."

Into this larger pattern of mendacity about his past life arises the question of Obama's discussion of his faith, perhaps the most singular and outrageous of his lies.

Contradictions

Asked about the religion of his childhood and youth, Obama offers contradictory answers. He finessed a March 2004 question, "Have you always been a Christian?" by replying: "I was raised more by my mother and my mother was Christian." In December 2007 he confirmed this in stronger words: "My mother was a Christian from Kansas. . . . I was raised by my mother. So, I've always been a Christian." In February 2009, however, he offered a completely different account:

> I was not raised in a particularly religious household. I had a father who was born a Muslim but became an atheist, grandparents who were non-practicing Methodists and Baptists, and a mother who was skeptical of organized religion. I didn't become a Christian until . . . I moved to the South Side of Chicago after college.

He further elaborated this answer in September 2010, saying: "I came to my Christian faith later in life."

Which is it? Has Obama "always been a Christian" or did he "become a Christian" after college? Self-contradiction on so fundamental a matter of identity, when added to the general questioning about the accuracy of his autobiography, raises questions about veracity; would someone telling the truth say such varied and opposite things about himself? Inconsistency is typical of fabrication: when making things up, it's hard to stick with the same story. Obama appears to be hiding something. Was he the areligious child of irreligious parents? Or was he always a Christian? A Muslim? Or was he, in fact, something of his own creation—a Christian/Muslim?

Obama provides some information on his Islamic background in his two books, *Dreams* and *The Audacity of Hope* (2006). In 2007, when Hillary Clinton was still the favored Democratic candidate for president, a number of reporters dug up information about Obama's time in Indonesia. Obama's statements as president have provided important insights into his mentality. The major biographies of Obama devote little attention to this topic, both the friendly ones (such as those by

David Maraniss, David Mendell, and David Remnick) and the hostile ones (such as by Jack Cashill, Jerome R. Corsi, Dinesh D'Souza, Aaron Klein, Edward Klein, and Stanley Kurtz).

I shall establish his having been born and raised a Muslim, provide confirming evidence from recent years, survey the perceptions of him as a Muslim, and place this deception in the larger context of Obama's autobiographical fictions.

"I Have Never Been a Muslim"

Obama readily acknowledges that his paternal grandfather, Hussein Onyango Obama, converted to Islam. Indeed, *Dreams* (p. 407) contains a long quote from his paternal grandmother explaining the grandfather's reasons for doing so: Christianity's ways appeared to be "foolish sentiment" to him, "something to comfort women," and so he converted to Islam, thinking "its practices conformed more closely to his beliefs" (p. 104). Obama readily told this to all comers: when asked by a barber (p. 149), "You a Muslim?" for example, he replied, "Grandfather was."

Obama presents his parents and stepfather as nonreligious. He notes (in *Audacity*, pp. 204–05), that his "father had been raised a Muslim" but was a "confirmed atheist" by the time he met Barack's mother, who in turn "professed secularism." His stepfather, Lolo Soetoro, "like most Indonesians, was raised a Muslim," though a non-practicing, syncretic one who (*Dreams*, p. 37) "followed a brand of Islam that could make room for the remnants of more ancient animist and Hindu faiths."

As for himself, Obama acknowledges numerous connections to Islam but denies being a Muslim. "The only connection I've had to Islam is that my grandfather on my father's side came from that country," he declared in December 2007. "But I've never practiced Islam. . . . For a while, I lived in Indonesia because my mother was teaching there. And that's a Muslim country. And I went to school. But I didn't practice." Likewise, he said in February 2008: "I have never been a Muslim . . . other than my name and the fact that I lived in a populous Muslim country for 4 years when I was a child I have very little connection to the Islamic religion." Note his unequivocal statement here: "I have never been a Muslim." Under the headline, "Barack Obama Is Not and Has Never Been a Muslim," Obama's first presidential campaign website carried an even more emphatic statement in November 2007, stating that "Obama never prayed in a mosque. He has never been a Muslim, was not raised a Muslim, and is a committed Christian."

"Barry Was Muslim"

But many pieces of evidence argue for Obama having been born and raised a Muslim:

(1)　*Islam is a patrilineal religion*: In Islam, the father passes his faith to the children; and when a Muslim male has children with a non-Muslim female, Islam considers the children Muslim. Obama's grandfather and father having been Muslims—the extent of their piety matters not at all—means that, in Muslim eyes, Barack was born a Muslim.

(2)　*Arabic forenames based on the H-S-N trilateral root*: All such names (Husayn or Hussein, Hasan or Hassan, Hassân, Hasanayn, Ahsan, Muhsin, and others) are exclusively bestowed on Muslim babies. (The same goes for names based on the H-M-D root.) Obama's middle name, Hussein, explicitly proclaims him a born Muslim.

(3)　*Registered as Muslim at SD Katolik Santo Fransiskus Asisi*: Obama was registered at a Catholic school in Jakarta as "Barry Soetoro." A surviving document correctly lists him as born in Honolulu on August 4, 1961; in addition, it lists him having Indonesian nationality and Muslim religion.

(4)　*Registered as Muslim at SD Besuki*: Although Besuki (also known as SDN 1 Menteng) is a public school, Obama curiously refers to it in *Audacity* (p. 154) as "the Muslim school" he attended in Jakarta. Its records have not survived, but several journalists (Haroon Siddiqui of the *Toronto Star*, Paul Watson of the *Los Angeles Times*, David Maraniss of the *Washington Post*) have all confirmed that there too, he was registered as a Muslim.

(5)　*Islamic class at SD Besuki*: Obama mentions (*Audacity*, p. 154) that at Besuki, "the teacher wrote to tell my mother that I made faces during Koranic studies." Only Muslim students attended the weekly two-hour Koran class, Watson reports:

> two of his teachers, former Vice Principal Tine Hahiyari and third-grade teacher Effendi, said they remember clearly that at this school too, he was registered as a Muslim, which determined what class he attended during weekly religion lessons. "Muslim students were taught by a Muslim teacher, and Christian students were taught by a Christian teacher," said Effendi.

Andrew Higgins of the *Washington Post* quotes Rully Dasaad, a former classmate, saying that Obama horsed around in class and, during readings of the Koran, got "laughed at because of his funny pronunciation." Maraniss learned that the class included not only studying "how to pray and how to read the Koran," but also actually praying in the Friday communal service right on the school grounds.

(6) *Mosque attendance*: Maya Soetoro-Ng, Obama's younger half-sister, said her father (namely, Barack's stepfather) attended the mosque "for big communal events," Barker found that "Obama occasionally followed his stepfather to the mosque for Friday prayers." Watson reports:

> The childhood friends say Obama sometimes went to Friday prayers at the local mosque. "We prayed but not really seriously, just following actions done by older people in the mosque. But as kids, we loved to meet our friends and went to the mosque together and played," said Zulfin Adi, who describes himself as among Obama's closest childhood friends. . . . Sometimes, when the muezzin sounded the call to prayer, Lolo and Barry would walk to the makeshift mosque together, Adi said. "His mother often went to the church, but Barry was Muslim. He went to the mosque," Adi said.

(7) *Muslim clothing*: Adi recalls about Obama, "I remember him wearing a sarong." Likewise, Maraniss found not only that "His classmates recalled that Barry wore a sarong" but written exchanges indicating that he continued to wear this garment in the United States. This fact has religious implications because, in Indonesian culture, only Muslims wear sarongs.

(8) *Piety*: Obama says that in Indonesia, he "didn't practice [Islam]," an assertion that inadvertently acknowledges his Muslim identity by implying he was a nonobservant Muslim. But several of those who knew him contradict this recollection. Rony Amir describes Obama as "previously quite religious in Islam." A former teacher, Tine Hahiyary, quoted in the *Kaltim Post*, says the future president took part in advanced Islamic religious lessons: "I remember that he had studied *mengaji*." In the context of Southeast Asian Islam, *mengaji Quran* means to recite the Koran in Arabic, a difficult task denoting advanced study.

In summary, the record points to Obama having been born a Muslim to a non-practicing Muslim father and having lived for four years in a fully Muslim milieu under the auspices of his Muslim Indonesian stepfather. For these reasons, those who knew Obama in Indonesia considered him a Muslim.

"My Muslim Faith"

In addition, several statements by Obama in recent years point to his Muslim childhood.

(1) Robert Gibbs, campaign communications director for Obama's first presidential race, asserted in January 2007: "Senator Obama has never been a Muslim, was not raised a Muslim, and is a committed Christian

who attends the United Church of Christ in Chicago." But he backtracked in March 2007, asserting that "Obama has never been a practicing Muslim." By focusing on the practice as a child, the campaign is raising a non-issue, for Muslims (like Jews) do not consider practice central to religious identity. Gibbs added, according to a paraphrase by Watson, that "as a child, Obama had spent time in the neighborhood's Islamic center." Clearly, "the neighborhood's Islamic center" is a euphemism for "mosque"; spending time there again points to Obama's being a Muslim.

(2) He may have made faces and horsed around in Koran class but Obama learned how to pray the *salat* in religion class; his former teacher at Besuki, Effendi, recalls that he would "join the other pupils for Muslim prayers." Praying the *salat* in of itself made Obama a Muslim. Furthermore, he still proudly retains knowledge from that long-ago class: in March 2007, Nicholas D. Kristof of the *New York Times*, witnessed as Obama "recalled the opening lines of the Arabic call to prayer, reciting them [to Kristof] with a first-rate accent." Obama recited not the *salat* itself but the *adhan*, the call to prayer (typically chanted from minarets). The second and third lines of the *adhan* constitute the Islamic declaration of faith, the *shahada*, whose very utterance makes one a Muslim. The full *adhan* in its Sunni iteration (skipping the repetitions) goes as follows:

> God is the greatest.
> I testify that there is no deity but God.
> I testify that Muhammad is the Messenger of God.
> Come to prayer.
> Come to success.
> God is the greatest.
> There is no deity except God.

In the eyes of Muslims, reciting the *adhan* in class in 1970 made Obama a Muslim then—and doing so again for a journalist in 2007 once again made Obama a Muslim.

(3) In a conversation with George Stephanopoulos in September 2008, Obama spoke of "my Muslim faith," only changing that to "my Christian faith" after Stephanopoulos interrupted and corrected him. No one could blurt out "my Muslim faith" unless some basis existed for such a mistake.

(4) When addressing Muslim audiences, Obama uses specifically Muslim phrases that recall his Muslim identity. He addressed audiences both in Cairo (in June 2009) and Jakarta (in November 2010)

with "as-salaamu alaykum," a greeting that he, who went to Koran class, knows is reserved for one Muslim addressing another. In Cairo, he also deployed several other pious terms that signal to Muslims he is one of them:

- "the Holy Koran" (a term mentioned five times): an exact translation from the standard Arabic reference to the Islamic scripture, *al-Qur'an al-Karim.*
- "the right path": a translation of the Arabic *as-sirat al-mustaqim*, which Muslims ask God to guide them along each time they pray.
- "I have known Islam on three continents before coming to the region where it was first revealed": non-Muslims do not refer to Islam as *revealed.*
- "the story of Isra, when Moses, Jesus, and Mohammed . . . joined in prayer": this Koranic tale of a night journey establishes the leadership of Muhammad over all other holy figures, including Jesus.
- "Moses, Jesus, and Mohammed, peace be upon them": a translation of the Arabic *'alayhim as-salam*, which pious Muslim say after mentioning the names of dead prophets other than Muhammad. (A different salutation, *sall Allahu alayhi wa-sallam*, "May God honor him and grant him peace," properly follows Muhammad's name, but this phrase is almost never said in English.)

Obama's saying "Peace be upon them" has other implications beyond being a purely Islamic turn of phrase never employed by Arabic-speaking Jews and Christians. First, it contradicts what a self-professed Christian believes because it implies that Jesus, like Moses and Muhammad, is dead; Christian theology holds him to have been resurrected, living, and the immortal Son of God. Second, including Muhammad in this blessing implies reverence for him, something as outlandish as a Jew talking about *Jesus Christ.* Third, a Christian would more naturally seek peace *from* Jesus rather than wish peace on him.

(5) Obama's overblown and inaccurate description of Islam in the United States smacks of an Islamist mentality. He drastically overestimates both the number and the role of Muslims in the United States, announcing in June 2009 that "if you actually took the number of Muslims Americans, we'd be one of the largest Muslim countries in the world." (Hardly: according to one listing of Muslim populations, the United States, with about 2.5 million Muslims, ranks about forty-seventh largest.) Three days later, he gave a bloated estimate of "nearly 7 million American Muslims in our country today" and bizarrely announced that "Islam has always been a part of America's story. . . .

[S]ince our founding, American Muslims have enriched the United States." Obama also announced the dubious fact, in April 2009, that many Americans "have Muslims in their families or have lived in a Muslim-majority country." When ordering religious communities in the United States, Obama always gives first place to Christians but second place varies between Jews and Muslims, most notably in his January 2009 inaugural speech: "The United States is a nation of Christians and Muslims, Jews and Hindus and non-believers." Obama so wildly overestimates the Muslim role in American life that they suggest an Islamic supremacist mentality specific to someone coming from a Muslim background.

In the aggregate, these statements confirm the evidence from Obama's childhood that he was born and raised a Muslim.

"My Whole Family Was Muslim"

Several individuals who know Obama well perceive him as Muslim. Most remarkably, his half-sister, Maya Soetoro-Ng, has stated: "My whole family was Muslim." Her whole family, obviously, includes her half-brother Barack.

In June 2006, Obama related how, after a long religious evolution, he "was finally able to walk down the aisle of Trinity United Church of Christ on 95th Street in the Southside of Chicago one day and affirm my Christian faith" with an altar call. But when his pastor at Trinity United, the Rev. Jeremiah Wright, was asked (by Edward Klein, *The Amateur*, p. 40), "Did you convert Obama from Islam to Christianity?" Whether out of ignorance or discretion, Wright finessed the question, replying enigmatically: "That's hard to tell." Note his not rejecting out of hand the idea that Obama had been a Muslim.

Barack's thirty-year-old half-brother who met him twice, George Hussein Onyango Obama, told an interviewer in March 2009 that "He may be behaving differently due to the position he is in, but on the inside Barack Obama is Muslim."

"His Middle Name Is Hussein"

Muslims cannot shake the sense that, under his proclaimed Christian identity, Obama truly is one of them.

Recep Tayyip Erdoğan, the prime minister of Turkey, has referred to *Hussein* as a "Muslim" name. Muslim discussions of Obama sometimes mention his middle name as a code, with no further comment needed. A conversation in Beirut, quoted in the *Christian Science Monitor*, captures the puzzlement. "He has to be good for Arabs because he is a Muslim," observed a grocer. "He's not a Muslim, he's a Christian," replied a customer. No, said the grocer, "He can't be a Christian. His middle name is Hussein." The name is proof positive.

The American Muslim writer Asma Gull Hasan wrote in "My Muslim President Obama,"

I know President Obama is not Muslim, but I am tempted never-theless to think that he is, as are most Muslims I know. In a very unscientific oral poll, ranging from family members to Muslim acquaintances, many of us feel . . . that we have our first American Muslim president in Barack Hussein Obama. . . . [S]ince Election Day, I have been part of more and more conversations with Muslims in which it was either offhandedly agreed that Obama is Muslim or enthusiastically blurted out. In commenting on our new president, "I have to support my fellow Muslim brother," would slip out of my mouth before I had a chance to think twice. "Well, I know he's not really Muslim," I would quickly add. But if the person I was talking to was Muslim, they would say, "yes he is."

By way of explanation, Hasan mentions Obama's middle name. She concludes: "Most of the Muslims I know (me included) can't seem to accept that Obama is not Muslim."

If Muslims get these vibes, not surprisingly, so does the American public. Five polls in 2008–09 by the Pew Research Center for the People and the Press asking "Do you happen to know what Barack Obama's religion is?" found a consistent 11–12 percent of registered American voters averring that he's really a Muslim, with much larger percentages among Republicans and Evangelicals. This number increased to 18 percent in an August 2010 Pew survey. A March 2012 poll found about half the likely Republican voters in both Alabama and Mississippi seeing Obama as a Muslim. Pew's June–July 2012 survey found that 17 percent saying Obama is a Muslim and 31 percent not knowing his religion, with just 49 percent identifying him as a Christian. This points to an even split between those who say Obama is a Christian and those who do not.

That those who see him as Muslim also overwhelmingly disapprove of his job performance points to a correlation in their minds between Muslim identity and a failed presidency. That such a substantial portion of the public persists in this view points to a bedrock of reluctance to take Obama at his word about being a Christian. This in turn reflects the widespread sense that Obama has played fast and loose with his biography.

"He Was Interested in Islam"

While attending school in Indonesia, Obama famously attended Koranic class; less known, as he recalled in March 2004, was his "studying the Bible and catechisms" at the Asisi school. As each of these classes were intended just for believers, attending both was irregular. Several of his former teachers there confirm Obama's recollection. Here are three of them on this topic:

- Obama's first-grade teacher at Asisi, Israella Dharmawan, recalled to Watson of the *Los Angeles Times*: "At that time, Barry was also praying in a Catholic way, but Barry was Muslim. . . . He was registered as a Muslim because his father, Lolo Soetoro, was Muslim."
- Obama's former third-grade teacher at Besuki, Effendi, told Anne Barrowclough of the *Times* (London), that the school had pupils of many faiths and recalled how students attended classes on their own faiths— except for Obama, who alone insisted on attending both Christian and Islamic classes. He did so even against the wishes of his Christian mother: "His mother did not like him learning Islam, although his father was a Muslim. Sometimes she came to the school; she was angry with the religious teacher and said 'Why did you teach him the Koran?' But he kept going to the classes because he was interested in Islam."
- An administrator at Besuki, Akhmad Solikhin, expressed (to an Indonesian newspaper, the *Kaltim Post*, January 27, 2007, translation provided by "An American Expat in Southeast Asia," quote edited for clarity) bafflement at Obama's religion: "He indeed was registered as Muslim, but he claims to be Christian."

This double religiosity, admittedly, is being discussed at a time when Obama is an international personality and when the nature of his religious affiliation had taken on political overtones; still, that three figures from his Indonesian past independently made this same point is striking and points to the complexity of Barack Obama's personal development. They also raise the inconclusive but intriguing possibility that Obama, even at the tender age of six through ten, sought to combine his maternal and paternal religions into a personal syncretic whole, presenting himself as both Christian and Muslim. In subtle ways, he still does just that.

Discovering the Truth

In conclusion, available evidence suggests that Obama was born and raised a Muslim and retained a Muslim identity until his late twenties. Child to a line of Muslim males, given a Muslim name, registered as a Muslim in two Indonesian schools, he read Koran in religion class, still recites the Islamic declaration of faith, and speaks to Muslim audiences like a fellow believer. Between his nonpracticing Muslim father, his Muslim stepfather, and his four years of living in a Muslim milieu, he was both seen by others and saw himself as a Muslim.

This is not to say that he was a practicing Muslim or that he remains a Muslim today, much less an Islamist, nor that his Muslim background significantly influences his political outlook (which, in fact, is typical of an American leftist). Nor is there a problem about his converting from Islam to Christianity. The issue is Obama's having specifically and repeatedly lied about his Muslim identity. More than any other single deception, Obama's treatment of his own religious background exposes his moral failings.

Questions about Obama's Truthfulness

Yet, these failings remain largely unknown to the American electorate. Consider the contrast of his case and that of James Frey, the author of *A Million Little Pieces*. Both Frey and Obama wrote inaccurate memoirs that Oprah Winfrey endorsed and that rose to #1 on the nonfiction bestseller list. When Frey's literary deceptions about his own drug taking and criminality became apparent in 2006, Winfrey tore viciously into him, a library reclassified his book as fiction, his agent dropped him, and the publisher offered a refund to customers who felt deceived.

In contrast, Obama's falsehoods are blithely excused; Arnold Rampersad, professor of English at Stanford University who teaches autobiography, admiringly called *Dreams* "so full of clever tricks—inventions for literary effect—that I was taken aback, even astonished. But make no mistake, these are simply the tricks that art trades in, and out of these tricks is supposed to come our realization of truth." Gerald Early, professor of English literature and African American studies at Washington University in St. Louis, goes further: "It really doesn't matter if he made up stuff. . . . I don't think it much matters whether Barack Obama has told the absolute truth in *Dreams From My Father*. What's important is how he wanted to construct his life."

How odd that a lowlife's story about his sordid activities inspires high moral standards while the US president's autobiography gets a pass. Tricky Dick, move over for Bogus Barry.

Part V

Individuals and American Islam

20

Stealth Islamist: Khaled Abou El Fadl

Which Muslims in the West support Islamism, which do not?

Those who have Al-Qaeda connections or deal in terrorism are relatively easy to classify, once they are found out. The state has ways to investigate and punish illegal activities. In September 2003, for example, Taysir Alony, a star reporter for the Al-Jazeera television network, was arrested in Spain on charges of belonging to Al-Qaeda.[1] In the United States, Abdurahman Alamoudi, "a well-heeled advocate who had represented American Muslims in White House meetings,"[2] was arrested on terrorism-related charges.

But what about individuals who apparently break no laws but promote an Islamist agenda in a legal fashion, sometimes from within the heart of the Establishment? One case is that of the renowned Swiss-French intellectual Tariq Ramadan, hailed by some as a moderate—a man who has stayed within the law but is believed by some to have Al-Qaeda connections.[3] Another is Bashir Nafi, who teaches at the University of London but in *February* 2003 was indicted at a US District Court in Florida as someone who "supported numerous violent terrorist activities associated with the Palestinian Islamic Jihad."[4]

Then there is the case of Khaled Medhat Abou El Fadl. Born in 1963, he is a professor of law at the University of California in Los Angeles, visiting professor of law at Yale Law School, President George W. Bush's appointee to the Commission on International Religious Freedom, a consultant to the Texas Department of Criminal Justice, an expert state witness on major cases, an advisor to major law firms, and a writer for prestigious publications.[5] As this listing of his achievements suggests,

Abou El Fadl has a reputation as a "Muslim moderate." Here are a few of his exuberant press clippings:

- *The Boston Globe*: Abou El Fadl is "a moderate voice urging Muslims in the United States and elsewhere to speak out against radical elements of Islam."[6]
- *The Jerusalem Post*: one of the few Muslims who "take a stand despite the [personal] risks" in favor of a "pluralistic, tolerant and non-violent Islam."[7]
- *Los Angeles Daily News*: "a leading critic of Islamic radicalism."[8]
- *Los Angeles Times*: a "longtime champion of human rights."[9]
- *National Review*: "one of the most formidable weapons in the battle against Islamic fundamentalism."[10]
- *The New Republic*: a heroic moderate who announces, "There may need to be sacrificial lambs. I'm going to play this role and speak my conscience."[11]

To judge from Abou El Fadl's press, he is a path-breaking and fearless antidote to extremism. But there is a body of other evidence suggesting that he is something other than the "moderate voice" his admirers believe or hope him to be.

Wahhabi Menace

Abou El Fadl's signature issue, the one that has most established his reputation as a moderate, involves his outspoken opposition to the Saudi regime. But one can be an Islamist, and even a radical one, and also take a stand against Wahhabism. Ayatollah Khomeini, and indeed the entire school of Shi'ite radicalism, provides a dramatic example of this pattern. After a confrontation with Saudi security forces during the pilgrimage to Mecca in 1987, which left hundreds of Iranians dead, Khomeini raged against "these vile and ungodly Wahhabis, [who] are like daggers which have always pierced the heart of the Muslims from the back."[12]

Abou El Fadl, another such anti-Wahhabi Islamist, fits into an Egyptian tradition, currently called the "New Islamists," that is outspokenly critical of Wahhabism. Sheikh Muhammad al-Ghazali (1917–96), a leading New Islamist, remains one of Abou El Fadl's chief intellectual influences. Although Ghazali had earlier taken refuge in Saudi Arabia, he felt free to criticize the dominant interpretation of Islam there, especially as concerns women. He also wrote a book in 1989 that accused the Wahhabis of a fanaticism that harms the reputation of Islam. Raymond William Baker recounts how Ghazali "directly attacked Saudi religious scholars, whom he charged with mistaking the backward, inherited customs of the Arabian Peninsula for Islam and its revelation and then arrogantly seeking to impose their limited understanding on others."[13] The Muslim Public Affairs Council of Los Angeles, with which Abou El Fadl was once closely affiliated, has a generally New Islamist outlook; it explicitly "rejects many of the ideas espoused by the doctrine of Wahhabism."[14]

Despite Abou El Fadl's general antipathy toward Wahhabi and Saudis, he nevertheless has offered excuses for them. The Wahhabis, he says, "do not seek to dominate—to attain supremacy in the world. . . . They are more than happy living within the boundaries of Saudi Arabia."[15] This statement ignores the Saudi regime's policy since the 1960s of spending billions of dollars to spread the Wahhabi ideology abroad, precisely in an effort to dominate.[16] Abou El Fadl declares there has been "no examination" of the extent to which objectionable materials are found in Saudi-funded religious schools and mosques outside the kingdom, calling for congressional hearings to learn more about this.[17] But the US government has already closed down several Saudi-funded institutions in the United States, such as the Institute of Islamic and Arabic Sciences in America.[18] As Stephen Schwartz, author of *The Two Faces of Islam*, notes, "There is no doubt about official Saudi funding of Wahhabism, and there is little or no need for further expenditure of federal funds holding hearings on it."[19]

Finally, Abou El Fadl has been known to place his talents at the service of Saudi-funded terrorists. In November 1995, for example, he provided sworn testimony in an "Affidavit in Support of Application for Bail" for Mousa Muhammed Abu Marzook, a top Hamas official, assuring the court that, "pursuant to Islamic law," Abu Marzook was obligated to abide by any bail agreement he would reach with the US government.[20]

Shari'a Paramount

In common with other Islamists, Abou El Fadl wants Muslims to live by Islamic law (the Shari'a), the law that among other things endorses slavery, execution for apostasy, the repression of women, and treats non-Muslims as second-class citizens. "Shariah and Islam are inseparable," he has written, "and one cannot be without the other." In a revealing passage, he confesses that his "primary loyalty, after God, is to the Shariah."[21] Given that Islamic law is Abou El Fadl's academic specialty, this profound allegiance to its goals has great significance and provides a key to his outlook.

To make Islamic law more appealing, he blurs or conceals some of its unpleasant realities. Consider the sensitive issues of adultery, jihad, and relations with non-Muslims.

Adultery: A Nigerian woman, Amina Lawal, was convicted of adultery and sentenced to death by stoning in March 2002. When asked about this case by talk-show host Oprah Winfrey, Abou El Fadl replied that the Nigerian authorities had made a mistake because "The punishment for adultery is really a symbolic punishment. It's a punishment that is designed to make a point about how bad this crime is."[22] This is nonsense, for the punishment of adultery is brutal, deadly, and real. It has been applied repeatedly in recent years, notably in Iran and in Afghanistan under the Taliban. It is deceitful to pretend that Islamic law's *hudud* punishments (prescribed in the Koran) are merely symbolic.

Jihad: Abou El Fadl hides the historic meaning of this term (i.e., the expansion of Muslim-ruled territories primarily through the use of force) and instead variously defines it as "the struggle waged to cleanse oneself from the vices of the heart" or "to strive hard or struggle in pursuit of a just cause."[23] In a sleight of hand, he substitutes his own Koranic reading of this word, blithely discarding a millennium of interpretation by Muslim scholars and rulers.[24] Using his definition, he concludes that jihad is "a good thing." More ominously, he denounces those who "carelessly dump on jihad,"[25] accusing them of "prejudicial, dangerous talk" reminiscent (so he wrote) of Nazi preparations for the Holocaust.[26]

Jizya: Abou El Fadl treats in like fashion the *jizya* tax, a discriminatory and humiliating poll tax imposed exclusively on non-Muslims by their Muslim rulers. He renders it into something historically quite unrecognizable—"money collected by the Islamic polity from non-Muslims in return for the protection from the Islamic state."[27] Again, this is deception to excuse a discriminatory practice.

Andrew Bostom of Brown University concludes from a close reading of Abou El Fadl's work on jihad and *jizya* that his omission of evidence, "combined with an excessive reliance on sacralized, whitewashed historiography, refutes the prevailing notion that El Fadl is engaged in a sincere effort to instill fundamental change in Islam."[28]

Abou El Fadl's efforts on behalf of Shari'a go further. Serving as the academic reviewer for the "Origins of Islamic Law" unit put out by the Constitutional Rights Foundation, he is at least associated with, if not the author of, an analysis that forwards a new amendment to the US Constitution, enabling Shari'a-like blasphemy laws to encroach on traditional US notions of freedom of religion. The proposed amendment reads: "The First Amendment shall not be interpreted to protect blasphemous speech. States shall be free to enact anti-blasphemy laws as long as they prohibit offensive speech against all religions."[29]

Islamist Prejudices

Abou El Fadl harbors the Islamist's typical hostility toward the West, blaming it for whatever ails Islam and Muslims. Islamist terrorism, for example, he deems "part of the historical legacy of colonialism and not the legacy of Islamic law."[30] By holding that "Islamic civilization has been wiped out by an aggressive and racist European civilization,"[31] he in one swoop exculpates Muslims for everything they do.

Nor is the problem restricted to the colonial past. In the United States, he finds, the "demonization of Muslims is well-camouflaged"[32] and he cites unnamed and unspecified "plots and conspiracies" against Muslims.[33] Along with Islamist organizations,[34] Abou El Fadl after 9/11 falsely issued alarmist predictions about "an explosion of hate crimes against Muslim and Arab Americans, both by police and by ordinary citizens."[35] (Federal Bureau of Investigation statistics showed 481 reported anti-Islamic hate crime incidents listed in 2001, 155 in 2002, and 149 in 2003.)[36]

Abou El Fadl, like all Islamists, objects to analyses of Islam that use such terms as "militant Islam," even calling use of this term "ideological ravings."[37] And like all Islamists, he relentlessly disparages true Muslim liberals and freethinkers such as Salman Rushdie and Taslima Nasrin for promoting what he calls "secular fundamentalism."[38] Ibn Warraq is (the pseudonym of) an ex-Muslim who has written scholarly works critical of the Koran, the life of Muhammad, and the Islamic religion. Asked about him, Abou El Fadl describes Ibn Warraq's work as nothing but propaganda and wrongly dismisses his work as derivative: "If you already know what Islamophobes and Orientalists believe, this author has nothing original to add."[39]

Along these same lines, Abou El Fadl shows the typical Islamist's bias against non-Muslims. In early 2003, shortly after President Bush appointed Noah Feldman, a New York University law professor, to serve as legal advisor to the Coalition Provisional Authority in Iraq,

Abou El Fadl expressed rage to a Boston-area seminar on "Islam and Democracy" that a Jew should be selected for this task.[40]

Terror and Denial

Abou El Fadl promotes the standard Islamist line exonerating Muslims from responsibility for terrorism. He testified to the 9/11 commission in December 2003 that "Statistically, after the attacks of 9/11, Muslim and Arab terrorism was responsible for 2 percent of the sum total of terrorist incidents taking place in the United States."[41] This statement runs wildly contrary to common sense and every analysis. Specifically, Robert Leiken surveyed 212 suspected and convicted terrorists implicated in North America and Western Europe between the first World Trade Center bombing in 1993 and December 2003. He found that "86 percent were Muslim immigrants, the remainder being mainly converts [to Islam] (8 percent) and African American Muslims."[42]

Further to exonerate the American Muslim population, Abou El Fadl claimed before the commission that terrorists in most cases are "outsiders . . . on the margins of American-Muslim society."[43] In fact, the record shows that in most cases of *jihadi* violence on US soil, the terrorists come from within the bosom of the American Muslim community.[44]

Having dissociated Muslims from terrorism, Abou El Fadl then railed against US counterterrorism measures. He characterized the overdue steps taken post-9/11 (such as the use of secret evidence and heightened surveillance) as the government having "turned against" American Muslims.[45]

Given his similarity of viewpoint with the Islamists, it comes as little surprise to find that Abou El Fadl maintains cordial relations with two of the most extreme Islamist institutions in the United States:

Holy Land Foundation: The Holy Land Foundation (HLF), an Islamic "charitable" organization, was closed down in December 2001 on grounds that it was collecting money "used to support the Hamas terror organization."[46] Abou El Fadl had contributed funds to it and publicly defended HLF, lauding its professional accountability and documentation.[47] In common with a bevy of Islamist groups, he portrayed its shuttering as evidence of "the systematic undermining of Muslim civil liberties" in the United States.[48]

Council on American-Islamic Relations: CAIR is the (Saudi-funded)[49] attack-dog of Islamist institutions in the United States, well known for intimidating those who disagree with it,[50] for being listed by the US government as an unindicted co-conspirator in a terrorism-funding trial,[51] for apologizing for Osama bin Laden,[52] for employing five persons subsequently arrested on terrorism-related charges,[53] for being and for declaring its intent to make Islam "dominant" in the United States.[54] CAIR is criticized by other Muslim organizations, such as the Islamic Supreme Council of America[55] and MuslimWakeUp.com.[56]

But Abou El Fadl lavishes praise on CAIR's "civility and grace," appreciates its "important role," and thanks it "for setting an example" for all Muslims. He presents himself as thoroughly in tune with CAIR's sense of victimhood, its resentments against American society, and its goal of promoting radical Islam. "Our voice," he wrote to CAIR, "must be loud, resounding, and even deafening." He declares himself "in brotherhood" with CAIR, gushes over its "admirable work," and promotes it as a "shining example" of Muslim leadership. He requests CAIR's help on the basis that he and it share opponents; expresses a hope that CAIR's influence will spread on university campuses; and invokes blessings on it ("May God aid you in your efforts and amply reward you for standing in justice and truth").[57] Abou El Fadl even helps CAIR fundraising efforts.[58]

This is not to say that Abou El Fadl approves of everything American Islamist organizations do. His "biggest problem" with them, he has said, has to do with their lack of "intellectual grounding" in Islamic tradition. His criticism concerns their lack of sophistication and cultural depth, not their goals. He laments that

> among American Muslim organizations, the intellectual and moral grounding—not just in the Islamic texts but in the pluralities of the Islamic tradition—is woefully, woefully absent. There has not been a serious movement among these organizations to create educational institutions that would attempt a critical understanding of the tradition they claim to represent. There are practically no such institutions, or even attempts to preserve the knowledge of Islamic law. These organizations remain activist, with a lot of energy but without direction.[59]

In other words, he rues their not being more effective.

Islamist Nonetheless

Ultimately, Abou El Fadl is engaged in developing a more sophisticated way of presenting Islamism. He works toward the same goals as are more brazenly radical groups like CAIR, but he takes care to present his views in a more acceptable fashion.[60] In some cases, this leads to differences between him and them. As a fêted favorite of the Establishment, he must distance himself from some of their particularly unacceptable positions (for example, he condemns suicide bombings against Israeli civilians). This is admittedly better than silence, but it hardly signals moderation. With rare exceptions, Khaled Abou El Fadl's differences with the overt Islamists are those of style, not substance.

Some Muslim observers have come to this same conclusion. Haroon Siddiqui of *The Toronto Star* writes that Abou El Fadl "does not fit the mould of a 'moderate' taking on 'militants.'"[61] Muqtedar Khan of the Brookings Institution finds it "scary" that Abou El Fadl wants the Shari'a to be central in Muslim life.[62]

The case of Abou El Fadl points to the challenge of how to discern Islamists who present themselves as moderates. This is still possible to do with Abou El Fadl, who has left a long paper trail; it is harder with those who keep their opinions to themselves.[63] In either case, the key is old-fashioned elbow grease: reading, listening, and watching. There is no substitute for research. It needs to be done by White House staffers, district attorneys, university search committees, journalists, Jewish defense agencies, and churches. Failing proper research, Islamists will push their way through Western institutions and ultimately subvert them.

Notes

1. *El Mundo* (Madrid), Sept. 18, 2003.
2. *The Washington Post*, Dec. 1, 2003.
3. *Le Parisien*, Nov. 13, 2003.
4. Attorney General, "Indictments," Feb. 20, 2003, at http://www.usdoj.gov/ag/speeches/2003/02202003pressconference.htm.
5. For his self-description, see http://www.scholarofthehouse.org/abdrabelfad.html.
6. *The Boston Globe*, Nov. 30, 2002.
7. *The Jerusalem Post*, Sept. 13, 2002.
8. *Los Angeles Daily News*, Aug. 14, 2003.
9. *Los Angeles Times*, Aug. 14, 2003. It also praises his "unflinching scholarship" that breaks "intellectual ground with bold social critiques," Dec. 29, 2000.
10. Rod Dreher, "Inside Islam: A Brave Muslim Speaks," *National Review Online*, Jan. 8, 2002, at http://www.nationalreview.com/dreher/dreher010802.shtml.
11. Franklin Foer, "Moral Hazard," *The New Republic*, Nov. 18, 2002.
12. Quoted in Martin Kramer, "Tragedy in Mecca," *Orbis*, Spring 1988, p. 245.
13. Raymond William Baker, *Islam without Fear: Egypt and the New Islamists* (Cambridge: Harvard University Press, 2003), pp. 97–8.
14. Muslim Public Affairs Council, *A Review of U.S. Counterterrorism Policy* (n.p, 2003), p. 5, fn. 13.
15. "The Gil Elan Show," KKOL (1300 AM, Seattle), Dec. 22, 2002, on tape.

16. Dore Gold, *Hatred's Kingdom: How Saudi Arabia Supports the New Global Terrorism* (Washington: Regnery, 2003), esp. chap. 8.

17. *The Wall Street Journal*, Nov. 10, 2003.

18. Ibid., Dec. 3, 2003.

19. Ibid., Nov. 18, 2003.

20. United States District Court, Southern District of New York, Nov. 16, 1995.

21. "Dr. Abou El Fadl's Response to CAIR," July 20, 2002.

22. *The Oprah Winfrey Show*, Oct. 4, 2002, transcript.

23. Khaled Abou El Fadl, *The Place of Tolerance in Islam* (Boston: Beacon Books, 2002), p. 19.

24. Khaled Abou El Fadl, "Peaceful Jihad," in Michael Wolfe, ed., *Taking Back Islam: American Muslims Reclaim Their Faith* (n.p.: Rodale, 2002), pp. 37–38.

25. Larry Witham, "Muslims See Wordplay as Swordplay in Terrorism War," *The Washington Times*, July 24, 2002.

26. Zachary Block, "One Man's War on Terror," *Brown Alumni Magazine Online*, Nov./Dec. 2002.

27. Abou El Fadl, *The Place of Tolerance*, p. 21.

28. Andrew G. Bostom, "Khaled Abou El Fadl: Reformer or Revisionist?" SecularIslam.com, May 2003.

29. Constitutional Rights Foundation, "Blasphemy! Salman Rushdie and Freedom of Expression."

30. *Los Angeles Times*, Aug. 22, 2002.

31. "What Became of Tolerant Islam?" *Los Angeles Times*, Sept. 14, 2001.

32. *The Toronto Star*, Nov. 24, 2002.

33. "Dr. Abou El Fadl's Response to CAIR," July 20, 2002.

34. For example, the Council on American-Islamic Relations issued a pamphlet, *Guilt by Association*, in July 2003 that made these points at greater length.

35. "What Became of Tolerant Islam?" *Los Angeles Times*, Sept. 14, 2001.

36. CNN, "Hate Crimes Decrease in 2002," Nov. 12, 2003; Federal Bureau of Investigation, *Hate Crime Statistics 2003*, November 2004.

37. "'Human Rights' Must Include Tolerance," *Los Angeles Times*, Aug. 12, 1997.

38. *Los Angeles Times*, Sept. 18, 1994.

39. *The Boston Globe*, Aug. 17, 2003.

40. Personal communication from Ray Freed, Dec. 2, 2003. Abou El Fadl did not reply to the author's repeated queries for comment on this matter.

41. "Statement of Khaled Medhat Abou El Fadl to the National Commission on Terrorist Attacks upon the United States," Dec. 8, 2003. Abou El Fadl did not reply to the author's repeated queries for a source for the 2 percent figure.

42. Robert S. Leiken, *Bearers of Global Jihad? Immigration and National Security after 9/11* (Washington, DC: Nixon Center, 2004), p. 6.

43. "Statement of Khaled Medhat Abou El Fadl."

44. For a detailed look at this phenomenon, see the case of Rashid Baz, examined in Uriel Heilman, "Murder on the Brooklyn Bridge," *Middle East Quarterly*, Summer 2001, especially the section on "Community Support," pp. 29–37. Other cases that exemplify this pattern include these incidents: July 1980: an Iranian dissident killed in the Washington, DC, area; Jan. 1990: an Egyptian

freethinker killed in Tucson, Arizona; Nov. 1990: a Jewish leader killed in New York; Jan. 1993: two CIA staff killed outside agency headquarters in Langley, Virginia; Feb. 1993: six people killed at the World Trade Center; Feb. 1997: a Danish tourist killed on the Empire State building; July 2002: an employee and a traveler on El Al killed at Los Angeles International Airport; Aug. 2003: an American killed by his former Saudi friend in Houston.

45. "Statement of Khaled Medhat Abou El Fadl."

46. "Remarks by the President on Financial Fight against Terror," White House news release, Dec. 4, 2001.

47. *Los Angeles Times*, Dec. 7, 2001.

48. "Dr. Abou El Fadl's Response to CAIR," July 20, 2002.

49. Daniel Pipes, "CAIR's Saudi Masters," June 5, 2003.

50. Daniel Pipes, "An American Rushdie?" *The Jerusalem Post*, July 4, 2001.

51. United States of America vs. Holy Land Foundation for Relief and Development, List of Unindicted Co-conspirators and/or Joint Venturers," May 29, 2007.

52. Council on American-Islamic Relations-Southern California Action Alert, "CAIR Demands Removal of Billboard Stereotyping Muslims," Oct. 28, 1998.

53. Daniel Pipes, "CAIR's Legal Tribulations," June 27, 2003.

54. Speech given by Omar M. Ahmad on July 2, 1998, reported in *San Ramon Valley Herald*, July 4, 1998.

55. Jake Tapper, "Islam's Flawed Spokesmen," Salon.com, Sept. 26, 2001.

56. Ahmed Nassef, "Listen to Muslim Silent Majority in US," *The Christian Science Monitor*, Apr. 21, 2004.

57. "Dr. Abou El Fadl's Response to CAIR," July 20, 2002.

58. Council on American-Islamic Relations, "Fundraising Dinner in the Defense Fund of Ahmad Adnan Chaudhry," *press release, Feb. 10, 2001.*

59. *Khaled Abou El Fadl, Sohail Hashmi, Qamar-ul Huda, and Zainab Al-Suwaij,* "Islam and the Prospects for Democracy," *Center Conversations,* Ethics and Public Policy Center, Oct. 20, 2003.

60. For a premier example of this, see his apologetic for Islam being democratic: Khaled Abou El Fadl, "Islam and the Challenge of Democracy," *Boston Review*, Apr.–May 2003. This issue of *Boston Review* has been reprinted as Khaled Abou El Fadl et al., *Islam and the Challenge of Democracy* (Princeton: Princeton University Press, 2004).

61. *The Toronto Star,* Nov. 21, 2002.

62. Muqtedar Khan, "The Priority of Politics," *The Boston Review*, Apr.-May, 2003.

63. I have listed a series of questions that can help to discern moderates at "Do You Believe in Modernity?" *The Jerusalem Post*, Nov. 26, 2003.

21

Waging Jihad through the American Courts

On March 20, 2002, officers from the FBI, customs, immigration, and the Bureau of Alcohol, Tobacco, Firearms and Explosives (ATF), raided nineteen offices and residences in Virginia and Georgia in the largest action against suspected terrorism financing in American history. One of the targets of "Operation Green Quest" was the Washington, DC-area residence of Iqbal Unus, a nuclear physicist, along with his wife, Aysha Nudrat, and their eighteen-year-old daughter, Hanaa.

The Unus family responded to the raid by filing an implausible but important lawsuit two years later in the US district court for Eastern Virginia. The three plaintiffs claimed there had been no probable cause to search their house, they further alleged a "conspiracy to violate [their] Constitutional rights," and they sought punitive damages from several individuals associated with the raid:

- David Kane the US Immigration and Customs Enforcement special agent who signed the 106-page affidavit that justified the search;
- Rita Katz, a private counterterrorism specialist and director of what is now called the SITE Intelligence Group; and
- "All unknown named federal agents . . . who searched plaintiffs' home." Those agents, the Unus family claimed, "knew or should have known that the affidavit did not contain probable cause for the search . . . for financial documents." (The agents, later named, numbered eleven in all: four customs agents, four Internal Revenue Service agents, an Immigration and Naturalization Service agent, a Secret Service agent, and a postal inspector.)

These defendants together stood accused of conspiring to "contrive allegations" that documents relevant to the financing of terrorism were located at their house. In plain English, the Unus family alleged that Kane, Katz, and the federal agents fabricated reasons for the raid.

In other words, the Unus family ascribed responsibility for the search of their house, a sovereign decision of the US government, to specific federal employees and, even more bizarrely, to a private person (Katz) who had never served as a US government employee. They justified suing Katz because she had claimed in her autobiography, *Terrorist Hunter* and on the CBS program *60 Minutes*) to having unearthed the information that led to Kane's affidavit. Accordingly, the Unus family deemed her "the impetus" behind the search warrant and the source for its "every piece of information."[1]

The Unus lawsuit, finally settled in 2009, warrants scrutiny because it fits a common pattern of what I call predatory exploitation of US courts by Islamists. It raises several questions: What did the Unus family hope to achieve from its lawsuit? How does this incident fit into the larger scheme of Islamist ambitions? How can this abuse of the US legal system be prevented?

The Lawsuit

The main target of the raids was a small office building at 555 Grove Street in Herndon, Virginia, the site of over a hundred closely related commercial companies, think tanks, religious organizations, and nonprofit charities controlled by a handful of individuals, known collectively as the "Safa Group," after one of the major companies in that network, or the "SAAR network," after the initials of Sulaiman Abdel-Aziz al-Rajhi, the Saudi financier alleged to have funded the enterprises.

Kane's affidavit stated that several members of the Safa Group "maintained a financial and ideological relationship with persons and entities with known affiliations to the designated terrorist Groups PIJ [Palestinian Islamic Jihad] and HAMAS." The affidavit connected Iqbal Unus to the Safa Group in two main ways. First, it said he worked for the Safa Group via e-mail accounts registered to his home address, serving variously as manager, officer, director, or administrative and billing contact. He acted in these capacities for such Safa Group companies as the International Institute of Islamic Thought, the Fiqh Council of North America, the Child Development Foundation, the Sterling Charitable Gift Fund, Sterling Management Group, and the International Islamic Charitable Organization.

Second, the internet registration for the Fiqh Council of North America's website, http://www.fiqhcouncil.org/, "identifies Iqbal Unus as the billing and administrative contact for this domain, with an email contact address of iqbalunus@aol.com. According to records received from America Online, the email account iqbalunus@aol.com is subscribed to by Iqbal Unus at 12607 Rock Ridge Road in Herndon." (This fact had particular relevance in justifying a search of the Unus residence).

This documentation, the US government argued, established the Green Quest raids as "completely lawful." The judge in the Unus case, Leonie M. Brinkema, agreed. In January 2005, she made short shrift of the Unus family's argument, dismissing it not just with prejudice[2] but with disdain: "there's no way in which Ms. Katz could ever be held liable under this fact scenario."[3] Further, she found the Unus family's claim against Katz "frivolous, unreasonable, or groundless," and ordered it to pay her $41,105.70 to reimburse her legal expenses.

Subsequent rulings confirmed this decision: in November 2007, Brinkema granted a government motion to throw out the remaining part of the Unus case, which focused on tactics the government agents on entering their house, rejecting the Unus family claims to false imprisonment, assault and battery, conspiracy, and unconstitutional search and seizure.

In May 2009, a three-judge panel of the Fourth US Circuit Court of Appeals unanimously upheld Brinkema's decision, finding that "the plaintiffs have failed to sufficiently identify any factual misrepresentations in the Affidavit, and therefore, have failed to identify how Katz caused any injury." The appellate court reversed Brinkema only on one small but significant point—her ruling that the Unus family must pay Katz's $41,105.70 for her legal fees, on the grounds that Unus' allegations did deserve "serious and careful consideration in a court of law." The Unus legal effort apparently completely bombed.

Purposes

This, however, is too narrow a prism through which to see the Unus lawsuit. Its goal would seem not to be to prevail in the courtroom but to attain multiple objectives outside the courtroom:

- To divert counterterrorism investigators, specialists, and prosecutors. The lawsuit forced Kane, Katz, and the others to waste time working with lawyers and explaining to judges an enormously complex investigation rather than proceeding with further counterterrorism efforts. (The Unus' own lawyer admitted it took her eight hours a day for five months to understand the Kane affidavit.)[4]

285

- To silence these same counterterrorists, who for the years during which the court proceedings took place could not speak freely about Unus or related subjects.
- To obstruct their work. For example, Unus argued that law enforcement officers must be instructed about Muslim customs before searching a Muslim-owned residence.[5]
- To distract attention. The Unus case followed on several other (ultimately successful) prosecutions of the Safa Group. Abdurahman Alamoudi, one of its major figures, signed a plea agreement in 2003 admitting his illegal financial dealings with Libya, a designated terrorist state, and participating in a plot to assassinate then-Saudi Crown Prince Abdullah; he is currently serving a twenty-three-year prison sentence. Soliman Biheiri, also closely tied to the Safa Group, was convicted in 2003 and sentenced to thirteen months and a day in prison, following which he was to be deported. Youssef Nada, another associate, was designated a terrorist sponsor by the US Treasury Department and the United Nations Al Qaeda Sanctions Committee, while his Bank Al Taqwa was placed on the Terrorist Exclusion List.
- To glean information useful for Unus to defend himself from a possible indictment, which he might have feared given that some of his associates had been already brought to trial.
- To bankrupt private individuals who try to expose terrorists. Katz's legal bill came to $41,105.70 and she also faced two other related lawsuits. (Soon after Katz in May 2003 described on television her role in the raids and the alleged links of the Safa Group to terrorist organizations, two Safa Group organizations sued her, the SITE Institute, and CBS for defamation, seeking $80 million in compensation. Subsequently they dropped their case against all three defendants. A chicken farm in Georgia, also raided in March 2002 and described by the Kane affidavit as "a Safa Group company," filed a similar lawsuit for an unspecified amount.)
- To garner publicity for Islamists and win them sympathy as victims of government persecution.

More broadly, predatory lawsuits fit a pattern of Islamists exploiting the West's own tools against itself, as in their hijacking of airliners, reliance on the Internet, and (in Spain) swaying the political landscape via elections. Long-shot suits such as the Unus one also reap wider benefits for Islamists:

First, by ascribing responsibility for sovereign US governmental actions to private individuals such as Katz, they bolster a conspiracist trend to undermine its authority. Thus has Richard Perle been blamed for the Bush administration's decision to overthrow the Saddam Hussein regime and Steven Emerson and I held responsible for a federal raid on InfoCom Corporation in September 2001 as well as for Operation Green Quest itself.

Second, Islamists make a practice of misusing the legal system with predatory lawsuits against individuals, organizations, and companies who, like Katz, dare report on them:

- The Holy Land Foundation for Relief and Development, deemed in 2001 a "Specially Designated Global Terrorist Entity," sued the *Dallas Morning News*, four of its reporters, and its parent company Belo Corp., accusing them of defamation.
- The Global Relief Foundation sued the *New York Times*, ABC News, the Associated Press, the *Boston Globe*, the *Daily News*, Hearst Communications, and seven journalists for reports in 2001 that it was funneling money to terrorists.
- Seven Dallas-area Muslim groups sued Joe Kaufman of "Americans Against Hate" for an article detailing ties between the Islamic Circle of North America and terrorist groups (Hamas, Hezbollah, and possibly Al Qaeda).
- The Islamic Society of Boston brought a law suit against seventeen defendants after news outlets and Jewish groups alleged that the ISB had connections to terrorist organizations and had purchased land from the City of Boston for below-market value
- Khadija Ghafur, superintendent of the now-defunct Gateway Academy, initiated a libel suit against the Anti-Defamation League on the grounds that its stated concerns (about the academy having connections to the terrorist organization Al-Fuqra and using taxpayer funding to provide religious instruction) were in fact part of ADL's "long-standing effort to denigrate Muslims as part of their advocacy for Israel."
- CAIR brought a defamation lawsuit against former Representative Cass Ballenger (a Republican from North Carolina), after he spoke of having reported CAIR to federal authorities as a "fundraising arm for Hezbollah." CAIR also filed suit alleging "libelous defamation" against Andrew Whitehead of Anti-CAIR for his terming CAIR "a terrorist supporting front organization" founded by members of Hamas.
- CAIR-Canada, CAIR's Canadian adjunct, sued David Harris, formerly of the Canadian Security Intelligence Service, along with Ottawa's CFRA radio station, because Harris, speaking on CFRA, noted that 70 percent of funds raised by CAIR-CAN go to CAIR and suggested that the Canadian government should look into CAIR-Canada's relationship with CAIR.

Finally, Islamists make life difficult for the US government itself by bringing lawsuits against agencies tasked with maintaining security:

- A Georgia chicken farm alleged to be part of the Safa Group won much attention for suing the government because its attorney, Wilmer

Parker, a former assistant US attorney, claimed that federal prosecutors "knowingly made false statements" to obtain the search warrant for the raids. The lawsuit was dismissed.

- Five US Muslim citizens got CAIR and ACLU support to sue the US Customs and Border Patrol for detaining them upon their return from an Islamic conference in Toronto, a conference that the patrol believed was a potential meeting place for terrorists. The suit was dismissed.
- Abdel Moniem Ali El-Ganayni, a nuclear physicist of Egyptian origins, sued the Department of Energy after it revoked his security clearance following an investigation that revealed he had "knowingly established or continued sympathetic association with a saboteur, spy, terrorist, traitor, seditionist, anarchist, or revolutionist, espionage agent, or representative of a foreign nation whose interests are inimical to the interests of the United States." Win or lose, the Islamists' legal gambits disrupt the work of law enforcement.

Such predatory lawsuits also carry risks, however. Not only are they expensive and likely to go down in flames, as did the Unus effort, but they can backfire and wreak damage on the plaintiffs, who look foolish when they must suddenly drop lawsuits. CAIR did so in its case against Andrew Whitehead and KinderUSA in its case against Yale University Press and Matthew Levitt of the Washington Institute for Near East Policy. Worse yet, Enaam Arnaout, director of the Benevolence International Foundation (BIF), made statements in BIF's suit against the US government that led to his being charged with obstruction of justice, convicted, and sentenced to 121 months in jail.

Policy Recommendation

The Unus and other lawsuits point to an abuse of the legal system in need of remedy. Fortunately, important steps toward such a remedy do exist, albeit usually only for private individuals: that would be Anti-SLAPP legislation, where SLAPP stands for "Strategic Lawsuits against Public Participation." A SLAPP, according to the California Anti-SLAPP Project, generally is "a (1) civil complaint or counterclaim; (2) filed against individuals or organizations; (3) arising from their communications to government or speech on an issue of public interest or concern." When these conditions are met, the court can make the plaintiff pay the defendant's attorney's fees and other legal costs.

The legislation works. The ADL filed an anti-SLAPP motion against Khadija Ghafur, prompting the court to dismiss her case. KinderUSA dropped its lawsuit as soon as the defendants made an anti-SLAPP motion, even before the court ruled on it. But Anti-SLAPP statutes are only spottily available; nearly half the states and the federal government have not enacted them. Also, in too many instances the legislation is too narrowly construed by courts, making it an ineffective tool for defendants. For example, in the ISB case, the judge denied an anti-SLAPP motion on the grounds that only activities directly related to petitioning the government, not media activities, are protected by Massachusetts' anti-SLAPP statute.

It is time to enact a uniform, federal anti-SLAPP legislation, as is now being proposed under the name of the "The Citizen Participation in Government and Society Act." Among other benefits, this will protect researchers and activists dealing with Islamism and terrorism from predatory use of the legal system. If the war against Islamism is to be won, all avenues of attack, including the courts, need to be battened down.

Notes

1. Deborah St. John, "Transcript of Motions Hearing," in Iqbal Unus et al. vs. David Kane et al., Jan. 11, 2005, p. 31.
2. Leonie M. Brinkema, "Order," in Iqbal Unus et al. vs. David Kane et al., Mar. 11, 2005, p. 3.
3. Leonie M. Brinkema, "Transcript of Motions Hearing," in Iqbal Unus et al. vs. David Kane et al., Jan. 11, 2005, p. 7.
4. St. John, "Transcript of Motions Hearing," p. 27.
5. St. John, "Transcript of Motions Hearing," p.33.

22

A Palestinian in Texas: Riad Hamad

Riad Elsolh Hamad, fifty-five, left his family's apartment in Austin, Texas, to get some prescription drugs on April 14, 2008. The immigrant from Lebanon and middle school computer teacher never returned home. Three days later, the police found his body, bound with tape, floating in nearby Lady Bird Lake, and concluded that "all signs indicate this may have been a suicide."

Hamad's family indicated that he had been under stress lately and even suicidal. And with good reason: the Federal Bureau of Investigation along with the Internal Revenue Service had searched his house on February 27, 2008, when the FBI declared him a "person of interest" in a criminal investigation.

Despite this cloud around the dead man, local news outlets reported nothing but kind words and high praise for him. After Hamad's family issued a statement describing Riad as a "peace activist who worked tirelessly on behalf of those less fortunate than him and was loved and admired by many members of the local, as well as international community," the press duly picked up on this moniker and regularly called him a "peace activist."

Television station KVUE quoted Joshua Howell, assistant manager at the office where Hamad had a postal box, recalling him as "always in a good mood. Never upset. Never even heard him say a harsh word about anybody." The principal at the school where he taught sent a letter to students' parents calling Hamad "a longtime and valued" member of the faculty whose "love and passion for education touched us all." At Hamad's memorial service, retired Episcopal Priest Edward M Hartwell praised "his humanitarian work to help the children of Palestine [as] some of the most creative and effective work that I know of."

Hamad himself boasted of his peaceable approach to politics: "All of our work is very transparent. We don't work with any militant group or violent group, or anybody with a militant affiliation."

That was the Riad Hamad praised by family, friends, admirers, and even himself. But Hamad had another side, the one that brought the FBI to search his house, that got him fired from Austin Community College for "making racist slurs and sexist jokes in the classroom," and that made him a foul presence in my life. Thanks to the recent testimony by a former ally of Hamad who has turned against him, several years later, we now know something approaching his full story.

The Summons

Hamad brought himself to my unwelcome attention in early June 2006 by sending me, via certified mail, a summons to appear in court in Austin. The document bore a scrawled, unkempt handwriting on a form issued by the US District Court, Western District of Texas, informing me that Hamad was suing Campus Watch and me for libel. (Campus Watch being a project of the Middle East Forum, he was effectively suing the Forum.)

This turned out to be the second amended complaint; I found myself in good company, as the summons also listed the Center for the Study of Popular Culture (now known as the David Horowitz Freedom Center), David Horowitz personally, the Center for Jewish Community Studies, the State of Texas, Joe Kaufman, Americans Against Hate, MilitantIslamMonitor.org, and an internet provider called CB Accounts. Hamad proceeded to file another three amended complaints and in them he tacked on yet more defendants (Freerepublic LLC, Jim Robinson, Laurence Simon, and Dotster Inc.)

His was a *pro se* summons, meaning that Hamad, a non-lawyer, had filled it out by himself and was representing himself—i.e., it cost him next to nothing to sue one and all.

Hamad charged each of us with twenty-one offences: libel and slander, malicious libel, malicious slander, defamation of character, defamation of character with intent to cause mental anguish, libeling and slandering a business name, defamation through fraud of a business name, interference with a business contract, tortious interference with a business contract, conspiracy to interfere with a business contract, interference with interstate commerce, interference with Internet commerce, conspiracy to interfere with Internet commerce, intentional infliction of mental anguish with the intent to injure, invasion of privacy, fraud, negligence, gross negligence, disparagement of a business name, disparagement of business products, and dilution of a business name.

In compensation for this long list of alleged abuses, Hamad demanded from his many defendants $5 million in compensatory damages, $10 million for his loss of income, and $50 million in exemplary and punitive damages. Nor was that all: he sought a permanent injunction against our calling his business an "Islamic charity" or he personally a "Muslim fundamentalist." He wanted a Department of Justice investigation into us for "criminal and racketeering work as lobbyists for a foreign country [i.e., Israel] without the proper permits and licenses." He also insisted on public apologies by us in ten media outlets chosen by him, as well as payment for his court costs and "any and all other relief that Plaintiff might show that he is entitled to in a jury trial."

Hamad gave insight into his mentality and his motives in the course of his lawsuit. His discovery requests of David Horowitz are particularly colorful, including:

- Document the "Religious affiliation of members of the board of CSPC, its affiliates and editors of Frontpagemag.org."
- Provide a "Blood and urine sample of David Horowitz . . . to identify his ethnicity and religious affiliations."
- "Identify any and all staff of the Israeli embassy that David Horowitz and CSPC are associated with, amounts of money paid for their services by the Israeli embassy."
- Answer whether "David Horowitz is a devout Jews [sic] and observes the Sabbath."
- Answer whether "David Horowitz eats pork and violates Jewish traditions."
- Answer whether "David Horowitz is not a Semite and pretends to be Jewish to gain sympathy for his views and make money."

This summons came as a total surprise, as a I had previously never heard of or mentioned Riad Hamad. Sleuthing revealed only the slightest and most indirect connection between us: Hamad had created and headed an organization called the Palestine Children's Welfare Fund (PCWF) and in a *January 18,* 2004, weblog entry, "Lamyaa Hashim, Supporting Burqas and Suicide Bombers," I had quoted Joe Kaufman who alluded to PCWF as follows:

> The site belongs to the medical director for the Palestine Children's Welfare Fund, Rosemary Davis

That's it. I quoted fifteen words from someone who mentioned who worked for Hamad's organization. For this glancing reference, my prorated share of payments to Hamad would come to my share of at least $65 million, or about a million dollars per word.

What is the PCWF? NGO Monitor analyzed the organization in 2003 and found its primary mission to be "propagating the delegitimization of Israel." As a 2007 summary by NGO Monitor put it, "Gaza-based PCWF openly exploits children's issues for radical politicized agendas that promote the conflict. These activities are entirely inconsistent with its claims to be a humanitarian organization." By way of example, NGO Monitor tells about PCWF's children's drawing contest in which

> The judges rewarded, almost without exception, entries that featured fierce and violent hatred of Israel. The winning picture features a fire, in the shape of a map of Israel and the Palestinian Authority, consuming the Star of David with the word "Israel" written inside the flag. Another entry depicted a Palestinian flag dropping flames on an Israeli flag and burning Israelis standing next to it. Such activities serve only to advance a culture of violence and hatred.

In brief, PCWF is as crude and hate-mongering as its leader.

The Lawsuit

Hamad might have been a *pro se* plaintiff but I could not take the chance of being a *pro se* defendant and so turned for representation to the law office of Levine Sullivan Koch & Schulz, L.L.P., which specializes in defamation issues. We responded to Hamad with a motion to dismiss on June 29, 2006, citing three grounds:

> First, this Court lacks personal jurisdiction over Pipes and MEF. Neither Pennsylvania defendant has had any contact with Texas that would establish either general or specific jurisdiction.

> Second, even if the Court had jurisdiction, plaintiff himself admits that his defamation claim is barred by the one-year statute of limitations because any alleged publication occurred "as late as July 2004."

> Third, plaintiff has not pled facts sufficient to allege that Pipes and MEF published any defamatory statements about him. Indeed, he cannot do so: Neither defendant has ever written a word about him or engaged in any action that would justify plaintiff's hauling them into a Texas court.

My motion also noted that Hamad is a *pro se* plaintiff with a history of filing what one judgment against him (*Hamad v. Austin Community*

College) called "patently frivolous" litigation efforts that "repeatedly abuse the legal system."

Three days before this motion to dismiss, Judge Sam Sparks of the Western District of Texas had already dismissed with prejudice Hamad's case against David Horowitz. On July 25, he dismissed the case against me and later awarded me court costs. For good measure, Sparks called Hamad a litigant with "a history in this Court of filing lawsuits without merit for the purpose of harassment and making outrageous allegations."

Undaunted by his failure to gain any legal traction, Hamad appealed. This prompted Judge Sparks to issue an even more vehement order on September 6 in which he characterized Hamad's complaints as espousing "no legal theory for which recovery can be made against any of the multitude of defendants sued in this case" and dismissed his pleadings on the grounds that they were "not filed for any purpose and simply harass and cause unnecessary delay or needless increase in the cost of litigation." Sparks again granted my motion to dismiss, agreeing with all three of my claims, ruling that the court cannot exercise jurisdiction over the Middle East Forum or myself (because of our lack of connections to Texas); that Hamad filed after the statute of limitations had expired; and that I never made defamatory statements concerning Riad Hamad. He also ordered Hamad to pay me a $1,000 penalty.

For a second time, Hamad responded belligerently, this time going public with his claims against we defendants. Talk about libel! He announced to the world on September 14 (including a comment sent to the Campus Watch website) that we

> are engaged in criminal activities and fraud upon the public by collecting donations amounting to tens of millions of dollars. The donations are being used to fund illegal activities in the United States and Israel and with the knowledge of the government of the United States and the judicial branch.

Four days later, Hamad sent out an appeal to his mailing list, stating that "closely linked" websites "are using false information and collection donations . . . to attack and discredit Arabs, Muslims" and asking for at least one thousand people to call the office for internet crimes belonging to the attorney general of Illinois.

Encouraged by the court's attitude toward Hamad, I requested on October 6 that he be compelled to pay my court costs. On January 17, 2007, Judge Sparks delivered his final judgment and granted my request for fees totaling $12,915. Sparks made clear his intense irritation with Hamad:

> Plaintiff Riad Elsolh Hamad first filed this wholly frivolous claim on April 13, 2006. Since that time, his "Petition" has gone through five revisions. None of the five Amended Petitions was authorized by the Federal Rules or leave of this Court, and not one version of Hamad's complaint states any claim for which relief can be granted under any law of the United States or the State of Texas against any defendant. The Court dismissed Hamad's complaint with prejudice in its second incarnation in an Order dated June 26, 2006. Nevertheless, Hamad has continued to file Amended Petitions presenting claims for relief identical to the ones dismissed in the Second Amended Petition. Each Amended Petition merely drags yet another group of defendants into the same unintelligible morass of vitriolic accusations for which no basis in law has ever been established. Moreover, Hamad continues to name dismissed parties as defendants in his repetitive pleadings.

The next fourteen months saw several more rounds of the same: Hamad appealing and all the judges turning down every aspect of every effort of his, culminating with a March 12, 2008, judgment by the 5th Circuit Court of Appeals slamming Hamad for his "ten year history of filing frivolous suits in this court." The appeals court upped the award to me to $32,944.50 in attorney's fees.

As Gerald Steinberg of NGO Monitor noted, Hamad's lawsuit "was a clear attempt to use the courts and intimidation to prevent independent analysis and exposure of the incitement by anti-Israel NGOs."

The Search

By early 2008, however, Hamad had other and larger concerns on his mind. Two weeks before, on February 27, 2008, the Federal Bureau of Investigation and Internal Revenue Service had jointly raided his house. Brandon Darby, a former leftist, anti-Zionist, and longtime friend of Hamad who now works for conservative causes and on behalf of Israel, has explained how this raid came to pass:

Darby, who had helped Hamad raise money and recruit "human shields" against the Israel Defense Forces and himself almost went to the Palestinian territories for that purpose, wanted to create a group, to be called Critical Response, to send medics into war zones such as Lebanon and Darfur to help civilians. Hamad liked this idea, regaling Darby with plans to use the cover of medics to place explosives on motorcycles and booby-trap ambulances in Israel to kill Jews. Hamad also devised a plan using the PCWF to send money to Hamas and Hezbollah. Darby recounted at Breitbart.com:

> Hamad had approached me and shared that he had been able to skim off money [from PCWF] that he intended sneak to Palestinian comrades in Israel. I asked him why he needed to sneak anything when he was able to send funds legally. He responded with a detailed analysis of all the ways suicide bombers could get through checkpoints and achieve their goals. I declined and he told me that I had fallen back into my white privilege, but would come back to the revolution soon.

This talk of violence, Darby reports, caused him to rethink his relationship with Hamad. "I couldn't sleep and I debated within myself if I should go to the FBI." Learning from another left-wing activist about Hamad's plans to set up "a fake business to help Hamad funnel money for Palestinians" then nudged Darby to confront Hamad. The two met for coffee. On hearing of Darby's disapproval, "Hamad responded by saying it would be good for white people to get caught in the war on terror and that people would limit what the government could do if the war on terror had whites in Guantanamo instead of just Arabs."

That settled matters. Darby agonized over his past actions—"wondering if my previous support and efforts for the Palestinian Children's Welfare Fund meant I had blood on my hands"—and resolved to stop Hamad. "I ended up meeting with the FBI. They were kind and gracious. Hamad and the Palestinian Children's Welfare Fund were raided."

The search warrant focused on fraud, not terrorism, as indicated by the supporting financial affidavit:

> RIAD ELSOLH HAMAD failed to file his federal income tax returns for the years 1999 through 2003 and 2005, evaded payment of his federal income taxes for the years 1999 through 2006, and is engaged in preparing false documents used to obtain federally subsidized loan from various University of Texas campuses. The affidavit will show that HAMAD earned taxable income from the Austin Independent School District (AISD). HAMAD also runs/operates the Palestinian Children's Welfare Fund (PCWF) which he claims raises money for the children of Palestine. HAMAD sends large amounts of money to the Middle East and/or to charities that forward the funds to the Middle East. The disposition of these funds is unknown at this time, A large amount of these "donated" funds have also been traced into various stock accounts controlled by Riad Hamad and/or his son Abdullah Hamad.

An investigator with the Internal Revenue Service put the last part more bluntly: "Riad Hamad, with the assistance of his son, Abdullah Hamad, his ex-wife, Diana Hamad, and his daughter, Rita Hamad, are using the 'donated funds' for personal use and not paying federal income taxes on these funds."

Lacking a news account, here is how Hamad himself reported the raid on his house: a dozen federal agents, armed with a search warrant based on probable cause to investigate wire fraud, bank fraud and money laundering, "searched every nook and cranny" of his apartment and took away "more than forty boxes of papers, files, computers and CDs."

The Suicide

After the raid, Darby recounts,

> I heard from Hamad one last time. He called me and said it was "just a matter of time." I asked what he meant. He told me of the raids and said they had taken all of his documents, and that I would know soon. He said he had to go and he did. His body was found in Austin, TX in Lady Bird Lake a few days later. He apparently chose not to face the consequences of his actions.

Even in death, Hamad perpetuated a fraud. First, he wrote a letter to his circle, creating the premise for violence against him (all spellings and ellipses exactly as in the original):

> besides the government harassment, the hateful environment from some students at school because I am an Arab and a Muslim . . . and their racist comments, I have been getting phone calls around midnight by some one saying "where is your camel." and last . . . a car was vandalized about two years ago . . . last night around 1 30 in the morning . . . someone rang the bell and ran away . . . and you could hear all the dogs in the neighborhood barking when the person who rang the bell ran away. . . . A real loving environment towards Arabs and Muslims . . .

(Reflecting back on his lawsuit, one sees the source of his fantasies about harassment, hateful environment, and racism.)

Second, evidence suggests that Hamad staged his death to make it appear that he wanted the honor of being murdered when in fact he checked out on his own. Based in part on the autopsy, a police statement asserted:

> When the body was removed from the lake, tape was found around the eyes, and the hands and legs were loosely bound. The bindings

of his hands and legs and placement of the tape were consistent with Hamad having done this to himself. Detectives know that Hamad walked from his vehicle to the water on his own based on evidence retrieved from the scene.

At this time, the Austin Police Department does not suspect foul play was involved. Witnesses and family members have confirmed with police that Hamad had extreme stressors in his life. This incident is still an ongoing investigation, but all signs indicate this may have been a suicide. According to the preliminary results from the Medical Examiner's Office there were no signs of trauma to the body or signs of a struggle.

Even Paul Larudee, Hamad's colleague and the last known person to speak to Hamad before his death, says that Hamad "did take his own life but he took it with a view of fueling the speculation that has in fact accompanied his death." Translation: He wanted it to appear like a hit job. Despite his skepticism about Hamad's demise, Larudee insists "I still think he was a hero."

The Conspiracy Theory

Palestinian extremists, Islamists, leftists, and assorted conspiracy theorists accepted Hamad's fakery. According to Ibrahim Dremali of the Islamic Center of Greater Austin, who says after an autopsy he washed Hamad's body, which was "cut all from the right shoulder all the way to the stomach, and from the left shoulder all the way to the stomach again, and from the stomach all the way to the bladder, . . . from all the back of his skull is completely cut, is empty completely, empty. . . . His wrists were all slit open and cut. . . . His eyes actually dropped all the way down. . . . It is a barbaric act. . . . Like somebody is eating the body. . . . This is a message for all Muslims." Dremali said it appeared as "something in the jungle, an animal attacking another animal."

Kurt Nimmo, a prominent conspiracy theorist, asked "Is it possible a neocon hit team or as likely a Mossad 'bayonet' team took out the school teacher Riad Hamad?" Radio host Alex Jones and others spoke ominously of Israeli attack squads surveilling Hamad's house. Some even accused "sociopathic FBI informant Brandon Darby" of killing Hamad. Years later. a Twitter site (riad_hamad) keeps the theories alive.

In contrast to these lurid accounts, the Travis Country medical examiner, David Dolinak, who inspected Hamad's body on the morning of April 17, found nothing alarming. Quite contrary to Dremali's description of the body being variously cut up, the medical examiner reporter found little to report:

IDENTIFYING MARKS AND SCARS:
A 10 inch vertical scar is in the lateral aspect of the right thigh. There are no tattoos.

EVIDENCE OF THERAPY [meaning needle puncture marks, surgical stitches, etc.]
None.

EVIDENCE OF INJURY:
None. . . .

BODY CAVITIES:
The organs are normally developed and are in their normal locations. The diaphragms are intact. There is no fluid accumulation in the pleural cavities or the pericardial sac. There is no fluid accumulation in the peritoneal cavity. There are no pleural adhesions or abdominal adhesions.

HEAD:
There is no subscalp blood extravasation. The calvarium is intact. The dura is intact. There is no epidural or subdural blood. . . .

MUSCULOSKELETAL SYSTEM:
No fractures of the clavicles, sternum, ribs, vertebrae, pelvis or extremities are detected.

Dolinak concluded that he saw "No evidence of traumatic injury" and that Hamad "died as the result of drowning."

Conclusion

Hamad died as a he lived, in a miasma of hate and duplicity. Darby informs me that "Riad publicly claimed to be a Christian but when he died it became evident that he had been lying and was actually a Muslim." We, the victims of his lurid and manic lawsuits never saw a dime of the money he owed us. His embezzlement and skipping on taxes having caught up with him, he perpetrated his final and grandest fraud—a pretend-murder. Not surprisingly, his venomous Palestine Children's Welfare Fund is now defunct, reduced to a homepage plaintively stating that "PCWF website coming again soon to carry on some of the great work of Riad Hamad."

Some observations about Hamad: First, the lofty praise for this wretch would make one think him a decent man, pointing to how political sympathy creates blinders. Second, even as he lived in the civilized quiet of Austin, Texas, Hamad contaminated his adopted home by importing political nihilism from the Middle East. Third, I may be out nearly $33,000 in court costs, but it was not all lost; Hamad's legal assault inspired me to expose this malign excrescence of anti-Zionism. Finally, if one truly is judged by the quality of one's opponents, we who defend Israel are thriving.

Most Muslim immigrants are law-abiding and constructive citizens in the West. But Hamad's case fits into a persistent pattern of immigrants who bring with them the bad habits imbued by the tyrannical politics and radical ideologies. Combining Islamic supremacism with cynical disdain, they despise all that is non-Muslim, import a mélange of extremist ideas, and act free of moral constraints. Consequently, they engage disproportionately in antisocial behavior, criminal activities, and terrorism. Reluctantly, I concluded almost a decade ago that "Muslim visitors and immigrants must undergo additional background checks." I reiterate this now, lest more Riad Hamads be allowed in.

23

Lefty for Radical Islam: Dennis Kucinich

Keith Ellison and Andre Carson receive considerable attention as the first two Muslims to serve in the US Congress. The novelty of their presence, however, should not obscure the fact that Congress includes other representatives, invariably on the left wing of the Democratic party, who also carry water for Islamist interests and causes.

Not themselves Muslim, their relative obscurity attracts less attention to them and may make them more effective. For example, When the US House voted 390–5 in 2009 in favor of a resolution concerning Israel's right to self-defense against Hamas, Carson voted for the resolution and Ellison voted "present." In contrast, Dennis J. Kucinich, Gwen Moore, Ron Paul, Nick Rahall, and Maxine Waters cast the "no" votes. In addition to those five, their ranks also include Cynthia McKinney, Gregory Meeks, and James Moran.

Kucinich, a representative from the Cleveland area from 1997 until 2013 whose primary loss in 2012 signaled the apparent end of his political career, offers the single best example of this phenomenon, having gone further down this path than any other national elected official and receiving more attention for it, particularly during his campaign for president of the United States in 2004.

Kucinich's far-left positions on a range of topics (most memorably, a promise to establish a Department of Peace) did not exactly burn up the campaign trail then but his platform did resonate among more than a few Democratic voters in a fractured race; he won 8 percent of the vote in Utah and Washington state, 9 percent in his home state of Ohio, 16 percent in Maine, 17 percent in Minnesota, and an impressive 26 percent in Hawaii. (Comparable efforts in a 2008 campaign for president fell flat, with him nowhere winning over 2 percent of the vote.)

This respectable showing brought considerable news coverage to his 2004 campaign that in turn uniquely exposed the candidate's positions and activities vis-à-vis Islamism.

Kucinich's Positions

Already before 2004, Kucinich had displayed a soft spot for Islamism, defined as the ideology seeking to apply Islamic law (the Shari'a) world-wide. For example, he insisted on accepting a $500 donation in 1997 from Washington's then-reigning Islamist, Abdurahman Alamoudi. Only after Alamoudi was arrested in 2003 on charges of taking money from Libyan intelligence, charges which landed him a long jail term, did Kucinich finally return the 1997 contribution.

In his 2004 presidential campaign, Kucinich adopted key elements of the radical Islamic message and worked closely with North America's most aggressive Islamist group, the Council on American-Islamic Relations (CAIR). He echoed its line about American Muslims having "suffered much over the last few years" and their having "been scape-goated and they've been subject to profiling and have been subject to law enforcement practices which are truly repugnant in a democracy." He presented key policies (opposition to the Iraq war and the Patriot Act, "support of Palestinian rights") as being Muslim-friendly. He even argued that his proposals for universal healthcare and expanded public education "are consistent with their [Islamic] religious beliefs about providing for the less fortunate and the needy."

Kucinich identified himself closely with American Muslims, calling them the bellwethers of the US government's "intolerance, surveil-lance, and oppression." At times, he waxed lyrical: "In its suffering the Muslim community is helping America to transform. We're defend-ing all Americans, all liberties. Stand up and live your faith: Celebrate Islam. Promote and share understanding. This country owes you a debt of gratitude." At other times, he got emotional: when he denounced the deportation of an illegal Muslim immigrant from Venezuela, the Cleveland *Plain Dealer* described his eyes "brimming with tears" as he declared his intent "to move heaven and earth" to keep her in the country.

A reporter described how, in one remarkable meeting with Muslims, Kucinich quoted the Koran with "the passion of an itinerant preacher" and roused the audience to get on its feet and chant "God is great"

(*Allahu Akbar*). To another Muslim audience he announced, "I keep a copy of the Koran in my office."

(In this, Kucinich anticipated former British prime minister Tony Blair, who announced in June 2011: "I read the Koran every day. Partly to understand some of the things happening in the world, but mainly just because it is immensely instructive.")

His campaign website had one special page devoted to Arab Americans and another devoted to Muslims. Some Kucinich campaign literature was translated into Arabic. Of special interest is the page lauding his "long record of making himself accessible to the Muslim community":

> He has hired or taken as interns a number of Muslim Americans. [*DP comment*: for example, Souheila Al-Jadda served on his House staff.] He meets regularly with his Muslim and Arab-American constituents in Cleveland. In his presidential campaign he has spoken several times at CAIR events, the only candidate to do so—and in spite of getting some very negative press from right-wing commentators for it. [*DP comment*: judging by the "Muslims for Kucinich" website, this is a reference to me] He also spoke at the ISNA [Islamic Society of North America] convention on August 30, 2003.

In addition, the site went on, Kucinich "created the post of National Muslims for Kucinich Coordinator on his campaign staff." In all, "Muslims working as campaign volunteers, including the National Muslims for Kucinich Coordinator, have found not only the candidate himself but also his staff to be welcoming and indeed eager to work with them and to reach out to the Muslim community."

Kucinich also touted his support among Muslims, naming Islamist organizations as proof:

> Leaders in national Muslim organizations like CAIR, ISNA, and the American Muslim Alliance have expressed support for Kucinich's candidacy. A group of nearly 100 supporters, ordinary Muslims from around the country, have organized an email list to receive updates on the campaign and learn about volunteer opportunities. The membership of this group has tripled in the last month [*DP comment*: this page is not dated, so it is not clear which month is referred to] and continues to grow on a daily basis. There does not seem to be any comparable organized group of Muslims supporting any of the other candidates.

In return for these expressions of solidarity, Kucinich looked for Muslim electoral support. Not surprisingly, Kucinich urged Muslims to vote as a block so as to enhance their political muscle; this not only followed the Islamist organizations' line but presumably reflected his hope to be the beneficiary of their votes.

Kucinich's Calendar

The candidate devoted extensive time and effort to addressing and meeting Muslims in person. MSNBC noted, for example, how he made sure "mosques and Muslim organizations are on his agenda as he stumps around the country." A partial listing from the height of the primary season included:

- *November 30, 2003*: Kucinich spoke at CAIR's Seventh Annual Fundraising Banquet outside of Washington, DC
- *December 20–21*: Kucinich electronically addressed the annual convention of the Muslim Public Affairs Council and won 17 percent support in its straw poll, coming in second behind Howard Dean.
- *December 30*: At the behest of CAIR, Kucinich visited the Islamic Society of the Tampa Bay Area, was "shown around a free medical clinic, full-time Muslim school and food pantry for the needy," and he met with CAIR members. CAIR's communications director in Florida, Ahmed Bedier, announced his approval of Kucinich: "We can feel the sincerity and the emotions and see that he believes what he is saying. It's rare to find someone in Washington like that."
- *January 13, 2004*: CAIR's Ahmed Bedier praised Kucinich for carrying "with him the flag of true patriotism and the message of inclusiveness and peace."
- *January 25*: Kucinich appeared at a presidential campaign forum in Houston co-hosted by CAIR.
- *January 27*: Steve Cerny, Virginia co-chair of Kucinich for President, sent out a memo addressed to "Muslim Supporters of Kucinich for President," that began with "Assalaamu Alaykum" (normally a phrase only used among Muslims) and pleaded with recipients to attend an organizing meeting on January 31. Cerny told about "a major presence at the big Eid celebration at the DC Armory" on, February 1, other Eid celebrations, and at "as many mosques as we can" on February 6. Cerny also told about plans to print thirty thousand flyers targeted to the Muslim community, the campaign's lists of registered Muslim voters and its plan to call them "to remind Muslims of the election and ask their support for Kucinich."
- *January 29*: The Detroit-based Arab-American Political Action Committee gave Kucinich over two-thirds of the votes cast by its members in an endorsement for president. (Another report indicated that Kerry received no votes.)

- *February 1*: Kucinich started the day "at an Islamic Festival at the University of New Mexico where he told attendees that, as president, he would work to rebuild relations between the Muslim community and the US government."
- *February 3*: Kucinich spent one and a half hours at the Idriss Mosque in Seattle, half an hour with the leaders and an hour with the community. The invitation made two statements of note: (1) This event "may include salat al-maghrib, observed by Representative Dennis Kucinich." (2) Kucinich, not the mosque, initiated the event when he "requested to meet with the local Muslim Community."
- *February 28*: Kucinich visited the Masjid Omar ibn Al-Khattab in downtown Los Angeles and discussed Iraq, education, and the prison system with about sixty-five persons.
- *March 8*: At an event sponsored by CAIR's San Antonio office, Kucinich met with a reported 400 Muslims. Sarwat Husain, the head of that office, announced at the occasion: "Even if he doesn't win [the presidency], he can represent our voice in Congress."

After 2004

Kucinich continued along the same path of reaching out to Arabs, Muslims, and Islamists even after the 2004 campaign. For example, his website long continued to list "Arab Americans" as an "issue."

He visited the Middle East in 2006 during the Hezbollah-Israel war and focused exclusively on the destruction caused by Israel and did not visit the scenes of Hezbollah attacks in Israel.

In June 2007, the US House of Representatives voted 411 to 2 for Resolution 21, "Calling on the United Nations Security Council to charge Iranian leader Mahmoud Ahmadinejad with violating the 1948 Convention on the Prevention and Punishment of the Crime of Genocide and United Nations Charter because of his calls for the destruction of the State of Israel." Kucinich (along with Ron Paul) was one of the two to vote against the resolution.

In 2008, according to the far-left Inter-Press Service, Kucinich alone of the presidential candidates attempted to court the Muslim vote. That same year, he condemned US policy vis-à-vis Iran but not Iranian policy vis-à-vis the United States and called for establishing a "National Commission on Truth and Reconciliation" which he wanted to "have the power to compel testimony and gather official documents to reveal to the American people . . . the underlying deception" that was the Bush administration's response to 9/11.

Kucinich called on Muslim support in 2009, stating that the health care issue offers Muslims "the opportunity to reach out to people of all faiths. This is a teachable moment for Muslims, whose every greeting has peace in it. Get involved in the current debate."

In a 2010 interview with *Turkish Policy Quarterly*, Kucinich fawningly addressed Turks and their Islamist government: "To my Muslim brothers and sisters in Turkey I say Selamunaleykum. We should be extending peace to each other. Turkey is an open, democratic, pluralistic democracy and the US should promote respect for Islam." Also in 2010, Kucinich adopted the Islamist line that drone strikes against Al-Qaeda targets conducted by the Bush and Obama administrations have helped stoke "fanaticism and radicalism."

Kucinich reportedly was the only member of Congress publicly to condemn the Obama administration's 2010 authorization to assassinate Anwar al-Awlaki, the US citizen and terrorist sponsor in Yemen accused of ties to several attacks in the United States. He was probably the only member in 2011 to praise the government of Syrian dictator Bashar al-Assad for showing "a willingness to listen" to the opposition that he was at that moment massacring.

Conclusions

Although Kucinich cut an eccentric figure among the Democrats running for president—seeking the Islamist vote in 2004 was a sure way *not* to reach the White House—his close association with radical Islam was innovative and pathbreaking.

This is confirmed by Howard Dean's following in Kucinich's footsteps during his own 2004 presidential campaign. The National Council of Pakistani Americans relates, for example, how Dean met in Milwaukee with about one hundred members of the newly formed Muslim Electorate Council of America (MECA). In so doing, it states, he "helped Muslims create a precedence that no American Presidential aspirant should ignore" and it portrays this event as going beyond what Kucinich did:

> Dennis Kucinich also went to a few Muslim functions. However, those functions were arranged by major national organizations as part of their fund raising efforts. Those meetings were not organized on election 2004 issues. "What we witnessed in Milwaukee is a new phenomenon. Muslim voters are making a bold statement and creating a grassroots movement of political empowerment without the influence of major political establishment," said Dr. Aslam Abdullah, the founding director of MECA.

Can we anticipate future Democratic candidates promising to espouse Muslim interests (as defined by CAIR and its ilk) to the White House? I expect so. More broadly, one sees a growing connection between the Left and radical Islam, as plumbed by David Horowitz in *Unholy Alliance* (Regnery) and by me in a number of articles. Among many other consequences, a long-term sorting out of votes is currently underway; as I wrote in 2003, "Arabs and Muslims, for all their sympathy for Republican economics, will vote Democratic, and Jews, for all their agreement with the Democrats on abortion, will vote Republican."

Index